Timely, framing the biblical arguments in light of contemporary settings. . . . For more than forty years, Hesselgrave has issued a clarion call to frame missions in light of the Bible, and we need a generation of people more like him if we are to maintain fidelity to missions in the future. Readers will find ideas of his with which they agree and others with which they disagree—but they will know why Hesselgrave takes the stances he takes.

—A. SCOTT MOREAU, chair and professor,
Department of Missions and Intercultural Studies
Wheaton College Graduate School

Why is it that no one has as yet thought of what Hesselgrave has done in *Paradigms in Conflict*? Each of the ten issues will provide a wonderful opportunity for study groups, missions classes in colleges, seminaries, and churches to develop a biblical missiology for the twenty-first century. The bibliography alone is worth the price of the book; however, the engagement of the conversation on each issue with some of the key stakeholders is sure to draw many into a most invigorating and useful analysis of our practice in our missionary programs as measured by the Scriptures.

—WALTER C. KAISER JR.
President, Gordon-Conwell Theological Seminary
Colman M. Mockler Distinguished Professor of Old Testament,
Gordon-Conwell Seminary

Sometimes one wanders through a familiar area only to discover new concepts, which may not really be new at all. They may pose opportunity mixed with danger. The ten questions that Hesselgrave examines are just such a blend. Missiologists have faced these issues for a long time. Yet, in a new millennium they take on new meanings, sometimes with dangerous implications. This book is a clarion call for cautious progress rooted soundly in and determined only by absolute biblical truth. As missiologists and practitioners alike reflect on and shape the future of evangelical missions, this work will prove essential to those tasks, and Hesselgrave will continue to be viewed as one of the most prophetic voices of our age.

—KEITH E. EITEL
Dean, Fish School of Evangelism and Missions
Southwestern Baptist Theological Seminary

Writings by Hesselgrave invariably provide a balance between the biblical, historical, and practical in presenting missiology with cutting-edge relevance. Changes throughout the world are accelerating as we move into the twenty-first century, having a significant impact on how we fulfill our Great Commission task. These insights by Hesselgrave will be a valuable tool for academicians and practitioners who are serious about understanding and using these turning points to advance God's kingdom.

—JERRY RANKIN, President
International Mission Board,
Southern Baptist Convention

As usual, Hesselgrave is sensitive to today's missiological environment. This book is no exception. His insights are of important value in assessing present and future trends. I commend it for wide use in our classrooms.

—BOB LENZ, editor
Occasional Bulletin,
Evangelical Missiological Society

Hesselgrave handles tough, controversial missions issues with irenic tone and spirit. At the same time, he leaves no doubts about where he stands. Scholarly and biblical, his work is infused with missionary spirit and passion. His wide range of inquiry goes beyond the usual missiological formulations and includes fresh, innovative ideas and approaches.

—JIM REAPSOME, former editor
Evangelical Missions Quarterly

PARADIGMS IN CONFLICT

10 Key Questions in
Christian Missions Today

David J. Hesselgrave

Kregel
Academic & Professional

Paradigms in Conflict: 10 Key Questions in Christian Missions Today

© 2005 by David J. Hesselgrave

Published by Kregel Publications, a division of Kregel, Inc., P.O. Box 2607, Grand Rapids, MI 49501.

Library of Congress Cataloging-in-Publication Data
Hesselgrave, David J.
Paradigms in conflict: 10 key questions in Christian missions today / by David J. Hesselgrave.
    p. cm.
Includes indexes.
    1. Missions—Theory. I. Title.
BV2063.H438   2006
266—dc22   2005024117

ISBN 0-8254-2770-3

Printed in the United States of America
06 07 08 09 / 5 4 3 2

*To the officers and members
of the Evangelical Missiological Society—
past, present, and future.*

Contents

List of Illustrations

Foreword

Ralph D. Winter

BOOKS LIKE THIS DON'T HAPPEN VERY OFTEN. They couldn't. There are very few people in the world who could write a book like this.

I have known and respected Dr. Hesselgrave for many years. As this book reveals, he possesses a beautiful balance of scholarly rigor, common sense, and practical perspective!

In *Paradigms in Conflict*, Dr. Hesselgrave selects a balanced array of truly pressing issues in Christian global outreach. He explores a wide range of different approaches to those issues, but he does not leave it there. His own best judgment is also boldly but humbly presented.

I cannot think of anyone better qualified to attempt so magnificent a challenge. It takes a lifetime to gain the perspective, the wisdom, the sheer knowledge of detail that this book so freely offers to the reader. It is not going to go out of date anytime soon. It should be in the library of every serious believer.

—RALPH D. WINTER
Frontier Mission Fellowship
Pasadena, California

Foreword

Andreas J. Köstenberger

I FIRST BECAME ACQUAINTED with David Hesselgrave's thought in 1985–88 during my M.Div. studies at Columbia Biblical Seminary. There, several of his books, including *Communicating Christ Cross-Culturally* (Hesselgrave 1978) were course texts. During doctoral work at Trinity Evangelical Divinity School from 1990 to 1993, I came across his interchange with John R. W. Stott (Hesselgrave 1991; Stott 1991). Hesselgrave's perceptive critique of Stott's "incarnational model" of missions confirmed my own conclusions that John's missions model is best described as representational rather than incarnational. That is, the church is called to represent Christ by proclaiming his message of salvation and forgiveness in the power of the Spirit. It is not John's understanding that we must somehow "re-incarnate the risen Christ," as it were, in our missionary endeavors.

After publication of my dissertation, *The Missions of Jesus and the Disciples according to the Fourth Gospel* (Köstenberger 1998), Dr. Hesselgrave and I began to correspond about our mutual concern that Christ's message should reach the ends of the earth. We also shared the proposition that missiology must be firmly grounded in a biblical theology of missions. Thus, this opportunity to write a foreword for *Paradigms in Conflict* comes after many years of interacting with Dr. Hesselgrave and his ideas.

This work provides a substantive biblical treatment of the most critical challenges facing missiology at the beginning of the twenty-first century. It will be an enduring contribution to the evangelical missions movement at this important juncture. Such heart-stirring ideas deserve to be heeded by all who have heard God's call to missions in Scripture.

The first chapter, "Sovereignty and Free Will," is an appropriate discussion with which to open the book, since issues related to divine sovereignty and human free will constantly surface in Christian mission. While systematic theologians regularly discuss this topic (most recently in the context of the "open theism" controversy), it is less often that one reads a treatment of this question from the pen of a missiologist.

Yet Hesselgrave shows convincingly that, ultimately, the issue of God's sovereignty and human "free" will is one of great missiological import. Arguing that "the best way to deal with the relationship between divine sovereignty and human responsibility is to go to the biblical text and, employing sound principles of exegesis, attempt to see what the text actually says," Hesselgrave treats the reader to a thorough treatment of the key text on the subject, Romans 9–11. Countering an individualism that is concerned primarily for God's plan "for me," Hesselgrave reminds us that God's plan for *our* history is but part of his larger plan for *all* history.

In chapter 2, Hesselgrave deals with the question of the destiny of the unevangelized, adjudicating between the positions of *restrictivism* (those unevangelized in this life are lost), *inclusivism* (there are other ways of salvation), and *universalism* (all will eventually be saved). Christians must continually wrestle with the standard questions, "What about people who never hear the gospel?" "Would a loving God send a sincere person who has never heard about Christ to hell?" and "How can people be held responsible if they do not believe in a Christ of whom they have not heard?"

After reviewing the Bible's teachings, Hesselgrave concludes that only by hearing and believing in Christ during this life can men and women be saved. He urges that gospel proclamation and mission are imperative to lead people to salvation.

Another knotty topic is approached in chapter 3: "How should we approach adherents of other faiths?" Citing at the outset his paternal grandfather by the same name, an ordained minister in the Universalist Church, Dr. Hesselgrave chronicles the two Parliaments of World Religions in 1893 and 1993 and their aftermath. He also investigates the beginnings of the World Council of Churches in 1948.

After defining the term "religion," Hesselgrave sketches out a "theology of religions" from Romans 1:18–3:31. All humans are sinful and rebellious toward God by nature, choice, and the decree of God and need the salvation in Christ provided by God, who seeks lost sinners.

Applying his study of Scripture, Hesselgrave describes interreligious encounters, including those with Judaism and Islam, as invasions into enemy territory. While this unflinching presentation is sure to offend advocates of toleration and open-ended dialogue, it is faithful to the biblical record.

Chapter 4 discusses the proper Christian response to poverty and the poor. Until the World Congress of Evangelism in Berlin in 1966, conservative evangelicals gave priority to evangelizing the world and discipling the nations. This began to change by the time of the International Congress on World Evangelization in Lausanne in 1974, where holism started to eclipse prioritism. Liberation theology taught that the church's mission, properly conceived, is to promote justice in society and establish *shalom* ("peace") on the earth.

Holism, in its revisionist and restrained permutations, held that Christians ought not to force an unnatural dichotomy between people's spiritual and physical conditions. Prioritism continued to uphold the primacy of the church's evangelistic mandate. After a thorough investigation of the word *poor* in both Testaments with a focus on Isaiah 61:1 and Luke 4:18, Hesselgrave concludes that the biblical "good news" has to do with the salvation of sinners, not merely or even primarily liberation from economic oppression as liberation theology affirms.

Against a revisionist holism, Hesselgrave reiterates that the "primary concern of our Lord and the heart of biblical missions have to do with meeting spiritual needs, not with meeting physical, material, or social needs."

At least for me, the highlight of Hesselgrave's book is chapter 5 on models of incarnationalism and representationalism. There are those who take their cue from Thomas à Kempis, who urged the imitation of Christ, or Charles Sheldon, who in his 1897 novel *In His Steps* raised to paramount importance the question, "What would Jesus do?" Touching on the social gospel as espoused in the first part of the twentieth century, liberation theology, and post-Vatican Roman Catholicism, Hesselgrave arrives at the most influential proponent of an incarnational missiological paradigm: John R. W. Stott.

Noting that incarnationalists span a considerable spectrum from "left" to "right," Hesselgrave discusses this paradigm within the matrix of three major views of Christ and his mission: (1) liberationism as espoused by Gustavo Gutierrez and others; (2) holism, represented by Stott in his influential 1975 book *The Christian Mission in the Modern World*; and (3) conversionism. Stott defines mission as "everything the church is sent into the world to do," but Hesselgrave affirms a representational model that accentuates the discontinuity between Jesus' mission and the mission of his followers. Hesselgrave understands the former in terms of life-giving in a primary sense and the latter in terms of bearing witness to Jesus and the gospel.

Another hot topic is the reality of "power encounters" and "truth encounters." In chapter 6, Hesselgrave provides a thumbnail sketch of how such encounters worked in the church of Acts and how they operated through medieval times. He also discusses the concept of *power encounter* as it has come to be used in contemporary missiology. Hesselgrave turns to a pertinent investigation of Jesus' instruction in John 13–17. Here the revealed truth of God is essential to the Christian encounter with the world, and the role of the Holy Spirit is absolutely vital as he has inspired the apostolic testimony, preserves and unifies believers, enables their missionary witness, and convicts the world. This biblical focus provides an important corrective to the emphasis on power encounter.

Chapter 7 addresses Ralph Winter's concern that missionaries go to the field either overprepared or unprepared, a phenomenon he calls the "re-amateurization of mission." A corollary concern is John Piper's lament that the professionalization of ministry patterns Christian ministry after the world's attitude of pride and self-promotion rather than fostering humility and self-abnegation. Hesselgrave stresses the role of the *divine call* in missions and advocates "the right kind of professionalism" in pursuing God's mission. At the same time, Hesselgrave decries the self-orientation of much of the North American missionary enterprise.

Chapter 8 takes up yet another issue over which missionaries have struggled, the question of form and meaning in the contextualization of the Christian message. Hesselgrave affirms the plenary verbal understanding of biblical inspiration. From his viewpoint in that paradigm, he conducts a brief overview of the history of inspiration and contextualization. He stops to offer substantive critiques of the important contributions to the debate, Charles Kraft's *Christianity in Culture* (1979) and Eugene Nida's "dynamic equivalence" approach to translation. In light of biblical inerrancy, Hesselgrave also expresses concerns with gender sensitive translations. Hesselgrave's grounding of contextualization in a high view of Scripture is exactly what is needed to inform and correct the contemporary scene.

Chapter 9 is less foundational but still of considerable missional consequence, the paradigms from which to view the relationship between missionary efforts and the imminence of Christ's return. How does apocalypticism and millennialism relate to missions? Through Jesus' eschatological discourse in Mark 13 and its parallels, Hesselgrave sets forth a premillennial view of evangelization. He notes that many are too preoccupied with trying to pinpoint the exact timing of Christ's return. This, he adds, was also true of Jesus' first followers. Rather than providing a pattern for a "countdown," Hesselgrave suggests that the Lord's "signs" were given to be used as "prophetic alerts." We must avoid presumption and use what Scripture says about Christ's return to motivate wise investment in the work of Christ.

Chapter 10, "The Kingdom of God and the Church of Christ," opens with the text of a note from the late Donald McGavran. McGavran urges Hesselgrave to establish "The American Society of *Christian* Missiology," which ought to be focused squarely on fulfilling Christ's "Great Commission."

At the beginning of the twentieth century, mainline denominations supplied 80 percent of the missionary force. At the end these denominations supplied only 6 percent of overseas missionary staff. The causes for this remarkable shift are several, but among them, Hesselgrave blames the near demise of ecumenical mission on inroads of liberalism, the social gospel, and historical criticism. Ecumenists have undercut their own ministry as well by broadening the definition of *mission* to include everything the church does in the world and even what God does outside the church.

Over Winters's notion of "kingdom mission," Hesselgrave calls the church to engage in "Great Commission mission," which makes disciples by preaching, baptizing, and teaching the peoples of the earth. As Christ is building his church, he will bring his kingdom.

Through these paradigm conflicts that involve evangelical missiology, Hesselgrave takes the reader on a whirlwind tour through missions history, a representative exegesis of relevant Scripture, and an adjudication of theological and missiological questions that are most critical for the missionary enterprise at the beginning of the twenty-first century.

By the nature of this approach, each chapter is a bare introduction that could be expanded into a book-length treatment. Some books on these matters already exist. But that is not the point. We do not need another narrow-focused, detailed tome on inclusivism vs. restrictivism or some other topic. We need the wide-ranging, far-reaching views that Hesselgrave provides.

There are very few, if any, who could have written such a work. I commend the book particularly because of three features:

1. Its *integrative nature*. Hesselgrave shows how various topics usually treated in isolation from one another are interrelated.
2. Its *biblical orientation*. Hesselgrave does not merely pay lip service to the notion that missions thinking ought to be grounded in Scripture. He self-consciously roots the treatment of every subject in biblical revelation in arriving at a sound conclusion.
3. Its *missiological thrust*. Unlike biblical or systematic treatments that lack connection to God's purpose in His kingdom, Hesselgrave keenly keeps missions firmly in view as he traverses the questions that have generated extensive debate.

All those interested in the Christian missionary enterprise will enjoy reading this delightful, well-written book. Hesselgrave has put all of us in his debt by turning his long experience into a gold mine from which to extract correction, a strategy, and action. We dare not miss this God-given opportunity, for the sake of those lost without Christ and the gospel and for the greater glory of him who in his great love sent his Son to die so that we, in him, may have eternal life.

—ANDREAS J. KÖSTENBERGER
Professor of New Testament and Greek
and Director of Ph.D. and Th.M. Studies
Southeastern Baptist Theological Seminary

References

Hesselgrave, David J. 1978. *Communicating Christ Cross-Culturally.* Grand Rapids: Zondervan.

———. 1991. "Holes in 'Holistic Mission.' " Trinity World Forum 15.3: 3.

Köstenberger, Andreas. 1998. *The Missions of Jesus and the Disciples according to the Fourth Gospel.* Grand Rapids: Eerdmans.

Stott, John R. W. 1991. "An Open Letter to David Hesselgrave." *Trinity World Forum* 16.3: 1.

Preface

DURING MY SEMINARY DAYS in the 1940s, foreign missions seemed to be largely a matter of whether we were willing to go to "the last, the least, and the lost."

When the 1940s gave way to the 1950s and my family headed to Japan, missions assumed a new aura of reality but still retained a romantic idealism. We were, after all, going to an occupied nation whose god had just abdicated and whose people were just waiting to hear the gospel and embrace the true and living God.

Or, so we were told.

After over a decade on the mission field in Japan, my wife Gertrude and I responded in the mid-1960s to a request from the Board of Overseas Missions of the Evangelical Free Church and Dean Kenneth Kantzer of Trinity Evangelical Divinity School that I consider joining their faculty as associate professor of mission. Their School of World Mission and Evangelism had not yet been inaugurated, but a flood of incoming students, including many headed for the mission field, made it necessary to hire additional faculty and offer a more complete slate of missions courses. Of course, additional faculty and courses were not all that was needed, because in those days there was still an acute lack of suitable textbooks and teaching materials in the area of Christian missions.

Today, after a generation and longer, everything has changed. During the last forty years, we have witnessed the rise of new schools and departments of missions, the revitalization of professional missiological

19

societies and the formation of new ones, the initiation of new learning opportunities and degree programs, and a veritable flood of missions books and information systems. Moreover, the past forty years have been marked by numerous missiological controversies and a plethora of missions strategies (many of them already eclipsed or forgotten). But during this time, Third-World churches and missions have grown until they are assuming ever-increasing importance in the global missionary enterprise of this twenty-first century.

Many missionaries of my generation have retired. Some have died, and those who remain are about to lay aside their armor. Even though the swords of those who remain may still be sharp, their ability to wield them and press the battle show evidence of weakness. In any case, I have felt it desirable to leave behind some small legacy to those who will tread a similar missionary path—albeit a more precipitous and slippery one—in the twenty-first century. Incomplete and inadequate as it certainly is, this book is primarily directed to those missionaries, although I hope that those who will send them will study it as well.

My thesis is this: *Although changes there must and will be, the future of Christian missions will depend more on changes that are not made than it will on changes that are made.* Amidst a crescendo of cries for radical change in missions, the thesis of this book may seem untenable. But the more one thinks about the uniqueness and sovereignty of Jesus Christ and the trustworthiness and truthfulness of Scripture, the more tenable it will seem.

In support of this thesis I have elected to deal with ten topics under current discussion that in my view constitute turning points or paradigm conflicts that need to be resolved in Protestant missions. In considering them and to avoid frustration and promote understanding, I encourage readers to take note of the following:

First, chapter titles are phrased to indicate that the respective pairs are not just competing ("either/or") but, at least to some degree, may also be complementary ("both/and"). Though one of each set of alternatives will be more hopeful and less hurtful, that does not necessarily mean that there is no truth whatsoever in the other.

Second, from my perspective biblical missiology is informed by three basic types of source materials: (1) biblical theology; (2) missionary experience (history), and, (3) the social sciences. Though severely limited at best, I have attempted to bring relevant materials from each of these source areas to the discussion of each of the ten topics. Here and there I have also included highly personal notes and experiences in an effort to enhance understanding and add human interest.

Third, my objective has been to provide a text that will serve as a unitive study of the situation in which missionaries find themselves at the beginning of this new century. It is also a series of essays meant to reflect individual investigation of the selected topics. This approach makes for some redundancy, of course. But it is my hope that redundancy will make it possible to grasp the argument and flow of each chapter without depending on the materials of preceding and succeeding chapters.

It is, of course, impossible to express individually the gratitude due all the colleagues with whom I have labored. From them I have learned so much of that which, however imperfectly, is reflected in this book. Those colleagues are now widely scattered across the globe, and not a few of them have been promoted to glory. But of the many who also have instructed, encouraged and helped in noteworthy ways, I want to mention the following:

- of the Evangelical Missiological Society, Drs. Norman Allison, Kenneth Gill, Keith Eitel, Michael Pocock, Gailyn Van Rheenen, Bob Lens, and Elisabeth Lightbody, who evaluated the manuscript or otherwise encouraged its publication.
- of First Evangelical Free Church of Rockford, Illinois, Mrs. Nancy Carlson and Mrs. Mary Anderson-Hendershot, who assisted with graphics.
- of Kregel Publications: Jim Weaver, Stephen Barclift, Amy Stephensen, Moriah Sharp, and their associates.

In addition, I want to express sincere thanks to my colleagues, Dr. Andreas Köstenberger and Dr. Ralph Winter, for providing forewords and otherwise encouraging me in so many ways.

Lastly, I want to recognize the members of my family: my wife, Gertude, without whose patience, kindness, and caring this book would be impossible; my son Dr. Ronald Hesselgrave, who often prevents me from settling for easy answers; my son D. Dennis Hesselgrave and his wife, Carolyn; my daughter Sheryl Ann Kroeker, and her husband, Marty; and their respective families. They all know and serve the same Lord and together constitute the kind of extended family that makes it easy to concentrate on the twin tasks of researching and writing.

Finally, a word about paradigms. As a modern physicist, Thomas Kuhn found Aristotle's *Physics* to be all but incomprehensible because Aristotle wrote out of a totally different mindset or "paradigm." Like many neologisms, this word came to be widely used in many disciplines, including missiology. "Mission paradigms" seem to come in various "sizes." The idea of a "radically new paradigm" is that mission must change its very meaning and direction. It is perhaps more usual to use *paradigm* as a synonym for *model* or *pattern*. Some of the alternative "sets" dealt with in this book can be thought of as mission models that co-exist with and even complement one another. Most, however, have at least the potential of becoming competing and conflicting models. How we think about and choose among these models will shape the future of Christian mission. May we choose prayerfully and wisely.

—DAVID J. HESSELGRAVE
Rockford, Illinois

Chapter 1

Sovereignty and Free Will

An Impossible Mix or a Perfect Match?

Oh, the depth of the riches and wisdom and knowledge of God! How unsearchable are his judgments and how inscrutable his ways!

—Romans 11:33

Prologue

WHEN HE INVITED ME TO SPEAK, the pastor also informed me that almost half of the seven or eight hundred in the congregation would be members of Campus Crusade for Christ. That was encouraging, because Campus Crusaders are especially eager to hear the Word. Speaking to them would be sheer delight. It would also be challenging because it meant that the majority of the congregation that Sunday morning would be relatively young. What would be a suitable topic?

After some prayerful reflection, I settled on the topic and, upon being introduced, announced it to the congregation. In measured words I said, "This morning I would like to speak on the subject, 'God loves you and has a wonderful plan.'" Then I paused. All Campus Crusaders and most everyone else knew that the first of the "Four Spiritual Laws" is "God loves you and has a wonderful plan *for your life.*" I assured them that I knew that also, but that the phrase *for your life* is practically meaningless unless what we were about to study in Romans 9–11 is eternally true and totally trustworthy.

With that as an introduction, the courteous and attentive audience became even more so—especially my Crusade friends. For the next forty-five minutes we zeroed in on what the apostle Paul had to say about the magnificent missionary plan of our great and mighty God.

No wonder the Serpent's ploy was so persuasive: "You will be *like God, knowing good and evil"* (Gen. 3:5, emphasis mine). Adam and Eve could not have foreseen it, but countless men and women yet unborn would spend a lifetime of study without solving the problem of good and evil to their own satisfaction, much less God's. And there in Eden that knowledge supposedly was available just for the eating of some forbidden fruit.

From a purely human point of view, one of life's greatest problems is that we humans simply do not know everything. It seems easier to accept our inability to *do* everything than to accept our inability to *know* everything. Real or imagined, it is the mysteries, imponderables, enigmas, riddles, conundrums, and antinomies of human existence that prevent many of the world's peoples from embracing divine revelation. To cope with enigma, people invent their own answers. Taoists manage to combine the *yin* and *yang* into the Tao. Buddhists pose the imponderable "What is the sound of one hand clapping?" to facilitate enlightenment. Marxists resolve thesis and antithesis into a synthesis that becomes a new thesis.

Meanwhile, thoroughgoing skeptics remain suspicious of this whole business.

Now none of this should be too surprising to the Christian. After all, people who are ignorant of the true God devise false gods, not just wrong answers. What is surprising is that, much like our first parents, even we believers are often tempted to press beyond both the boundaries of human finitude and the strictures of divine revelation to satisfy inquiring minds—our own or someone else's. Divine revelation may be quite acceptable until what is revealed seems to clash with human reason and logic. Then we go to work to solve the disconnect. In the process, we sometimes succeed in getting revelation and even God himself all bent out of shape.

The problem to be faced in this chapter can be expressed in quite simple terms: *What part does God play, and what part do people play, in all events but especially in those having to do with sin and salvation? What are their respective roles in all of history but especially in salvation history? What parts do God and people play in the whole of Christian missions but especially in the fulfillment of the Great Commission?* Although our present discussion focuses on differences between Calvinism and Arminianism, it does so only because that is where issues having to do with divine sovereignty and human free will constantly and consistently surface in Christian missions.

The Nature of the Question and Categorization of Answers

Questions having to do with the sovereignty of God and the free will of man are at the heart of a debate that has been with us for centuries and give every indication of being with us for a long time to come. Clothed in theological jargon, this kind of discussion may appear to be one in which only theologians and philosophers have either the interest or the capability to participate. This particular discussion, like most all others of lasting import, begins as a theological discussion. However, it soon becomes apparent that much more than theological positioning is at stake. For example, if systematic theology is involved, so is biblical theology. If biblical theology is concerned, so is practical theology. If practical theology is involved, our discussion is concerned not only with the way we think but also with the ways in which we pray, worship, serve, and witness.

Put another way, when we inquire into the relationship between God's sovereignty and human free will, we are inquiring into foundational questions having to do with everything from the very nature and attributes of God himself to the meaning and method of Christian missions. What part do sinners play in their salvation? Do saved sinners "elect" God, or has he already elected them? Do they exercise saving faith, or is faith as well as salvation a gift of God? Does God determine not only the course of human history but also personal histories—yours and mine? Or are humans free to write their own ticket and reap the results, whether good or bad?

Christian apologists and missionaries alike will find it impossible to avoid questions such as these if they are responsible to their calling. Answers given throughout Christian history have been so diverse and divisive that otherwise responsible missionaries are sometimes driven to despair. But they should take heart. They should be ready to give reasons for their hope in Christ. At the same time they should remember that we all see through a glass darkly. Even responsible and reputable Christians known for their scholarship, integrity, and devotion to Christ are sometimes at odds with one another on these matters. After all, we are not obliged to agree with one another on all matters—just to love and attempt to understand one another.

As they have tried to reconcile sovereignty and free will and answer related questions, Christian scholars have come up with very different and even contradictory ideas. In a recent book on the subject, and one to which I refer several times in this chapter, C. Gordon Olson deals with three views, to which I add two moderate views—moderate Calvinism and moderate Arminianism. Olson himself has come to espouse what he calls a "mediate theological view" (Olson 2002, 50–52). It will be left to readers to determine whether Olson's view is tenable and sufficiently different from moderate Calvinism and moderate Arminianism to occupy a special position between them. Be that as it may, building on Olson's work, our modified categorization is as follows:

1. Augustinian deterministic Calvinism—God alone determines all events independently of man's will, including those having to do with salvation and lostness.
2. Moderate Calvinism—Man's free will is limited and God's sovereignty and foreknowledge operate in such a way that saving grace is restricted to the elect.
3. A mediate theological view—God's sovereignty and man's free will are somehow synergistic, working together in ways that ac-

complish his plan and purpose, including those matters having to do with salvation and lostness.

4. Moderate Arminianism—God has limited his sovereignty and shown his love in such a way that his grace is extended to all on the condition of repentance and faith in the gospel of Christ, with the expectation that all are free to accept or reject it.

5. Open theism or extreme Arminianism—God's sovereignty is subject to the limits of his foreknowledge and the largeness of his love so that man's freedom is unimpeded in any way or to any degree.

I will not so much attempt to make a case for or against any of these positions as to shed light on some of the basic issues involved that have an impact on our understanding of the nature of God and Christian missions.

Missions in the Light of Calvinism and Arminianism

Later in this chapter we look specifically at some of the things that Scripture, and especially the book of Romans, has to say about these matters. First, however, we begin with an affirmation of God's great plan of redemption, reconciliation, and restoration. We begin with promises made to Adam as the head of our race, to Abraham as the father of faith, and to the faithful in Israel and the church. We begin with Jesus Christ, Son of God and Savior of the world, Messiah of Israel, and Head of the church. Then we examine two opposing viewpoints on sovereignty and free will, Calvinism and Arminianism, to take note of the impact these theological systems have on our understanding of the God of the Bible and the mission of the church.

John Calvin and Calvinism

Deeply devoted to Augustine (354–430) as well as to his own under-standing of Scripture, John Calvin (1509–1564) held that God rules and overrules human affairs in such a way that nothing happens apart from his own counsel and will. *All* events, including evil events, are ordained by him. Nevertheless, he held that God is not at all unjust and man is responsible. Following Augustine, Calvin seems to have been quite willing to leave this mystery unresolved because he believed that it squared with the teachings of the Bible.

As for human redemption, Calvin taught that, though God hated sin in man, he also found in man that which he loved. He therefore devised a plan according to which Christ would bear sin and provide salvation in the fullness of time. Calvin's teaching seems to have implied double predestination—that is, that some people are predestined to be saved and others are predestined to be lost. Salvation is a gift of God, given wholly by his grace and through faith—faith which itself is a divine gift. In his foreknowledge, God knew those who would be saved and sends his Holy Spirit to engender in them the kind of faith that accepts what has been done for them in Christ. Concerning both the elect and the reprobate, Calvin wrote,

> [Paul] concludes that God hath mercy on whom he will have mercy, and whom he will he hardeneth (Rom. 9:18). You see how he refers both to the mere pleasure of God. Therefore, if we cannot assign any reason for his bestowing mercy on his people, but just that it so pleases him, neither can we have any reason for his reprobating others but his will. When God is said to visit his mercy or harden whom he will, men are reminded that they are not to seek for any cause beyond his will (Calvin 1953, 224).

Both of the great Reformers, Calvin and Martin Luther (1483–1546), were impressed with the majesty and sovereignty of God. Both held to the historic creeds of the church and to the authority of the Scriptures. Both believed in predestination and in salvation by faith. Both believed that the Great Commission (Matt. 28:19–20) was given to, and fulfilled by, the apostles.

All of the first wave of Reformers have been faulted for not seeing the need or urgency to send missionaries to the "heathen." More so than Luther, Calvin seems to have viewed mission primarily in terms of societal transformation. From 1541 to 1564, Calvin devoted considerable effort to making of Geneva a truly Christian society. As for Luther, he thought primarily in terms of expanding the influence of the church so as to encompass more territory and peoples.

In 1555, Calvin did send a group of French Huguenots with four clergymen to found a colony for persecuted Protestants on the Bay of Rio de Janeiro. And Luther sent his pastor and colleague, Jan Bugenhagen (1485–1558), on expeditions to the low countries, Pomerania, and Scandinavia, much as we send out short-term missionaries today.

Therefore, although none of the leading first-generation Reformers, Luther, Calvin, or Huldreich Zwingli (1484–1531), looked at missions and the Great Commission in the way we do, they and some of their most prominent followers, including Theodore Beza (1519–1605) and Philip Melancthon (1497–1560) did exhibit a larger evangelistic concern. And later on in the sixteenth and seventeenth centuries, Hadrian Saravia (1530–1612), John Eliot (1604–1690), Justinian von Welz (1621–1688) and others within the Lutheran and Reformed churches came to reflect a view that was more like today's conception.

Still, the fact that Protestant missions made such little headway for two hundred years after the Reformation did have theological reasons. When in about 1664, von Welz issued a call to the churches to assume the responsibility of evangelizing the world, almost all of his colleagues thought him a dreamer at best and a heretic at worst.

"The holy things of God are not to be cast before such dogs and swine," was one reaction, as quoted by J. Herbert Kane in *A Global View of Christian Mission* (Kane 1971, 76). Much later in the 1790s, hyper-Calvinists in Scotland refused to support William Carey (1761–1834) in his mission to India, declaring that the "conversion of the heathen" would have to wait until God did it. The title of Carey's work, *An Enquiry into the Obligation of Christians to Use Means for the Conversion of the Heathen* (1792), indicates the difficulties Carey had with certain Calvinists (Neill 1965, 261). And when, a little over a decade later in 1806, American students were driven under a haystack by rain and spent the time praying for the world, they kept records in code because they were persuaded that Calvinists would think of their ideas as absurd (Olson 2002, 384).

There is another side to this predestinarian coin, however. In discussing Calvinism's contribution to nineteenth-century Protestant missions, Roger Greenway notes that Calvinist missionaries played a major role in missions to Africa, Asia, and Latin America in particular. He credits in part the emphases on God's sovereignty in missions and God's lordship over all places and every aspect of life. He also insists that the importance of the glory of God in Calvinist theology was a motivating influence for carrying out evangelism. The Westminster Shorter Catechism begins, "The chief end of man is to glorify God and to enjoy him for ever" (Greenway 2000, 155–56).

Jacob Arminius and Arminianism

In the late sixteenth century a student of Beza, Jakob Arminius (1560–1609), became a Reformed pastor in Amsterdam. Well-educated and eloquent, he attracted large audiences. At the time, certain Dutch Reformed ministers known as the remonstrants took issue with the view that God decreed certain men to be lost and others to be saved. They held:

- that Christ died for all and not just for the elect;
- that salvation is by faith alone given from God's grace and through rebirth; and
- that God does not predestine any person to be either lost or saved but
- that all who accept God's grace are saved, and those who reject it are lost.

When Arminius left his pastorate and became a professor at the University of Leiden, he set out to refute these remonstrants. Instead, he was persuaded by them. Arminius died before the controversy eventuated in the calling of a synod of Reformed church leaders at Dordt or Dordrecht in the Netherlands (1618–19). At the Synod of Dordt, a five-point Calvinism was set out to refute the ideas popularized by Arminius. The remonstrants were excommunicated.

Arminius and others who held to more moderate Calvinist doctrines came to be known as Arminians. Many who were basically of that persuasion played important roles in launching the modern missionary movement from the Continent in the seventeenth century; from England at the end of the eighteenth century; and from America at the beginning of the nineteenth century. Included were the Pietists Philip Spener (1635–1705) and August Francke (1663–1727) of Halle; Ludwig von Zinzendorf (1700–1760) and the Moravians of Herrnhut in Germany. William Carey (1761–1834) moved to this position after his rejection by some members of his own presbytery and it became the theological position of his Baptist missions board.

According to Charles Van Engen, Arminianism has made five major contributions to Protestant missions thinking and activity.

1. The belief that Christ died for all has provided missionary motivation.
2. The emphasis on conversion and a relationship with Christ has been an impetus for evangelism and revival.
3. The stress on prevenient grace has meant that Arminians are open to the workings of God's grace in righting the wrongs caused by sin and in openness toward cultures.
4. The call for religious freedom from the state has provided for a more freewheeling and creative approach to missions.
5. The emphasis on freedom in working cooperatively with God has given impetus to world evangelization and social reform. (Van Engen 2000, 76–78)

Not all observers will evaluate some of these emphases quite as positively as does Van Engen. Some will find here a certain anthropocentrism and experientialism that can be overreaching and even counterproductive. However, as in the case of Calvinism, most of the really deleterious influences of Arminian theology and missiology emanate from extreme forms of it.

Analyzing and Avoiding the Extremes

True teachings can be pressed to the point where other teachings, equally true, are lost sight of and the teachings so tenaciously held and extremely stretched are left alone to explain all relevant phenomena. Partial truth, while still truth, is not the whole truth even though it may be made to function as though that were indeed the case. Calvinism can be maintained and expounded in such a way that it makes (or *appears* to make) God out to be the Author or Determiner of everything that happens and man the victim of God's decisions. Arminianism can be maintained and expounded in such a way that it makes (or *appears* to make) man out to be the sole determiner of his fate and God the loving but limited landlord of the human estate.

Augustinian Deterministic Calvinism

Augustine's idea was that God's sovereignty is exhaustive, comprehensive, and deterministic of all events, not just the salvation event. That view was argued by the Synod of Dordt (1618–19) and in the Westminster Confession of Faith (1647). However, Augustine's determinism was thought to be extreme by some. Melancthon anticipated Arminian theology and sent the Lutheran Church in that direction with the Augsburg Confession (1530). Arminius and the remonstrants strongly rejected Augustine's pessimism about human ability.

As one would anticipate, determinists such as Augustine, Calvin, Jonathan Edwards (1703–1758), and Charles Hodge (1797–1878) have been succeeded by contemporary interpreters such as John Piper, Ray Ortlund Jr., R. C. Sproul, and Harold Camping. But, by the same token, these determinists have critics who believe that their teachings lead to hurtful consequences. C. Gordon Olson is one of them. He expresses appreciation for the scholarship of these men, but he finds their methodology flawed and some of their conclusions extreme and believes that they unnecessarily polarize believers. He maintains that some of their statements on predestination and election go beyond the biblical text; that some of their assertions go beyond Calvin's own statements; and that the frequent charge that Arminians and most evangelicals today are Pelagian or semi-Pelagian is divisive (Olson 2002, 441–46).

Entertaining a related but still different concern, Ralph Winter takes issue with what he calls a "passive Augustinian neo-Platonism" that experiences catastrophic illness and other bad events and then concludes that "it must have been God's will." Winter points out that, despite his deterministic position, Edwards died in an effort to spare Indians by trying out a vaccine on himself. He did this in the face of Augustinian/ Calvinistic fellow clergy who said that he was "interfering with Divine Providence" (Winter 2001, 6). Winter credits the open theist Gregory Boyd with a substantial insight when, in *God at War,* Boyd maintains that sickness is the "work of the devil, and not the will of God" (Boyd 1997, 183; quoted in Winter 2001, 5). Winter advances the idea that research and other undertakings directed toward the eradication of disease-bearing microbiological organisms are part of our Christian duty in the war against evil (see chap. 10). And he insists that this understanding and approach would have tremendous appeal to educated Hindus, whose worldview makes Brahman out to be the source of suffering and evil.

To the extent that Calvinists state or defend their position in extreme ways, criticisms such as those of Olson and Winter merit a hearing. Most evangelicals take exception to the notion that the God and Father of our Lord Jesus Christ is the Author of evil. They take exception to a scenario where humans dance puppet-like on a string that reaches from heaven and to the accepting and supposedly "faith-full" response, "God killed my baby." The God of the Bible becomes an impersonal god like Brahman or a deity like Allah who rules by fiat decree and whose love is confined to submitters only.

However, not all extremists are of a determinist bent. Some are free-willist.

Open Theism and Extreme Arminianism

At the free-willist, Arminian end of the theological spectrum is a view of God that became quite prominent about the turn of the century. Sometimes called extreme Arminians, open theists such as Gregory Boyd, Clark Pinnock, John Sanders, Richard Rice, and William Hasker take exception to the classic view of God held by the church fathers and Reformers (Pinnock 1996; Boyd 2001). They deny that God is omniscient in the sense that he has absolute foreknowledge of all future events. Whether by self-limitation or simply by virtue of the fact that future events have not yet occurred and therefore cannot be known, God's sovereignty is circumscribed. He simply does not have foreknowledge that encompasses all future happenings. Even if he may somehow be

able to orchestrate certain events crucial to his purposes (e.g., such as
the crucifixion of Christ), he cannot know the free actions of individuals
that culminate in such events. Open theists emphasize that God's love is
such that humans are free to make their own choices. Often surprised
by the calamities that overtake his children, God "feels" with them in
their difficulties and sometimes "changes his mind" in response to their
entreaties and prayers.

Criticisms of open theology are numerous and serious. Most basic is
the criticism that open theism flies in the face of the orthodox and biblical
teaching that one of God's attributes is a foreknowledge that is comprehensive and absolute. Furthermore, in denying God's omniscience, open
theists also diminish his omnipotence, immutability, and ability to effect
his plan for history. As Bruce Ware writes,

> And what do we make of God's providential oversight of the
> unfolding of human history? Deficient knowledge and wisdom
> surely mean that neither we nor God can be certain about just
> what will happen in the end. Will God succeed in fulfilling his
> goals? Will history move in the direction he hopes it will? Are
> God's predictions and promises sure? The only answer open the-
> ists can give to these questions is that they are hopeful that God
> will somehow pull it off. . . . In short, the God of open theism
> suffers greatly from this lack of knowledge and it affects his
> plans, wise counsel, predictive ability, and providential control
> of history. (Ware 2000, 20)

E. Calvin Beisner goes so far as to say that open theism constitutes an
"evangelical heathenism." His view is that open theists remake God in
accordance with their own image of him. He dates the invasion of open
theology into the modern missions movement to the 1930s and 1940s
with the moral government theology of Gordon C. Olson (1907–1989;
not to be confused with C. Gordon Olson, also cited in this chapter).
An engineer and informal Bible teacher associated with the organization
Men for Missions, Gordon C. Olson was influenced by revivalist Charles
G. Finney (1792–1875) and theologian Lorenzo D. McCabe (1817–1897).
Beisner appeals to a number of theologians and contends that Finney

tended to elevate philosophy over Scripture. McCabe took Arminius's and John Wesley's ideas of human freedom and carried them entirely too far. Influenced by Finney and McCabe, Olson promoted the idea that "God's foreknowledge was necessarily limited by human free will" (Beisner 1996, 17). Abandoning the classical doctrine of the omniscience of God and taking his findings to their "logical" conclusion, Olson taught that such classical doctrines as original sin, human depravity and moral inability, the atonement, and justification are also wrong.

Beisner's criticism of Olson's open theism (and moral government theology) is indeed severe, but there has been no shortage of other critiques and by no means do all of them stem from Calvinistic determinism and the doctrine of foreordination.

One of the earliest criticisms of open theism was that of William Lane Craig (Craig 1987, esp. 27–37). In Craig's view, foreordination cannot be the only, or even the best, argument against open theism. First, Craig surveys the vast amount of biblical data that confirms what Christians have known and believed from apostolic times, namely, that God has absolute knowledge of the past, present, and future. Accordingly, he maintains that the plain and overwhelming testimony of Scripture is that open theology/theism cannot be true.

Second, he argues that God's foreknowledge includes knowledge of our sinful intentions, thoughts, and behaviors. But since God cannot be the author of evil, it is not possible that he foreordained these sinful occurrences. Sinful activities "are therefore truly free acts, or contingents, and God's knowledge of them is thus foreknowledge of future free actions" (quoted in Olson 2002, 451).

Third, Craig upholds the concept of middle knowledge—the notion that God knows the future in its entirety, and he knows the events that could take place but *actually do not*. For example, Jesus said that if the mighty works he did in Galilee had been performed in Sodom, Tyre, and Sidon, those cities would have repented (Matt. 11:20–24). This demonstrates a knowledge not only of what actually happened but what might have happened under different circumstances. Having knowledge this extensive, God has the ability to choose between the free choices of human agents by ordering circumstances without effecting the actual choices themselves.

The primary stage upon which this controversy will be played out is a theological one. But a theological issue is also a missiological issue by definition. Recalling the pilgrimage of McCabe, we cannot disregard the possibility—even the likelihood—that denial of God's omniscience will lead to changes in or rejection of doctrines intrinsic to biblical missions. This will be apparent in chapter 2. As we will see (pp. 56–57), some open theists refashion the love of God in such a way as to make heaven not universally obtainable but bordering on the inescapable. God's mercy becomes so wide and human freedom so extensive that only those who actually choose hell can be expected to go there. To the extent that open theists go to such an extreme, not only is the sovereign God of the Bible diminished by human freedom, but Christian mission is diminished as well.

Mediating Proposals and Options

The best way to deal with the relationship between divine sovereignty and human responsibility is to go to the biblical text and, employing sound principles of exegesis, attempt to see what the text actually says. Of course, the Scriptures must be read and studied within the contexts of the historical and contemporary churches, so we must give consideration to whatever the best minds and hearts of the church have had to say and do. Church and missions history provides us with numerous correctives if we are prepared to learn from history. But ultimately we must go to the Bible for ourselves and study the text "in its original historical-cultural and grammatico-literary, as well as its theological, context," as William Larkin admonishes us (Larkin 2001, 1). Philip Schaff long ago wrote, "The Bible gives us a theology which is more human than Calvinism, and more divine than Arminianism, and more Christian than either of them" (cited in Olson 2002, 32).

In identifying basic views on this subject, C. Gordon Olson does not give special attention to either a moderate Calvinism or a moderate Arminianism. Rather, he identifies his own view as being the "mediate theological view" and provides an extensive explanation without mentioning other parallel views. Perhaps he feels that his view is unique. Perhaps it is. Here I will look at Olson's "mediate" view alongside that of a moderate Calvinist and a moderate Arminian. None of the three views comes out of an attempt to work out some kind of "friendly compromise." All three are sincere attempts to wrestle with what the Bible actually has to say on this critical issue, thereby opening the door to continuing dialogue. All three proposers are wholeheartedly committed, not only to the authority of Scripture, but also to Christian mission.

D. A. Carson and Grant R. Osborne are colleagues in the New Testament department of Trinity Evangelical Divinity School (TEDS) in Deerfield, Illinois. C. Gordon Olson completed his doctoral studies at TEDS. The reference used in briefly summarizing the positions of Carson and Osborne is a publication of the Ministerial Association of the Evangelical Free Church of America in which their views are compared and contrasted (Keynes 2001). Carson has written an entire book on the topic (Carson 1994). For Olson's position we will look at his book, *Beyond Calvinism and Arminianism* (Olson 2002).

The Mediating Perspective of a Calvinist: D. A. Carson

Carson approaches the problem as a Calvinist and argues for "compatibilism" (Keynes 2001, 1–10; see also Carson 1994; Carson 2000). In his view, God is absolutely sovereign but never in a way that mitigates human responsibility. His sovereignty is never to be understood to mean that anything and everything that happens does so as a result of God's direct doing and therefore man is not really free. Divine sovereignty and human free will are not antithetical because God stands behind good and evil "asymmetrically." That is, God stands behind good in such a way that he causes good, and it is to be credited to him. Evil, on the other hand, is occasioned by secondary causes. God himself is not responsible for evil nor is he to be charged with that responsibility.

The Bible yields numerous illustrations of compatibilism. For example, when Joseph's brothers were confronted with the evil they had done in selling him into slavery, Joseph said, "Do not fear, for am I in the place of God? As for you, you meant evil against me, but God meant it for good, to bring it about that many people should be kept alive, as they are today" (Gen. 50:19–20). Two very different intentions were involved in that single act. The fact that God used it for good and deserved credit for that did not mitigate the fact that Joseph's brothers meant it for evil and therefore they had to bear responsibility for what they did. Joseph gave God credit for the good, but God alone was in a position to judge Joseph's brothers.

Joseph's experience presaged a similar and infinitely more important event, namely, the crucifixion of Christ which, in accordance with God's perfect plan effected salvation but without absolving those who actually crucified him of responsibility for that heinous crime.

Carson clears up a number of difficulties that arise out of mistaken assumptions and misinterpretations of the biblical text, but he is quite ready to concede that, though compatibilism offers a logical and biblical way of better understanding the tension between divine sovereignty and human freedom, compatibilism itself remains something of a mystery.

The Mediating Perspective of an Arminian: Grant R. Osborne

Approaching the question from an Arminian perspective, Osborne says that both Calvinists and Arminians do well to approach their differences with a good measure of humility. Not only does the Bible present us with a large number of verses that support both positions, but a careful reading of the Bible as a whole would seem to indicate that God is not as interested in this issue as we are. Furthermore, there is no indication that this issue was a subject of debate in the early church.

That having been said, Osborne is concerned that extreme forms of both views be rejected (Keynes 2001, 10–13). He is persuaded that a correct understanding of Arminianism would answer to excesses of both positions. Arminianism, he says, does hold to God's omniscience, his sovereignty, and even to the predestination of those who will believe. At the same time, human depravity means that, faced with a decision for Christ, the person who does not know Christ will reject him apart from the convicting power of the Holy Spirit. Predestination grows out of that foreknowledge. So repentance and faith is "simply the way we participate in the saving work of God (Rom. 3:21–4:25)" (12).

One way of reconciling freedom and divine foreknowledge is middle knowledge (referred to above) according to which God knows all possible worlds in which humans exercise free will and God actualizes the possible world that conforms to his will. But of greater interest than satisfying the biblical tension between sovereignty and freedom is Osborne's twin interests of helping the church to avoid both doctrinal aberrations and ecclesiastical divisions with reference to this question.

The "Mediate Theological View": C. Gordon Olson

Olson's missionary text *What in the World Is God Doing?* (Olson 2003) and his *Beyond Calvinism and Arminianism* (Olson 2000) are of special interest because they reflect the musings and investigations of a missiologist who has wrestled with these issues and arrived at an understanding that he believes to be satisfying and biblical.

Olson first attempted to divest himself of unwarranted assumptions and undertook a thoroughgoing inductive study of the biblical text as it relates to Calvinism and Arminianism. He reaches a view that is actually more Amyraldian (i.e., basically Calvinist but more Arminian with respect to the doctrine of grace). But since Olson himself simply calls it a "mediate theological view" I will attempt to briefly summarize what is involved and leave it at that.

There are three major movements in the development of Olson's mediate position: (1) a new awareness that philosophical assumptions play a major role in Calvinist extremism; (2) an extensive inductive study of the biblical text; and (3) the emergence of a new position. Let's look at what is involved.

First, Olson credits Calvinist J. Oliver Buswell Jr. with "sensitizing" him to a philosophical error that had been a determining factor in his own thinking up to his reading of Buswell. The error was the commonly held notion that God cannot foreknow that which he has not determined. Buswell's response to that idea reminds us of William Lane Craig's position above and is unequivocal. He writes:

> [Jonathan] Edwards and [Lorraine] Boettner thus come to the conclusion that, since God is omniscient, there can be no free or contingent event.
>
> But it is presumptuous for man to claim to know what kind of things God could or could not know. *There is a mystery*

in knowledge which will probably never be resolved for us.
Nevertheless, even human knowledge is an observable fact. For
men to declare that God could not know a free event in the future
seems to me sheer dogmatism. (Buswell 1962, 1:46; emphasis
mine)

Olson holds that Buswell's insight is devastating to both extreme Calvinism and extreme Arminianism. Olson likewise takes aim at another
unwarranted assumption by saying that the certainty of a future event
need not necessarily mean that the event has been divinely determined.

Second, having disabused himself of these "unwarranted assumptions," Olson proceeds with an inductive study of the biblical text that
includes relevant word studies, an examination of texts crucial to the
cases of extremists, a special study of passages that bear most intimately
on the sovereignty of God as sovereignty relates to salvation, and so on.
Only by undertaking a careful reading of this book will the reader be
able to appreciate the comprehensiveness of his study.

Third, as one would expect, the "mediate view" to which Olson arrives is both comprehensive and complex. Nothing approaching justice
can be done to it in this venue, but by simply pointing to some baseline
conclusions that relate most intimately to the sovereignty/free will issue,
perhaps readers will get a sense of his thinking.

1. God limited the exercise of his sovereignty by creating moral beings and delegating certain authority to them.
2. Since the fall did not erase God's image, depravity does not mean
   that man cannot respond to God's initiatives.
3. Although Christ's death is particularly efficacious for believers, it
   is potentially available to all.
4. Election/foreordination is based upon foreknowledge.
5. The conviction of the Spirit immediately prepares sinners for
   faith.
6. The new birth is conditioned upon repentant faith.
7. God's calling to salvation is not irresistible.
8. God declares sinners to be righteous by repentant faith alone,
   apart from works.

9. Christ's charge is to proclaim salvation on God's terms. (Olson 2002, 33–44)

In essence, Olson's mediate position holds that by virtue of his omniscience and foreknowledge God orchestrates and orders events of his choosing without coercing the wills of the moral agents involved in them. Certain men and women may not incline themselves to follow God's will and for that they will be held accountable. But by his Spirit, an omniscient and omnipotent God can work in both the world of his making and the lives of his creatures in such a way as to counteract evil and effect his own plan and purpose.

Sovereignty, Freedom, and God's Plan according to Paul

One Bible passage frequently referred to in connection with the issue is Romans 9–11. Given the fact that the early Christians entertained existential questions just as puzzling and even perplexing as the theoretical questions we face, it is not surprising that the Spirit led missionary Paul to write to these issues as they relate to the larger plan of God in church and missions.

The Two Meanings of "Mystery"

The word *mystery* (Gk. *mystērion*) comes into play here. The term is used twenty-seven times in the New Testament (twenty-two times in the singular). The word is derived from *muo,* which means to shut one's mouth and from that idea comes the basic meaning of "silence," and by extension, "secret." The word has various related meanings in the New Testament, but primarily it is used to refer to sacred truth or information or teaching that would not be known to human intelligence unless and until God chooses to reveal it by his Spirit. Accordingly, Paul speaks of the "mystery of the gospel" (Eph. 6:19), the "mystery of Christ" (Col. 4:3), the "mystery" having to do with Christ and the church (Eph. 5:32), and, in the chapters before us, the "mystery" of God's plan for the partial hardening of Israel, the inauguration and completion of the "times of the Gentiles," and the restoration of Israel (Rom. 11:25).

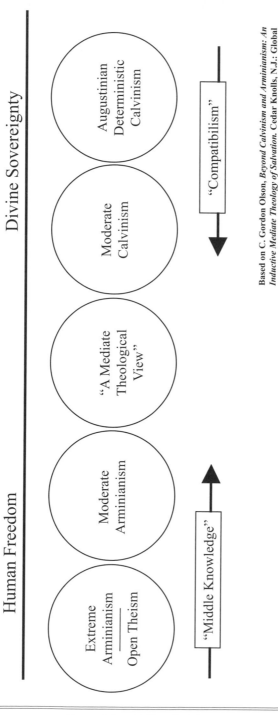

Human Freedom

Divine Sovereignty

Extreme Arminianism / Open Theism

Moderate Arminianism

"A Mediate Theological View"

Moderate Calvinism

Augustinian Deterministic Calvinism

"Middle Knowledge"

"Compatibilism"

Based on C. Gordon Olson, *Beyond Calvinism and Arminianism: An Inductive Mediate Theology of Salvation.* Cedar Knolls, N.J.: Global Gospel Publishers, 2002:50-52.

Figure 1. Free Will and Divine Sovereignty

It is of the utmost importance that we recognize the profound difference between this (primary, but not sole) use of *mystērion* in the New Testament and the meaning of the English word *mystery* as commonly defined in our dictionaries and used in ordinary conversation (i.e., something beyond human comprehension). As is often said, New Testament mysteries are "revealed secrets"—known, but only by virtue of divine revelation. English dictionary mysteries, on the other hand, are "known to be incomprehensible" or, at least, largely so.

Paul highlights both types of mystery in Romans 9–11 and it is of the essence that we understand this to be the case. Paul did not write these chapters primarily to solve human conundrums of either the first or the twenty-first century. He wrote them to answer questions growing out of divine revelation, especially those having to do with God's plan for his people Israel.

What about God's promises to Abraham, his disposition of Israel as a nation, and the relationship between believing Jews and Gentiles in the church of Jesus Christ? These were the "mysteries" with which Paul and his readers were concerned (Rom. 11:29; Eph. 3:4, 6, 9). Granted, in answering these and still other questions related to God's plan for Israel, Paul dealt with other perplexing issues as well. But Paul was mainly concerned with the faithfulness of God, his great redemptive plan for the world, and the place of Israel and the church in that plan. Roman Christians, and other believers, desperately needed to understand the nature of the true God and the divine plan for all peoples and especially his own. Answers to the questions were available, but only by virtue of divine revelation.

It is reassuring that, nearly a century and a half ago in his commentary on Romans, Charles Hodge, distinguished between these two types of mysteries (Hodge 1859, 277). Recognition of that simple distinction no doubt contributed to some emphases that do not ordinarily characterize Reformed theology, such as his insistence that God makes his salvation available to all; that God's offer of mercy is to be extended to all; and that "whosoever calls on the name of the Lord shall be saved" (256–57). While the identity of the Jewish nation has to do with a separate debate, Hodge also took a position more common to Arminians that the "[Jewish] nation, as such, shall acknowledge Jesus to be the Messiah, and be admitted into his (God's) kingdom" (278).

The Mystery of the "Partial Hardening of Israel" and God's Plan

Frederick Godet called the book of Romans the "cathedral of the Christian Faith" (Godet 1970, introduction). Certainly it is one of the most concise and yet incisive theologies ever penned. It was most likely written about A.D. 58 to the fledgling church at Rome. Though Paul had not yet visited the church, he knew a number of the believers there (Rom. 16:3–16) and something of their trials. Jews, for example, had already been expelled from Rome by the Emperor Claudius (ruled 41–54) and some were perhaps returning with predictable anxieties. Christians undoubtedly were aware of precursors of the kind of persecution that was about to be unleashed under Nero (ruled 54–68). It was no simple matter to figure out what in the world God was doing.

Look at it this way. As the "apostle to the Gentiles," Paul wanted believers in Rome to understand not only what God was doing but also his own message and mission. Accordingly, he laid out the basics of God's eternal and magnificent plan of redemption. As he proceeded to unfold the doctrines of sin, justification, sanctification, and glorification, the Roman believers must have been overawed by the greatness and majesty of it all. At the same time, they were living in a time of transition. The "people of God" had come to include many people other than Jews. In fact, in the church the distinction between Jew and Gentile had been erased. There was no preference. Or was there? What about God's prior election of Israel? Had God's plan and promises to Abraham, Isaac, and Jacob failed? If so, and God was unable to work out his plan for Israel, what about the promises and plan for all Christians as disclosed in Romans 1–8? To put it in another way (and in a way some may prefer to put it), what kind of God is he after all? Is he forgetful of his promise? Changeable? Unknowing? Limited?

Paul deals with questions such as these in Romans 9–11. Many commentators think of these chapters as constituting a parenthesis between the doctrinal chapters that preceded them and the practical chapters that follow. But if these chapters constitute a parenthesis, it must be one of the most important parentheses ever penned. A consideration of Paul's teachings at this point should be sufficient to convince us of that. Take note of Paul's points:

As concerns God's sovereignty in his dealings with Israel—Romans 9:1–29. Paul affirms that Israel is indeed a special people of God, and that the promise of God to Abraham (Gen. 12:1–3 et al.) has not failed. But not all natural descendents ("children of the flesh"—v. 8) are children of the promise because God chose as his special children the descendents of Abraham through Isaac and Jacob. And he did so of his own sovereign will before they were born and could show themselves to be good or bad.

But wait a minute. Paul's answer, based on divine revelation, elicits a question that emanates from human curiosity: How can God hold Hagar, Ishmael, Esau, and their progeny responsible when he is the one who did the choosing? How does one get around that problem? And Paul only compounds that mystery when he adds that it all depends on God's will and purpose, not on human will and works. Why? Because God purposes that his power be proclaimed throughout the whole world.

Human questioners of every century really get their comeuppance here. "Who, after all, do God's creatures think they are to question God's decisions?" asks Paul. Since when does the pot question the potter as concerns its shape? These rhetorical questions are straightforward and to the point. They are also rather unsatisfying if we persist in pursuing human perplexities. But if we are willing to take our lumps and return to what God has chosen to reveal of his will and plan, more light will be forthcoming.

Paul goes on to say that the sin of Israel would be sufficient ground for their rejection as a nation. But since all Israelites were not rejected there must be more. And there is: God's promise to Abraham, his commandments through Moses, his judgment on Pharaoh's Egypt, his messages of mercy through Hosea and Isaiah—all are still valid. God in patience endured vessels of wrath in order to make vessels of mercy. God fashioned for himself a people who were not a people, a "beloved" who was not beloved, and "sons of the living God" who were nobodies. So says Hosea. And so it is. Apart from God's mercy corporate Israel would have ended up like Sodom and Gomorrah. But because God is patient, loving, and merciful, a remnant will be saved and "carry out [God's] sentence upon the earth fully and without delay." So says Isaiah. And so it is. There are no ifs, ands, or buts here precisely because, in the final analysis, the fulfillment of God's plans and promises does not depend upon "human will or exertion." It depends on God himself.

As concerns man's freedom to respond to God—Romans 9:30–10:21. In this section of the parenthesis, Paul speaks more to issues having to do with human will and the ability to respond appropriately to God. In the closing verses of chapter 9, Paul says that the difference between the larger nation of Israel on the one hand, and the "remnant" of Israel and believing Gentiles on the other, is that the former relied on the law and attempted to attain righteousness by works while the latter exercised faith and attained the righteousness that comes by faith. Corporately, Israel "stumbled over Christ" and was (temporarily) rejected. A remnant of Jews and many Gentiles believed in Christ and have been (eternally) saved.

The eternal purpose of God being to show forth his own power and mercy through Christ, human freedom basically consists in inclining heart and mind toward or away from God and his revelation. All lesser freedoms flow from this fundamental one. And even here it is the Holy Spirit who is at work. Illumination, conviction, salvation—all are aspects of his work of grace. Acknowledgment, repentance, faith—God has every right to expect these by way of grateful response. If this is not enough to completely quiet our human curiosity, it nevertheless is essential to understanding the plan of God.

These truths bring us to one of the greatest missionary passages in the entire Bible—a passage we must look at in some considerable detail in the chapter that follows on the fate of the unevangelized. At this point, we confine ourselves to the shortest and simplest way of summarizing Paul's teaching in these verses as it relates to the present discussion: God's eternal and unchangeable purpose and plan is that in this age of grace his "new people," the church, preach the gospel to people everywhere so that "whosoever will" may call upon the name of the Lord and be saved (Rom. 10:14–17). It is our responsibility and privilege to go and preach to worldlings. It is their privilege and responsibility to hear and believe.

As concerns the brilliance and glory evident in the divine plan—Romans 11:1–36. Paul himself must have been overwhelmed as he unraveled the threads of God's magnificent plan for Israel and the nations as outlined in the first thirty-two verses of Romans 11. God did not reject Israel even though they temporarily rejected him. As in Old Testament times so today in this age of grace, there is a Jewish remnant who will believe when the gospel is preached. Though Israel as a nation has been removed from the olive tree and the Gentiles grafted in, this arrangement is temporary. The salvation of Gentiles will move Israel to jealousy and faith, the "times of the Gentiles" will come to an end, and Israel will be grafted into the olive tree again. If Israel's trespass has blessed the world through the death and resurrection of Christ, just imagine what their turnaround will mean, not only for them but for the entire world. Truly through Abraham all will be blessed.

What began with a human query in Romans 9:1 ends in *gloria Dei* in Romans 11:33–36. Human curiosity may not be fully satisfied, but the all-important answer to the question with which Paul began this section of Romans is now so clear and compelling that Paul himself can hardly contain himself. No person had any inkling of what God would do with his chosen people. No one was in a position to offer God counsel as to how he should proceed, once they rejected him. No people of earth merited either his saving grace or the revelation of his grace. Yet being as all-knowing as he is, he conceived the plan. Being as loving as he is, he made it possible. Being as all-powerful as he is, he will carry it through:

> Oh, the depth of the riches and wisdom and knowledge of God! How unsearchable are his judgments and how inscrutable his ways! . . . For from him and through him and to him are all things. To him be glory forever. Amen. (Rom. 11:33, 36)

Conclusion

Curious things happen in human forums. For years, members of the Evangelical Theological Society (E.T.S.) engaged in a debate on the theological position of open theology as it has been expressed by some who consider themselves evangelical. The debate finally came down to the question of whether two members who espouse open theism, Clark Pinnock of McMaster Divinity College, Hamilton, Ontario, and John Sanders of Huntington (Indiana) College, should be expelled from the E.T.S. Many discussions and almost an entire issue of the *Journal of the Evangelical Theological Society* (June 2002) were devoted to the question. Many expected that they would be expelled at the annual meeting in Atlanta, Georgia, in November 2003, but accommodations were made and that action was not taken.

A report in *Christianity Today* related, "Most members of the E.T.S. believe such teaching [i.e., open theism] not only departs from the overwhelming testimony of Christian thinkers through the ages but also calls into question God's own accuracy in biblical prophecy." If that is so, ordinary mortals might wonder how it could be that its proponents could be exonerated in the councils of astute twenty-first-century evangelical theologians (Neff 2004, 21). But it appears that open theists have not been exonerated. Very likely the open theology discussion has not been closed. As E.T.S. President David Howard Jr. of Bethel Seminary later reported, "Open theism has not been cleared. The issue was the connection to inerrancy."

It seems that, after all had been said and done, the issue ultimately did not come down to whether open theism is acceptable. Since the theological basis of the E.T.S. rests on a shared belief in the inerrancy of the Bible, the real issue is whether a member can opt for open theism and still hold to the inerrancy of Scripture. Both Pinnock and Sanders claim to believe in inerrancy, so in the final analysis the question becomes, "What does inerrancy mean?" (see further discussion of that issue in ch. 8). According to Howard, "Upholding inerrancy will probably require incorporating an expanded definition of the term in the ETS constitution. That will require an 80 percent vote and a long process" (Neff 2004, 22).

In short, rather than resolve the problem of open theism, well-meaning theologians have taken on another problem that just aggravates matters. We have left the question of the nature of God and moved to a discussion of the nature of revelation. Some observers might be justified in using this debate as *prima facie* evidence that theologians do not solve problems. Rather, they only create problems to be solved.

But that conclusion is unwarranted. If anything, all of this simply proves that, like everyone else, theologians have limitations, both individually and corporately. It also may well prove that, when it comes to the question before us, there is a point at which acceptance of the complementarity and even synergy of God's sovereignty and man's freedom actually can enlighten our minds, strengthen our faith, encourage our service, and reinforce our mission. By the same token, there is a point past which the clash and tension between divine sovereignty and human free will do just the opposite.

It is incumbent upon us all, then, to recognize our finitude, avoid extremes seemingly necessitated by human reason or bias, and simply accept God for who he is and Scripture for what it says. Then we should trust ourselves to the faith and service of an all-knowing, all-powerful, wholly just, and ever-loving God. Parallel rails of a railroad track seem to run together if one looks far enough into the distance. But, given human reason and experience, we know that they do not actually meet. They just appear to do so. The sovereignty of God and the free will of humankind appear to run on parallel tracks and, no matter how far we gaze into the future, it seems that they cannot possibly come together.

But given divine revelation, a full measure of faith, and an appropriate supply of humility, we eventually will come to understand that they *come together.* It just *appears* that they cannot do so. In another dimension of space and time they actually can and will. In the end, divine sovereignty and human free will prove to be a perfect match, not an impossible mix.

Christ staked his whole life and ministry on it. We can stake ours on it too.

Epilogue

"I would like to speak this morning on the topic 'God Loves You and Has a Wonderful Plan . . . Period.'" It was the "period" that initially ruffled that part of my audience that was "in the know." They were so conditioned to hearing and repeating "God loves you and has a wonderful plan *for your life"* that my topic seemed to be not only truncated but almost heretical.

For forty minutes or so we devoted our minds to thinking with Paul as he showed how an awesome God melded the vagaries of Abraham's faith, the hardness of Pharaoh's heart, the steel of Joseph's character, and (miracle of miracles) the horrendous crucifixion of his beloved Son by his chosen people. His plan was such that he could provide and proclaim the life-giving gospel to all peoples. As we proceeded in the text, our hearts sang with Paul: "Oh, the depths of the riches and wisdom and knowledge of God! . . . For from him and through him and to him are all things. To him be glory forever. Amen."

Then and only then did the true significance of the "therefore" in Romans 12:1 become apparent. If our God was both willing and capable of effecting such a wonderful plan for Israel, for his church, and for the whole world, is it not reasonable that we freely present our bodies in sacrificial service to him? And is it not reasonable to believe that, whatever twists and turns our life might take, sooner or later we will discover that his plan for our life is as "good and acceptable and perfect" as has been his magnificent plan for all of history (Rom. 12:2)? After all, his plan for *our* history is but part of his larger plan for *all* history, is it not?

As they departed church that morning, some of our hearers remarked, "You know, I never thought of it that way." That's a bit odd, isn't it? The Holy Spirit inspired Paul to think and write about it that way almost two thousand years ago.

References

Beisner, E. Calvin. 1996. *Evangelical Heathenism: Examining Contemporary Revivalism.* Moscow, Idaho: Canon.

Boyd, Gregory A. 1997. *God at War.* Downers Grove, Ill.: InterVarsity.

———. 2001. *God of the Possible: A Biblical Introduction to the Openness of God.* Grand Rapids: Baker.

Buswell, J. Oliver. 1962. *A Systematic Theology of the Christian Religion.* Vol. 1. Grand Rapids: Zondervan.

Calvin, John. 1845 E.T. *Institutes of the Christian Religion.* Trans. by Henry Beveridge. Calvin Translation Society; various editions.

Carson, D. A. 1994. *Divine Sovereignty and Human Responsibility: Biblical Perspectives in Tension.* Grand Rapids: Baker.

———. 2000. *The Difficult Doctrine of the Love of God.* Wheaton, Ill.: Crossway.

Craig, William Lane. 1987. *The Only Wise God: The Compatibility of Divine Foreknowledge and Human Freedom.* Grand Rapids: Baker.

Godet, Frederick Louis. 1883. *A Commentary on the Epistle to the Romans.* One volume edition reprint, Grand Rapids, Zondervan, 1970.

Greenway, Roger S. 2000. "Calvinism." In *Evangelical Dictionary of Evangelical Missions,* edited by A. Scott Moreau. Grand Rapids: Baker.

Hodge, Charles. 1859. *Commentary on the Epistle to the Romans.* 17th ed. Philadelphia: William S. & Alfred Martien.

Kane, J. Herbert. 1971. *A Global View of Christian Mission: From Pentecost to the Present.* Grand Rapids: Baker.

Keynes, William. 2001. *The Open View of God: A Critique.* Minneapolis: EFCA Ministerial Association.

Larkin, William J. 2001. "The Role of Biblical-Theological Methods in Missiological Research." *Occasional Bulletin, Evangelical Theological Society* 16.1 (Winter): 1–8.

Neff, David. 2004. "Open to Healing." *Christianity Today,* January, 21–22.

Neill, Stephen. 1965. *A History of Christian Missions.* Grand Rapids: Eerdmans.

Olson, C. Gordon. 2002. *Beyond Calvinism and Arminianism: An Inductive, Mediate Theology of Salvation.* Cedar Knolls, N.J.: Global Gospel.

———. 2003. *What in the World Is God Doing: The Essentials of Global Missions: An Introductory Guide,* 5th ed. Cedar Knolls, N.J.: Global Gospel.

Pinnock, Clark, et al., eds. 1996. *The Openness of God: A Biblical Challenge to the Traditional Understanding of God.* Downers Grove, Ill.: InterVarsity.

Van Engen, Charles. 2000. "Arminian Theology." In *Evangelical Dictionary of World Missions,* edited by A. Scott Moreau. Grand Rapids: Baker.

Ware, Bruce A. 2000. *God's Lesser Glory: The Diminished God of Open Theism.* Wheaton, Ill.: Crossway.

Winter, Ralph D. 2001. "A Blindspot in Western Christianity." Paper published by Frontier Missions Fellowship, Pasadena, Calif.

Chapter 2

Restrictivism and Inclusivism

Is This Missions Trip Really Necessary?

So faith comes from hearing, and hearing through the word of Christ.

—Romans 10:17

Prologue

WE WERE NEW TO JAPAN, and we were entering a new field of service. Mr. and Mrs. Miyata and the only daughter we knew about had come to faith in Christ. It seemed a bit unusual when they invited us to visit them one afternoon.

Welcomed and served the usual green tea and some bean cake, our visit began with the usual social pleasantries. But it soon became apparent that the Miyatas had something more serious to talk about. We were invited into an adjacent room. There on the lacquerware table and flanked by flowers was the picture of a beautiful Japanese girl. In somber tones and somewhat haltingly, Mr. and Mrs. Miyata took turns telling us why they had invited us to their home. They explained that it was the anniversary of the untimely death of their older daughter. She had died during the war because of complications brought on by malnutrition. Ordinarily they would have gone to the temple for a Buddhist rite, but now that they were Christians they had invited us to come and read Scripture and pray.

Before we did that, though, they wanted an answer to a very important question: Their daughter had died without hearing about the Lord Jesus. What would God do with her?

What about people who never hear the gospel? Can anyone be saved without actually hearing the gospel and believing in Christ? Does God have some other way to heaven? Would a loving God send a sincere person who has never heard about Christ to hell? Is it possible that un-evangelized people will have a chance to hear and believe the gospel after death? How can people be held responsible if they do not believe in a Christ of whom they have not heard?

Questions having to do with the destiny of the unevangelized are many and varied. Every inquirer has reasons for asking and phrasing the question as he or she does. Skeptics may desire to reinforce their unbelief. Cynics may want to embarrass believers. Apologists may be trying to resolve a stumbling block to faith. Ordinary believers may be seeking answers for their own peace of mind. Witnessing Christians may be inquiring on behalf of others. There is about as much speculation concerning this question as any other—partly because we Christians tend to be uncomfortable with our own answers. Worse, the more biblical the answer the more uncomfortable we often become. It seems God often takes special delight in pushing us out of our intellectual comfort zones. This may turn out to be one of those occasions.

Basic Interpretations and Certain Speculations

The importance of the problem can be demonstrated by both the intensity of debate and the extensiveness of literature. It might be helpful to simply put forth some proposals offered by various scholars, even though we cannot stop to evaluate them at this point.

Allen Tuneberg observes that some arguments relating to the unevangelized are basically emotional (e.g., sympathy). Others are deductive (e.g., a loving God would not send anyone to hell). Others are exegetical (e.g., all will be reconciled to God in accordance with 1 Cor. 15:22). He identifies ten positions regarding the destiny of "those who are unin-formed about Christ" (Tuneberg 1992):

1. inclusivism;
2. qualified universalism;
3. extended probation;
4. general revelation as an avenue to saving faith;
5. extraordinary applications of the atonement;
6. "faith that would have been" (i.e., if the person had heard the gospel);
7. agnosticism;
8. traditionalism (i.e., restrictivism);
9. annihilationism and conditional immortality; and
10. degrees of punishment in hell

One immediately sees that, while all of these options relate to God's disposition of the unevangelized, some have as much to do with broader questions. In fact, some of these responses have to do with the inability of theologians to come up with answers that satisfy even themselves.

Types of Positions

Focusing specifically and solely upon what God will do with "those who have never heard the gospel," John Sanders proposes a rather simple typology: restrictivism, wider hope, inclusivism, and universalism (Sanders 1992). When one analyzes his *wider hope* category, it does seem that it can logically be subsumed under inclusivism. So we will settle here for three major categories of answers: restrictivism, inclusivism, and universalism. We will evaluate them and put forward a case that may seem both sane and scriptural to many Bible-believing Christians. Here are the basic categories:

Restrictivism—the unevangelized (in this life) are lost. Most conservative missionaries of the modern era have at least tended toward this restrictivist position. Hudson Taylor, for one, is widely reported as saying that he would not have gone to China had he not believed that the Chinese were lost and needed Christ.

Even when they basically agree with Taylor, however, conservatives today tend to be somewhat more restrained. For example, Ajith Fernando agrees with Taylor that Scripture teaches that those who do not hear the gospel of Christ are lost. Fernando, however, takes great pains to explain what the Scripture has to say about degrees of punishment. He concludes that the degree of punishment of the unevangelized lost will reflect what they knew (Fernando 1987, 132).

This inclination toward a more nuanced exclusivism is evident in Christopher Little's study *The Revelation of God Among the Unevangelized* (Little 2000). Little maintains that people need to hear and believe the gospel of Christ, but he broadens the scope of special revelation beyond Scripture to include oral tradition, miraculous events, dreams, visions, angels, and human messengers of the biblical gospel (Little 2000, 118–31). Little is not a traditional restrictivist, but he still stands in that tradition in his emphasis on special revelation and his insistence that precedence be given to biblical revelation and authority when evaluating the validity of other sorts of special revelation.

Inclusivism—salvation is accessible apart from special evangelization. As William Crockett and James Sigountos say, this idea is not new:

> At every period in history, great saints have held this view. Christians such as Justin Martyr (ca. 100–165), John Chrysostom (ca. 347–407), Huldrych Zwingli (1484–1531), and John Wesley (1703–1791) believed that God would save the unreached who earnestly sought him—even though they might never have heard the gospel. (Crockett and Sigountos 1993, 259)

As is true of restrictivism, inclusivism comes in different packages.

Some say that salvation is universally accessible during this life. J. N. D. Anderson takes this position in *The World's Religions*, which has had some circulation in Christian schools (Anderson 1976). Anderson draws upon the example of Cornelius (Acts 10) and concludes that God saves all people who recognize their spiritual need and throw themselves on the mercy of God, irrespective of whether they actually hear and believe the gospel. Anderson says that the virtuous unevangelized person may "wake up, as it were, on the other side of the grave to worship the One in whom, without understanding, he had found the mercy of God" (Anderson 1976, 235).

Some advocates of what is currently called "wider hope," on the other hand, contend that all will ultimately be evangelized, if not before, then after, death. Repelled by restrictivism, Clark Pinnock writes:

> The implication of popular eschatology [i.e., restrictivism] is that the downtrodden of this world, unable to call upon Jesus through no fault of their own, are to be rejected for eternity, giving the final victory to the tyrants who trampled them down. Knowing little but suffering in this life, the unevangelized poor will know nothing but more and worse suffering in the next. (Pinnock 1992, 183)

Understood this way and without the caveats offered by most restrictivists, it is understandable that Pinnock believes God's love to be so defining of his character that many unevangelized (in this life) will have a "grace-filled postmortem encounter" with Christ and go to heaven (Pinnock 1992, 169–72). In the final analysis, Pinnock says (at least as I understand him) that the only ones who will eventually go to hell are those who actually choose to go there.

We will return to Anderson's case for inclusivism. For a studied response to various forms of inclusivism, see Ramesh Richard, *The Population of Heaven* (Richard 1992).

Universalism—all will be saved. Taking cues from such men as Origen (ca. 185–254) and Friedrich Schleiermacher (1768–1834), twentieth-century theorists such as C. H. Dodd, John A. T. Robinson, John Hick, and Paul Knitter qualify as universalists by this definition. Though their reasoning follows somewhat differing paths, they all end up at a God whose enduring love and eternal purposes enfold all.

Universalism is not really an option for Bible-believing Christians and will not be considered in our discussion. But that is not to say that universalism is not a threat to the Christian faith or that it is not necessary to acknowledge its existence.

Ancillary and Subordinate Notions

In illustrating the positions on God's disposition of the unevangelized highlighted above, then, it is important to take note of the various notions that have been used to explain or support them, such as the following:

1. *Extrabiblical modes of special revelation* (Little).
2. The *"acceptability"* of *God-fearers* (Anderson).
3. A *"grace-filled postmortem encounter"* with God (Pinnock).
4. Treatment of the call to whatever gods are known as a reaching out to the true God (Knitter). Just as Christians are saved through the name of Jesus, people of other faiths can find salvation through the names they call upon for salvation.
5. *"The Melchizedek factor"* (Don Richardson). Richardson more or less assumes that Melchizedek in Genesis 14:18–20 (cf. Ps. 110:4; Heb. 7:1–7) knew God through general revelation and that same general revelation can be found in other religions. This knowledge often makes it easier for adherents to come to Christ and be saved.
6. *Implicit Christians or implicit-faith* (Millard Erickson). Those who never hear the gospel can nevertheless be saved if they have responded to God in the sense of seeking "glory and honor and immortality" (Rom. 2:7). God will save them because, if they would have heard the gospel, God knows that they would have accepted it.
7. *Annihilationism/conditionalism* (John R. W. Stott). Strictly speaking, annihilationism is the doctrine that the death of the wicked involves the extinction of their being. The concept has taken different forms, but it is the work of John R. W. Stott that has attracted the most attention among conservative evangelicals. Stott believes that no person is actually immortal until an immortal soul is given at conversion. Therefore, people who are not saved do not survive death in any form. Stott calls this "conditional immortality" (Edwards and Stott 1988, 313–20).
8. *Agnosticism* (C. S. Lewis). Some simply confess that they do not know what God will do with those who have not heard of Christ. Though he does not give evidence of a thoroughgoing study of

Scripture on the topic, C. S. Lewis probably thought long and hard before he wrote the following lines:

Is it not frightfully unfair that this new life should be confined to people who have heard of Christ and been able to believe in Him? But the truth is God has not told us what His arrangements about the other people are. We do know that no man can be saved except through Christ; we do not know that only those who know Him can be saved through Him. (Lewis 1952, 50)

These ideas and authors are representative of ideas that have been set forward either to complement or to reinforce basic biblical teaching on the fate of the unreached. Each view should be measured against the clear teaching of Scripture. When unanswered questions remain, as they invariably will, believers are called upon to confess the limits of our understanding and make additional proposals only with a good deal of humility, sobriety, and tentativeness.

I often recall the example of my former dean, Kenneth Kantzer. Following an Urbana missionary convention, he was queried by a Chicago reporter concerning God's disposition of those who have never heard the gospel. After explaining the singular responsibility they bear to respond to whatever light God may give, Kantzer went on to say something like the following:

Holy Scripture indicates that all people are sinners and worthy of judgment, that people are responsible for the light he gives them, and that God is both loving and just. In answer to your question and in the final analysis, the most that we can possibly say on the basis of Scripture is that every person might be immortal until such time as that person chooses to turn his or her back on the light God gives.

I think Kantzer was right. I know that his answer was neither flippant nor evasive. It assumed a complete and thorough investigation of all that Scripture says on the subject. He was not proposing conditional immortality. He was simply saying that we are not in a position to make a

A Basic Typology:

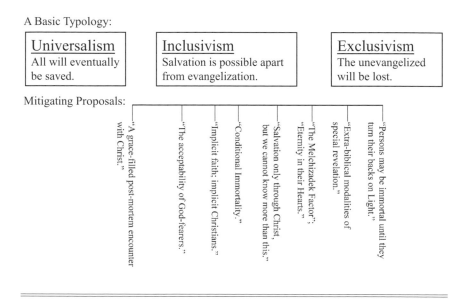

Figure 2. The Destiny of the Unevangelized

judgment or to speculate that there are people who actually have followed the light God has given them and then died without receiving further light.

So what *does* Scripture say? I propose that we employ Kantzer's "light" metaphor as used by John and also the "sound motif" used by Paul to advance an inquiry into the subject. The "light motif" is widely used in relation to divine revelation and spiritual understanding and is one of the apostle John's favored metaphors to present Christ and the gospel. The apostle Paul, on the other hand, seems to favor the "sound" concept. "Hearing" in a very special sense of the word is right at the heart of Paul's argument for missions in Romans 10—a passage we will look at quite closely (see pp. 65–69). Interestingly enough, when Carl F. H. Henry assigned a title to one of his books on this general subject, he called it *God Who Speaks and Shows* (Henry 1976).

Sound and light.

Speaking and showing.

Hearing and seeing.

What could be more simple? What could be more profound? I trust that it will not seem that I misrepresent or trivialize world evangelization to refer to it as God's spectacular "sound and light show."

Five Incontrovertible Teachings

A common difficulty in broaching questions relating to the unreached is that, instead of beginning with what we know and are assured of, we are prone to begin with what we do not know and are not assured of. There can be little hope of achieving a meeting of minds, or even rest in our own mind, unless we begin with our basic beliefs instead of with our nagging doubts.

What are some of those beliefs? I would suggest that there are at least five fundamental and relevant biblical teachings on which we should be able to reach a consensus. Employing the biblical metaphors of light and sound, let me state these teachings, display them in the Gospels and Epistles, and comment on each in turn.

Number 1: The true Light enlightens everyone—everyone has heard. Referring to Christ, John writes:

> In him was life, and the life, was the light of men. . . . The true light, which enlightens everyone, was coming into the world. (John 1:4, 9)

Referring to creation, Paul writes:

> For what can be known about God is plain to them, because God has shown it to them. For his invisible attributes, namely, his eternal power and divine nature, have been clearly perceived, ever since the creation of the world, in the things that have been made. So they are without excuse. (Rom. 1:19–20)

Then, quoting Psalm 19:1, Paul says:

> Their voice has gone out to all the earth, and their words to the ends of the world. (Rom. 10:18)

Jesus Christ is both the source and personification of light and truth—indirectly through creation, conscience, history, and reason and directly through his incarnation, the Scriptures, and, at times, other modes of special revelation.

Everyone who has ever come into the world has seen his light and heard his voice. For reasons of God's design or human doings or both, some have received more light and some less. But all have been enlightened to some degree. Some have heard more clearly and some less so. But all have heard to some degree. From time immemorial theologians have espoused and expounded two kinds of revelation: *general* and *special*. The distinction should not be pressed too far because in a profound sense they were designed to go together. But all people of every place and every time have received general revelation. Many—probably many more than we have sometimes been led to believe—have received special revelation as well.

Number 2: People love darkness more than God's light and turn a deaf ear to God's voice.

John writes:

> And this is the judgment: the light has come into the world, and people loved the darkness rather than the light because their deeds were evil. (John 3:19)

With special reference to Israel but in words applicable to all, Paul writes:

> God gave them a spirit of stupor, eyes that would not see and ears that would not hear, down to this very day. (Rom. 11:8)

And, drawing again upon the Old Testament, Paul concludes:

> None is righteous, no not one; no one understands, no one seeks for God. All have turned aside; together they have become worthless; no one does good, not even one. (Rom. 3:10–12)

That is indeed harsh language, so Paul must have experienced some measure of relief in being able to quote the likes of Moses, David, and Isaiah in these passages. But his own case had already been made in Romans 1–2. Primal peoples (tribalists; those looked down upon by "cultured" folk) learned of God through the world that Christ had made, but, far from glorifying and thanking him, worshipped idols of their own making (Rom. 1:20–23). And, despite the witness of creation, reason, and conscience, supposedly sophisticated Greeks and Romans acted in the same way as did those they looked down upon (2:1–16). Finally, enlightened not only by general revelation but also by the law, God's chosen people, the Jews, prided themselves in possessing it but utterly failed in the performing of it (vv. 17–29).

Darrell Bock notes that, in the Epistles "the term *ignorance* most often describes the lifestyle of the saved before conversion" (Bock 1993, 122). Not only have men and women not been passed by in the dispensing of revelation, their lifestyle reflects their refusal of it. All discussions concerning the fate of the unevangelized purporting to be biblical must take this into account.

Number 3: The degree of judgment is proportionate to the intensity of the light seen and the clarity of the Word that is heard.

John records the admonition of Jesus:

While you have the light, believe in the light, that you may become sons of light (John 12:36)

Paul writes:

For all who have sinned without the law will also perish without the law, and all who have sinned under the law will be judged by the law. (Romans 2:12)

The question is often posed as to whether God is just in judging the unevangelized. There are at least three answers to this question. Henry says questions having to do with God's justice are not to be answered on the basis of empirical investigation but on the basis of his nature. God does not stand under some external norm of justice. He *is* just. Justice is the very foundation of his throne (Ps. 89:14; Henry 1996, 254).

Second, as seen above, the Scriptures indicate that additional revelation is given or withheld on the basis of what we do with the revelation already vouchsafed. Light comes in different ways, at different times, and in differing degrees of intensity. God's Word comes in different ways, at different times, and with differing degrees of clarity. Human opportunity and responsibility is to respond by receiving and obeying the light and Word given, not light and Word not given. Upon the basis of their response, women and men are judged worthy of receiving more truth, but, if found unworthy, God removes the truth already given.

Third, people will be judged on the basis of what they have done with divine revelation. In his Sermon on the Mount, Jesus said, "If then the light within you is darkness, how great is that darkness" (Matt. 6:23 NIV). When denouncing people in Chorazin, Bethsaida, and Capernaum for their refusal to repent, Jesus said that their judgment would be greater than that of Tyre, Sidon, and even Sodom. Why? Because they were unrepentant in spite of the great miracles he had performed in their midst (11:20–24).

Also, the apostle John says that at the Great White Throne judgment, not one but two books will be opened: the book of life and the book of works. On the basis of the gospel we know that names appearing in the former book are there because of grace—what Christ has done in granting salvation. On the basis of biblical teachings such as those above, we know that those whose names appear in the latter book will be judged on the basis of their works—what they have done in response to the revelation of God's will and word.

Number 4: The missionary calling to proclaim the gospel is vital to the plan of God.

Concerning John the Baptist as Christ's forerunner, John the Evangelist writes:

He came as a witness, to bear witness about the light, that all might believe through him. He was not the light, but came to bear witness about the light. (John 1:7–8)

Paul begins his letter to the Romans with the following words:

> Paul, a servant of Christ Jesus, called to be an apostle [i.e., missionary], set apart for the gospel of God. (Rom. 1:1)

And near the end of the same book he says:

> And thus I make it my ambition to preach the gospel, not where Christ has already been named, lest I build on someone else's foundation, but as it is written, "Those who have never been told of him will see, and those who have never heard will understand." (Rom. 15:20–21)

To a significant degree, the modern missionary enterprise rests on an awakening to the fact that the Great Commission was directed not only to the first-century disciples of Christ but to his disciples today as well. That should be enough to convince us of the need to disciple the nations.

But there is more. In all his writings Paul takes the missionary calling, his own and that of others, with utmost seriousness. In the tenth chapter of Romans, where he describes the place of missions in God's grand plan for the ages, he includes one of the most compelling challenges to be found anywhere in Holy Scripture: to reach all peoples with the gospel. In that great chapter he employs what was probably a well-used formulation of faith at the time (vv. 9–10) and follows it with a series of rhetorical questions designed to establish the necessity of "going with the gospel." His argument in verses 13–16 is as simple as it is irrefutable:

1. Everyone who calls on the name of the Lord will be saved.
2. How will they call on one in whom they have not believed?
3. How can they believe in one of whom they have not heard?
4. How can they hear without someone preaching to them?
5. How can anyone preach to them unless someone is sent?

The rhetorical style of Paul's argument in Romans 10 adds to its persuasiveness. As far as Paul is concerned, no rejoinders are necessary. No way out is anticipated. No other options are offered.

Number 5: Only by hearing and believing in Christ during this life can men and women be saved.

The Lord's commission leaves believers with no alternative. They must go and proclaim the gospel. The Lord's command leaves unbelievers with no alternative. They must hear and believe the gospel.

John was quoting Jesus himself when he wrote:

> I am the light of the world. Whoever follows me will not walk in darkness, but will have the light of life. (John 8:12)

> As long as I am in the world, I am the light of the world. (John 9:5)

Writing under the inspiration of the Holy Spirit, Paul wrote,

> I am under obligation both to Greeks and to barbarians, both to the wise and to the foolish. . . . For I am not ashamed of the gospel, for it is the power of God for salvation to everyone who believes. (Rom. 1:14, 16)

Concentrate on what Paul is saying in Romans 10:17 and on what happens at the "end of the line" when the missionary preaches the gospel and unreached people hear it (see Lightfoot n.d., 154–58 on *pistis;* Verbrugge 2000, concerning this and other lexical data).

First, look at the *faith* by which the righteous will live. Faith (*pistis*) can be passive or active. On the one hand, it refers to trustworthiness, whether of the immutable purpose and promises of God or the "good faith" or honesty of men. On the other hand, as active faith, it is used as "faith" and "belief" and refers to the "teachings of our Lord, enforced and explained by St. Paul, the foremost place in the phraseology of Christian doctrine" (Lightfoot n.d., 157).

In this active sense *pistis* has shades of meaning that are not always clearly distinguishable in the biblical text. It can, for example, be objective or subjective. Used objectively it refers to

- Christ's *commands* (*entolē*) in the Great Commission (Matt. 28:20);

- his *teachings* (*didachē*), which the Holy Spirit would bring to the remembrance of the apostles (John 14:26);
- the *gospel* (*euangelion*) that would be preached in all the world (Matt. 24:14);
- the *preached word* (*kerygma*) through which people are saved (1 Cor. 1:21); and
- the *word or message* in itself (*rhēma*; see pp. 68–69).

In fact, it can refer to the whole body of revealed truth to which Jude refers when he exhorts us to "contend for the faith that was once for all delivered to the saints" (Jude 3). We refer to this faith as the "Faith of our fathers, holy faith" (Faber 1849).

As a Christian virtue, the active sense of *pistis* most often denotes subjective trust or belief. It is the kind of faith to which the writer of Hebrews refers in the oft-quoted verse, "Now faith is being sure of what we hope for and certain of what we do not see" (Heb. 11:1 NIV). It is being more certain of the reality of what is believed in than we would be if we could smell, taste, see, or touch it. It is the kind of faith we have in mind when we sing, "My faith looks up to thee, thou Lamb of Calvary, Savior divine" (Palmer 1830).

We sometimes pit these two aspects of faith against each other by saying that one is creed or doctrine while the other is a personal "living" faith. Or we refer to one as knowledge *about* God and the other as *actually knowing* God. Such distinctions can be useful, but they can also be grossly misleading. Paul and the New Testament writers use *pistis* as both the revealed truth of God in Scripture and the trusting response of a person to God. The intimate connection between the objective and subjective aspects of faith is of great importance. Like hydrogen and oxygen in water, they go together. Moreover, in the New Testament, *pistis* is used with reference to God, not with reference to human beings or natural means such as a missionary strategy or methodology.

As Paul uses the word in Romans 10:17, we are probably correct in thinking that an active subjective faith is primarily in view, but the faith by which those declared righteous will live must have both objective and subjective elements in it.

Second, look at the *hearing* that is involved. Just as faith is not just any kind of believing, so hearing in this verse is not just any kind of hearing. When "hearing" (*akouō*) is used intransitively (i.e., without an object) if refers to hearing per se (e.g., Matt. 11:15: "He who has ears, let him hear"). When used transitively (i.e., with an object) *akouō* can refer to hearing something (e.g., Acts 9:7: "they *heard* the sound" NIV) or to hearing the meaning or message (e.g., 22:9: "My companions saw the light, but they did not *understand* the voice of him who was speaking to me" NIV), depending on the sentence construction. It is in this latter sense that *akouō* is used in Romans 10:17, as when we inquire whether someone "got the message." We are not inquiring as to whether someone heard the words, but whether someone heard and understood what was communicated.

It is imperative that we understand that, in addition to those obligations placed upon missionaries to go and proclaim God's truth in a culturally understandable way, God places an obligation upon hearers to listen with open minds and hearts to understand what is being communicated. A Russian proverb says that men are like donkeys; to get them to go in the right direction one must grab them by the ears. One approach to Bible translation has it that the translator's goal is to produce a text that "grabs the ears" of the reader and creates the impact that the text had on its original hearers/readers. Not so. The goal is to transmit the original meaning of the text insofar as the translator is able. Hearers/readers have a responsibility to "get the message" and respond to it.

Third, look at the message that must be delivered in Romans 10:17. Yet another all-important word is to be found in this verse. We referred to it above. It is the Greek word translated "word." Usually it is the Greek *logos* that is translated as "word" as, for example, in John 1:1. But since *rhēma* and not *logos* is used in Romans 10:17, "message" may be allowable here. But even "message" does not capture the larger meaning of the Greek. Used in the singular, *rhēma* refers to a word or message that is appropriate for a particular audience or occasion. Used in the plural (*rhēmata*) it refers to an entire speech, discourse, sermon, or exposition.

In verses Romans 10:8 and 17 Paul uses the singular form, *rhēma,* indicating that an appropriate message is to be conveyed. However, lest the missionary preacher think that his or her particular insights take precedence in determining what is or is not "appropriate" to the unbelieving auditors and particular occasion, Paul indicates that it is the "*rhēma* of faith" (v. 8) and the "*rhēma* of Christ" (v. 17) that engender true faith and transform lives. Those phrases serve to center preaching in the "faith once for all delivered to the saints" and Christ who alone, in any ultimate sense, is the "light of the world."

James Montgomery Boice concludes that the bottom line of Paul's argument here is that people must believe in Christ before they can call on him. They must hear Christ before they can believe. There must be preaching of the Word if people are to hear Christ. He concludes that for Christ to be proclaimed to such people, preachers must be sent to them (Boice 1993, 1242).

The Unevangelized in Acts: Two Critical Encounters

Review once more the various views taken with respect to God's disposition of the unreached (pp. 55–57). The incontrovertible teachings of the Gospels and Epistles almost demand that one subscribe to a restrictivist position.

Interpretations that support inclusivist views strain to support that understanding from the textual evidence. Two of the texts most often used to support inclusivism are found in the book of Acts. One is Peter's message to Cornelius and his household and the other is Paul's Athenian address.

The Conversion of Cornelius (Acts 10:1–11:18)

Cornelius was a Gentile God-fearer—devout and reverent before God and generous to the poor. Obviously he had responded positively to the Jewish faith of his neighbors, perhaps more so than did they (Acts 10:1–2). The day came when Peter was commanded to set aside the strictures of his Jewish upbringing and go to Caesarea to proclaim Christ to Cornelius and his family.

Our question here is simple: Was that trip really necessary?

Some seem to think that Peter's trip to Cornelius's home in Caesarea was nice but not really necessary. In this view, God saves all people who recognize their spiritual need and throw themselves on the mercy of God, whatever specific understanding of Christ and his salvation they have.

For example, even though the epilogue of the first edition of Anderson's textbook on world religions does not refer to the Cornelius episode (Anderson 1950, 190–96), by the time the fourth edition was published some twenty-five years later, Anderson makes much of it. He especially emphasizes Peter's words, "Truly I understand that God shows no partiality, but in every nation anyone who fears him and does what is right is acceptable to him" (Acts 10:34–35). From the story of Cornelius and these words especially, Anderson concludes that someone with the virtues of a Cornelius who never hears the gospel may "wake up, as it were, on the other side of the grave to worship the One in whom, without understanding, he had found the mercy of God" (Anderson 1976, 235).

Anderson does go on to say that his interpretation should not be understood as lessening our missionary responsibility.

Others believe that the trip was necessary, but for a different reason. Ralph Winter and the German scholar U. Wilchens (Marshall 1980, 190) believe that, as God-fearers, Cornelius and his household were already saved when Peter arrived. They prefer to emphasize the fact that Peter and all who were present that day needed to understand that "the whole dichotomy between circumcized and uncircumcized is irrelevant, and the Gentiles who did not follow the law abjectly were as acceptable to God as Jews, both equally able to find 'repentance unto life' (11:18)" (Winter 2004, 2).

This for certain is a primary, if not *the* primary, teaching of the larger passage so we can agree that the gospel makes the dichotomy between circumcision and uncircumcision irrelevant. We may also agree with Winter when he maintains that evangelization would be speeded up if missionaries were to highlight the greater glory of God—a glory discoverable in the whole of creation from the astral to the microbiological, and we can certainly agree when Winter affirms that both the glory of God and the missionary message culminate in the "face of Jesus Christ."

The more traditional view, however, correctly concludes that Peter's trip was necessary to the salvation of Cornelius and his household. In Acts 11 Peter recounts the entire experience for the benefit of elders of the Jerusalem church. He quotes Cornelius's explanation of why he had sent representatives to Joppa to bring Peter to his home in Caesarea. Peter says that Cornelius "told us how he had seen an angel appear in his house and say, 'Send to Joppa for Simon who is called Peter. *He will bring you a message through which you and all your household will be saved'*" (vv. 13–14, emphasis mine).

Also important to this interpretation of the Cornelius encounter is a correct understanding of the usual English translation "acceptable" in Acts 10:35 and "saved" and "message" in 11:14. Acts 10:34–35 says, "So Peter opened his mouth and said: 'truly I understand that God shows no partiality, but in every nation anyone who fears him and does what is right is acceptable to him.'" The Greek word used for "acceptable" in verse 35 (*dektos*) is a general term that could also be translated "accepted," "agreeable," or "approved." The verb form often had to do with receiving someone with hospitality, prepared to entertain them. It is highly questionable exegetical practice to read more into the text.

As for the Greek word used for "saved" in Acts 11:14 (*sōzō*), it appears in Greek literature in the general sense of "saving, rescuing, healing, or delivering from some peril or evil." In the New Testament, however, it is often used in the sense of saving or delivering from final ruin or judgment. Most scholars interpret it that way in this context.

As for the word translated "message," it is familiar to us from our analysis of Romans 10:17. The Greek word is *rhēma* (singular). In Acts 11:14 it is this *rhēma* that culminated in repentance and faith on the part of Cornelius and his household, the giving to them of the Holy Spirit, and the command of Peter that they be baptized in the name of Jesus Christ (Acts 10:44–48).

We do not know the conditions under which God might be pleased to send a missionary (or an angel or dream or vision or special sign). We do not know how many Cornelius-like people there might be in the world. We do not know what the consequences would have been had Cornelius not obeyed the Lord and sent for Peter. These and still other questions can (and must) be left to the often inscrutable ways of a righteous and loving God. But we know that Cornelius followed the light God gave him. By hearing and responding to the preached *rhēma,* he and his entire household were saved. And with I. Howard Marshall, we know that

Peter's argument [to critics of the circumcision party in Jerusalem] proved convincing. Not only was incipient criticism reduced to silence, but rather the audience expressed their praise to God that he had granted *to the Gentiles* as well as the Jews the opportunity of repenting of their sins and thus of obtaining eternal life ([Acts] 5:20; 13:46, 48). This opportunity was provided in the preaching of the gospel. (Marshall 1980, 198)

Paul's Address to the Athenians (Acts 17:16–34)

No single episode in the life and ministry of the apostle Paul has drawn so much attention from commentators as Acts 17:16–34. It is a compelling text for those who seek guidance as to principles of communicating the Christian message to cultured pagans. This may be one of the most famous sermons ever preached. Besides its place in Scripture, it is engraved on a bronze plate secured to the side of Mars Hill in Athens.

The question is "Was it necessary that the sermon be preached?" It is the same question we considered regarding Cornelius, but the circumstances are entirely different. The Athenians were indeed Gentiles, not God-fearing proselytes. They were cultured, sophisticated pagans. Paul even quoted their philosophers and applied their pagan claims about Zeus to the true God. His strategy raises many issues regarding missionary communication, but they are relevant here only insofar as they help answer the basic question about the need for the gospel to be heard.

If those cultured Athenians were to be saved, was it absolutely imperative that Paul preach the gospel and that they repent and believe it?

Missions scholars have given much time and energy to an examination of the missionary significance of Paul's Athenian address, including the well-known evangelical Don Richardson. I would not be surprised to learn that his study of Acts 17 provided the impetus for his research into the basic teachings of a variety of worldviews and religious traditions, although I do not know that to be the case.

Tite Tiénou has said that he believes Richardson's research and his understanding at this point are flawed (Tiénou 1993). An overview of the Richardson–Tiénou debate helps clarify the issues. Richardson's proposals are put forward in his book *Eternity in Their Hearts* (Richardson 1981). Tiénou's response bears the same title, only posed as a question: *Eternity in Their Hearts?* (Tiénou 1993).

In his book, Richardson has gathered a host of illustrations from a variety of sources and religions to prove that they all shine considerable "spiritual light" on the character of the true God. He calls general revelation the "Melchizedek factor" (Gen. 14:18–20; Heb. 7:1–7) and believes that general revelation acts in such a way as to make it easier for adherents of non-Christian religions to understand special revelation (the "Abraham factor"—Gen. 12:1–3) and come to Christ. In this sense, these ideas are "redemptive," though not "redeeming" (Richardson 1986, 59). Cases where this might not hold true are accounted for on the basis of the "Sodom factor" (Gen. 19:1–29). Richardson places an extremely high value on the recognition of general revelation in non-Christian religious systems.

From his perspective as an African and a theologian, Tiénou finds Richardson's approach to be mistaken and misleading. One of his reasons applies to our present inquiry: Tiénou says that Richardson's work has implications Christians should not accept regarding "the value of general revelation (do other religions save?) and the final destiny of the heathen (will God save everyone?)" (Tiénou 1993, 213).

He notes Richardson's acknowledgment that a person cannot be saved apart from the gospel. But does this caveat still hold with the greatly inflated value Richardson places on general revelation and the "redemptive" role assigned to it? This analysis of general revelation, Tiénu says, is based upon personal emotions rather than sound theology. These can easily lead to error:

> There is no theological reason why someone cannot use Richardson's approach to claim that non-Christian religions do redeem. If we leave such a door open, someone will inevitably walk through. Richardson's book provides no clear reason why we should not continue down the road toward universalism.
>
> If the question is, does general revelation save? the answer is no. Revelation does not save, Jesus Christ does! Yet Scripture never rules out the possibility that some might come to a saving

knowledge of God through general revelation. God has not given us an easy test for determining people's salvation based on what kind of revelation they have. Consequently, no attempt to simplify the complex picture painted by Scripture is adequate. Let us therefore be content with the sobriety of Scripture. (Tiénou 1993, 215)

There is very much to applaud in these paragraphs by Tiénou. However, the fact that "Scripture never rules out" the possibility of salvation through general revelation is an argument from silence. If Scripture does not *rule it out*, neither does it *rule it in*. Has Tiénou himself perhaps gone too far? It would be better to follow the lead of Kantzer: If one hazards to go beyond the bounds of explicit biblical teaching, do so only when inference will allow it and then only tentatively and with trepidation.

Understandable human emotions cause Richardson and many others to invest too much ethical and spiritual currency in non-Christian attitudes, philosophies, and religions. Look again at Paul's Athenian discourse, the events leading up to it, and its aftermath. It is possible to read much that seems to be positive and affirming about Athenians and their religion here. Paul complemented the Athenians for being "devout" (Acts 17:17) and "very religious" (v. 22). The fact that they acknowledged an "unknown god" provided an "opening wedge" for introducing the true God was a plus. It is instructive to realize that Paul knew his audience and was familiar with their philosophical and religious writings (v. 28).

But look closely at the background of Paul's sermon. Luke says that Paul was so "provoked" at the idols that he reasoned with those Athenians every day (v. 16). Some learned Athenians called Paul a babbler, and others said he preached deities that were foreign to them when he preached Jesus and his resurrection (v. 18). Paul's message was "strange to their ears" and "new." In fact, Athenians loved to hear anything new, and it was only on that basis that they wanted to hear what Paul had to say at all (vv. 19–21).

Now, review the message itself. Paul's sermon was suited to the occasion and audience. But Paul's discourse was not simply a motivational speech or a "seeker" sermon. It gave unmistakable evidence of the true nature of Athenian history, minds, hearts, need, and hopelessness. Darrell Bock, for

Restrictivism and Inclusivism   **75**

example, points out that Paul used a "decidedly mixed term" *(seboō)* to describe their worship (v. 17). He did not hesitate to call attention to their ignorance (v. 30). He made it clear that the true God demands repentance (v. 30), and that a day of judgment was coming (v. 31; Bock 1993, 122–23). Richard Wolff maintains that their fear of their own deities proves that the Athenians were ignorant of the true God (Wolff 1961, 42).

Perhaps the most significant aspect of Paul's preaching in Athens was not that it addressed the ignorance that was not dispelled by general or natural revelation, but that it accentuated the Athenian need for special revelation. As we will see in the next chapter, Gregory Beale points out that Paul's statements actually alluded to very specific Old Testament references that "convey truths about God's 'special' redemptive revelation" (Beale 2004). So, although the word *rhēma* is not used here in either the singular or plural, one would be hard pressed to find a more succinct and scintillating example of the use of passages that, when taken together, become integral parts of the larger story of redemptive history. Though the word *euangelion* is not used, the Athenian speech seems to be a classic example of "evangelizing," of communicating the gospel of special revelation.

In sum, it would seem to be a colossal blunder to find communication stratagems here without rediscovering the importance of proclaiming the gospel message to all who will listen.

Finally, notice the response of the Athenians (vv. 32–34). Some mocked. Some procrastinated. Only a few believed and joined Paul. But light—the brilliant light of the divine Word—was preached to all to the extent that they were willing to listen. And to all were given both the opportunity and the responsibility of following the light. If Athenian gods and religion were sufficient for salvation, then their situation was made worse by rejecting Christ. Nevertheless, because saving faith comes from a right hearing of the true gospel, it was worth proclaiming that gospel a thousand times over. Few may have been saved that day, but, in time, Athens became home to a great church. In eternity, heaven will be the home of many Athenian saints.

Henry would concur with this. He writes, "The biblical passages that most pointedly clarify universal knowledge of God are Acts 17 and Romans 1" (Henry 1976, 248). There we learn that, though general revelation does yield some knowledge of God, there is no "ubiquitously shared common ground" between the assumptions and content of heathen religions and biblical revelation (see pp. 109–10). In the final analysis, those who have never heard the gospel face judgment because they have rejected the light of general revelation (Rom. 1:20–21). But perhaps it is also true that they are "immortal" (in the sense in which Kantzer used that word) until they have done so. At any rate, though Paul's stay in Athens may have been a matter of convenience, his Areopagus climb and speech were necessary.

Conclusion

In announcing a forthcoming missions conference, Southern Baptist Seminary professor Russell D. Moore puts the problem we have been exploring in terms of a man on an island:

> If a man is stranded alone on an island from infancy until death and never hears the Gospel of Jesus Christ, where will he spend eternity? Do the trees and rocks provide the man with enough evidence to point him savingly to Christ's atoning death? Or will he be viewed as innocent because he was ignorant of the only way to salvation? (Robinson 2003, 1)

Moore argues that "the answer to the question of the 'man on the island' separates the pure biblical gospel from non-biblical expressions of it."

We generally concur. But that is not to say that, when one takes account of all that Scripture has to say on this matter, a clear and simple conclusion is easy to come by. There are numerous pertinent passages that require painstaking study. There are many subsidiary questions for which Bible writers do not supply specific answers.

The challenge here is threefold. First, we are challenged to embrace all that the Bible says about the fate of the unevangelized without dismissing or defacing any of it. What Moses wrote long ago applies here: "The secret things belong to the LORD our God, but the things revealed belong to us and to our children forever, that we may follow all the words of this law" (Deut. 29:29 NIV).

Second, we are challenged to avoid going beyond what the Bible says about God's final disposition of the unevangelized except in a most tentative fashion. Paul's admonition to the Corinthians comes to mind. He wrote, "I have applied all these things to myself and Apollos for your benefit, brothers, that you may learn by us not to go beyond what is written" (1 Cor. 4:6).

Third, we are challenged to do what we can to make the gospel available to as many people as possible. None other than our resurrected Lord said, "Go into all the world and proclaim the gospel to the whole creation" (Mark 16:15).

Of the charge that it would be unfair of God to judge the unevangelized, Henry had this to say:

> To accuse God of misconduct, to fault him and disparage his elective grace, is to forget that God himself is the standard of truth and justice and love. Scripture nowhere derives its doctrine of truth, justice, and love from heathen sources. The perversion of truth, justice, and love is what makes humans heathen. God's fairness is demonstrated because he condemns sinners not in the absence of light but because of their rebellious response. His mercy is demonstrated because he provides fallen humans with a privileged call to redemption not extended to fallen angels. He continues to extend that call worldwide even while some rebel humans spurn it as unloving and unjust and prefer to die in their sins. All are judged by what they do with the light they have, and none is without light. (Henry 1993, 255)

Epilogue

As kindly and as clearly as the limitations of culture and language allowed, I reminded the Miyatas that Japan had had the light of the gospel for generations and that their daughter may have known and believed more than they were aware of. Then I rehearsed the truths to which they committed themselves when they decided to follow Christ as Savior and Lord, and asked basic questions such as "Do you believe that God has forgiven *all* your sin?" "Have you trusted Christ and Christ *alone* as your

Savior?" and "Do you mean to say that all your hopes for this life and the life to come have been placed in him?"

To these questions all three gave univocal and unhesitating assent. Then in measured tones I asked, "Do you really mean what you have said?" They thought for a few moments and then each replied in the affirmative. I felt justified in continuing, "Dear friends, if you can trust the true God and his Son to forgive your sin, to guide your footsteps while on earth, and to save your soul for all eternity, will you not also entrust your daughter to him in the knowledge that he is a righteous God who will always do what is right?"

This time there was something of a pause, but after a few moments the answer came: "Yes, we will."

Over the next four years we were with the Miyatas regularly and we met them periodically over subsequent years. At no time have they ever, even once, brought up the question of their daughter's destiny. I sincerely believe that they really meant it when they committed their daughter to an altogether righteous God, of whom Abraham said, "Will not the Judge of all the earth do right?" (Gen. 18:25). I think that we too must act upon what we understand and believe on the basis of God's Word—and leave the rest to him.

References

Anderson, J. N. D., ed. 1950. *The World's Religions.* 1st ed. Grand Rapids: Eerdmans.

————. 1976. *The World's Religions.* 4th ed. Grand Rapids: Eerdmans.

Beale, Gregory K. 2004. "Other Religions in New Testament Theology." In *Biblical Faith and Other Religions: An Evangelical Assessment.* Edited by David W. Baker. Grand Rapids: Kregel.

Bock, Darrell L. 1993. "Athenians Who Have Never Heard." In *Through No Fault of Their Own? The Fate of Those Who Have Never Heard.* Edited by William V. Crockett and James G. Sigountos. Grand Rapids: Baker.

Boice, James Montgomery. 1993. *Romans.* Vol. 3, *God and History: Romans 9–11.* Grand Rapids: Baker.

Crockett, William V., and James G. Sigountos. 1993. "Are the 'Heathen' Really Lost?" In *Through No Fault of Their Own? The Fate of Those Who Have*

Never Heard. Edited by William V. Crockett and James G. Sigountos. Grand Rapids: Baker.

Edwards, David L., and John Stott. 1988. *Evangelical Essentials: A Liberal-Evangelical Dialogue.* Downers Grove, Ill.: InterVarsity.

Faber, Frederick W. 1849. "Faith of Our Fathers."

Fernando, Ajith. 1987. *The Christian's Attitude Toward World Religions: Responding to the Idea That Christianity Is Just Another Religion.* Wheaton, Ill.: Tyndale.

Henry, Carl F. H. 1976. *God, Revelation, and Authority.* Vol. 2, *God Who Speaks and Shows.* Waco, Tex.: Word.

————. 1993. "Is It Fair?" in *Through No Fault of Their Own? The Fate of Those Who Have Never Heard.* Edited by William V. Crockett and James G. Sigountos. Grand Rapids: Baker.

Lewis, C. S. 1952. *Mere Christianity.* New York: Macmillan.

Lightfoot, J. B. N.d. *The Epistle of St. Paul to the Galatians.* Grand Rapids: Zondervan.

Little, Christopher. *The Revelation of God Among the Unevangelized: An Evangelical Appraisal.* Pasadena, Calif.: William Carey Library 2000.

Marshall, I. Howard. 1980. *The Acts of the Apostles: An Introduction and Commentary.* Tyndale New Testament Commentaries. Grand Rapids: Eerdmans.

Palmer, Ray. 1830. "My Faith Looks Up to Thee."

Pinnock, Clark H. 1992. *A Wideness in God's Mercy: The Finality of Jesus Christ in a World of Religions.* Grand Rapids: Zondervan.

Richard, Ramesh P. 1992. *The Population of Heaven: A Biblical Response to the Inclusivist Position on Who Will Be Saved.* Chicago: Moody.

Richardson, Don. 1981. *Eternity in Their Hearts.* Ventura, Calif.: Regal.

Robinson, Jeff. 2003. "Conference to Answer, 'What About the Man on the Island?'" In *Towers,* a publication of Southern Baptist Theological Seminary, Louisville, Ky., 1.11 (10 February): 1, 3.

Sanders, John. 1992. *No Other Name: An Investigation into the Destiny of the Unevangelized.* Grand Rapids: Eerdmans.

Tiénou, Tite. 1993. "Eternity in Their Hearts?" In *Through No Fault of Their Own: The Fate of Those Who Have Never Heard.* Edited by William V. Crockett and James G. Sigountos. Grand Rapids: Baker.

Tuneberg, Allen C. 1992. "Contemporary Views in Reference to the Doctrinal

View of the Evangelical Free Church of America." Doctor of Missiology major project, Trinity Evangelical Divinity School.

Verbrugge, Verlyn, ed. 2000. *The NIV Theological Dictionary of New Testament Words*. Grand Rapids: Zondervan.

Winter, Ralph D. 2004. Personal letter to David J. Hesselgrave, 4 July.

Wolff, Richard. 1961. *The Final Destiny of the Heathen*. Ridgefield Park, N.J.: Interdenominational Foreign Missions Association.

Chapter 3

Common Ground and Enemy Territory

How Should We Approach Adherents of Other Faiths?

For all the gods of the peoples are worthless idols, but the Lord made the heavens.

—Psalm 96:5

Prologue

ONE HEIRLOOM ALREADY PASSED on to my oldest son is a small shell-covered purse. It was a prized possession of my paternal grandfather, David Fivored Hesselgrave. Grandfather was said to have been an avid student of the Scriptures and became an ordained minister in the Universalist Church. When the First World Parliament of Religions was held in Chicago in 1893, Grandfather was probably one of its most enthusiastic attendees. It was there that he purchased the purse bearing the Parliament inscription. It was there that he listened to the likes of the Jainist "chosen one," Virchand Gandhi, and the prominent Hindu philosopher Swami Vivekananda.

Most historians credit the 1893 Parliament with opening America to religions foreign to both our continent and our culture. And therefore by the time the Second World Parliament of Religions was celebrated in Chicago's Palmer House in 1993, the situation was completely different.

Not only were almost all major (and many "minor") world faiths represented—most of them had found a home in America. This time organizers attempted to build on Vivekananda's statement in his address of welcome to the World Parliament on September 11, 1893, "We believe not only in universal toleration, but we accept all religions to be true."

Discussions relating to religion and the particular religions often encounter roadblocks. Few subjects are fraught with more passion and a greater diversity of opinions. Open discussions often generate more heat than light, and even scholarly dialogues become mired in minutiae and often yield little that is conclusive or helpful.

As for the Christian mission to people of other religions, in the public arena the very idea of missions is challenged by a pervasive relativism and loss of absolutes, a general misunderstanding of what it means to be tolerant of other faiths, and repeated appeals to be appreciative of religious diversity. In the theological arena, the discipline of missions is challenged by a diversity of views as to the relationship between Christianity and other world religions. In the missions themselves, there are various opinions on how to relate to adherents of other religions and communicate the gospel to them.

Where, then, should we begin, and how should we proceed? Since the nature and meaning of mission is discussed in various places in this book we will briefly review the history referred to above and discuss the meaning and significance of "religion" and "religions." Then we can better consider various aspects of the missionary encounter with other faiths in the light of Scripture.

Two Parliaments of World Religions and Their Aftermaths

The religious context of the last decades of the nineteenth and the first decades of the twentieth centuries did not augur well for solid, scriptural answers to questions having to do with the encounter between Christians and adherents of other religions. At the end of the nineteenth century, thinking about religion was influenced by the rise of the social gospel movement, the inroads of higher criticism, and the World Parliament of Religions.

Then came the significant but inclusive Edinburgh Missionary Conference in 1910 and the modernist-fundamentalist debates. Various alliances formed, including the International Missionary Council (I.M.C.). Discussions considered the Christian mission to non-Christian religions in I.M.C. during the 1920s and 1930s, and a "Laymen's Missionary Inquiry After 100 Years" was conducted to evaluate the first century of missions from North America.

Rufus M. Jones of Haverford College and William Ernest Hocking of Harvard promoted the Layman's Missionary Inquiry. It put forward a "reconceptualized mission" that idealized religion and depicted particular religions as ways of thinking about a final truth to which all aspired. The aim of Christian missions was to contribute to that goal. "We desire," wrote Hocking, "the triumph of that final truth: we need not prescribe the route." The Christian missionary "will look forward, not to the destruction of these religions, but to their continued co-existence with Christianity, each stimulating the other in growth toward the ultimate goal, unity in the completest religious truth" (Hocking et al. 1932, 44).

The Inquiry was undertaken by the initiative of certain individuals. It was not inaugurated by any ecclesiastical body as such, and its findings were subscribed to by only one denomination. But it reflected disenchantment with traditional missions on the part of more than a few. Indeed, some liberals went so far as to say that, so extensive and pervasive are the truth and good of other religions, Christian missions are no longer necessary.

Unequivocal answers to these and similar ideas were not long in coming from within the I.M.C. The most definitive and exhaustive response emanated from the voice and pen of the professor of the history of religions at the University of Leiden, Hendrik Kraemer. At the behest of the I.M.C., Kraemer prepared a response to the Inquiry for the World Missionary Conference at Tambaram, Madras, India, in 1938 and published it in *The Christian Message in a Non-Christian World* (Kraemer 1938). Kraemer's very formidable arguments were debated in Madras, and the arguments of that book and other works (see Kraemer 1957; Kraemer 1962) resonated with some.

But these contributions were largely eclipsed by World War II and its aftermath. The World Council of Churches began in 1948. The I.M.C. was absorbed into the World Council in 1961. Important ecumenical gatherings were convened in 1947, 1952, and 1954 (Brown 1957, 35–46). All of these meetings were more or less occupied with war and peace and a renewed and overriding concern for church unity. As a result, Kraemer's arguments for Christian uniqueness and exclusivism never received the attention they deserved.

Unlike their ecumenical counterparts, post–World War II evangelicals were primarily concerned with reaching new peoples and planting new churches. The "common ground" of their central concern had more to do with available means of communicating the gospel to adherents of other faiths. For half a century and more, macro-strategies and micro-strategies for world evangelization found their way from the headquarters of evangelical missions and the halls of evangelical schools to the mission fields of the world. A case could be made that evangelicals were better prepared to encounter other faiths on their own turf than they were to meet representatives of those faiths at the 1993 Second World Parliament of Religions.

When six thousand delegates met in the centennial Parliament, the common ground they pursued was a unifying statement on global ethics. An intermediate goal was a "mystical experience of pluralism." Delegates were admonished to "ditch their doctrines." They united in singing "Leaning on the Everlasting Arms," but only after excising Jesus' name and changing the lyrics to "Oh, what fellowship. Oh, what joy divine. I can feel the fellowship all around." The nine-page statement was carefully crafted so as to avoid even one mention of the word *god*, lest Buddhists and others be offended by its inclusion (Hirsley 1993; Jones 1993).

With plenty of time to prepare, conservative evangelicals might have done well to schedule a simultaneous consultation devoted to the uniqueness of Christ and his gospel. As it was, some of them opposed any identification with the Parliament; others attended as observers; and most settled for the fact that Charles Colson was invited to address an audience at a peripheral event midway through the proceedings. Without settling long-standing and irritating issues having to do with establishing common cause with each other, evangelicals continued various efforts to exploit "common ground" strategies for evangelizing adherents of other religions.

Without minimizing the importance of issues having to do with intra-faith cooperation, it is the latter quest with which we concern ourselves here. But to do so in a hopeful and helpful fashion, we should "begin at the beginning," lest we trip over unstated preunderstandings and assumptions later on.

Religion and Particular Religions

The Bible does not use the word *religion*; that term was inherited from Cicero (106 B.C.–43 B.C.). We will opt here for the understandings of religion of Lucius Lactantius (260–330) and Augustine of Hippo (354–430), who used the linking or binding idea inherent in the Latin word *religare* "to tie or bind again." In its broad concept, *religion* has to do with linking, or reconnecting people to the divine, supernatural, or transcendent, however conceived. Particular religions, then, can be thought of as the various systems of faith and worship that attempt to make this linkage or reconnection possible.

What, then, is the source of religion in general and the various religions in particular? As one might expect, philosophers, psychologists, and anthropologists come up with very different answers and explanations. Logically, however, there are only four possible answers to the source question: the source of religion must be God, humanity, Satan, or some combination of the three. The position that seems to be in accordance with Scripture is that God is the author of religion in the sense that he has created human beings as *worshiping* beings and has sought fellowship with them. In terms of the particular religions, however, he can be regarded as the "author" of the *true* religion only. All other religions find their source in people, Satan, or people and Satan acting in collaboration.

Of course, to say this opens up a "Pandora's box." We are immediately confronted with questions about what distinguishes a "true" and a "false" religion, the presence or absence of truth in various religions, and why God would allow false religions to exist in the first place. Exclusivists, inclusivists, and pluralists clash as they try to answer such questions:

- Exclusivists believe that only one religion is true (or, at the very least, superior).
- Inclusivists believe that truth is to be found in all religions.
- Pluralists subsume all religions under an overarching truth or reality of which all are reflections and to which all aspire.

The position taken here is basically the Christian exclusivism of Edmund Perry:

> Since from the viewpoint of Gospel faith the one only True and Living God is the God of Abraham, Isaac and Jacob, the Father of our Lord Jesus Christ, and since the Gospel alone brings men to this God, all other faith claims and systems lead men away from him. Religion is therefore, first of all, the *generic* term comprehending the universal phenomenon of men individually and collectively being led away from God in manifold ways by divers claims and systems. Religion in this generic sense exists of course only in the *specific* religions, each of which is a concrete manifestation or actualization of a particular people being led away from God in a particular way by a particular schema, but as a descriptive term "religion" expresses the unity of human life being oriented and organized away from the God of Gospel faith through the diversity of creeds, codes, myths, cults and ways of worship. (Perry 1956, 88)

No doubt Perry's lines will raise the eyebrows of most and the temperatures of many. But they accord well with the words of the psalmist above and, as we will see, with the general tenor of Scripture. In agreeing with Perry at this point, the words of C. S. Lewis come to mind: "I was not writing to expound something I could call 'my religion,' but to expound 'mere' Christianity, which is what it is and was what it was long before I was born and whether I like it or not" (Lewis 1952, viii).

We will not pause here to quibble about the precise definitions of Perry's "Gospel faith" and Lewis's "mere Christianity." Perry delineates the gospel in terms of the "biblical story of a *promise* [to Abraham—Gen. 12:2–3], a *person* [Jesus Christ—Acts 13:32–33] and a *people* [the family of Christ, the church—Eph. 5:25]" (Perry 1958, 26). As is well known, Lewis gives considerable space to *myth* in the early history of humankind. In both cases we might have hoped for a more extended discussion of the authority of the biblical text itself.

As for Perry's definitions of *religion* and *particular religions* they also entail a semantic problem because, according to his understanding, Christianity itself does not really qualify as a "religion." But if that is a problem when it comes to general usage, it is no problem at all for Perry. In his view it is Christ and not Christianity that restores relationship with God in a way that religions as such only purport to provide. And with that proposition we find ourselves in complete agreement.

A Theology of Religions: A Brief Introduction

If Genesis and Exodus are crucial to the *story* of the "religious human being," the first three chapters of Romans are crucial to his *theology.* In writing to the Romans, Paul introduces his letter by testifying to a central theme informed by both divine inspiration and personal experience. He says, "The gospel is the power of God for salvation to everyone that believes. . . . For in it the righteousness of God is revealed . . . as it is written, 'The righteous shall live by faith'" (Rom. 1:16–17, author's translation). In the chapters that follow, he lays out God's revelation concerning sin, justification, sanctification, glorification, mission, and Christian living—the major doctrines with which religion is concerned.

At this point, we primarily consider Paul's doctrine of sin (or *hamartiology* after the Greek term meaning "sin") as he develops it in Romans 1:18–3:31. These chapters translate the stories of Genesis and Exodus into a basic theology of human relationship with the Creator God and also with gods of humanity's own making.

First, Paul writes about what is variously called primal religion, tribal religion, animism, dynamism, and, sometimes, folk religion (each of which has its own nuances but all of which are at least similar). He says that from the very beginning the Creator God's eternal power and divine nature were made known by virtue of the things he made, but people did not glorify nor thank him. Instead, they deliberately set off in a direction that caused them to be deranged in their thinking, darkened in their affections, derelict in their worship, and depraved in their behavior (Rom. 1:18–32).

It is imperative to understand Paul's teaching here. Though he doesn't use the term *grace*, Paul furnishes us with a perfect demonstration of its significance . Grace is usually defined in terms of the "unmerited favor of God," but that is only the half of it. Etymologically and theologically, grace is *both* God's goodness and gifts extended to people, unmerited to be sure, *and human recognition of God's goodness and thankful reception of his gifts.* Full-orbed grace must have both elements. Paul is saying that, from the very first, God graciously made his power and Godhead known, but instead of responding by giving him glory and gratitude, people chose to make idols and worship or "link up" with those idols instead of with their Creator God.

Second, Paul goes on to deal with people groups that are thought of (and think of themselves) as being more "civilized" or as practicing religions that are more "developed" and sophisticated (Rom. 2:1–11). Romans and Greeks, for example, celebrated the proud philosophies expounded on Mars Hill in Athens and in the Roman Forum. Paul knows them, as he knows about the degraded worship of Delphi and the unconscionable atrocities of the Coliseum. Actually, the religions of Greece and Rome could not survive philosophical reflection. Brahmanism (subsequently elaborated into Hinduism), Buddhism, Judaism, Christianity, and Islam "are the only religions that have produced great systems of thought, exhibiting their content in a speculative and rational form" (Rees 1930, 1250).

No matter how complex their philosophies and embellished their religions, those who look down their noses at primal worship are just as degraded, according to Paul. These sophisticates will find a law that judges themselves to be just as unworthy if they look at their own . . .

- *nature* (*physis*, or "essence; disposition; natural instinct"),
- *heart* (*kardia*, or thoughts, mind, feelings), and
- *conscience* (*syneideisis*, or co-perception, moral consciousness).

Third, Paul looks at his own people and their religion (Rom. 2:12–29). Jews boast of a covenant extending back to Abraham and a circumcision that sealed it. Jews boast of the law given through Moses and the injunctions that forbid the worship of any god but Yahweh. However, their proud monotheism is not attended by proper behavior, so the name of God is blasphemed among Gentiles (v. 24). True circumcision is an affair of the heart, and obedience to divine law is a matter of both letter and spirit.

Paul concludes that all who are outside of Christ are abject sinners, whatever their religious affiliation, level of devotion, or race. This is so, even though the only true God has continually revealed his *person, attributes, and goodness*. Paul's conclusion is disconcerting, but look at his propositions in Romans 3:10–12:

> No one is righteous, no not one.
> No one understands.
> All have turned aside and
> become worthless.
> No one does good, not even one.

By nature, all of us proudly resist the notion that these propositions apply to us, but, of course, they do apply. Moreover, we even resist the idea that they apply to all adherents of all religions on the face of the earth. Certainly there must be some people somewhere who seek God of their own accord. Can't we at least categorize them as "seekers," if not "saints," or "good," if not "perfect"? Can we not call them something other than "abject sinners"?

As kind and courteous as is the inclination to gentle down the force of these words, the effect of doing so is both *un*kind and unscriptural. Such kindness denies what God says and also what he is. He is the merciful "seeking God" who always seeks out sinners (and, in his grace, transforms sinners into seekers before transforming them into sons). Our first inclination is to hide from God, just as did our first parents.

Less obviously, however, any attempt to blunt the force of Paul's argument is *un*kind because it thwarts God's saving purpose. God "has consigned all to disobedience, that he may have mercy on all," says the apostle (Rom. 11:32).

All are sinners by nature, by choice, and by decree of God.

"That's bad," we say.

Well, yes, but also, no.

Why no? *Because in his mercy God saves sinners. That's the only kind of people he saves.*

For the history of religions, look first at Genesis. It all begins there. But for a biblical theology of what happened back there in the beginning—a theology of humanity and his religion and religions—look at Romans. The basics are all there.

Interreligious Encounters: Invasions of Enemy Territory

In a day of pluralism, inclusivism, and relativism, to say nothing of a twisted understanding of religious tolerance, the idea that the various religions constitute enemy territory seems hopelessly biased. Delegates at the First World Parliament of Religions suspected that religion should bring people together, not tear them apart. By the time of the Second World Parliament, delegates were certain that unity should be the goal of religion.

And what about the good that is evident in all religions? When a Buddhist says, "Do not do unto others what you would not want others to do to you," is that not another way of expressing the Golden Rule? When a Muslim recites the words "God is all-forgiving, all-compassionate," is he not speaking the truth about God? Are those who share such teachings *enemies* to each other?

"Even those parts of another religion which might appear to be lofty and uplifting," according to Kraemer, "prove to be parts of a whole that is under the judgment of God" (Kraemer 1962, 136). When Edmund Perry speaks of the various religions as leading men and women *away* from God, he is thinking of religions as indivisible wholes. These are *systems* that Satan, disguised as an "angel of light," employs to predispose adherents to *dis*believe in the Christ of the biblical gospel. That, after all, is the crux of their problem: *The first concern of biblical faith has to do with reconnecting people to God, and Christ is the only connection.* Missionaries almost invariably find themselves confronting "good" people who are predisposed to misunderstand, misrepresent, and disbelieve

Jesus Christ. In this profound sense missionaries easily find themselves frustrated and located in "enemy territory."

We will more or less confine this part of our discussion to anecdotal materials relating to those religions systems. But as we proceed, we must remember that Christianity itself is by no means monolithic. Throughout church history and still today, some great churches and throngs of so-called Christians have yielded to the wiles of Satan and given ground to him. This being so, "Christian lands" themselves often constitute enemy territory in the senses that Kraemer and Perry indicate, and therefore call out for missionary witness.

Primal Religions as Enemy Territory

It goes without saying that primal religion (tribalism, animism, dynamism, etc.) exists not as one religious system but as many, each with its own deities, intermediaries, remedies, and rituals. In many ways, tribal peoples, such as those of sub-Saharan Africa and the islands of the South Pacific, have proved to be fertile soil for missionary endeavor. But they have also proved to be resistant. Would-be Christian converts often find themselves repairing to local medicine men under the cover of darkness. Syncretism is more the norm than an exception.

Central to primal or animistic religions is the "high god" who is too far away to connect with people in the round of daily affairs. Lesser gods, good and evil spirits, ancestral spirits, and various sources of power are near at hand. So are the shamans, medicine men, sorcerers, and workers of magic who provide the best hope for manipulating the lesser gods and spirits. The work of tribal religion is to continually enlist intermediaries to appease the spirits and fend off evil by means of prescribed rituals, medicines, amulets, and power words.

Primal religionists are "easily reached" but "hard to win." They lack or automatically misconstrue the categories we use—*Creator God, Redeemer, Savior, sin, salvation, faith,* and even *missionary.* Primal religionists are predisposed to think of the Creator God of Genesis as far removed; the Christ of the Gospels as a miracle-working medicine man or shaman; prayers and the ordinances as powerful words and rituals; and missionaries as something other than just bearers of a divine message.

The very system often conspires to remake missionaries into something other than the humble heralds and disciplers they are called to be.

Brahmanism and Hinduism as Enemy Territory

Indian syncretism presents its own set of dangers. A well-known Christian apologist proposed that we confront Hinduism head-on. His idea was that all religions have to face up to the principle of noncontradiction. This apologist understood monism as a philosophical system, but he did not fully appreciate that it also is a way of life in India. At the existential level, we are challenged by Brahmanism as it has evolved into modern Hinduism.

Intellectually we can understand that, if Brahman is the Absolute and the only "real Reality," all else must be complementary and not "really" contradictory. Even Ego (the *Atman* or individual Self or Soul) *is* Brahman. However, the further one goes into monism, the more frustrating it tends to become. How does one carry on serious conversation in a context in which contradictory philosophies of six divergent schools of Hindu thought accommodate each other? To visit temples and crematoria and walk through the slums of Bombay or New Dehli, realizing that Hinduism establishes the apologetic for justifying contradictory ritual and social inequity. It is almost more than a sensitive soul can bear.

Hindu accommodation of mutually contradictory ideas seemed most incredulous to me as I began doing research on the religion. I happened upon a Hindu apologetic prepared for Westerners by one of India's eminent philosophers and a president of India in the 1960s, Sarvepalli Radhakrishnan (1888–1975). In light of the new awareness of Indian religion that followed the First World Parliament of Religions and in the wake of philosophical and doctrinal controversies that plagued Protestantism and paved the way for the Laymen's Inquiry, Radhakrishnan explained Hinduism in a way that made it plausible for India and almost appealing to the West. His work, *The Hindu View of Life,* was first published in 1927, but has had numerous printings and was followed by several similar works.

By the time Radhakrishnan has worked his philosophical and semantic alchemy, all gods, however low or high; all spirits, however numerous; all idols, however crass; and all mediators, however diverse, can be accommodated and even celebrated. All worship forms, from the grossest expressions of *bhakti* (devotion) to the strictest expressions of *dharma* (law), can be validated and appreciated. In his view, even caste (and the *varna,* or segregation on the basis of color that was its original basis) is necessary for society to progress. Principles of *samsara* (the wheel of birth and rebirth), *karma* ("action" or cause and effect), and *adhikara* (degrees of spiritual perception) are employed to explain everything.

One of Radhakirshnan's most arresting statements cuts against the grain of popular wisdom:

> In a sense, Hinduism may be regarded as the first example in the world of a missionary religion. Only its missionary spirit is different from that associated with the proselytizing creeds. It did not regard it as its mission to convert humanity to any one opinion. For what counts is conduct and not belief. Worshippers of different gods and followers of different rites were taken into the Hindu fold. (Radhakrishnan 1927, 28)

Radhakrishnan may have been more than a historian at this point. He may have been something of a prophet. Hinduism not only maintains a tight grip on its own, but it also attracts postmodern outsiders. It is like a giant web that looks dirty and repellant until viewed in shades of philosophy and interpreted in ways that shield some of its gross aspects. Then the true God is swallowed up in a false reality. Christ may be counted, along with Rama, Krishna, Gautama, and others, as one of the ten most prominent *avatara,* or incarnations. Sin is not so much defiance of God as denial of self. And, given a right understanding of *karma*, the prayer of the penitent, is both superstitious and futile—like asking God to abrogate his own law (Radhakrishnan 1927, 53).

The one who masquerades as an "angel of light" must have labored diligently to devise this system. And he must have worked overtime to predispose its adherents to accept and disseminate it.

Buddhism as Enemy Territory

If tradition is to be trusted, Buddhism was founded by Gautama Buddha about six centuries before the Christian Era. *Gautama* (or *Gotama*) was the name of his particular subset of the Sakya clan. *Buddha* means "Enlightened One" or "Awakened One." It is in that concept of awakened enlightenment that the essence of Buddhism is to be found. After years of arduous and unrewarded searching, Gautama sat down under a pipal tree to meditate one day. It was there that he awakened to the truth. And it was from there that he went forth to preach the true *dharma* (law).

Buddha's message was one of the most radical ever conceived. It reflected the basic worldview and the fundamental concepts of Gautama's native India, such as *karma* and rebirth. But Buddha replaced Brahman with Nirvana and the doctrine of the soul (*atman*) with "no-soul" (*anatman*). Buddha's worldview was that nothing is permanent; all is in flux (*annica*). People have no personal or individual identity. Life is inevitably characterized by the kind of suffering (*dukkha*) that accompanies human attachments of any sort. The human problem is ignorance. The solution is to overcome suffering by treading an eightfold path that leads to various levels of enlightenment (*moksha*) including, eventually, nirvana. Nirvana is the state of bliss that accompanies the cessation of desire and absorption (or reabsorption) into the All-embracing Brahman.

As the Buddha, Gautama took issue with the religiosity of India expressed in its worship and social arrangements and especially in the necessity to conform. If he could not accommodate Hinduism, neither could Hinduism accommodate him. His was a different message and mission.

Buddhism developed around the world in two primary forms: *hinayana* and *mahayana*. Though Buddhists may take exception to this usual way of distinguishing these major schools, it is nevertheless descriptive. Hinayana means "small boat or raft." In Hinayana Buddhism, enlightenment and nirvana are arrived at by individual effort. Mahayana means "large boat or raft" and is the kind of Buddhism where enlightenment and Nirvana are arrived at by the mercy of Buddha and the merits of the bodhisattvas who have postponed buddhahood in order to help others who are "on the Path." Gautama Buddha and all of his successors have pointed followers in a direction that not only does not lead *to* the Christ, who alone is the way, the truth, and the life, but in fact lead their followers away from him.

Judaism as Enemy Territory

Judaism as a term dates to Hellenistic times. It is used in only one passage in Scripture. In Galatians 1:14 Paul says that he was so zealous for the "traditions of his fathers" that he was advancing in Judaism above others of a similar age. The word *Judaism (Ioudaismos)* was comparatively new, but its "traditions" were old and its "faith" even older.

As Christians we owe so much to our Jewish forbears that it is hard to contemplate the idea that the Jewish faith constitutes enemy territory. Such an idea smacks of anti-Semitism, and there is not the slightest bit of room for that in biblical Christianity. As a follower of Christ, Paul says that to his Israelite kinsmen belong the adoption, the glory, the covenants, the giving of the law, the worship, and the promises. To them belong the patriarchs. From their race, according to the flesh, came the Christ (Rom. 9:4–5).

But it is at the person of the Christ that we part company. Later in that same chapter (Rom. 9:32–33) Paul quotes Isaiah and says that the Jews "stumbled over the stumbling stone" (i.e., Christ). Judaism clung tenaciously to the law and summarily rejected Jesus as either Christ or Lord.

Judaism has changed markedly throughout the past two centuries. Today's Jews are divided into groupings ranging from the outspoken atheists of Reform Judaism and uncommitted agnostics of Conservative Judaism to Orthodox Jews who are faithful to Jewish rites and rituals. Within this wide-ranging set of belief options, all are recognized as Jews. The only belief that brings exclusion from the Jewish community is that Jesus is the Messiah and Lord.

There are historical reasons for this insistence that messianic believers must be pushed from the family, but the chief reason is that the religious establishment has from the start been implacably at enmity with Jesus as the promised Christ or Messiah. The rejection of that identification is what motivated the Jewish leaders to seek Jesus' death in the first place. Paul faced enmity because his gospel did not make room for the "traditions" (Gal. 1:14). By "traditions," he probably meant the additions to, and interpretations of law that would be collected and edited as the Mishna in about the year 200.

After the destruction of Jerusalem in A.D. 70, opposition to Christians became intense due to the teachings of Yochanan ben Zakkai, a disciple of Rabbi Hillel. Gamaliel, who taught Paul, would have studied under Hillel at about the same time as Zakkai, who by all accounts lived to an extraordinarily old age of well over a hundred years and therefore exerted a long-lasting inflence. Zakkai was leader of the Pharisees during the first Jewish revolt and helped save Judaism from disintegration by his efforts and the influence of his school in Jamnia.

Zakkai's hatred for Jesus remains, reinforced by many centuries of mutual hostility and violence committed in the name of Christ. There is today a concerted effort to dispel the claims of Christ from serious consideration among the Jewish people (Kaplan et al 1976; Moore 1996, esp. 307–91). Never will I forget the response of an otherwise affable Jewish rabbi from New York as we conversed at the Western Wall in Jerusalem in 1968. When the discussion turned to a consideration of the messiahship of Jesus, he suddenly became irritated. As he walked away, he muttered in anger, "We Jews will never consider that man!"

Any evangelism among Jews means an invasion into enemy territory. Jesus said so when he faced Jewish leaders who laid claim to being Abraham's children while rejecting Jesus himself. In one of his "hard sayings," he said, "You are of your father the devil, and your will is to do your father's desires" (John 8:44). Paul said something similar when writing to the Romans. He wrote, "*As regards the gospel,* they are enemies of God for your sake" (Rom. 11:28, emphasis mine).

That's bad news. But there is good news too. The unbelief of the Jews resulted in the gospel being preached to the Gentiles. And the acceptance of the gospel by Gentiles will someday eventuate in the salvation of the Jews (Rom. 11:11–12).

Islam as Enemy Territory

In the sixth century of the Christian Era, a young member of the Quraysh tribe of Mecca joined the caravans that for centuries had traveled from Egypt in the south to Damascus in the north. At twenty-five he was employed as chief merchant by a rich widow named Khadija and became ever more familiar with the religions of Palestine, although the versions of Judaism and Christianity he encountered were both aberrant forms. But Muhammad was captivated by a desire to cleanse the shrine in Mecca of its idolatry and superstition.

His devotion to prayer and meditation culminated in a series of visions and revelations from the angel Gabriel. Encouraged by Khadija, whom he married, he began writing these messages down on pieces of wood, stone, leather, or whatever was available. In time he came to be accepted as the "final prophet" of the religion of Islam (literally meaning in Arabic "surrender" or "submission").

But, in a profound sense, Islam did not begin with Muhammad. Muhammad himself dated it to a line stretching from Adam to Noah to Moses to Abraham. It is at that point that he deliberately made a choice that was destined to rival the decision of the Jews to reject their Messiah in terms of its impact upon world history. Muhammad opted for Abraham's line but through the Egyptian concubine Hagar and their son Ishmael rather than through his wife Sarah and their "son of the promise," Isaac. In doing so he also aligned himself, at least spiritually, with Isaac's firstborn, Esau, who sold his birthright to his younger brother Jacob for some red pottage. Jacob's name was changed to "Israel" (i.e., "strength with God"), Esau's name was changed to "Edom" (i.e., "red"). Like Ishmael before him, Esau the hunter gathered up his belongings and journeyed east to the biblical Mount Seir, part of a mountain range extending 120 miles from the Dead Sea to the Gulf of Akabah. The Egyptians called it "The Red Land," and "Edom" is the Hebrew or Canaanitish translation.

In addition to their blood and territorial relationships, Ishmaelites and Edomites became related by marriage when, along with Hittite and Horite wives, Esau married Ishmael's daughter Mahalath. Subsequently, both intermarried with Temanites, Kadmonites, Nabatheans, Midianites, Yemenites, and other tribal groups in the general area. In accord with God's promises to Abraham, Hagar, and Ishmael, many of these peoples prospered, largely as a result of the caravan traffic intersecting Egypt, Petra, Palmyra, Damascus, and other great cities. Only gradually and over the centuries as the caravan traffic gradually gave way to shipping did this change. Then those hardy Arabic peoples came upon harder times. Finally, many of them were forced to abandon their cities and wander over barren lands while fending for themselves as best they could.

The Bible is replete with references to these peoples, especially to Esau and the Edomites who became more or less representative (perhaps because Esau personally chose to sell his birthright). According to the Old Testament account, Joseph was sold to Ishmaelites who took him to Egypt. Edomites refused passage to the Israelites when they came out of Egypt and often took sides with Israel's enemies during the conquest of Canaan. Obadiah prophesied that the house of Joseph would prevail over the house of Esau. Malachi quoted Yahweh as saying, "I have loved Jacob but Esau I have hated. I have laid waste his hill country and left his heritage to jackals of the desert" (Mal. 1:2–3).

Immediately upon opening the New Testament we are introduced to a genealogy that traces the lineage of the Christ child to Abraham through Isaac and Jacob (Matt. 1:2). We also meet Herod the Great, who was an Edomite (Greek *Idumean*—Matt. 2:1), as well as the last independent king to reign in Jerusalem. Herod set out to destroy the baby Jesus by killing all male children of about his age around Bethlehem. It was one of his sons, Herod Antipas, who governed Jesus' home area of Galilee. It was Herod Antipas who mocked Jesus during his trial and then returned him to Pilate.

The writer of Hebrews warns believers not to be sexually immoral (*pornē*) and unholy (*bebēlos*) like Esau, who "sold his birthright for a single meal" and was turned down when he "desired to inherit the blessing" later on (Heb. 12:16–17). Paul quotes Malachi 1:2–3 in Romans 9:13. He urges the Galatians not to return to the slavery of the law and dependence on the flesh represented by Hagar and her son, but to embrace the freedom proffered by God's grace as symbolized by Sarah and Isaac (Gal. 4:21–31).

Note that I am not arguing that Muhammad was an Edomite by ethnic origin. Geneological relationships among Arab peoples are notoriously difficult to establish. At the same time, a careful reading of the life and career of Muhammad reveals a remarkable "kinship" between Muhammad and the line of Esau. Esau and the Edomites can be viewed as something of a biblical prototype for Muhammad and his successors. This is not to say that all Muslims are alike in culture and attitude. However, an understanding of Esau and his progeny provide some basis for understanding of such intricacies as the Muslim ambivalence toward Jesus and his followers, the nature of *jihad*, and the Muslim conception of heaven.

The current political and religious climate has motivated even some who represent themselves as Christians to argue that Muhammad was a great and good man, that Allah is a totally fitting name for the God of the Bible, and that the *Qur'an* contains high praise for Jesus. Such apologists seem sure that Shi'ite and Wahhabi (radical Sunni) fundamentalists do not represent Islam, the religion of peace. They believe that *jihad* can be interpreted as the give-and-take of interfaith dialogue.

The facts argue for a different construction of reality. What is known of Muhammad shows him to be a complex leader who fits his time, as merciless as he was clever. The Allah of the *Qur'an* is very unlike the Triune God of the Bible. Isa (Jesus) of Islam is nothing like the crucified and resurrected Christ. When everything said about Jews, Christians, and other "unbelievers" is set out from the *Qur'an* and *Hadith*, the ultimate result is persecution. Until Islamic law, *shari'a*, guides all lands and peoples, at least one meaning of the complex concept of *jihad* is that Islam is at "war" with the world until all embrace Islamic peace.

It is impossible to understand Islam without taking into account this biblical background and the bad choices of Abraham, Esau, and, of course, Muhammad himself. A key to understanding Islam is that little Greek word *bebēlos* in Hebrews 12:16. The primary meaning of *bebēlos* is "accessible" or "available to be trodden on." By extension it means unhallowed, profane, or irreligious as opposed to *hieros*, or "sacred." In the final analysis, Islam is promoted by the sword, prophesies a judgment of works, and promises a heaven of fleshly delights (for men). Far from being spiritual in the biblical sense, it is the archetype of what may be termed "secular religion." It enfolds countless millions of upstanding and peace-loving adherents and other millions of nominals and folk religionists. But whatever their status, the vast majority of Muslims convert to the God of the Bible and his crucified, risen Son only with great difficulty and often at a tremendous price.

The Missionary Quest for Common Ground

Throughout the history of the missionary movement and, in America, especially since the early years of the twentieth century, missiologists and missionaries have concerned themselves with finding the best ways to approach adherents of non-Christian faiths. Obviously there must be *some* common ground or else communication would be impossible. But where is it? What is its nature? How can we discover it? What are its boundaries? These are not easy questions. But they must have answers.

Numerous proposals have contributed to discussions of common ground. Discovering points of contact, building bridges of understanding, finding redemptive analogies and "eye openers," establishing identification with respondents, engaging non-Christians in dialogue—all have their advocates. All are characterized by certain assumptions and applications. Most can be understood rhetorically, philosophically, sociologically, anthropologically, and psychologically as well as religiously. Many of them have at least some validity—some more and some less. Our primary interest here has to do with the possibility of establishing common ground on spiritual and religious bases.

Problematic Approaches to Establishing Common Ground

1. *A common search.* At first blush, understanding the missionary quest for common ground might seem to be a rather simple matter. It grows out of the notion that religion itself represents a search for God or truth or salvation, as the case might be, while particular religions represent various ways of going about that search. William Ernest Hocking's (1873–1966) "fulfillment approach" to common ground is an early example of this. Contemporary examples can be found in the proposals of Leonard Swidler, John Hick, Willard Oxtoby, and Hasan Askari. If I understand him correctly, Swidler, for example, thinks of humans as evolving toward a kind of utopia in which freedom of thought and action is somehow guided by mutual love and respect. Religion serves both as the expression of, and the vehicle for, achieving that kind of culture and society. "Human nature," he writes, "is directed at an open-ended, endless, in-finite [*sic*] all-embracing, comprehensive knowing and loving

and knowing freely acting. That total knowing and loving and knowing freely acting that humans, both individually and communally have created over the centuries is Religion, and the Culture that matches it" (Swidler 1992, 115).

Swidler's rather cryptic lines suggest that he believes that Religion with a capital *R* somehow enlists adherents of all religions old and new in this common effort to create a "Global Culture" of knowledge, love, and freedom.

As interpreted by John Hick, the common search takes on an evangelical flavor. He believes that the teachings of religions are different but complementary. They represent a variety of ways in which humankind can achieve salvation:

> These resources [i.e., various religions] have at their heart, I want to suggest, an awareness that the great purpose of religion is salvation, or liberation, as an actual transformation of human existence; and a recognition that this is taking place (though in conjunction with quite different systems of belief) within other "houses of faith" as well as one's own. (Hick 1985, 5)

From a human perspective, Hick's understanding certainly seems to merit consideration:

- Did not Augustine say that man is restless until he finds rest in God?
- Did not Pascal talk about a void in the human heart that can only be filled by God himself?
- Did not the prophet Jeremiah say, "You will seek me and find me. When you seek me with all your heart, I will be found by you, declares the LORD" (Jer. 29:13–14)?
- Did not Jesus speak to the Samaritan woman about a thirst that could be quenched only by the "living water" that he gives (John 4:14)?
- Did not Peter's hearers on Pentecost seek a way to right the wrong they had done when they inquired, "Brothers, what shall we do?" (Acts 2:37).

- Was not Paul's invitation on Mars Hill based on the intense desire of Athenian philosophers to know about his "new teaching" (Acts 17:19)?

Surely lost men and women have been engaged in a quest for God or for something that he alone can give from time immemorial. The missionary quest for common ground should be an easy one. The search for common ground is the almost universal involvement in another, larger quest for God and truth or hope and salvation.

Perhaps that is common ground, or perhaps not. Who did the searching after the fall? Not Adam and Eve. They were not "seekers"; they were "hiders." And that is in line with Paul's words: "No one seeks for God. All have turned aside" (Rom. 3:11–12).

God is the "Seeker." Jesus said, "The Son of Man came to seek and to save the lost" (Luke 19:10). Seeming exceptions to this understanding may, in fact, support it. Jeremiah, after all, was speaking on God's behalf to a covenant people whom God had called and blessed. And the response of repentant Jews on Pentecost (Acts 2:37–41) did not represent people reaching out for God so much as a loving God reaching out to his erring children.

The Lord Jesus speaks very directly to this issue. Far from endorsing the notion that people are engaged in a common search for God and his gifts of grace, Jesus said, "No one can come to me unless the Father who sent me draws him" (John 6:44). By nature people seek for substitutes but not for him. Perry is right when he avers that the various religions represent ways in which humankind is being led *away* from God, not *toward* him.

It is right that missionaries pray that they might be led to people in whose hearts and minds there has been a providential working of God's Spirit. But it is wrong to assume that the search for God (or for that which he alone can supply) is common. That idea is in stark contrast to biblical teachings, which indicate that it is God who searches and God who draws men and women to himself. Ever since Eden, people have been running *away* from God. We have been hiding; he has been seeking. We are the rebellious sinners; he is the loving God.

2. *Religious similarities.* The "similarity approach" to establishing

common ground is both very popular and very problematic. Its proponents seek out teachings and practices in the various religions that appear to be the same or similar to presumed counterparts in Christianity, hoping to build bridges of understanding thereby. But it is extremely difficult to compare the various religions, especially so when the Christian faith is involved. For that very reason, comparative religions as a discipline of study has tended to give way to the history of religions. Nevertheless, for various reasons and with varying degrees of success, comparisons continue to be made.

In a frequently used reference work, Eric Sharpe attempts to define and explain some fifty words that have special and correlative meanings in the world's religions. His objective is to promote understanding of comparative religion in general and the several religions in particular (Sharpe 1971, 115).

Swidler takes a somewhat different tack. He selects seven words (*redemption, liberation, enlightenment, nirvana, heaven, communism,* and *salvation*) that he believes to be descriptive of the "goal of religion" and proceeds to explain how these words are used and what they mean within the contexts of the various religions (Swidler 1992, 12–17). As we have seen, Swidler's objective is to bring to light commonalities and complementary aspects of religion to promote unity and a new society.

In works that already have become evangelical missions classics, Don Richardson emphasizes the importance of discovering redemptive analogies and what he calls "eye-openers" (e.g., the "peace child" idea and ritual among the Sawi people of West Irian in New Guinea) that will enable non-Christian peoples to understand the gospel (Richardson 1974; Richardson 1981). Richardson's goal is to make the gospel understandable and to facilitate conversion.

It seems fair to say that all three authors are of the opinion that there are similarities between Christian and the non-Christian faiths that, properly understood and exploited, will facilitate both understanding and the fulfillment of God's "mission" for the church as they understand it. But, even though there may be some truth to this idea, the approach is problematic in any case and especially so if one holds to the absolute uniqueness of the "faith that was once for all delivered to the saints" (Jude 3). Both philosophically and theologically, a communication approach that is overdependent upon the discovery and utilization of similarities is open to question.

Here again, Hendrik Kraemer is helpful. He points out that the attempt to catalogue similarities "on such subjects as the idea of God and of man, the conception of the soul or of redemption, the expectation of an eternal life or the precedence of the community over the individual, etc., is an impossible thing." In the first place, no religion is an assortment of spiritual commodities that can be "compared as shoes or neckties" (Kraemer 1962, 134–35). On the contrary, every religion is a unity or individual whole in which each teaching, myth, or ritual must be understood in relationship to all else. In the second place, when exposed to the light of God's revelation in Christ and the Scriptures, even those parts of another religion that might appear to be lofty are parts of a whole that is under the judgment of God (Kraemer 1962, 136).

Kraemer's words are in accord with Perry's understanding of religion and particular religions. Moreover, what he says is quite easily demonstrated by the kind of holistic examination advocated by both authors. Though conceived of as a "high god" in Chinese religion, for example, Shang-ti hardly qualifies as being analogous to the God of the Bible if one takes all of Chinese religion into account. Similarly, the "three bodies of Buddha," the mercy of Amida, and the faith displayed in Mahayana—all such so dimly reflect supposed counterparts in Christianity as to be entirely misleading if taken to be anything approaching mirror images. It would be quite a stretch to agree that the Allah of the Qur'an has been divested of the qualities of the pre-Islamic moon god of Muhammad's Quraysh tribal people and has taken on most of the qualities of the God of the Bible. But even if we attempted to do so, Allah's very nature (and not just Muhammad's misunderstanding of the Trinity) would make the deity of Christ impossible.

Readers will have to judge the validity of redemptive analogies such as Richardson's well-known "peace child" for themselves (Richardson 1974). That that particular analogy functioned well early on in the communication of the gospel to the Sawi seems to be beyond question. However, the peace child of Sawi tribalism is light years removed from the Prince of Peace of biblical revelation. Sooner or later—and the sooner the better—the difference must become as crystal clear to Sawi believers as it is to the missionaries. To the degree that it does not, Sawis will inevitably be more syncretistic, less Christian.

Dissimilarities may in fact prove to be more useful than similarities in communicating Christ and the gospel. This often is the way that new knowledge and understandings are attained. After all, the Christian faith (in its revelation if not always in its practice) is absolutely unique. There is no other faith *like* it. No other God; no other Christ; no other Calvary; no other empty tomb; no other redemption; no other salvation; no other heaven. That being the case, when the objective is to convert and disciple people, communication often will be enhanced by pointing out differences. People need to know that sin in Scripture and *tsumi* in Shinto are not the same, or even similar in the final reckoning. Neither is grace in the gospel like *karuna* (mercy) in Mahayana. Nor is Trinity in Christian faith like *trimurti* (the three high gods) in Hinduism or biblical inspiration like *wahy* (authoritative relation) and *ilham* (less authoritative "inspiration") in Islam. Such pairs can be more clearly communicated by means of contrast than by supposed similarity.

Plausible Approaches to the Search for Common Ground

1. *Points of contact.* It is customary for missiologists to speak of finding points of contact between missionaries and their hearers. Rhetoricians speak of establishing "identification" with the audience.

It is not difficult to find examples of this kind of approach in the New Testament. Since the Lord Jesus "came to his own" (i.e., his own people—John 1:11), he did not have many encounters with those of other religions. We do have the example of his use of a water metaphor when speaking to the Samaritan woman at the well as recorded in the fourth chapter of John.

Examples are more readily found in the ministry of the apostle Paul. His statement that he became "all things to all men so that I may by all means save some" (1 Cor. 9:22 NASB) is often pointed to in this connection. We see his approach to Athenians on Mars Hill in Acts 17. He drew attention to Athenian religiosity by noting that they had erected an altar with the inscription "To the unknown god" (vv. 22–23). He quoted their own poets (probably Epimenides and Aratus) to show them that they had some foundation for believing that God the source of life is also near at hand (vv. 27–28).

It would be easy to read too much into these references to Greek religion and philosophy, however. Since the "unknown god" was unknown, Paul did not obligate himself to empty the Greek concept of false notions. And Paul quickly moved from the general idea offered by the Greek writers to the specifics of special revelation and Christ's incarnation. Far more significant was Paul's declaration that the gods the Athenians did worship were idols, and their vaunted philosophy grew out of ignorance (vv. 29–30).

Points of contact have significance, but they also have definite limitations. Even acts of generosity and kindness designed to overcome animosity and suspicion in making initial contacts can be misinterpreted. It was just such a misinterpretation that led to the deaths of Jim Elliot, Pete Fleming, Ed McCully, Nate Saint, and Roger Youderian on January 8, 1956 as they tried to establish themselves among the Huaorani (then called the Auca) in Peru. Similar disasters have occurred for like reason. Kraemer assesses points of contact this way:

> There is only one point of contact, and if that one point exists, then there are many points of contact. This one point of contact is the disposition and attitude of the missionary. . . . Such is the golden rule, or, if one prefers, the iron law in this whole matter. The way to live up to this rule is to have an untiring and genuine interest in the religion, the ideas, the sentiments, the institutions—in short, in the whole range of life of the people among whom one works, *for Christ's sake and for the sake of those people.* (Kraemer 1962, 140)

2. *Interreligious dialogue.* Generally speaking, missionaries are less comfortable with dialogical communication than with monologue preaching and teaching. In a chapter on dialogical communication of the gospel, however, John R. W. Stott reminds us that the Lord Jesus "seldom if ever spoke in a declamatory, take-it-or-leave-it style. Instead, whether explicitly or implicitly, he was constantly addressing questions to his hearers' minds and consciences" (Stott 1975, 61).

Whereas among liberals interreligious dialogue is often proposed as a means of discovering common ground with non-Christians, among conservatives it should be regarded more as a means of disseminating the gospel. Whereas among liberals interreligious dialogue is proposed as a means of establishing commonality, among conservatives it should be recognized that authentic dialogue will often lead to controversy and disputation.

Bypassing some of the complex Old Testament examples, such as Elijah's contest with the prophets of Baal (1 Kings 18), look at dialogue in the New Testament. The New Testament introduces the word from which our term *dialogue* is derived. It appears almost exclusively in its verb forms (*dialegomai* and *dialogizomai*). Though the Gospels make it clear that Jesus never hesitated to enter into the give-and-take of two-way conversation, there is no clear indication that Christ employed "interreligious dialogue" as we understand the concept. In the one place in which the cognate verb *dialogizomai* ("to converse or discuss with") is used regarding an encounter between Jesus and the Pharisees, the emphasis is probably on discussion, but a confrontation is involved (Luke 5:21–24).

Dialegomai and *dialogizomai* are used more prominently in connection with the apostle Paul. He engaged in dialogue in the synagogues (Acts 17:2, 17; 18:4, 19), in the marketplace (17:17), in the school of Tyrannus (19:9), and in the church at Troas (20:7, 9). In each of these cases, it is apparent that Paul's intention was to establish the truth of the gospel, not find common ground with his audience. In one context—Paul's defense before Felix—*dialogue* is used in a negative frame of reference. Paul tells the court that his Jerusalem accusers did not find him "dialoguing" or causing riots in Jerusalem or in its temple and synagogues (24:12).

From Scripture and history, it seems safe to conclude that interreligious dialogue is a questionable means of establishing common ground. On the other hand, it seems to be powerful for communicating the gospel and convincing hearers of gospel truth when undertaken at the risk of inviting debate and dissension. Careful inquiry supports the conclusion of Gottlob Schrenk, when he writes,

> In the New Testament there is no instance of the classical use of *dialegomai* in the philosophical sense. In the sphere of revelation

there is no question of reaching the idea through dialectic. What is at issue is the obedient and percipient acceptance of the Word spoken by God, which is not an idea, but the comprehensive declaration of the divine will which sets all life in the light of divine truth. (Shrenk 1964, 95)

Positive Approaches to Establishing Common Ground

Some approaches to establishing common ground, when properly understood, do seem to be almost entirely positive.

Christian rational presuppositionalism. Though it is not uncommon for missiologists to think of differences between Hindu-Buddhist monism and Judeo-Christian theism as being almost unbridgeable philosophically, Carl F. H. Henry takes exception with this notion. True, given the notion that the Brahman embraces all in oneness, there can be no room for the law of noncontradiction. This would seem to nullify both Western rationalism and Christian revelationism as bases for common ground. But Henry says that is not so:

> There is, in fact, no perspective, oriental or occidental, that would not be assisted by a good course in logic, or that does not soon sacrifice universal validity if it neglects the law of contradiction. The laws of logic are not a speculative prejudice imposed at a given moment of history as a transient philosophical development. Neither do they involve a Western way of thinking even if Aristotle may have stated them in an orderly way. The laws of valid inference are universal; they are elements of the imago Dei. In the Bible, reason has ontological significance. God is himself truth and the source of truth. Biblical Christianity honors the Logos of God as the source of all meaning and considers the laws of thought an aspect of the imago. (Henry 1990, 109–10)

I am not saying that the missionary to Hindus and Buddhists should not understand and reason from "within" their all-encompassing monistic worldview. My point is that Henry must be correct. Whatever the worldview or ways of thinking, there is but one truth and one logic—both grounded in the person and nature of the Creator God. He is Truth and the Source of truth. He is the basis of logical validity and the "law of noncontradition" because he cannot deny himself (2 Tim. 2:13). He is the basis of propositional truth and the "law of correspondence," because it is impossible for him to lie (Heb. 6:18).

Christian rational presuppositionalism is neither racial nor cultural. It is philosophical and theological. Insofar as the missionary is truly Christian, the unshakable but humble conviction that the God of the Bible is the God of truth underlies anything that he or she might be, think, understand, do, or say. Only to the degree that persons of any race or culture come to know him will they be able to think his thoughts after him. Only to the degree that they think his thoughts after him will they be able to think rightly about creation, religions, and their own condition.

Biblical theology. The concept of biblical theology developed because of the need to distinguish between theologies based upon church tradition and theologies developed on the basis of Scripture. Over time, however, the meaning of "biblical theology" has tended to take on the meaning imposed by whatever church, school, or group is employing the term. In this book the term is almost invariably used to refer to theology that is not only based on the Bible itself but also on the unfolding revelation of the Bible story as it proceeds from Genesis to Revelation. In various contexts we have emphasized the importance of communicating that larger story and not just fragments of it or lessons growing out of it. Here I would emphasize the importance of using the approach of that kind of biblical theology as a basis for establishing common ground.

Gregory Beale writes, "The New Testament writers typically do not make reference to specific pagan religions, philosophies, and their belief systems. Some of the exceptions to this, as is well known, are 1 Corinthians 15:53; Titus 1:12; Acts 14:11–18; and, above all, Paul's address to the Athenians in Acts 17:16–34" (Beale 2004, 79). Beale is correct, but was the Mars Hill address so exceptional in this regard? Beale himself takes special notice of the biblical underpinnings of Paul's Mars Hill address and how he applied basic teachings from the Old Testament. At first Paul's words to the Athenians may seem to be grounded in general or natural revelation. Upon closer examination, however, they are seen to be grounded in Scripture:

"God who made the world" (v. 24)—Genesis 1:1;

"He himself gives to mankind life and breath" (v. 25)
—Genesis 2:7; Isaiah 42:5;

"He made from one man" (v. 26)—Genesis 1:28;

"Having determined . . . the boundaries of their dwelling place"
(v. 26)—Deuteronomy 32:8; and

"That they should seek God" (v. 27)—Isaiah 55:6.

It is Beale's contention that Old Testament teachings and events basic
to redemptive history lie behind Paul's statements both in his Athenian
address and other proclamations of the gospel. Paul did establish common
ground. He did not call attention to the Septuagint. But his references
were clear enough that he could have gone back later and explained the
connections in this initial proclamation. That is important because biblical theology in the sense we use the term here is essential to discipling
the *ethnē*.

Missional theology. Paul G. Hiebert has suggested that "missional
theology" is especially important when presenting the gospel to those
of other religions and cultures. While systematic theology is needed for
an understanding of such concepts as God, humanity, sin, and salvation,
missional theology enables missionaries to see how these concepts function in the beliefs and practices of non-Christian respondents. After all,
it is what *they* believe and practice that helps determine whether they
will be converted to Christ and whether they will mature in the Christian
faith (Hiebert and Tiénou 2002).

The idea of "missional theology" has its own baggage, but as an anthropologist, Hiebert is calling upon missionaries to do what Kraemer
says is so necessary—namely, to take an "untiring and genuine interest
in the religion, the ideas, the sentiments, the institutions" of the people
among whom they work. It is that kind of "close-up" indigenous understandings and practices that the missionary must take into consideration
if the gospel is to be contextualized effectively.

In fact, in knowing not only *what* respondents think about God, humanity, sin, and salvation but also *why* they think and behave as they do, the missionary is sometimes enabled to show them where their faith is misguided and how to find truth in biblical faith.

An example is the annual Obon festival, which is celebrated in Japan. When it comes in mid-summer, many Japanese invite the spirits of departed ancestors into their homes for a brief time of celebration and respite and then accompany them back to their burial places. The dead must then depart for another year of suffering in the netherworld. Obon draws on entirely Buddhist notions of the world, the "divine," human beings, evil, judgment, and salvation. Japanese celebrants, however, may take little notice of this. Most of them may not even know the underlying story of how Mokuren prevailed upon the Buddha to lift the veil so that he could get a glimpse of his mother in the netherworld. The reluctance of the Buddha to do so was understandable, for when the veil was lifted, Mokuren saw his mother being crucified in one of the ten hells (*obon* means to be crucified upside down). Brought to a level of awareness, the story of Obon furnishes a vivid backdrop for relating the meaning of Christ's cross.

Understood this way, missional theology enables us to stand where others stand, temporarily making *their ground* common ground for the contextualizing of the gospel.

Missionary self-exposure. Kraemer is quoted above (p. 106) as saying that "there is only one point of contact, and if that one point exists, then there are many points of contact. This one point of contact is the disposition and attitude of the missionary" (Kraemer 1963, 140). Do we sometimes despair in our quest for common ground? Does it seem that *all* attempts are bound to fail because of *their* obduracy and *our* inability? No. Look again at what Jesus and Paul and other writers of Scripture have to say about humankind in its natural state. Review Paul's assessment in Romans 1–3. Clearly, what is common to all of us is our sinful state before a holy God. That is the common ground on which both Christian missionaries and their non-Christian hearers stand. We must not only admit it; we must insist upon it. If there is any one key that unlocks the door to common ground it is "missionary self-exposure."

Why so?

First, part of the attraction of most religion systems is that very human persons have somehow attained the status of "saint." True adherents emulate or even worship them without ever having seen either those men and women, or themselves for that matter, as "sinners" in the biblical sense of the word. Now if the missionary comes as another "saint," how can those adherents be expected to know what a "sinner" is? After all, the truth is that Christ Jesus saves only sinners. So sin and sinnerhood can and must be explained. But how much easier to understand if they are permitted actually to *see* a sinner.

Second, as was true of Christ himself, skeptics are constantly on the lookout for the foibles and failings of anyone who lays claim to being "good" or possessing "truth." Christ's contemporaries could find no fault in him. But the same is not true of us. Our auditors have little difficulty in discovering our inability to live up to their standards or our own, much less God's. Unless we sincerely confess that we too are subject to temptations and failings and in need of divine forgiveness, we deny them the privilege of witnessing the operations of divine grace.

Third, we have Paul's example of self-exposure. He always made it clear that he preached Christ and not himself, that he himself was weak and unworthy of being Christ's ambassador, and that he was foremost among sinners (1 Tim. 1:15). Invariably, the common ground between Paul and his auditors, whether in Athens, Berea, Corinth, or Ephesus, was that all alike were sinners. Once saved, all Christians were merely sinners saved by grace.

Sooner or later the whole world must discover that its sickness is sin and the remedy is Christ. We missionaries should be able to identify with that. We have been, and in too many ways still are, part of that world.

Conclusion

The search for common ground has engaged many brilliant minds and dedicated hearts over an extended time. That fact alone argues that it is due careful consideration and has validity and value. But however that search might progress and whatever turns it might take, we must always remember that only the gospel of Christ has saving power. That gospel says that Christ saves sinners only.

	Problematic	Plausible	Positive
1. A common search	✓		
2. Religious similarities	✓		
3. Points of contact		✓	
4. Interreligious dialogue		✓	
5. Christian rational presuppositionalism			✓
6. Biblical theology			✓
7. Missional theology			✓
8. Missionary self-exposure			✓

Figure 3. The Missionary Potential of
Eight Approaches to the Quest for Common Ground

In the final analysis we need not search for common ground with those of other races and cultures, traditions and religions. We already stand together before a holy God. But how do we proceed from that point to an understanding of the gospel that those in other cultures will comprehend?

Epilogue

According to family records, which admittedly may be somewhat biased, Grandfather Hesselgrave was physically impressive and extremely bright. He was not beyond making serious mistakes, however. As a young man he assayed the future possibilities of two developing centers of commerce and communication—Chicago, Illinois, and Lodi, Wisconsin—and decided to homestead in the latter area. He was qualified to practice law and actually practiced it, but amid his other pursuits he never bothered to take the examination necessary to be recognized as a lawyer in Wisconsin.

His greatest mistake, however, was in his understanding of God. Grandfather was so impressed by the love of God that he found no place for God's righteous wrath. When a Universalist church was established in Lodi in 1875, the names of Grandfather and Grandmother Hesselgrave were at the top of the membership roster. And then there was the problem of that deep and positive impression that he carried away from the First World Parliament of Religions in Chicago in 1893.

After a time the Universalist congregation in Lodi dispersed. Later the church building was sold to a fledgling Evangelical Free Church congregation and, when the Free Church constructed a large and attractive sanctuary on the edge of town, the old church became a museum. Grandfather's son Albertus Leroy and his wife became born-again Christians. And his grandson was called to take his family to minister for Christ in Japan. There this grandson was privileged to preach the gospel and see the Spirit lead some Japanese away from the Shintoist and Buddhist religions or from no religion to faith in Christ.

I believe that Grandfather Hesselgrave was certainly sincere. But I also believe that he was sincerely wrong.

References

Beale, Gregory K. 2004. "Other Religions in New Testament Theology." In *Biblical Faith and Other Religions: An Evangelical Assessment.* Edited by David W. Baker. Grand Rapids: Kregel.

Brown, Robert McAfee. 1967. *The Ecumenical Revolution: An Interpretation of the Catholic-Protestant Dialogue.* Garden City, N.Y.: Doubleday.

Henry, Carl F. H. 1990. *Toward a Recovery of Christian Belief.* Wheaton, Ill.: Crossway.

Hick, John. 1985. "Religious Diversity as Challenge and Promise." In *The Experience of Religious Diversity.* Edited by John Hick and Hasan Askari. Brookfield, Vt.: Gower.

Hiebert, Paul G., and Tite Tiénou. 2002. "Missional Theology." *Mission Focus: Annual Review* 10: 29–42.

Hirsley, Michael. 1993. "When World's Religions Collide: Chicago Parliament Sees More Conflict Than Harmony." *Chicago Tribune* September 5, sec. 1, 5.

Hocking, William Ernest, et al. 1932. *Re-thinking Missions: A Laymen's Inquiry After One Hundred Years.* New York: Harper & Brothers.

Jones, Peter. 1993. "Curb Your Dogma: In the Midst of a Gloomy Week, One Bright Moment." *World*, 18 September, 22.

Kaplan, Aryeh, et al. 1976. *The Real Messiah.* New York: National Conference of Synagogue Youth.

Kraemer, Hendrik. 1957. *Religion and the Christian Faith.* London: Lutterworth.

————. 1938. *The Christian Message in a Non-Christian World.* London: Edinburgh House.

————. 1962. *Why Christianity of All Religions?* Translated by Hubert Hoskins. Philadelphia: Westminster.

Lewis, C. S. 1952. *Mere Christianity.* New York: Macmillan.

Moore, Philip. 1996. *The End of History: Messiah Conspiracy,* vol. 1. Atlanta: RamsHead.

Perry, Edmund. 1956. *The Gospel in Dispute: The Relation of Christian Faith to Other Missionary Religions.* Garden City, N.Y.: Doubleday.

Radhakrishnan, Sarvepalli. 1927. *The Hindu View of Life.* New York: Macmillan.

Rees, T. 1930. "God." In *The International Standard Bible Encyclopedia.* James Orr, general editor. Chicago: Howard Severance.

Richardson, Don. 1981. *Eternity in Their Hearts.* Ventura, Calif.: Regal.

————. 1974. *Peace Child.* Glendale, Calif.: Regal.

Sharpe, Eric J. 1971. *Fifty Key Words: Comparative Religion.* Richmond, Va.: John Knox.

Shrenk, Gottlob. 1964. "Dialogue." In *Theological Dictionary of the New Testament*, vol. 2. Edited by Gerhard Kittel; translated and edited by G. W. Bromiley. Grand Rapids: Eerdmans.

Stott, John R. W. 1975. *Christian Mission in the Modern World: What the Church Should Be Doing Now.* Downers Grove, Ill.: InterVarsity.

Swidler, Leonard. 1992. *The Meaning of Life? Some Answers at the Edge of the Third Millennium.* New York: Paulist.

Chapter 4

Holism and Prioritism

For Whom Is the Gospel Good News?

The Spirit of the Lord God is upon me, because the LORD has anointed me to bring good news to the poor.

—Isaiah 61:1

Prologue

WORLD WAR II WAS STILL recent history. After learning that I had volunteered for missionary service in Japan, my university professor stoically reported that he had just visited Japan. He found its cities in ruins and its people poverty-stricken and demoralized. Concerning my proposed mission he commented, "You might want to do some more thinking about that. My observation was that the Japanese people want a changed economic picture right now, not a pie in the sky by and by."

I was inclined to dismiss the remark as being more indicative of the professor's cynicism than of the general attitude of the Japanese people. After all, in report after report, evangelical missions leaders were saying that, as a result of their crushing defeat and the emperor's disavowal of deity, the Japanese were spiritually hungry and anxious to hear the Christian gospel.

Who would prove to be more correct, the missions leaders or my unbelieving professor friend? I, for one, was inclined to believe the former.

~

To a degree reminiscent of ecumenical publications of a generation ago, evangelical missions literature today focuses on the "poor." Articles discuss "the urban poor," "our mission to the poor," and "the church and the poor." Analysts ask "What about the poor?" and consider how we should be "walking with the poor." In fact, the word *poor* has taken on characteristics of what modern rhetoricians call a "god-term"—a word the meaning of which is more or less assumed and is so important that it tends to govern assumptions and feelings on a particular topic. As a god-term, to be "poor" means to be economically impoverished, devoid of the necessities of life, and, very often, part of an underclass that is disenfranchised and helpless to do anything to change prevailing circumstances.

Understood in this way, it is to be expected that concerned Christians inquire into such questions as, What are the reasons for widespread poverty in the world today? What can be done to ameliorate suffering and injustice? What is the responsibility of the church with respect to the poor? How does social action relate to evangelism? So, with increasing frequency and intensity and along with their more liberal counterparts, conservative evangelicals have concerned themselves with these and similar questions.

In this chapter we will ask different and even more basic questions: Who *are* the poor? Why are they special—*to God, that is?*

The Poor in Post–World War II Missiology

From the beginning of missions from America, Christian missions of almost every stripe have concerned themselves with a variety of ministries designed to meet the physical, social, and educational needs of people around the world. Traditionally, most missions have usually thought of these ministries as "secondary," "supporting," or "related." Priority has been given to preaching the gospel, winning people to Christ, and growing responsible churches.

In his introduction to the modern missions movement, church historian Edwin Scott Gaustad writes what he assumes to be an unassailable fact: "However much the missionary acts as teacher, doctor, or technical assistant, he remains primarily a missionary, an evangelist" (Gaustad 1966, 349).

After Vatican II (1962–65), Roman Catholic and ecumenical Protestant missions thinking tended to be increasingly occupied with concern for the world's poor and what ways and means could be found to liberate them from powerlessness and oppression. According to liberation theologians, the poor are engaged in a struggle for freedom and the kingdom of God is a liberating force. The poor are the object of God's special love and concern. As Emilio Castro, soon to become general secretary of the World Council of Churches, expressed it to me back in the mid-1970s, "If you want to know what God is doing and saying in the world, look to the poor. What the poor are doing and saying is what God is doing and saying. God is always on the side of the poor!"

About that time, the poor began to become increasingly prominent in the thinking of conservatives as well as Catholics and ecumenical Protestants. Right up to the World Congress on Evangelism held in Berlin in 1966, conservative evangelicals had tended to speak univocally and in accord with the conference theme: "One race, one gospel, one task." Priority was given to discipling the nations and evangelizing the world. But by the time of the First International Congress on World Evangelization (Lausanne, 1974), priorities had begun to change. From that time on, through the Consultation on the Relationship between Evangelism and Social Responsibility (Grand Rapids, Michigan, 1982), the Global Consultation on World Evangelization (Manila, 1989) and to the present hour, the poor have been at or near the top of the evangelical agenda.

Three Positions on the Poor: Liberationism, Holism, and Prioritism

Three very different views on social concern and the plight of the poor have developed. They can be placed on a continuum designed to help us consider our central question: *For whom is the gospel good news?*

1. *Radical liberationism.* As I use the term, *radical liberationism* draws heavily upon the Marxist view of class struggle and the biblical emancipation motif of Israel's exodus from Egypt. Liberationists tend to

equate the biblical notion of salvation from sin with the struggle of poor and oppressed people for justice.

Gustavo Gutiérrez, a Peruvian Roman Catholic priest who developed liberation theology, is representative. He consistently points to Scripture and draws upon biblical themes having to do with sin, self-denial, suffering, reconciliation, and salvation. He sometimes applies these themes to individuals, but his primary application is to the clash between classes, to social emancipation and cultural transformation. He endorses the *Populorum progressio* encyclical of Pope Paul VI (1967). Paul VI speaks of building a world where every person can live free from servitude imposed by other men or natural forces. Yet Gutiérrez criticized the encyclical for not giving "a more decided and direct thrust in favor of the oppressed, encouraging them to break with their present situation and take control of their own destiny" (Gutiérrez 1973, 34–35).

2. *Holism.* Depending on who is applying it, *holism* has a variety of denotations and connotations. Some emphasize ministering through word, deed, and sign. Others stress ministering to the whole person—spirit, mind, and body. Sometimes the emphasis is on transforming whole cultures and societies. At other times the emphasis is on transforming the whole world. The holism in view here promotes the partnership of social (and, sometimes, political) action with evangelism in ways that supersede traditional theory and practice. Holism of this kind comes in two forms, *restrained* and *revisionist.*

Revisionist holism does not go nearly as far as radical liberationism, but it does make evangelism and social action *full and equal partners.* The key words here are *full* and *equal.* Bryant Myers, for example, rejects "the dichotomy between material and spiritual, between evangelism and social action, between loving God and loving neighbor" (Myers 1999a; see also Myers 1999b).

James Engel and William Dyrness describe this kind of holism:

> *Partnership* [i.e., full and equal partnership] affirms that evangelism and social transformation are inseparable elements in Christ's kingdom that embraces all of creation (Lk. 4:18–20). The goal is *shalom*—a sense of human welfare and well-being that transcends an artificial distinction between the private and

public worlds. Shalom, by its very nature, is rooted in justice and compassion. (Engel and Dyrness 2000, 93)

Restrained holism, on the other hand, attempts to preserve the traditional priority for evangelism, while elevating social action. The place of church planting and development is less well defined as compared to the traditional position, however. In restrained holism evangelism and social action are made to be *more or less equal partners,* although a certain priority is reserved for evangelism. This kind of holism was espoused by the architects of the Lausanne Covenant (1974) and elaborated a year later by John R. W. Stott (Stott 1975). The framers of the Covenant wrestled with questions of social responsibility but preserved a clear priority that "in the service of the church evangelism is primary" (par. 6). In his "new understanding of mission," Stott held that John 20:21b is the most important statement of the Great Commission: "As the Father has sent me, even so I am sending you." That makes Jesus' mission a model for ours. Isaiah 61:1–2 as quoted by Jesus in Luke 4:18–19 succinctly characterizes the nature of Jesus' mission that we are to model: "He has anointed me to proclaim good news to the poor" (v. 18b; Hesselgrave 1990, 1–5).

3. *Traditional prioritism.* What I will call *traditional prioritism* recognizes the importance of all or most of those ministries that address the various medical, educational, economic, and social needs of individuals and societies. At the same time it sustains the time-honored distinction between the primary *mission* of the church and secondary or supporting ministries. With reference to spiritual transformation and social transformation, it gives priority to spiritual transformation. With reference to spirit, mind, and body, it gives priority to the spirit or soul. With reference to social action and evangelism, it gives priority to evangelism. In maintaining these priorities, however, it does not admit to being reductionistic either in the sense of neglecting social ministries on the one hand or confining cross-cultural work strictly to evangelism on the other. It simply retains priority for the kind of work described in the closing statement of the World Congress on Evangelism (Berlin, 1966) and promulgated some eight years prior to the Lausanne Covenant:

Our Lord Jesus Christ, possessor of all authority in heaven and
on earth, has not only called us to himself; he has sent us out
into the world to be his witnesses. In the power of his Spirit he
commands us to proclaim to all people the good news of salvation through his atoning death and resurrection; to invite them to
discipleship through repentance and faith; to baptize them into
the fellowship of his Church; and to teach them all his words.
(Johnston 1978, 368–69)

This high priority for evangelism motivated Billy Graham to support the Berlin Congress, *Christianity Today* to organize it, and Arthur
Johnston to defend it some twelve years later in his book *The Battle for
World Evangelism* (1978). That book, in fact, provides a detailed history
of major postwar enclaves that focused on this and related issues and
makes a solid case for the priority of world evangelization.

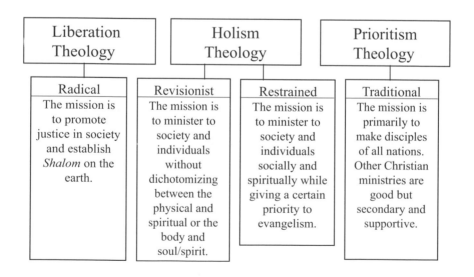

Liberation Theology		Holism Theology		Prioritism Theology	
Radical	Revisionist	Restrained	Traditional
The mission is to promote justice in society and establish *Shalom* on the earth.	The mission is to minister to society and individuals without dichotomizing between the physical and spiritual or the body and soul/spirit.	The mission is to minister to society and individuals socially and spiritually while giving a certain priority to evangelism.	The mission is primarily to make disciples of all nations. Other Christian ministries are good but secondary and supportive.

Figure 4. Missiological Responses to the Plight of the "Poor"

Holism an Inadequate "Missiological Cradle" for the Poor

Before undertaking a more in-depth consideration of poverty and the poor in those Scripture texts critical to our present discussion, let me briefly lay out a case against holism in simple terms—what a former colleague of mine would call "Peter Rabbit English." Our concentration here is on holism because, although liberation theology has been espoused by a few evangelicals in the past, it has hardly any evangelical advocates today. If holism fails to pass the test, liberation certainly fails as well because it relies on many of the same arguments.

The frame of the "holistic cradle" is constructed out of one fiber—namely, the notion that no priorities are allowable. That cradle hangs between two boughs, one of them can be labeled "reason" and the other "revelation." If either bough breaks, the cradle hangs precariously in midair. If both break, the cradle will fall and down goes cradle, the poor (i.e., as defined by liberationists and holists) and all.

Both boughs break. Why?

Because, unlike Hinduism, Christianity begins with an absolute dichotomy between the Creator and his creation. It proceeds by making very different valuations of body and soul, treasures on earth and treasures in heaven, and this world and the world to come. In fact, these dichotomies and the choices they necessitate attach to the essence of Christianity. C. S. Lewis makes this very clear when, in comparing the relative importance of the average life span with eternity, concludes: "Christianity asserts that every individual human being is going to live forever, and this must be true or false. Now there are a good many things which would not be worth bothering about if I were going to live only seventy years, but which I had better bother about very seriously if I am going to live for ever" (Lewis 1952, 159).

As a matter of fact, holists themselves do not seem to rest well in the ideological cradle they have constructed for the world's poor. Overlooking the fact that, without some kind of dichotomy, no priority is logically possible, liberationists and holists insist that God has a certain preference for the poor, is especially attentive to the plight of the poor, and takes special delight in answering the cries of the poor.

So much for *reason*. What about *revelation?*

Holists (and many liberationists as well) do pay attention to Scripture. First, they point to numerous passages that indicate that God himself is a God of love and compassion who cares deeply about the poor and distressed of the world. Second, they note that God insists that "true and faultless" religion (James 1:27) is concerned with justice and with caring for the poor and disadvantaged. Third, they resort to many noteworthy events in Scripture—the exodus from Egypt, the establishment of the theocracy in Canaan, the deliverance from Babylonian captivity, the Nazareth pronouncement of Christ, and much more—as models of social and even political concern. Fourth, they highlight the character of the kingdom envisioned by the prophets and proclaimed by Christ during his ministry on earth. Fifth, they point to the Great Commandment to love our neighbor as ourselves. Sixth, they often point out that, indirectly if not directly, the Great Commission entails a special concern for the poor and needy by requiring us to teach all Christ commanded. Seventh, they draw encouragement from the fact that the apostles and early believers had a special concern for widows, the poor, and the hungry.

Certainly no Christian missionary—in fact, no Christian—would deny either the truth or the significance of these points. Our concern is not with the observation that the Bible reveals God to be a God of compassion, that he has a special concern for the poor, and that he expects us to share in that concern. *Our concern is rather with what we judge to be interpretations or misinterpretations that obscure or obliterate biblical priorities for the work of the church around the world.*

An entire book would be required to deal with all such passages. Since that is impossible, the present discussion must be limited to a consideration of certain critical passages having to do with the poor. I choose the following passages and approach for four reasons. First, these passages are almost invariably cited as supporting holism (and liberationism). Second, concern for the poor has become a kind of shibboleth, a criterion or test for faithfulness. Third, if the meaning of *poor* in these key passages turns out to be something other than what the word ordinarily is interpreted to mean by holists, that may indicate that holistic interpretations of other relevant passages are similarly flawed. Fourth, and most important, a more accurate biblical understanding of *poor* may result in reordering our priorities and redirecting our prayers in ways that will give everlasting hope to the poor and bear eternal fruit in missions.

The Poor in the Old Testament (Isa. 61:1)

The Spirit of the LORD God is upon me, because the LORD has anointed me to bring good news to the poor. (Isaiah 61:1a)

Some commentators conclude that Isaiah was referring to the church here. Probably the majority of evangelicals assume that he was speaking of the Messiah and find reinforcement for their view in the fact that Jesus applied the passage to himself (Luke 4:17–21). Bypassing other questions, therefore, we simply inquire into the identity of the poor referred to by Isaiah in this messianic pronouncement. To identify the poor, we must examine lexical and textual/contextual data, as well as scholarly opinion.

Lexical Data: The Meaning of ʿănāō ("Poor")

Of about eight Hebrew words that the Holy Spirit could have led the prophet Isaiah to use in Isaiah 61:1 he chose to employ the Hebrew plural עֲנָוִים (ʿănāōim). The word can be translated "poor" either literally or figuratively. In its more literal meaning it refers to life circumstances. In its figurative sense it has to do with a state of mind. Which meaning is preferable here?

The NIV translators' decision to translate ʿănāō as "poor" does not really help us in this regard. The King James tradition has just as much exegetical proof for using the figurative sense of "meek." While ESV translators chose to render it "poor," they added the more ambiguous word *afflicted* in the margin. The NASB translators used "afflicted" in the text and added the alternative *humble* in the margin. All of these words and connotations are possible. Which is to be preferred?

Textual/Contextual Data: ʿănāō in Isaiah 61:1–2

The latter sections of Isaiah, from chapters 40–66, have stirred debates among Old Testament scholars that are beyond the scope of this volume. But most scholars can agree that, in its surrounding context, this particular text draws on the language and ideas of the "Jubilee Year" of Leviticus 25.

The Year of Jubilee. Certain requirements of the Jubilee Year seem clearly designed to raise people out of permanent economic poverty. There was not to be an underclass devoid of hope among God's people. The word *ʿānāō* was not used in Leviticus 25, perhaps because of its broader range of meanings to denote the afflicted, humble, and righteous poor. Both the subject of Leviticus 25 and the language used leave no question that the law is dealing with literal economic and circumstantial poverty. For example, land that could not be redeemed by the poor because they simply did not have enough money was to be returned to them anyway, lest their families be landless and destitute.

The times of Isaiah. By Isaiah's day, the situation had changed radically. The theocracy had long been replaced by a monarchy. The Assyrians decimated the northern tribes, and the Babylonians would one day be Yahweh's instrument of judgment in the south. Gleason L. Archer follows E. J. Young in thinking that Isaiah 1–39 is a stair rising from the Assyrian to the Chaldean periods. He believes that some discourses of chapters 50 to 66 describe conditions that prevailed in the reign of Manasseh (Archer 1964, 325). The circumstantial poor had little hope for a better life in the short term. Judgment involved the loss of both land and freedom.

Isaiah was concerned with both literal and figurative impoverishment. Economically and circumstantially, it was a sad hour for Yahweh's chosen people. Even so, the deplorable situation did not remove the obligation for sincere obedience.

The message of Isaiah. The Israelites had come to place great emphasis on certain outward religious observances: circumcision, Sabbath-keeping, fasting, and perhaps others as well. That being the case, the Israelites were prone to accuse God of disregarding these righteous deeds, of turning a deaf ear to their cries, and of leaving them to suffer at the hands of enemies less righteous than themselves.

Isaiah had to remind Israel that externals were not sufficient. Yahweh was still the God of the exodus from Egypt and the occupation of Canaan. He still demanded true worship—that they keep the Sabbath while not desecrating it and fast without neglecting justice and their needy neighbors (Isa. 41:17; 49:13; 51:21; 54:11; 58:1–59:15). Both literal and figurative poverty can be seen in these passages (on chs. 58–59, see Ellison 1952, 61).

In Isaiah 60 and 61, however, Isaiah looks to the future, and the focus changes. The earthly kingdom of the Messiah is in view. The coming of the Messiah will be infinitely more significant than that of anyone who led the exodus from Egypt. When Messiah comes, he will proclaim good news to the "poor" (*ănāōim*), bind up the brokenhearted, and proclaim liberty to captives and freedom to prisoners (61:1). He will proclaim the year of the Lord's favor (v. 2). He will comfort the mournful and give them garlands, the oil of gladness, and the mantle of praise (v. 3). He will see to it that ancient walls are rebuilt and ruined cities repaired; that strangers and foreigners are servants while Israelites are priests and ministers; and that Israel will eat of the wealth of Gentiles and claim their riches (vv. 4–6). Until that day comes, in the midst of their trials and injustices and until their vindication, those who are distressed, afflicted, humble, and meek in mind and spirit can take hope and comfort in the knowledge that Yahweh will not forget his promise nor will he abandon them to their enemies.

It seems quite clear from text and context that a subtle but significant change in meaning has occurred. The *ănāōim* in Isaiah 61:1 may be literally poor, but in the company of words such as *brokenhearted, captive, prisoner,* and *mournful, poor* takes on new meaning. It refers primarily to people to whom Isaiah's (and the anointed Messiah's) confirmation of the ancient covenant itself constitutes good news. It is good news to people who humbly look for the hope of Israel above and beyond anything else.

Corroborative Data: The Conclusions of Some Recognized Scholars

Does this make exegetical sense? Before turning to the New Testament, let us look at the conclusions of some scholars. Their testimony should help us to at least understand why, in the text, the margin, or both, most translators have been careful to point out that the poor referred to in Isaiah 61:1 are characterized by humility and meekness, not primarily financial poverty.

German Hebraist Franz Delitzsch (1813-1890) translates *ănāōim* in

Isaiah 61:1 "sufferers" (Delitzsch 1954, 424). Delitzsch argues that the literal blessings of the Year of Jubilee become spiritual blessings in Isaiah 61. "The vengeance applies to those who hold the people of God in fetters, and oppress them, the grace to those whom the infliction of punishment has inwardly humbled, though they have been strongly agitated by its long continuance (chap. 57:17)" (Delitzsch 1954, 427).

Then, with respect to those humble "sufferers" and their promised blessings he writes, "The gifts of God, though represented in outward figures, are really spiritual, and take effect within, rejuvenating and sanctifying the inward man; they are the sap and strength, the marrow and impulse of a new life" (Delitzsch 1954, 427).

Turning to a contemporary scholar, Darrell Bock first points out the importance of the Old Testament word ʿănāō: In the Old Testament, the ʿănāōim are "pious poor," the afflicted. God will exalt these afflicted ones (Luke 1:51–53) who have suffered for being open to God (6:20–23). "They are open to God and his way since they are frequently the first to recognize how much they need God" (Bock 1996, 136).

Bock suggests that it is the spiritual dimension that is bequeathed to the New Testament. Some scholars conclude that there is such a strong affinity between circumstantial poverty and the humble recognition of need for God that *poor* is almost a technical term for spiritual humility in the Old Testament: "The poor," they conclude, "are the humble, and the humble are the godly (Ps. 10:17; 14:5–6; 37:11; Zeph. 3:12–13)" (Elwell and Comfort 2001, 1062).

The Poor in the New Testament (Luke 4:18)

The Jews of Jesus' hometown of Nazareth had great difficulty in connecting the prophecy of Isaiah 61:1–2 to their carpenter-neighbor Jesus. To be sure, at first they were amazed at his use of this prophetic passage in the sermon they heard preached. Some may have even been open to part of what he was teaching. But they soon became furious and were ready to kill him.

Jesus simply did not conform to their expectations for the long-awaited Messiah. He even made odious comparisons between his proud fellow citizens and the people of Capernaum, a Sidonian widow, and a Syrian leper. There may have been some circumstantially poor people in the synagogue that day, but it is evident that there were few of the pious poor. It was the pious poor whom Jesus sought and to whom his message and ministrations were directed.

Lexical Data: Meanings of ptōchos, a Greek Word for "Poor"

But will the language, text, and contexts support this metaphorical and spiritual understanding of "poor" in Luke 4:18? As in the Hebrew, various Greek words can be rendered "poor." Again, each has its own meaning and nuance. The word used in Luke 4:18 is *ptōchos*. From the time of Homer in the ninth century B.C., *ptōchos* had referred to the condition of being reduced to begging or asking alms. In the New Testament, however, the meaning broadened to refer to the lack of anything. Literally, it meant to be poor and in need as opposed to being rich and wealthy. Figuratively, it meant to be spiritually poor and destitute of Christian virtues and eternal riches. The Greek adjective *penichros* and the noun *penēs,* referring to a person in need, seem more restricted to literal, circumstantial poverty.

For most occurrences of the Greek *ptōchos* (usually in the plural form, *ptōchoi*), the English "poor" fits in translation. Therefore, the respective contexts in which it is used must be studied carefully to determine exact meaning, whether literal circumstantial poverty or the figurative spiritual kind. Context usually clarifies meaning.

Several texts are illustrative and insightful in this regard.

1. Jesus spoke of the basic character of his kingdom in what are usually called the Beatitudes. The first pronounces a blessing on the *ptōchoi*. So that there be no misunderstanding, he referred to them as "poor in spirit" (Matt. 5:3). Obviously, more than the circumstantial poverty can be inferred when Matt. 5:3 and Luke 6:20 are both in view.

2. When Luke speaks of the widow who put two small copper coins into the temple treasury (Luke 21:1–3), he uses the adjective *penichros* in verse 2 to call attention to her poverty-stricken circumstances. But when Jesus commends her in verse 3 he uses

the word *ptōchos*. This could indicate that what was true of her economic condition was true of her mind and heart as well.

3. Jesus was resting in the house of Simon the leper when a certain woman poured costly perfume over his head (Matt. 26:6–13). Some disciples complained that the perfume could have been sold and the proceeds given to the poor (*ptōchoi*). Jesus, however, replied that the poor (*ptōchoi*) are *always* present. This implied that his presence, death, and burial provided an opportunity greater than giving to the poor. He insisted that the woman had used the perfume in a more timely and important manner than to sell it and give the proceeds away. Obviously, "poor" in this instance refers to literal, circumstantial poverty.

4. Following his ascension, Christ instructed the apostle John to write to the seven churches of Asia (Rev. 1:17–19). To the church in Laodicea, he employed the word *ptōchos* to describe the church's spiritual poverty. In a stinging rebuke he said that they thought of themselves as rich and wealthy—in need of nothing. Spiritually myopic, they didn't recognize the fact that they were actually "wretched, pitiable, *poor,* blind and naked" (3:17, emphasis mine). Their perception of themselves may well have been as literal as it was erroneous. Christ's perception had to do with their spiritual state. The meaning of *ptōchos* is figurative and spiritual.

In Luke 4:18, what is the meaning of *ptōchoi* in Jesus' proclamation of good news to the "poor"? For the word *ptōchos,* the lexical evidence alone is not conclusive. Robert Stein writes, "In Luke the term 'poor' does refer to an economic condition but not merely to economic status, for the poor and humble hope in God" (Stein 1992, 156). If this is so, the text and its contexts must inform our understanding of *ptōchoi*.

Textual/Contextual Data

One would think that, if indeed the Isaiah text referred to by Jesus here employed the Hebrew word *ʿănāō* to refer to the "pious poor," the humble, meek, and godly, Jesus probably used the Greek word *ptōchoi* in much the same way. But will closer examination of the context bear this out? Note the following.

1. Jesus broke off his reading of the Isaiah passage at a critical point. He read "To proclaim the year of the Lord's favor," but he closed the scroll without reading the rest of the sentence: "and the day of vengeance of our God" (Luke 4:19; cf. Lev. 25:10; Isa. 61:2). An all-important aspect of Messiah's complete mission—divine judgment—is evidently not in view. Various explanations have been given for this omission. But it seems evident that there cannot be social justice without the right kind of judgment, and Jesus did not come to judge between a man and his neighbor (Luke 12:14).

2. When his audience asked for a display of the miraculous signs expected of the Messiah and already a part of his Capernaum ministry, Jesus answered that miracles were not proffered to everyone. Their benefit was to that lesser number who received his teaching (Luke 4:23–31). The ensuing dialogue is instructive.

    First, Jesus said, "You will quote to me this proverb, 'Physician heal yourself,' What we have heard you did at Capernaum, do here in your hometown as well" (Luke 4:23). In other words, "If what you say is the fulfillment of Isaiah's prophecy, let's see you do here and now what reporters say you did in Capernaum." Skepticism . . . cynicism . . . They were too proud to admit that he was more than "Joseph's son."

    Second, Jesus spoke of Elijah and a poverty-stricken widow, knowing that his neighbors were well aware of this story and revered Elijah. Why did Elijah pass by a multitude of widows in Israel and seek out an obscure widow in Zarephath, of all places? Clearly Yahweh was looking for something other than religious ancestry and physical need as an occasion to demonstrate his power and compassion. He chose a woman who humbly recognized that she had desperate need for Yahweh and his mercy. Yahweh raised up a Sidonian widow to be his example.

    Third, Jesus referred to Elisha and Naaman the leper. Jesus knew that his neighbors were familiar with this story and that they revered Elisha. But why was Elisha sent to a Syrian leper who was an enemy soldier? Why not heal one or two or even an entire colony of lepers of Israel? Why, indeed, except that God chose this highly placed Syrian official and made him willing to wash himself in the dirty waters of the Jordan as the prophet directed. Evidently, Yahweh saw something in the heart of Naaman that he did not see in the hearts of the lepers in Israel and, seeing it, he did not allow either the Syrian's status or citizenship to prevent his healing. In Naaman he saw a humble recognition of need for the merciful Yahweh of Israel.

So why was it that Jesus' neighbors did not hear his message as the good news it really was? They were not "poor in spirit," and that's the kind of poverty Jesus had been sent to cure once and for all. The very fact that his Nazareth "friends" actually demanded miracles constituted prima facie evidence of something Jesus already knew: They were not "of a mind" to accept him or his message or his kingdom.

3. It does not make exegetical sense to interpret *ptōchoi* in Luke 4:18 literally while interpreting the parallel "prisoners," "blind," and "oppressed" figuratively. All should be in basic agreement. But, though "blind" can easily be literal or figurative, "prisoners" and "oppressed" seem to be mainly figurative in meaning. To take those words literally would so severely limit the message and mission of Jesus as to make him out to be little more than a miracle-working social revolutionary. Jesus released not one political prisoner.

4. Finally, it should be noted that the text lends little support to the idea that the *ptōchoi* constituted a distinct social class. There is no definite article in the original text, so it could be translated "to preach good news to poor people." Liberationists and holists often speak of "the poor" here as though an identifiable and recognizable social class were in view. That notion has little support from either the text or its context.

Corroborative Data: Conclusions of Bible Scholars

What are we to conclude from all of this with reference to the meaning of *ptōchoi* in Luke 4:18? We rest our case by drawing attention to the conclusions of several learned and trusted commentators.

The observation of Bock above emphasizes that the Hebrew "poor" in Isaiah 61:1 has the same or very similar meaning to the Greek quotation of it in Luke 4:18. Both refer to what he calls "pious poor." Bock describes these people as humble sufferers who knew their need for God, and accepted his message and ministrations (Bock 1996, 136).

I. Howard Marshall tends toward the same position as Bock, although he is reluctant to employ the term *pious poor*. He fears such a term may be misunderstood to mean people whose actions are calculated to win God's favor. He would emphasize their humility and meekness.

Marshall takes much more serious exception to the interpretation of Ronald Sider and others who say that, since the miracles in Luke 7:18–23 were physical (blind sighted, leprosy cured, deaf healed, dead raised), the same must be true of Luke 4:18–19 (Sider 1990, 45). Marshall thinks that line of reasoning is misleading on two counts. First, the physical miracles in Luke 7 were demonstrations of messiahship, not model responses of a compassion for human need. Second, along with the account of these miracles in Luke 7, Jesus adds that through them "good news is preached to the poor" (v. 22 NIV). That phrase recalls 4:18, where Marshall believes the good news mentioned is the announcement of salvation to those who are "poor" in a spiritual sense. His conclusion is that *ptōchoi* in Luke 4:18 "draws attention to the needy condition of the sufferer which God alone can cure. The poor are thus the needy and downtrodden whose wants are not supplied by earthly helpers. As Matthew makes clear, the meaning of the word is not restricted to literal poverty. . . . It was to such people [i.e., "spiritually impoverished"] that Jesus preached good news (*euangelizomai*)" (Marshall 1970, 121–23).

Next, we turn to a recent exposition by William J. Larkin Jr. (Larkin 1998, 152–69). Larkin's position could perhaps be categorized as *restrained holism*. He rejects liberationism and radical holism but insists that Jesus' announcement makes clear that the kingdom requirement is for economically rich people to share liberally with those who are economically poor. The materially poor could be expected to consider that to be "good news" indeed.

Nevertheless, Larkin recognizes the spiritual priority in Jesus' proclamation. He notes that in communicating the purpose of his coming as prophesied by Isaiah, Jesus quotes four infinitives and three of them have to do with preaching. The poor are *evangelized*; the prisoners have release; and the blind have sight *proclaimed* to them. The year of the Lord's favor or the Jubilee Year is *proclaimed*. "Luke, then, regards the primary activity of Jesus' ministry as preaching. Other tasks are present . . . but these either validate or become the content of the gospel message" (Larkin 1998, 158).

As for the economically poor, Larkin concludes,

> The poor are given hope of relief in the future and even now by means of the themes of eschatological reversal and economic repentance. But the final theme, economic discipleship, points to the priority that even the poor must give to the spiritual good news. The last poor person we meet in Luke is the destitute widow who gives to God through the temple treasury "all that she had" (21:3). Jesus, by approval of her act, relativizes the physical-economic need in favor of the spiritual. In Luke's gospel the final word about the poor is not the good news of what they will receive to alleviate their need, but the challenge of what they must give as part of the life of radical discipleship in devotion to Jesus. (Larkin 1998, 162)

By "Blessed are you who are poor" in Luke 6:20, Jesus means all who turn to the Lord, whatever their need. It was to bring the gospel to such people that Christ came (Matt. 11:5; Luke 4:18). Eighteenth-century Baptist theologian John Gill wrote,

> In Isaiah it is, "to the meek"; which design the same persons, and mean such as are poor in spirit, and are sensible of their spiritual poverty; have low and humble thoughts of themselves, and of their own righteousness, and frankly acknowledge that all they have and are, is owing to the grace of God: and generally

speaking, these are the poor of this world, and poor in their intel-
lectuals [*sic*], who have but a small degree of natural wisdom
and knowledge; to these the Gospel, or glad tidings of the love,
grace, and mercy of God in Christ, of peace, pardon, righteousness, life and salvation by Christ, were preached by him; and that
in so clear a manner, and with such power and authority, as never
was before, or since; and for this purpose was he anointed with
the oil of gladness above his fellows. (Gill 1999, 136)

Gill's understanding of the poor in the Isaiah passage is consonant
with the understanding of the poor in the Lukan passage advanced in this
chapter. This understanding also agrees with the use of words that can be
translated "poor" in relevant passages in the epistles. For example, citing T. E. Schmidt and Herman Ridderbos, Christopher Little notes that
the term *poor* has more of a "redemptive-historical" connotation than
it does an economic one, at least with regard to Paul's collection for the
"poor" at Jerusalem. He seems to agree with Dieter Georgi that the term
is sometimes used to refer to "the genuine eschatological people of God"
as a whole (Little 2005, 157).

Conclusion

Four conclusions can be quite confidently affirmed. First, we can
confidently conclude that the Christian gospel is both *true news* and
good news. It is true because God himself declared it to be true. It is
true as Jesus summarized it in John 3:16–18 and as Paul outlined it in
1 Corinthians 15:3–8. It is also true in its largest dimensions—in all
that God relates of his redemptive purpose in Scripture from Genesis
to Revelation. It is true not only in what it reveals about Jesus' sacrifice
and resurrection, but also in what it reveals about humanity's sin and
condemnation. It is true in what it reveals about both God's wrath and his
love (John 3:36).

It is good news for the very same reason. It is good because God
pronounced it good just as he pronounced creation "good" in the very
beginning. It is imperative that we recognize this to be the case. Otherwise we may yield to the temptation to tailor the gospel to the tastes of

sinners. Only the biblical gospel is really good news, and it is good quite apart from anything that you or I or anyone else in the world might think or feel about it.

Second, we can quite confidently conclude that, in announcing good news to the poor, both Isaiah and Jesus intended it to be the kind of news that, first and foremost, had to do with the salvation of sinners. When they spoke of the "poor" they referred primarily to people who recognized their sinful and needy state before a holy God and humbly reached out for mercy and grace.

Third, we can affirm that, at its heart, Christian mission (Great Commission mission, primary mission, essential mission) has to do with making the true and good gospel of Christ known to those who are most separated geographically, ethnically, and religiously from centers of gospel knowledge and influence. It does not follow from this that missions are absolved of a responsibility to respond to physically needy, economically deprived, and socially disadvantaged people. Jesus' Great Commandment to love our neighbors as ourselves; Paul's injunction to "do good to all people, especially to those who belong to the family of believers" (Gal. 6:10 NIV); and many additional Old and New Testament texts such as Micah 6:6–8; James 1:26–27; 2:14–17; and 1 John 3:17–18 argue just the opposite. Furthermore, literal and spiritual poverty often go together, as we have indicated. The circumstantially poor are often the first to recognize their spiritual poverty and reach out to the God of truth and grace. It does follow, however, that the primary concern of our Lord has to do with meeting spiritual needs, not with meeting physical, material, or social needs.

If the "poor" are first identified with poverty of mind and spirit and a humble recognition of need for God and his grace, then it simply will not do to place other kinds of need on equal footing with this in Christian mission. It is for that very reason that Carl Braaten faults holistic mission. He says that "it has contributed to such a great inflation in the meaning of mission, including virtually everything the church is doing, that there is a danger that evangelism, which is the heart of mission, will become buried in an avalanche of church activism, under the controls of a burgeoning bureaucracy" (Braaten 1985, 111).

Fourth, we conclude that missionaries should do their best to seek out individuals and people groups who, by whatever means, have been providentially prepared to hear, understand, and respond to the gospel of Jesus Christ. Missions historians are privy to scores of remarkable cases where God has been pleased to work so that certain persons or peoples are ready and even waiting to hear and receive the gospel message. Church growth leaders of a previous generation often emphasized the significance of recognizing and reaching receptive people groups. Missionaries and missions supporters of every generation do well to pray, prepare, plan, and proceed in ways that maximize the possibility of finding people whose hearts and minds have been prepared to receive the gospel gratefully and gladly.

At the height of a famine and intertribal war in Ethiopia, I happened to be ministering in a conference in Nairobi. A deeply troubled and exhausted missionary couple, fresh from that field, came to see me. They explained that they were the sole source of food and medicine for a large number of Ethiopian tribal people. Many were dying of starvation and disease, and there was never sufficient food to feed everyone, yet they were forced to feed soldiers before women and children. The war, the famine, the shortage of supplies, the vagaries of culture, and the unending suffering and dying—all had drained them psychologically, physically, and spiritually.

After a lengthy conversation punctuated by deep sighs and interrupted by tears, the anguished wife said somewhat haltingly, "Dr. Hesselgrave, we didn't really come for counsel. We just needed someone with whom to talk and pray. We wouldn't think of not going back. But we have to face it; there will not be enough food. One by one, we will watch them die. There is nothing else that we can do."

We talked. We prayed. I could offer encouragement and some limited cultural understandings, but little more. Before they left, however, I reminded them of something we all know but so easily forget: There was, after all, something else they could do for those poor Ethiopian peoples, even when they ran out of physical food. *They could offer them the Bread of Life. Dying now, the believing poor could live forever.*

We Christians constantly need to remind ourselves that "The Son of Man came to seek and to save the lost" (Luke 19:10). Amid all the good things that missionaries are called upon to do, they should never forget that their essential task is to seek out those who will humbly confess their sins and throw themselves upon the mercy of God available in

Christ Jesus. And among all the needs for which missionary intercessors might pray, they should pray that missionaries will be successful in that search.

After all, the reason for Jesus' coming is the reason for their going.

Epilogue

So who was right? What did postwar Japanese desire most—a "changed economy here and now" or a Christian gospel that offered forgiveness of sin and life everlasting?

Regarding the Japanese people as a whole, my skeptical professor was correct, and those optimistic missions leaders were wrong. Initially, hundreds of thousands of Japanese responded to the invitation to "believe the gospel and accept Christ," but most quickly reverted to their old ways. In fact, after half a century, the percentage of Christians in Japan is not appreciably higher than it was at the close of World War II. The Japanese have what they wanted. They are more wealthy in material terms than the vast majority of the peoples of the world. But most are spiritually impoverished and lost.

But that is not the whole story. Far outweighing all other considerations is the fact that thousands have faced up to their desperate spiritual state. They heard the gospel as the good news it really is, embraced Christ, and joined one of the small but vital Christian churches that dot the landscape from Hokkaido in the north to Kyushu in the south. I meet many of them every time I return to that land. My life, our world, and heaven itself would be infinitely "poorer" without them.

References

Archer, Gleason L. Jr. 1964. *A Survey of Old Testament Introduction*. Chicago: Moody.

Bock, Darrell L. 1996. *Luke: The NIV Application Commentary*. Grand Rapids: Zondervan.

Braaten, Carl. 1985. *The Apostolic Imperative: Nature and Aim of the Church's Mission and Ministry*. Minneapolis: Augsburg.

Delitzsch, Franz. 1954. *Biblical Commentary on the Prophecies of Isaiah*, vol. 2. Trans. by James Martin. Grand Rapids: Eerdmans.

Ellison, H. L. 1952. *Men Spake from God: Studies in the Hebrew Prophets.* London: Paternoster.

Elwell, Walter A., and Philip W. Comfort, eds. 2001. *Tyndale Bible Dictionary.* Wheaton, Ill.: Tyndale.

Engel, James F., and William A. Dyrness. 2000. *Changing the Mind of Missions: Where Have We Gone Wrong?* Downers Grove, Ill.: InterVarsity.

Gaustad, Edwin Scott. 1966. *A Religious History of America.* New York: Harper and Row.

Gill, John. 1999. "Luke." In *Exposition of the Old and New Testaments.* Electronic version 1.0. Paris, Ark.: Baptist Standard Bearer.

Gutiérrez, Gustavo. 1973. *A Theology of Liberation: History, Politics and Salvation.* Maryknoll, N.Y.: Orbis.

Hesselgrave, David. 1990. "Holes in 'Holistic Mission.'" *Trinity World Forum* 15.3 (Spring): 2–5.

Johnston, Arthur P. 1978. *The Battle for World Evangelism.* Wheaton, Ill.: Tyndale.

Larkin, William J. Jr. 1998. "Mission in Luke." In *Mission in the New Testament: An Evangelical Approach.* Edited by W. J. Larkin Jr. and J. F. Williams. Maryknoll, N.Y.: Orbis.

Lewis, C. S. 1952. *Mere Christianity.* New York: Macmillan.

Little, Christopher R. 2005. *Mission in the Way of Paul: Biblical Mission for the Church in the Twenty-first Century.* New York: Peter Lang.

Marshall, I. Howard. 1970. *Luke: Historian and Theologian.* Grand Rapids: Zondervan.

Myers, Bryant L. 1999a. "In Response . . . Another Look at Holistic Mission." *Evangelical Missions Quarterly* 35.3 (July): 287.

———. 1999b. *Walking With the Poor: Principles and Practices of Transformational Development.* Monrovia, Calif.: World Vision.

Sider, Ronald J. 1990. *Rich Christians in an Age of Hunger.* 2d ed. Dallas: Word.

Stein, Robert H. 1992. *Luke.* New American Commentary, vol. 24. Nashville: Broadman.

Stott, John R. W. 1975. *Christian Mission in the Modern World: What the Church Should Be Doing Now.* Downers Grove, Ill.: InterVarsity.

Chapter 5

Incarnationalism and Representationalism

Who Is Our Missionary Model—Jesus or Paul?

Therefore, we are ambassadors for Christ, God making his appeal through us. We implore you on behalf of Christ, be reconciled to God.

—2 Corinthians 5:20

Prologue

IT WAS RIGHT AFTER WORLD WAR II, and many Japanese in Takatsuki City had never seen a real, live missionary. This particular missionary happened to be a tall Swede from California named Calvin Hanson, but they knew nothing about him and very little about the Lord Jesus. Hanson introduced himself and filled out the required forms correctly, but he was shocked when his heating bill was addressed to "Mr. Jesus Christ." He returned to the city office and explained that he had come to teach the people about Jesus Christ, but that he himself was not Jesus Christ. A month passed, and another bill arrived addressed to Mr. Jesus Christ. In spite of his protestations, Hanson quickly became known as Mr. Jesus Christ among his neighbors. His scottish terrier was said to belong to Mr. Jesus Christ and was sometimes known as the "Christian dog."

On one occasion when the Hansons made a house call, they were met in the *genkan* (entry) by a little boy who quickly ran to his mother yelling, "Mother, Mother, Jesus Christ has come again."

The first name that occurs to many Christians when we think of emulating the life and person of Christ is Thomas à Kempis (ca. 1380–1471), who composed or collected the text of *The Imitation of Christ* over five hundred years ago. A classic of devotional literature, the book has appeared in more than a thousand editions and has been translated into most major languages. Its dominant theme is that love of Jesus is the highest good and meditation on the life of Christ will bring peace and godliness. Therefore, Christians should forsake the world and live a life of seclusion and self-denial, searching for God.

Just over one hundred years ago, a Congregational minister-theologian, Charles Sheldon (1857–1946), wrote the short but popular novel, *In His Steps* (1897). Sheldon was an advocate of the social gospel that was so prominent at the time. In his novel, the Reverend Henry Maxwell persuades his congregation to do nothing without first asking the question, "What would Jesus do?" As they learn to live like this, their whole community is changed.

Both à Kempis and Sheldon emphasized the imitation of Christ, but they had differing paths and differing ends in view. The spiritual life of the individual Christian was à Kempis's concern. Sheldon's concern was for the "christianization" of society. Both are still widely read. It might be fair to say that both were right.

Both were also wrong.

Tiptoeing Through Some Relevant History

Whether grappling with their own sinfulness or with the challenges of ministry in a fallen world, Christians have always looked to Jesus for guidance, as well as for redemption, when they looked for a pattern of right living as well as a source of salvation. This was especially true for advocates of the social gospel during the last decades of the nineteenth century and the early twentieth century. They believed that the business of the church is to order personal and community life according to the pattern provided by Jesus. Thus they would build his kingdom on earth.

Many became disillusioned, however, as they experienced the horrors of inhuman behavior demonstrated in World War I. For example, seeing the land of his forefathers, Germany, at war with his native land, the United States, Walter Rauschenbusch (1861–1918) became despondent in his final years. He had been a leading social gospel theologian.

By the end of World War I, the social gospel movement had lost much of its appeal, but aspects of its theology lived on. The search for direction by observing the ministry of Jesus still characterized many churches and their missions following World War II. Many Roman Catholic and mainline Protestant leaders became especially concerned with repositioning Christian missions. The Division of World Mission and Evangelism of the World Council of Churches commissioned Johannes Blauw to review and summarize studies on the biblical foundation of missions between 1930 and 1960 (Blauw 1962). His study and subsequent ones revealed a heightened emphasis on service and liberation motifs in the mission of Israel, Jesus, and the church (Verkuyl 1978, 94, 107).

Especially after Vatican II (1962–65), various forms of liberation theology became increasingly influential in Roman Catholic and conciliar church circles. The plight of the poor and disenfranchised, especially in Latin America where the church had played such dominant social and political as well as religious roles for many years, became a millstone around the neck of the church. Something had to be said about this state of affairs. More important, something had to be done. To find out what had to be said and done, church and missions leaders reexamined the mission and ministry of Jesus.

Liberation theology occasioned serious debate in both Roman Catholic and ecumenical Protestant circles, but evangelicals also entered into the debate. Almost from the beginning of the modern missionary movement, evangelicals had carried on extensive relief, medical, educational, and service ministries. But in the politically charged climate of the 1960s and 1970s, conservative evangelicals joined Roman Catholics and conciliar Protestants on the defensive. Not wanting to be branded as callous and uncaring, evangelicals attempted to maintain their traditional priority for world evangelization while searching for new ways to show concern for social issues in theory and practice. The Lausanne Covenant (1974) reflected this concern, and the "Manila Manifesto" of the Global Consultation on World Evangelization (1989) made deed ministry a primary interest.

One of several evangelicals to play a role in this process was the Anglo-Catholic John R. W. Stott. He advocated a new (for him) understanding of the Great Commission, according to which Jesus and his mission became *the* model for the church's mission. Incarnationalism gradually increased in importance in evangelical missiology.

Incarnational Missiology: Jesus as Model Missionary

Andreas J. Köstenberger points out that entire missiological paradigms have been built around various interpretations of John 17:18 ("As you sent me into the world, so I have sent them into the world.") and John 20:21 ("Jesus said to them again, 'Peace be with you. As the Father has sent me, even so I am sending you.'"). Köstenberger studied the mission of Christ as revealed in John's Gospel (Köstenberger 1998). We will focus on some of his conclusions.

Köstenberger begins his study by distinguishing between two very different models of missions ministry, an *incarnational model* and a *representational model*. He gives the following contrast:

> The "incarnational model" . . . sees Christ as present in the church so that the church can fashion its ministry after the model provided by Jesus during his earthly ministry. According to this view, the church is not just *representing* Jesus—it is Jesus working through his church today. The implication of this model appears to be a focus on the continuity between Jesus' mission and the church's mission. (Köstenberger 1998, 3)

Seldom carefully spelled out or defined, what is sometimes called "incarnationalism" provides a starting point for understanding incarnational as contrasted with representational missiology. The incarnational model focus is on continuity between Christ's incarnate earthly ministry and the contemporary ministry of the church today. Incarnationalism holds that the church's mission today is, in a very real sense, a continuation of the mission and ministry of Jesus Christ on earth.

What then *was* his mission?

What is ours?

To answer these questions, incarnational missiologists tend to drift toward less Scripture-centered ways of thinking. Some of the more avant-garde incarnationalists are primarily concerned with establishing *shalom* (i.e., peace, social harmony) in today's world, whether by interfaith dialogue or by involvement in actions promoting social and political justice. Both of these versions of incarnational mission attempt to build on principles and models developed from the history of God's people in the Old Testament and from Jesus in his kingdom mission. In either case, they propose that we continue doing what they see God doing throughout history and most significantly in the ministry of Jesus.

At the other extreme are incarnationalists who maintain a traditional concern for world evangelization and the verbal proclamation of the gospel, but who enjoin Christ's attitudes and behaviors upon the church and its missionaries today. It is worthwhile noting that, insofar as these more conservative proponents are missiologically informed, their proposals tend to mirror many ideas that grow out of such anthropological and communicational concepts as *identification*, *indigenization*, *accommodation*, *contextualization*, and *enculturation*.

It is not easy to understand, much less evaluate, a missiology so variegated. But its very fuzziness makes careful examination all the more important.

Incarnationalism: Foundations and Formulations

Incarnational missiology cannot be completely understood or evaluated apart from a basic understanding of three very different views of Christ's person, kingdom, and ministry: (1) liberationism; (2) holism; and, for want of a more precise term, (3) "conversionism."

Liberation-incarnationalists take their Old Testament cues from Israel's emancipation from Egypt as recorded in Exodus, from the servant passages in Isaiah, and from other select passages in the Old Testament prophets. They also look, of course, to Christ's incarnation and ministry, especially Jesus' announcement in Luke 4:16–20 (see pp. 128–35). Jesus is viewed as the great Liberator and Emancipator. His announcement of the kingdom "reveals to society itself the aspiration for a just society" and "opens up the promise and hope of complete union of all men with God," according to perhaps the most influential of liberation theologians (Gutierrez 1973, 281–82). Gustavo Gutierrez quotes Latin American bishops approvingly when they say,

> It is the same God who, in the fullness of time, sends his son so that, made flesh, he might come to liberate all men from *all* the enslavements to which sin has subjected them—ignorance, misery, hunger and oppression, in a word, injustice and hatred which have their origin in human selfishness. (Gutierrez 1976, 67)

While most contextualized theologies of the 1970s and 1980s ran their course, liberation theology lives on in liberation-incarnationalism. To be true to Christ and his kingdom and to carry forth his mission and ministry, it is the solemn obligation of the church to be the divine agent of a sociopolitical revolution whereby the oppressed achieve "total liberation" (Gutierrez 1976, 69).

Holism-incarnationalists seek the extension of Christ's kingdom over the whole of life and society. They don't think so much of priorities. They think of witness in terms of "word, deed, and sign" and of Jesus Christ as the Transformer of societies and cultures as well as individuals.

The pivotal work in opening the door to this kind holism was John Stott's seminal little 1975 volume, *The Christian Mission in the Modern World: What the Church Should Be Doing Now*. Stott supplemented it in 1992 with *The Contemporary Christian: Applying God's Word to Today's World*. While others, such as Bryant Myers, have produced more extensive prescriptions for holistic mission, Stott's influence has been far more extensive within the evangelical movement. During the 1970s, Stott started on a project that he and his followers were still working at over a quarter century later. Their aim was to mediate between the view that the central goal of world ministry is the proclamation of the Word of God and the view that it is about establishing *shalom*.

Stott holds John 20:21 to be the most important statement of the Great

Commission. When Jesus said "*As* the Father has sent me, *even so* I am sending you," Stott sees Jesus clearly making his mission a model for the church's mission (as in Luke 4:18–19). That means that sociopolitical action (deed) is a more or less equal partner with evangelism (Word) in Christ's mission and our own. Accordingly, the church's mission today consists of "everything the church is sent into the world to do" (Stott 1975, 30). Stott goes so far as to say that, since the church is to be salt and light, it is the failure of the church if a community deteriorates socially or physically (Stott 1975, 32).

While Myers and other holists are reluctant to make any distinctions between social action and evangelism, Stott adds certain caveats. He reserves a certain priority for proclamational evangelism. He maintains that the Incarnation was indeed a unique work of God that cannot be copied. What is to be imitated is the "principle of the incarnation." Nor can Christ's atonement be taken out of its unique purpose and historic reality. Christians cannot be saviors. Also, while insisting that the missiological task includes everything the church is "sent to do," Stott makes it clear that the ideal mission is not necessarily everything that the church actually does. Nevertheless, Stott "changed his mind," and many evangelicals have readily done the same.

Conversion-incarnationalists, in the sense in which I employ the term here, maintain clear priorities. They understand the mission of the church in terms of discipling the *ethnē* (i.e., peoples, people groups; Gentiles but not exclusive of Jews) by proclaiming the gospel, bringing people to Christ, baptizing converts, instructing them in the faith, and incorporating them into responsible reproducing churches. Christ is Messiah, Redeemer, Savior, and Lord—all of these and more. He is also our Model in the way he understood and carried out his mission, but undergirding all he said and did was the fact that "the Son of Man came to seek and to save the lost" (Luke 19:10).

Conversion-incarnationalists reject liberationism and are uncomfortable with at least some aspects of holism, but with or without careful attention to the risks involved they attempt to fashion contemporary missiology after the pattern and principles of Jesus more than those of the apostle Paul. Robert Coleman, for example, discovers the "master plan of evangelism" in the methods of Jesus (Coleman 1962) and notes that a

"Great Commission lifestyle" displays the incarnational dimension of his mission (Coleman 1992, 16).

Though laying unequivocal claim to being an incarnationalist, Ron Rogers speaks more specifically to what is involved in incarnational missiology (Rogers 2002, 43–58). As I understand the reasoning of Rogers, I would categorize him as a "conversion-incarnationalist." He says that, though such terms as *accommodation, identification, indigenization*, and *enculturation* are often used, it is *incarnationalism* that "sets forth the truly biblical model for cross-cultural ministry" and that Christ is "the model *par excellence* of a truly incarnational missionary ministry" (Rogers 2002, 44).

Rogers develops this thesis in two stages. First, he lays out the main features of Christ's ministry as God Incarnate: enfleshment; self-emptying; humanity; involvement; servanthood; sacrifice; and the cross. Second, he spells out the implications of Christ's incarnation for missionary endeavors today under headings of "renunciation," "identification," and "communication" (Rogers 2002, 44–52).

Rogers's essay is conservative and straightforward. His theology of the Incarnation is clearly biblical. While recognizing that many of his recommendations for effective missionizing could be inferred from the principles of applied anthropology and cross-cultural communication, he frames them within a conversionist brand of incarnationalism and looks to Jesus and his ministry as his authority and model. Nowhere in his essay does he suggest that our mission is a continuation of Jesus' mission in the sense that most liberationists and many holists believe it to be. But neither does he explicitly state that our mission is *not* a continuation of Jesus' mission in the sense that they believe it to be. He is an incarnationalist by virtue of his own insistence that he is one and by his use of Jesus as model. However, if pressed to identify him with either incarnationalism or representationalism as we have defined those positions, I would place him in the company of representationalists.

Implications and Applications of the Jesus Model

Obviously, the practical outworkings of incarnationalism will vary with the type of incarnationalism involved. In liberation theology and missiology, incarnationalism has been used to support all kinds of social and political activities, including participation in violent revolution. A colleague heard a self-acclaimed "evangelical liberationist" assert that, when following Jesus in Latin America today, "bullets are as important as Bibles." That, however, was a different time.

But setting aside the extremist forms of incarnationalism and assuming the most biblical forms of holistic and conversionist incarnationalism, what aspects of Jesus and his ministry have particular meaning for world ministry today? Some proposals have been built around these statements about Jesus:

1. Jesus' ministry was characterized by humble, self-sacrificial service on behalf of all people.
2. Jesus was willing to renounce his rights and privileges as the Son of God in order to identify with those he came to serve.
3. Jesus became poor and took the form of a servant in order to meet the needs of hurting people and carry out his mission to the poor and powerless.
4. Jesus did not hesitate to engage in a power encounter with the forces of the Evil One by casting out demons and otherwise demonstrating divine power.
5. Jesus immersed himself in the affairs of a local culture, joining in a wedding feast, attending a funeral, going on a "fishing trip," and participating in everyday life.
6. Jesus communicated, in both verbal and nonverbal ways, that people could understand. He spoke in the everyday language of the people.
7. Jesus spent most of his time training a few chosen disciples who would faithfully and effectively carry on his ministry.
8. Jesus gave priority to prayer and fellowship with his heavenly Father.
9. Jesus did not have a superiority complex but, rather, assumed a humble attitude in working with the people.
10. Jesus was willing to suffer and even die for the people he came to save.

By fulfilling his mission in this way, Jesus modeled attitudes, lifestyle, activities, and methods that are worth emulating in missions ministry today. Missions and missionaries should think as he thought, say what he said, and do what he did. In doing so, they continue his ministry. Stated in a most elemental way, that seems to be the essence of incarnationalism.

Representational Missiology: Paul as the Model Missionary

Scripture and the history of missions offer an alternative model for missions theory and practice—the representational model. The essence of it is described by Köstenberger:

> Another view, the "representational model," accentuates more keenly the *discontinuity* between the respective missions of Jesus and of his disciples. It acknowledges the uniqueness of Jesus' person and work while viewing the primary task of his disciples as *witnessing* to Jesus. While Jesus can be said to "give life" in a primary sense, the disciples' contribution is limited to their witness. (Köstenberger 1998, 3–4; emphasis mine)

Two words here become keys to understanding the difference between incarnationalism and representationalism. They are *discontinuity* and *witness.* As we will see in chapter 10, George Eldon Ladd believes that there is little difference between the gospel preached by the Lord Jesus and justification as preached by the apostle Paul (Ladd 1974, 216). In dialogue with the Jewish scholar Pinchas Lapide, Peter Stuhlmacher says something similar, although his words conflict with Paul's on the uniqueness of the gospel and ministry (Gal. 1:11–24; Eph. 3:1–13):

> Paul is not far from Jesus with his gospel of justification; indeed he is very close. This gospel is essentially based on the same Old Testament from which Israel, to this very hour, draws all of its strength for its faith. All of this harmonizes so well because, as Paul has already said, God is not only the God of the Jews but also the God of the Gentiles. And since he is the God both of the Jews and of the Gentiles he is the One before whom, and for

whom all of us live (Rom. 3:20ff.). (Stuhlmacher and Lapide, 1984, 27, 30)

Köstenberger is correct in saying that such an emphasis on continuity is replaced by an emphasis on discontinuity in the writings of representationalists. They recognize the unbroken line between the good news of salvation in the Old and New Testaments, and between the gospel of Christ and Paul's gospel, but the fact that Paul can declare that Christ has been crucified, has been raised from the dead, and has been seen by his disciples (1 Cor. 15:3–9) make the post-Passion gospel complete and distinct. Paul emphasizes the completed work of Christ, not details of His life on earth.

As for the word *witness,* that too is especially significant in the context of representationalism. Stott's reminder that "we are not saviors" is well taken, but it seems hardly needed except as a reminder not to be sidetracked by the beguilements of incarnationalism. Missionaries are not only "not saviors," they are "sinners saved by grace" and have no ground whatsoever for preaching to others apart from their witness to the saving power of the one and only Savior, the Lord Jesus Christ.

It should be stated that subscription to representational missiology does not oblige one to accept the notion that the ministry of the apostle Paul is the biblical model for today. The two concepts often go together, and they are treated together in this discussion. But we are not assuming that acceptance of one means the necessary acceptance of the other.

The Case for Representationalism in Preference to Incarnationalism

The kinds of incarnationalism we have categorized as liberationist and holistic collide with representationalism at critical points. Conversion-incarnationalism, in contrast, coexists with representationalism in a symbiotic relationship. However, to hold both positions at one time seems analogous to riding two horses at once—delightful in a circus but disastrous in a battle. In the final analysis, almost any version of incarnationalism creates or perpetuates more problems than does representationalism.

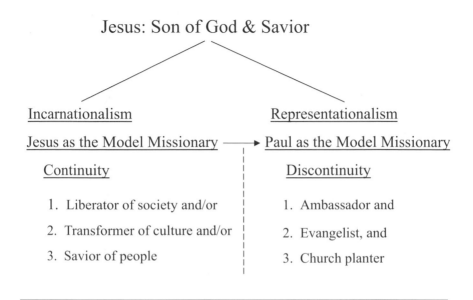

Figure 5. Incarnationalism and Representationalism

Incarnationalists and representationalists pose different (sometimes *very* different) answers to three fundamental missiological questions: (1) What are today's missionaries to be? (2) What are they to say? (3) What are they to do? Acknowledging a debt to Köstenberger's thinking in this area, I find good reason to choose representationalism as providing more biblical answers and so promising more for the future.

First, what are missionaries to be in the world? Are they in some sense incarnations or reincarnations or "duplications" of Christ? Or are they disciples, witnesses, representatives, and ambassadors of Christ? The answer seems obvious. In fact, only by resort to metaphorical language does the first option become thinkable.

Literally and biblically, missionaries are representatives of an authoritative Sender, sent to certain places and peoples to fulfill a prescribed task. This sender-sendee relationship changes with new generations, cultures, peoples, and prescribed tasks in the missions endeavor. The Son had one mission, the Twelve another, the Seventy or Seventy-two another (Matt. 10; Luke 10), and those who respond to the Great Commission of Matthew 28 and Mark 16 yet another. But the shape of the work changes with where we are in salvation history. At one point the mission revolved around the Jews, at another point the calling out of the church and, at another point it will be concerned more with the kingdom. By maintaining that the church's mission is a *continuation* of Christ's own personal mission, incarnationalism blurs these distinctions and becomes a source of confusion. Representationalism, especially as modeled by Paul, maintains continuity in the sender-sendee relationship but progression in the divine program of redemption (2 Cor. 5:20).

Second, what are missionaries to say in the world? The essence of the missionary message is the gospel *of Christ*—the good news of what God has accomplished in sending his only begotten Son into the world to die and rise again in order that the world might be saved. Representational missiology affirms the absolute uniqueness of Christ's incarnation, deity, and ministry, and also the atoning death, bodily resurrection, and complete fulfillment of Christ's redemptive mission.

In its insistence on new "incarnations" and continuing Christ's own mission, incarnationalism runs the risk of detracting from the uniqueness of his person and the fulfillment of his mission. This, in fact, is Köstenberger's primary concern with John Stott's incarnational approach. Köstenberger writes that Stott's kind of incarnationalism "seems to be at odds with the Fourth Gospel's presentation of Jesus' incarnation as thoroughly unique, unprecedented and unrepeatable (cf. especially the designation *monogenēs* in 1:14, 18; 3:16, 18). The incarnation is linked with Jesus' eternal preexistence (1:1, 14) and his unique relationship with the Father (1:14, 18)" (Köstenberger 1998, 216).

In the postmodern trend to downgrade theology and doctrine, it may seem picayunish to entertain the idea that a metaphorical use of Christ's incarnation could *obscure* his identity or *detract* from his mission. Incarnationalists quote Paul when he writes that "for me to live is Christ" (Phil. 1:21) and says that "Christ in us" is our "hope of glory" (Col. 1:27). However, in biblical teaching, the truth of the indwelling of Christ through the Holy Spirit is light years removed from the doctrine of the incarnation of Christ. As for maintaining the absolute uniqueness of Christ's incarnation, it must be remembered that the West faces pluralism, syncretism, new ageism, false Christs, and the disintegration of absolutes. The Eastern world faces the various *avatara* of Hinduism, the bodhisattvas and *manushi* buddhas of Mahayana, the numerous *kami* of Shintoism, the sectarian claims of cultic saviors, and the primacy of individual illumination.

Despite their own inadequacies and sinfulness, Christian missionaries must, above all else, represent the only Lord and Savior, Jesus Christ. He is the only person in God's entire universe and all of human history who was and forever will be both God and man. Therefore, he alone is able to bring sinners into a right relationship with a holy, living God.

Third, what is the missionary to do? If one takes Jesus' mission as a model, what is the contemporary missionary to do about those aspects of mission and ministry that are not repeatable? We do know, for instance, that we should at least emulate Christ's obedience to the Father, his willingness to lay aside heaven's glory, his wisdom in speaking to the Samaritan woman about water and to Nicodemus about a second birth, and his practice of prayer. But should we emulate his cleansing of the temple with a tongue-lashing and the sting of a whip? Can we repeat the casting out of legions of demons at the cost of a herd of swine or the raising of Lazarus to life when his body had already begun to decompose? Although some try to design their own mission around such miracles, not one can measure up.

By looking at Paul's mission in the context of the entire church's New Testament mission, Don N. Howell Jr. finds answers to the three questions before us (Howell 1998, 63–116). Howell comes to conclusions that are similar to our own, although he does not emphasize the "modeling" aspect of Paul's work. Howell writes,

> From the moment of his conversion, Paul understood the proclamation of the gospel of Jesus Christ to be his mission in life. But he was more than an itinerant evangelist. His aim was to bring the Gentiles to the obedience of faith (Rom. 1:5) and to organize his converts into self-governing churches. Paul energetically labored not to gain large numbers of converts but to present each person mature in Christ (Col. 1:28–29). Such maturity in the corporate congregation of believers is attained as each one exercises his or her gifts to the edification of the whole (Eph. 4:11–16). In short, Paul was a pioneering, church-planting evangelist. (Howell 1998, 70)

Representationalism—Foundations and Formulations

Representationalists almost always think of Paul as the model missionary. The other apostles and many "ordinary" believers played important roles in evangelizing their world and in establishing churches. But it was the apostle Paul whom God specially prepared, called, and used to evangelize and establish churches throughout the Mediterranean world of the first century. As Stuhlmacher says, "Historically it is beyond doubt that Paul worked as an apostle, and indeed more intensively and with greater lasting impact than all the other apostles of Jesus whose names we know" (Stuhlmacher and Lapide 1984, 27). Not only so, it was the apostle Paul through whom the Holy Spirit provided approximately half of the entire New Testament record.

For these reasons among others, representationalists generally look to Paul as their model. There would be no gospel, no church, and no mission apart from Christ, but it was Paul, acting as Christ's *ambassador* (from Greek *presbeuō*, "to act as a representative"), who explained the gospel, extended the church, and exemplified the mission.

Various missiologists indeed view Paul through somewhat different lenses. Some, such as Stuhlmacher and Arthur Glasser, have a special interest in Paul and his way of presenting the gospel because of a concern to witness to Jews. Glasser also points to Paul as an organizer and leader of "parachurch" missions. Some, such as Dean Gilliland, present Paul as multifaceted missionary theologian and practitioner. Some, such as Samuel Faircloth and I, focus on Paul as a model missionary and church planter. In fact, over the years Paul's ministry as a church planter has been a focal point in the writings of numerous missiologists, among them Henry Venn, Rufus Anderson, John Nevius, Roland Allen, Alexander Hay, and Melvin Hodges.

Five times Paul points to his own life and ministry as a model. First, in 1 Corinthians 4:16 he exhorts believers to imitate him in rejecting claims to superiority and in working for church unity. Second, the same exhortation in 1 Corinthians 11:1 occurs after Paul admonishes believers to follow him in using Christian liberty to be a slave to all men in order to win some of them (1 Cor. 9:22). The third exhortation occurs in Philippians 3:17, where Paul exhorts believers to follow his own example of humility and self-sacrifice, the kind Jesus demonstrated perfectly in his *kenosis* or self-emptying (Phil. 2:1–11). Fourth, Paul commends Thessalonian believers for having imitated him and other members of his missions team. They had received God's Word joyfully in spite of tribulation (1 Thess. 1:6). Fifth, Paul reminds the Thessalonian Christians that they should follow him in living a disciplined life. He had been willing to labor with his own hands so that he would not be a burden—all for the sake of the gospel (2 Thess. 3:7–9).

Although uniquely prepared, converted, and commissioned by Christ personally, both Paul's theology and mission were confirmed by the early church and its leaders. Barnabas introduced him to the church in Syrian Antioch. With Barnabas he was sent on his first missionary journey by that church. When his gospel and mission were questioned by those of the circumcision, he reported to the church and apostles in Jerusalem and was affirmed by them. When the apostle Peter in effect denied the universality of the gospel by his conduct, Paul challenged him to his face (Gal. 2:11–14). And when Barnabas and Paul parted, the Holy Spirit orchestrated events and revelation in such a way that Luke recorded the exploits of Paul and Silas rather than those of Barnabas and John Mark.

Paul and his associates were the center of some controversies, so that one might think the Antioch believers would be hesitant to send these men as their representatives. Not so. Led by the Holy Spirit, they "commended" Paul to the grace of God and sent him and his new associate Silas on their way (Acts 15:36–41). Subsequently, God provided Timothy in the place of John Mark and directed Paul's little team to spearhead the evangelization of Europe.

After looking at the full story of Paul, it would seem that the long line of representational missiologists who viewed him as a model missionary had good reason. In fact, Paul publicly called himself a model missionary in the representational sense of the word. At the end of a well-researched and convincing chapter on the Pauline model, Christopher Little concludes: "In the final analysis, it is impossible to separate Pauline missions from the missional task of the church in any age. Therefore, one can only conclude that the missiological basis for Pauline orthopraxy in Christian mission is beyond question" (Little 2005, 158).

Applying the Pauline Model

The Anglican missionary and theorist of the last century, Roland Allen, readily comes to mind when viewing the record of Paul's missionary practice. After service in China, Allen spent some forty years studying and writing about what biblical mission is and how to advance it. He prophesied that his works would not be greatly appreciated until after his death (which occurred in 1947), and that indeed proved to be the case. In the era following World War II, few evangelical students of missions graduated without at least a cursory knowledge of Allen and his theory of the "indigenous church."

Perhaps best known among Allen's works is *Missionary Methods: St. Paul's or Ours?* (first publication 1912). In the foreword to the first American edition of that book, Lesslic Newbigin downplays Allen's emphasis on Paul and his missionary methods, choosing rather to highlight "*the way of Christ* and His Apostles" (Allen 1962, i–ii; emphasis mine). However, as Kenneth Grubb's foreword to the 1962 American edition and Allen's own subtitle indicate, *Missionary Methods* isn't about the ministry of Christ and the other apostles. Allen centers on Paul's missionary message and methods of evangelizing people and planting churches as he was directed and energized by the Holy Spirit. Missionaries can only be helped and missiologists only informed by a careful reading of books that focus on Paul, such as *Missionary Methods*, *Planting Churches Cross-Culturally* (Hesselgrave 1990) and *Mission in the Way of Paul* (Little 2005).

According to those who advocate representational missions, some aspects of his ministry have implications and applications for today:

1. Paul's ministry was characterized by humble, self-sacrificial service in which he willingly gave up personal rights in order to identify with and meet the needs of people to whom he ministered (e.g., 1 Cor. 9:15–23).
2. Paul concentrated on centers of learning and commerce, from which the gospel could flow naturally to surrounding areas.
3. Paul labored with his own hands to provide for himself and his co-workers (Acts 18:1–4; 1 Cor. 4:12).

4. Paul considered himself an ambassador of Christ, and on Christ's behalf he urged men and women to be reconciled to God (e.g., 2 Cor. 5:20; Eph. 6:19–20).
5. Paul concentrated on raising up indigenous churches that would not be dependent upon either the missionaries or the churches that had sent them (Eph. 4:11–16).
6. Paul ordinarily did not spend a long time in each place, choosing rather to train and appoint local leaders who could carry the work forward after his departure (Acts 14:23).
7. Paul maintained contact with churches he had established, admonishing them on the basis of his apostolic calling and role as spiritual father to walk worthy of their calling (e.g., Eph. 4:1).
8. Paul encouraged believers in the churches he had planted to give liberally to care for the needy believers in Jerusalem (Rom. 15:25–27; 1 Cor. 16:1–3).
9. For the sake of the gospel, Paul made himself a servant of all, becoming "all things to all men" so that some might be saved (1 Cor. 9:22).
10. While maintaining his authority as one commissioned and sent by Christ on the one hand, Paul humbly confessed his unworthiness as a sinner and former persecutor of the church on the other (e.g., 1 Cor. 15:9–10).

Contemporary missiologists tend not to speak of *"indigenous* churches" today, and reservations are expressed to the relevancy of one or another aspect of Paul's methods. But one would be hard-pressed to find a more unerring guide to the fundamentals of a New Testament theology and practice than those that can be found in the writings and ministry of the apostle Paul.

Incarnationalism and Representationalism: Proposals

Defining Our Terms

As is so often the case, part of the disagreement between incarnationalists and representationalists is occasioned by a confusion of meaning, especially of the word *model. Model* is sometimes understood in the sense of *archetype* (i.e., "a prototype, original pattern, or defining paradigm") and sometimes in the sense of *example* (i.e., "a sample, typical pattern, or parallel paradigm").

Many incarnationalists—especially liberationists and holists, but also some conversionists—tend to use the word *model* in the sense of *prototype*. For them Christ's ministry is archetypal, that is to say, it is the defining pattern or paradigm for the church's mission today. In fact and as we have seen, they view the church's mission as a *continuation* of Christ's own mission. Other incarnationalists, however, use *model* more in the *pattern* sense of the word. They look at Jesus and the way he lived and ministered as an example of the way in which all of his followers should try to live and serve.

On the whole, representationalists tend to use the word *model* in this latter example or *typical pattern* sense. They tend to view Paul's ministry as an exemplary pattern for understanding and carrying out the Christian mission. Some representationalists, however, go further. They point to Paul and his mission as an *archetype* or *defining paradigm* that more or less defines what all true missionaries should at least attempt to be and do.

Armed with an understanding of this difference in meaning, perhaps we can better understand the theological foundations and practical implications of incarnationalism and representationalism. Note the various ways in which incarnational missiologists return to Jesus' incarnation and ministry to determine how to understand and practice the mission of the church. Then note the ways in which representational missiologists picture Paul, not as the *determiner* of Christian mission, but as the *defender and fulfiller* of what the Great Commission requires.

At the *example* level, advocates of these two approaches to missions can agree and learn from both Christ and Paul as models in how to do the work of mission. At the *archetype* level, however, the disagreement becomes more serious. In fact, we may be forced to choose between them, and, unless we choose wisely, both the church and its task may suffer.

Drawing Important Lessons

It is entirely proper, even requsite, for all Christians to look to Jesus as their Example as well as their Lord and Savior. The writer of Hebrews says so. According to him, Christ is not only the "founder and perfecter of our faith" (Heb. 12:2); he is also the "apostle [missionary] and high priest of our confession" (3:1). These same texts exhort us to "fix our eyes," and by implication our thoughts, on him (12:2). Paul made it clear that he himself was an "imitator" *(mimētēs)* of Christ (1 Cor. 11:1). There is a profound sense in which all who lay claim to being Christian—from Peter and Paul, to Thomas Aquinas and Thomas à Kempis, to Charles Sheldon and John Stott—look to Jesus Christ as the Model for life and work.

In that general sense at least, we are all "incarnationalists," if we must employ that term.

Perhaps the clearest and most positive biblical affirmation for a kind of incarnationalism is to be found in Philippians 2:5–11. Nowhere else in Scripture is the self-emptying, self-abnegation, and self-sacrifice of our Lord Jesus Christ more succinctly and poignantly portrayed. Nowhere in the Bible is God the Father's plan and purpose for Jesus and his mission more powerfully displayed. And nowhere is the exhortation more clear: "Have this mind among yourselves, which is yours in Christ Jesus" (v. 5).

This is clear indication of the fact that representationalists themselves stand to profit from looking to Jesus, not only directly, but through the lens provided by the apostle Paul and his attitude and labors. In a passage very often referred to in connection with his ministry, 1 Corinthians 9:19–23, Paul says that, although he is "free from all" he has made himself a "servant of all." To Jews he became as a Jew. To those under the law he became as one under the law. To those outside the law, as one outside the law. To the weak as weak. Why? For the sake of the gospel. To win men and women. To share the blessings of the gospel. And whom did he follow in all of this? Who other than Christ Jesus himself?

From a practical point of view, all Christians—and especially those who would serve in lands and among peoples other than their own—profit by emulating both Jesus and Paul as examples of humility, self-abnegation, and self-sacrifice.

Discriminating Between the Normative and the Descriptive

Both incarnationalism and representationalism are attended by the common hermeneutical problem of distinguishing between what is normative and what is only descriptive.

To illustrate this problem, we turn, first, to the work of a contemporary missiologist, Jonathan Bonk's *Missions and Money: Affluence as a Western Missionary Problem* (1991). In one or another sense of the word, Bonk is clearly an incarnationalist. In a scholarly and careful manner, Bonk deals with deep problems occasioned by the fact that so much of the modern missionary movement has represented an affluent West to a poverty-stricken Third World. Jesus "became poor" in coming into the world, and Bonk urges Western missionaries to adopt an "incarnational lifestyle" as a way of identifying with poverty-stricken peoples worldwide.

Ken Baker is one of those who find serious flaws in Bonk's proposal. Baker's problem is not so much with the idea that missionaries should simplify their lifestyle. Baker doesn't like the notion that an incarnational lifestyle is key to solving the problem of identification. He doesn't believe that this is the one biblically intended model or that relative affluence is an unbridgeable gap (Baker 2002, 16–24). While he sees important strengths in Bonk's proposals, Baker believes that Bonk errs in making Christ's simple lifestyle normative for missionaries working in the Third World. This disagreement is not one that can be defined away. It is not easily resolved at either the biblical or practical levels.

A second illustration comes from Roland Allen. We have already noted the emphasis that he gives to Paul's dependence upon the place and power of the Holy Spirit in missionary ministry (p. 157). That emphasis, among others, has made Allen's teachings attractive to many, especially to Pentecostals and charismatics. However, Allen himself was a high church Anglican, a sacramentalist rather than a Pentecostal. According to Allen, Paul could depart from fledgling churches without having given the considerable time needed to instructing them in Christian doctrine, precisely because he could leave them in the care of the Holy Spirit *and with the sacraments.*

Numerous representationalists, including some Pentecostals, have taken exception to this on grounds other than Allen's sacramentalism. They point out that there were places where Paul did not intend to stay for a long period and some places, such as Ephesus, where he did spend a considerable amount of time. Sometimes he left, not because he thought his work was done, but because he was forced to leave. He revisited and otherwise instructed the churches and left certain churches in the care of co-workers. It seems to read too much into the New Testament record to say that dependence on the Holy Spirit and the sacraments allow a missionary to plant a church and quickly move on without intensive instruction in faith and doctrine. This is a clearly a case of failing to distinguish between what is descriptive and what is normative.

Conclusion

In writing *In His Steps* at the turn of the twentieth century, Charles Sheldon accomplished at least two things. First, he undoubtedly helped many Christians to construct a kind of practical ethic around their answers to that seemingly simple question, "What would Jesus do?" Second, he affirmed many Christians in their commitment to a social gospel. This gospel was characterized by "the confident hope of Christian leaders that the application of Christian principles to the ordering of society would lead to the rectification of serious social evils and pave the way for the establishment of the kingdom of God on earth" (Handy 1991, 164–65). Undoubtedly many of those who were enamored with this kind of Christianity didn't realize that they were "profiting" at the expense of truth—the real gospel.

In embracing incarnationalism at the turn of the twenty-first century, its advocates accomplish at least two things. First, they reinforce practical Christian ethics and missiology. Look at the Sheldon-inspired slogan "WWJD" (i.e., "What would Jesus do?"). It is found on T-shirts, bracelets, and bumper stickers. I suppose an environmental ethic can be adduced around the droll question, "What would Jesus drive?" Such a tack might wean American believers and unbelievers from their infatuation with SUVs. Perhaps asking "What would Jesus eat" might encourage a more healthful diet.

In missions circles, of course, legitimate, positive lessons can be drawn from the actions and attitudes of Jesus. Jesus as missionary challenges today's missionaries to avoid arrogance and humbly serve the people to whom they are sent.

At the same time, there are other worrisome implications if incarnationalism is embraced in theology and missiology. For example, when Today's New International Version of the New Testament is packaged with the title *Walking With Jesus New Testament* (2002), is such a title appropriate? The New Testament is comprised of twenty-seven Spirit-inspired books, not just the four Gospels. In the same way, is it good missiology to advocate an approach that tends to diminish the absolute uniqueness of Christ as the Son of God?

Again we call attention to ongoing discussion about the necessity of "taking risks" in missions. We should think this "incarnation" risk through carefully. During Kenneth Scott Latourette's "great century of missions" (Latourette 1944) and Ralph Winter's "unbelievable years" (Winter 1970), most conservative missionaries were committed to obeying Christ's final command in much the same way as did the apostle Paul even when the cost of doing so was considerable. Others chose Christ as their model and "walked in his steps" but interpreted Christ and his ministry in ways that seemed to fit their own predilections and paradigms, much as we are being urged to do today. Either way one looks at the mission of the church, risks are involved. Let each be persuaded in his or her own mind as to which of these risks is worth taking.

Epilogue

Missionary Hanson did what he could to make it clear that, though he *represented* Jesus Christ, *he himself was not "Mr. Jesus Christ."* Change came slowly, but it did come—probably abetted by the ease with which Japanese can pronounce the name *Hanson*. But almost from the beginning, Hanson started an early morning Bible study that met daily from Monday through Friday. Though new to Takatsuki and relatively new to Japan, Hanson and his students benefited from his grasp of the language and his knowledge of Scripture. Over the next few years, a goodly number of Japanese came to know who Jesus really is. A thriving church was planted that has had an impact on the larger community for God for over a half century. Hanson's ministries were varied, but looking back at the Christian leaders who came out of those early morning Bible studies, Hanson says, "I have little doubt that that simple Bible study was the most effective thing I ever did during my years in Japan."

References

Allen, Roland. 1962. *Missionary Methods: St. Paul's or Ours?* Grand Rapids: Eerdmans.

Baker, Ken. 2002. "The Incarnational Model: Perception or Deception?" *The Evangelical Missions Quarterly* 37.1 (January): 15–24.

Blauw, Johannes. 1962. *The Missionary Nature of the Church: A Survey of the Biblical Theology of Mission.* New York: McGraw-Hill.

Bonk, Jonathan. 1991. *Missions and Money: Affluence as a Western Missionary Problem.* Maryknoll, N.Y.: Orbis.

Coleman, Robert E. 1964. *The Master Plan of Evangelism.* Westwood, N.J.: Revell.

———. 1992. *The Great Commission Lifestyle: Conforming Your Life to Kingdom Priorities.* Grand Rapids: Revell.

Gutierrez, Gustavo. 1973. *A Theology of Liberation.* Translated and edited by Caridad Inda and John Eagleson. Maryknoll, N.Y.: Orbis.

———. 1976. "The Hope of Liberation." In *Mission Trends No. 3: Third World Theologies,* edited by Gerald H. Anderson and Thomas F. Stransky. New York: Paulist.

Handy, Robert T. 1991."Social Gospel." In *New Twentieth Century Encyclopedia of Religious Knowledge,* edited by J. D. Douglas. 2d ed. Grand Rapids: Baker.

Hesselgrave, David J. 2000. *Planting Churches Cross-Culturally: North America and Beyond.* 2d ed. Grand Rapids: Baker.

Howell, Don N. Jr. 1998. "Mission in Paul's Epistles: Genesis, Pattern and Dynamics" and "Mission in Paul's Epistles: Theological Bearings." In *Mission in the New Testament: An Evangelical Approach,* edited by William J. Larkin Jr. and Joel F. Williams. Maryknoll, N.Y.: Orbis.

Köstenberger, Andreas. 1998. *The Missions of Jesus and the Disciples According to the Fourth Gospel: With Implications for the Fourth Gospel's Purpose and the Mission of the Contemporary Church.* Grand Rapids: Eerdmans.

Ladd, George Eldon. 1974. *The Presence of the Future: The Eschatology of Biblical Realism.* Grand Rapids: Eerdmans.

Latourette, Kenneth Scott. 1944. *The Great Century in Northern Africa and in Asia,* vol. 6 in *A History of Christianity.* New York: Harper.

Little, Christopher R. 2005. *Mission in the Way of Paul: Biblical Mission for the Church in the Twenty-First Century.* Ph.D. diss., Fuller Theological Seminary.

Rogers, Ron. 2002. "Why Incarnational Missions Enhances Evangelism Effectiveness." *Journal of Evangelism and Mission,* no. 1 (Spring): 43–58.

Stott, John R. W. 1975. *Christian Mission in the Modern World: What the Church Should Be Doing Now.* Downers Grove, Ill.: InterVarsity.

————. 1992. *The Contemporary Christian: Applying God's Word to Today's World.* Downers Grove, Ill.: InterVarsity.

Stuhlmacher, Peter, and Pinchas Lapide. 1984. *Paul: Rabbi and Apostle.* Translated by Lawrence S. Denef. Minneapolis: Augsburg.

Verkuyl, Johannes. 1978. *Contemporary Missiology: An Introduction.* Translated and edited by Dale Cooper. Grand Rapids: Eerdmans.

Walking With Jesus New Testament, Today's New International Version. 2002. Colorado Springs, Colo. Grand Rapids: Zondervan.

Winter, Ralph D. 1970. *The Twenty-Five Unbelievable Years, 1945 to 1969.* Pasadena, Calif.: William Carey Library.

Chapter 6

Power Encounter and Truth Encounter

What Is Essential in Spiritual Warfare?

For Jews demand signs and Greeks seek wisdom, but we preach Christ crucified, a stumbling block to Jews and folly to Gentiles, but to those who are called, both Jews and Greeks, Christ the power of God and the wisdom of God. For the foolishness of God is wiser than men, and the weakness of God is stronger than men.

—1 Corinthians 1:22–25

Prologue

SHORTLY AFTER THE CLOSE OF THE occupation period following World War II, the Japanese exhibited a significant degree of interest in Christianity. However, it was apparent that the American way of presenting a brief, largely uncontextualized gospel message and immediately calling for decisions to "accept Christ" was not resulting in the kind of conversions that would build solid Christian churches.

Many missionaries became frustrated and looked for answers. Missionary conferences and gatherings tended to feature special prayer for a spiritual awakening and revival on the one hand, and an intensive search for the kind of missionary strategy that would result in lasting conversions on the other. All were sincere. Some were almost desperate. A few were so desperate for the salvation of Japan that they determined to leave their respective homes and missions and come together in Toyama in central Japan. There they would devote themselves to prayer on behalf of Japan and its people until God would see fit to work mightily through them and other Christians in such a way as to bring salvation to that spiritually dark and needy land.

From the birth of the church and the beginnings of its mission, God's power has been displayed and his truth disclosed through Holy Spirit–filled believers. In the first century, the mission progressed and the church grew by virtue of both miraculous works and the ministry of the Word. We know something of that story, though not as much as we would like. We know even less of the spread of Christianity in the second and third centuries, but we do know that the church continued to grow in the eastern part of the Roman Empire and beyond. And we know that much of that growth occurred as a pagan world was confronted by missionaries armed with Holy Spirit–inspired truth and Holy Spirit–generated power.

A History of Power and Truth Encounters

The Acts Record

The bold outline of the establishment and expansion of the early church is well known. The church expanded from Jerusalem to Caesarea to Antioch to Troas to Macedonia and to Rome. The main feature of that expansion was, of course, the clash between God and Satan. That clash could be seen in encounters between true and false prophets, between church representatives and state authorities, and between divine and demonic spiritual powers.

There were two primary dimensions to those struggles. One had to do with *power and authority*. The other had to do with *truth and rightness*.

These two dimensions were intimately interrelated, both existentially and revelationally. For example, in Jerusalem at Pentecost the miraculous gift of glossolalia made it possible for all to hear the Word of God in their own language (Acts 2:6). Stephen's witness was twofold. He "did great wonders and signs among the people," and in the disputations that followed the people "could not withstand the wisdom and the Spirit with which he was speaking" (6:8–10). Paul "reasoned in the synagogue (in Corinth) every Sabbath, and tried to persuade Jews and Greeks" (18:4). Apollos "powerfully refuted" certain Corinthians (v. 28). When Paul moved on to Ephesus, he spent three months "reasoning and persuading" Jews in the synagogue (19:8) and a whole two years in the hall of Tyrannus "reasoning daily" with all who would listen (vv. 9–10). Right after that, we are told that God did such "extraordinary miracles by the hands of Paul" that some "itinerant Jewish exorcists" and "seven sons of a Jewish high priest named Sceva" invoked the name of Jesus and attempted to exert the same kind of power over evil spirits (vv. 11–15).

Truth encounters and power encounters mark the record of first-century church and mission.

The Early Centuries

After the first century, somewhat less attention was given to the church's mission to the Jews. The larger preoccupation was with pagans and paganism. The writings that make up the New Testament were translated into Syriac, Coptic, Gothic, and Latin so that they could be circulated among the churches. The gospel became available to a wide variety of peoples of the Near East, northern Africa, the Roman Empire, and beyond. Like the Jews of the first century, pagan peoples took offense at a religion that was so revolutionary, so demanding, and so uncompromising. Simple witness and sophisticated apologetic were closely allied. The church fathers attacked the failures and foibles of pagan religions on the one hand and defended the truth of the gospel on the other. In so doing, they played an important role in the mission of the church.

Something of the nature of those encounters is revealed in the third-century apologetic critique of the anti-Christian writer Celsus (d. ca. 180) by Origen (ca. 185–ca. 254). In his *True Discourse*, Celsus charged that Christians downgraded reason and required that people believe without examining the evidence, and they taught nothing of ethics that had not already been taught by the philosophers. Celsus complained that after the Resurrection, Jesus appeared only to believers and in secret. He said Christians were so simple-minded that they actually believed Jesus when he said that the kingdom of God was for the child, the poor, and the sinner. Origen refuted Celsus' charges in an able apologetic work, *Against Celsus.* Origen employed revelation but especially philosophy and logic to counter Celsus and build a compelling case for Christianity.

Christian apologists of the early centuries were well trained in Greek philosophy and rhetoric, well acquainted with the Scriptures, and personally transformed by the Holy Spirit. Origen, Irenaeus (late second century), Justin Martyr (ca. 100–165), Tertullian (ca. 160–ca. 220), Augustine (354–430), and others proved to be equal to every pagan challenge. They were resilient and resourceful souls. They were not carbon copies of one another either in doctrine and substance or in approach and strategy. Origen's teachings proved to be a significant mixture of Christianity and Platonism, but sometimes heretical. Irenaeus's *Against Heresies* proved equally significant and a more reliable statement of Christian beliefs.

Justin Martyr took the position that reason and faith are compatible. Tertullian's formula was *credo quia absurdum* ("I believe what is absurd"). Augustine's formula was *credo ut intellegam* ("I believe in order to understand"). Augustine concluded that all truth is God's truth and on that basis used much of what he had learned in "pagan" schools for kingdom purposes.

Although the record of the early centuries contains accounts of victories won through what we would call "power encounter," it was "truth encounter," in the tradition of the apostle Paul, that really came into its own with the church fathers. Nevertheless, even in their works, truth encounter did not stand alone, nor was it characterized by uniformity. It was reinforced by the powerful witness of transformed lives.

Two stories emanating from that early period in the history of church and missions are relevant and enlightening in this regard. One has to do with Origen and Gregory of Pontus (ca. 213–ca. 270), also called "Thaumaturgus" or "Worker of Wonders" (not to be confused with Gregory the Illuminator [ca. 257–ca. 337], who is credited with the Christianization of Armenia). Born and raised as a pagan in a prominent family, Gregory of Pontus went to Palestine in search of a fitting education. It was there that he came into contact with Origen, who was then a professor of philosophy at Neocaesarea (Caesarea on the Orontes). Through his study with Origen, Gregory became a Christian. Eventually he was appointed bishop of Neocaesarea. It became legend within the church that there were only seventeen Christians in Neocaesarea when Gregory became bishop and only seventeen pagans when he died some thirty years later.

The other story has to do with the brilliant Augustine. A hot-tempered but deeply introspective young man, Augustine was almost overwhelmed in his struggle with evil. One day he found his solitary way to a quiet nook in a garden. Thinking himself to be alone, he took note when a child's voice drifted from the other side of the garden wall. The voice of a child said, "Take and read." In front of him he found a copy of the book of Romans. Opening it, his eye fell on chapter 13: "not in rioting and drunkenness . . . but put ye on the Lord Jesus Christ, and make not provision for the flesh, to fulfil the lusts thereof" (KJV).

The child may have said the words as part of a game, but Augustine was arrested by the Word of God and was soon baptized by Ambrose (ca. 340–397). He established a monastic and missionary community and become bishop of Hippo in North Africa. He was one of the most brilliant proponents of Christianity in history. His autobiographical *Confessions* and his apologetic for the church, *The City of God,* are two of the most influential Christian books of all time.

After five centuries, the faith of a few obscure followers of Jesus had become the faith of much of the Roman world. Christianity had spread eastward to Central Asia and probably India and Ceylon and westward as far as Ireland. Among the reasons for this phenomenal growth, Kenneth Scott Latourette offers one as all-important:

> The motives which led non-Christians to embrace the faith were many and varied. We hear of an entire family, headed by the grandfather, who became Christian because they knew of a case of demon possession which was cured by invoking the name of Christ. In the fifth century in one section of Gaul numbers of pagans were converted because, when a plague attacked the herds,

the cattle of the Christians escaped or recovered and this was attributed to the use of the sign of the cross. One son of pagan parents in Gaul, who later became a distinguished bishop, was led to the Christian faith by struggling with the question: "What is the purpose of my life?" We are told of a fourth century Roman scholar and teacher of distinction who after prolonged and careful study asked for baptism. . . . Whence came these qualities which won for Christianity its astounding victory? Careful and honest investigation can give but one answer, Jesus. . . . It was through the sign of his cross or by the use of his name that miracles were wrought. It was true insight, even if exercised in derision, which named the members of the new faith Christians and in the city where non-Jews were won in large numbers. Without Jesus Christianity would never have been and from him came the distinctive qualities which won it the victory. (Latourette 1953, 105, 107–8)

Illustrations from the Middle Ages

With respect to the next thousand years, three giants of faith figure prominently in the "encounter history." First, Boniface (680–754), whose given name was Winfrith, was a famous English missionary to Holland and Germany who became known for his aggressive attacks on the very centers of paganism. He did not hesitate to physically dismantle pagan idols as a prelude to establishing churches and monasteries. He is best known for chopping down a sacred oak tree at Geismar that had been dedicated to the thunder god. After the thunder god did not retaliate against this act of vandalism, Boniface claimed the victory of Christ.

Thomas Aquinas (ca. 1224–1274), the Italian theologian and philosopher, was educated by the Benedictines but later joined the Dominicans. He was first influenced by Augustine but came to interact largely with the works of classical Greek philosophers—especially Aristotle. Instead of Augustine's "I believe in order to understand" credo, Thomas said, "I understand in order to believe." Among many writings are his *Summa Contra Gentiles, Summa Theologica,* and *Questiones Disputatae.* Most of his writings are thoroughgoing discussions on God's truth, power, and the nature of evil. Aquinas put much confidence in human intellect and the ability to employ reason to bring people to the truth. He used logical argumentation to defend the existence and nature of God and the reality of life after death. His idea was that, if he could bring them far enough by reason, people would soon be convinced of the truths of revelation. Aquinas had a profound effect on missionary thinking, especially until the time of John Calvin (1509–1564), who took issue with the idea that fallen people possessed the ability to reason their way to God. Nevertheless, Aquinas remains a powerful contributor to the discussion of evangelism and mission in the church.

Following his remarkable conversion, Ramon Lull (ca. 1235–1315) of Majorca spent almost a decade studying Arabic and other subjects at the University of Palma prior to teaching at the University of Paris. While at Palma he honed his debating skills by disputations with all sorts of unbelievers but especially with Jews and Muslims. He also began writing prolifically in the conviction that, if his arguments were sufficiently cogent, his opponents would be forced to relent and believe. He founded a missionary college on the island of Majorca and then, in 1292 undertook the first of his missionary journeys to Tunisia and Bugia, a city on the Mediterranean coast of Algeria.

Lull opposed the Crusades as a means of converting Muslims. He practiced what he preached and the ministry for which he had prepared. His arguments for the truth of the gospel resulted in the salvation of as many as five hundred persons, most from influential families. His arguments were also forceful enough to stimulate resistance and animosity in spite of his patience with friend and foe alike. Like the aggressive and power-oriented Boniface, the contemplative and reason-oriented Lull was killed by an angry mob.

Power Encounter in Contemporary Missiology

The lives of such missionary-evangelists provide a frame of reference for evaluating the encounter issues that are currently being discussed. Such theologians as Jack Deere and such missiologists as C. Peter Wagner have approached spiritual warfare in a grand way. Novelists such as Frank Peretti and ministry professionals such as John Wimber have been concerned with evil spirits and deliverance. More recently, missiologist and strategist Ralph Winter has proposed that Christians take up the challenge of researching and combating evil at the level of what we might call "microbe warfare" by taking a leading role in research designed to cure and eradicate killer diseases, including HIV (Winter 2000).

Others have tended to avoid the warfare approach in the conviction that the warfare metaphor itself is self-defeating. For example, taking a cue from James R. Moore, who attempted to show the negative effects of the war metaphor on post-Darwinian evolution controversies, some years ago Harvie Conn had already become extremely cautious at this point. While allowing that a metaphor such as "power encounter" has a certain limited value, he feared that it might foster polarization and antagonism. Accordingly, he devoted scant mention to it in his *Eternal Word and Changing Worlds* (Conn 1984, 49ff.).

Over the years Conn's fear has proved to have some validity. During the decade of the 1990s especially, questions and practices connected with spiritual warfare became most divisive among evangelicals especially. More recently, militant Islam and the "war on terror" have occasioned a debate on the advisability of using warlike metaphors in Christian discussions having to do with either missions or politics.

But whatever the terms used to describe it, Christians are engaged in a spiritual struggle. C. S. Lewis said,

> Enemy-occupied territory—that is what this world is. Christianity is the story of how the rightful king has landed, you might say landed in disguise, and is calling us all to take part in a great campaign of sabotage. . . . I know someone will ask me, "Do you really mean, at this time of day, to re-introduce our old friend the devil—hoofs and horns and all?" Well, what the time of day has to do with it I do not know. And I am not particular about the hoofs and horns. But in other respects my answer is "Yes, I do." I do not claim to know about his personal appearance. If anybody really wants to know him better I would say to that person, "Don't worry. If you really want to, you will. Whether you'll like it when you do is another question." (Lewis 1952, 36)

Alan Tippett on Power Encounter

We've glanced at some power encounters that took place through the centuries of the Christian era from apostolic times to the Reformation. The late Australian anthropologist-missiologist Alan Tippett was closely associated with power encounter. Tippett's approach closely paralleled that of Boniface. He wrote that "the Scriptures leave us with a clear picture of a battle being fought, of a conflict of powers, with a verdict of victory or defeat for mansoul" (Tippett 1969, 88).

The term *power encounter* itself appears in both Tippett's *Verdict Theology in Missionary Theory* (1969) and *People Movements in Southern Polynesia* (1971). In the latter he developed the thought that Polynesians "knew that power (mana) to save had to come from outside themselves. . . . But the superiority of that salvation had to be proved by practical demonstration. Somewhere there had to be an actual power encounter between Christ and the old god" (Tippett 1971, 160). Well-versed in the progress of Christian missions in the South Pacific, Tippett observed that most advances in that area took place when significant numbers of people converted to Christ as the result of a demonstration that the Christian God is more powerful than the local deities. With demonstrations of God's power, vis-à-vis pagan deities and evil spirits as recorded in Scripture and informed by both history and his background in anthropology, Tippett advocated a power encounter strategy, particularly where pagan gods and spirits elicit fear. He said, "At the level of actual conversion from paganism . . . no matter how many elements may be woven into the conversion complex in communal society, the group action . . . must fix itself in encounter at some material locus of power at some specific point in time. . . . Where such demonstrations occur churches begin to grow" (Tippett 1971, 169).

The Evolution of the Power Encounter Concept

Tippett and Donald McGavran could hardly have been expected to foresee the heightened emphasis soon to be placed on power encounter by their younger Fuller colleagues, Wagner and Charles Kraft (along with an influential advocate and friend of theirs, John Wimber). A new course, "Signs, Wonders and Church Growth," taught by Wagner and Wimber, was introduced into the curriculum of Fuller Seminary in the mid-1980s (but quickly dropped in 1986). At first, their understanding of power encounter retained much of its earlier meaning. A "power encounter" was a "a visible, practical demonstration that Jesus Christ is more powerful than the false gods or spirits worshipped or feared by the members of a given society or people group" (Otis 1999, 253; Wimber 1992, 29).

But gradually the term *power encounter* took on a much broader meaning and significance. That broader meaning was reflected in early definitions of the kind adopted by Neil Anderson, Timothy Warner, Opal Reddin, and others. Anderson is architect of the Freedom in Christ movement (Anderson 1990) and Warner has been one of its advocates. Power encounter here has to do with "spiritual warfare," especially as it pertains to victorious Christian living. Reddin's definition makes this clear:

> Power encounter is the demonstration by God's servants of God's "incomparably great power for us who believe" (Ephesians 1:19) based on the cross (Colossians 2:15) and the ministry of the Holy Spirit (Acts 1:8) in confrontation with and victory over the work of Satan and demons (Luke 10:19) in their attacks on God's children or their control of unbelievers resulting in the glory of God and in the salvation of the lost and/or the upbuilding of believers. (Reddin 1989, 4–5)

Clearly this understanding is more expansive than that of Gregory, Boniface, and Tippett (and even the Wimber definition). Traditionally, *power encounter* tended to be characterized by at least five distinctives. First, it had to do with cross-cultural missions, especially in a tribal context. Second, it amounted to an open confrontation between the divine and the demonic for the benefit of the unreached. Third, there was a certain precedence for power displays and less stress on "reasoned" presentations of the Christian faith. Fourth, missionaries intentionally planned for such encounters instead of waiting for increased openness to the gospel. Fifth, power encounter involved appropriate cultural components that increased the impact of encounters.

As power encounter thinking and strategy developed, however, it became more comprehensive. Finally it was described as synonymous with spiritual warfare itself—an aspect of all Christian life, work, and witness. Reinforced by Pentecostal theology and practice, this newer power encounter/spiritual warfare thinking came to be a significant feature of much evangelical missiology by the close of the twentieth century. In fact, evangelicals who believe "signs and wonders" to be essential for effective ministry came to be categorized as "third wave Pentecostals."

Third wave-type power encounter usually goes beyond demonstrating the power of the true God in the context of false gods. To engage in Christian ministry itself is to engage in spiritual warfare, and power encounter is an inherent part of it. Included are such supernatural phenomena as healing the sick, speaking in tongues, interpreting tongues, exorcising demons and territorial spirits, neutralizing poisonous bites, overcoming Satanic attacks of various kinds, and even raising the dead. Related practices include concerted prayer and fasting, the laying on of hands, anointing with oil, the use of special handkerchiefs and other objects, slayings in the Spirit, spiritual mapping, and prayer walking.

Examples of small- and large-scale power encounters are legion, but perhaps one of the most revealing was the 1999 Celebration Ephesus gathering orchestrated by C. Peter Wagner. Wagner's motive for holding the celebration was his desire to confront the "Queen of Heaven" worshiped in Abraham's hometown Ur of the Chaldees (mentioned in Jeremiah 7:16–18) and known in New Testament times as the goddess Diana. "Spiritual mapping" had revealed that, under Satan, this "Queen of Heaven" has numerous strongholds and that one of the principal ones is near Ephesus in Turkey. She is responsible for blinding the eyes of untold millions and keeping them in spiritual darkness.

This called for spiritual warfare prayer. So for a year before the 1999 celebration, Wagner led a group of intercessors in prayer at the Global Harvest Ministries' World Prayer Center in Colorado Springs, Colorado. Celebration Ephesus featured a large choir, an orchestra, "Levitical trumpeters," shofars, and dancers. It is reported to have attracted some five thousand people from sixty-two countries (Guthrie 2000, 77).

After Celebration Ephesus, the vice president of Global Harvest Ministries, Chuck Pierce, reported, "You could actually hear by the Spirit of the Lord an unlocking in the nations of the earth for his planned, future Harvest" (Pierce 2000, 2). All of this is in accord with Wagner's power encounter approach and his theology that "prayer should be spontaneous, frequent, aggressive, loud, expressive, and emotional" (Kennedy 2003, 37).

Spiritual Warfare and Power Encounter in Missions

Proponents draw upon various data to support power encounter's validity and importance to ministry in general and missionary ministry in particular.

First, power encounter squares with anthropological understandings and existential experience. Missionaries from the West sometimes tend to overlook the importance of spirits, demons, ghosts, and related rituals and artifacts that play a vital part in the daily life of a vast number of the world's peoples. But the West's blind spot—Paul Hiebert's "excluded middle"—does not change reality. The fact that in the West there is little overt interaction between physical and spiritual realities does not change the milieu in non-Western societies. People in these cultures often take it for granted that there is a "middle zone," a place where physical and spiritual forces and entities converge. In these societies, folk religion, shamans, witch doctors, priests, and medicine men must be taken into account. Incantations and prayers, potions and phylacteries, and amulets and talismans are important to the manipulation of various powers (Hiebert 1999). At one level or another, perceived or not, power encounters will occur when presenting Christ to such societies.

Second, power encounter squares with the biblical record and biblical theology. Old Testament history, accounts of Jesus' ministry, the Acts record, and epistles all refer to supernatural interventions and displays of spiritual power. Moreover, such interventions were and are to be expected. Jesus promised that believers would do "greater works" (John 14:12) and that they would "receive power" (Acts 1:8). He said that in his name they would cast out demons, speak in new tongues, pick up serpents and drink deadly poison without being harmed, and heal the sick by laying on hands (Mark 16:17–18).

In the days immediately following Pentecost, signs and wonders were *"regularly* done" by the apostles (Acts 5:12), and others. "Spiritual gifts," including demonstrations of spiritual power, were given by the Spirit to ordinary believers in the early church (1 Cor. 12:1–31). These gifts were to be "earnestly desired" (1 Cor. 14:1) and exercised in times of need (James 5:13–18).

Third, it is impossible to ignore the recent explosion in power encounter thinking and practice. If the case for power encounter draws on evidence from the Bible and Bible times, its explosion in popularity in recent years has a more recent historical context. The foundation was laid by the rise of an eschatology-driven triumphalist missiological theology at the end of the nineteenth century (Nevius 1968) and the related rise of the Pentecostal movement in the early twentieth century. More recently its impetus was fueled by the works of theologians Merrill Unger and John Warwick Montgomery, novelist Peretti, revivalist Vinson Synan, and others.

Growth of the movement warrants use of the word *explosion.* An unprecedented number of books and articles relating to power encounter have appeared—most of them in the decade of the 1990s (see, for example, Van Rheenen 1991; Stayne 1995; and Moreau 1997). The *Evangelical Dictionary of World Missions* (Moreau 2000) features lengthy articles on "Power Ministries," the "Theology of Power," and "The Powers," in addition to an article on "Power Encounter" itself.

Throughout the 1990s, the subject was featured in a number of evangelical enclaves and conversations and occasioned considerable controversy. For example, a paper by Robert Priest, Bradford Mullen, and Thomas Campbell on spiritual warfare and power encounter was read at the annual conference of the Evangelical Missiological Society (E.M.S.) in 1994 and was to have been included in a future volume of the E.M.S. publication series (as promised in Rommen and Netland 1995). However, the paper occasioned so much discussion that an entire volume of the publication series was given over to the subject. The volume was entitled *Spiritual Power and Missions: Raising the Issues* (Rommen 1995). Publication of that volume raised such reaction that E.M.S. leaders selected the topic "Mission and the Holy Spirit" as the theme for the 1996 annual conference (McConnell 1997). During that conference, noted Assembly of God historian Gary McGee expressed hope that discussions among practitioners and scholars would enable "evangelical Christians of all persuasions to grow in mutual understanding, work together for the advancement of the kingdom of God, and realize greater unity in the body of Christ" (McGee 1997, 94).

Some Central Issues Related to Power and Power Encounter

McGee's hope has been realized only to a very limited degree. Numerous disagreements on spiritual warfare and power encounter have emerged in discussions on missions and ministry practice in recent years.

Traditionally the major point of divergence between Pentecostals and non-Pentecostals has been in their respective responses to the theological question: Were signs and wonders and the more "spectacular" gifts of the Spirit (such as healing and tongues) to cease with the passing of the apostles, or were they meant to continue? Pentecostals have believed that, along with power for Christian witness and living, these special powers were intended to be part and parcel of Christian mission and practice until the return of Christ (Mark 16:15–18). Cessationists have maintained that both the need and divine provision for displays of supernatural power ceased with the completion of the New Testament (1 Cor. 13:8–10; Heb. 2:3–4).

Controversies as basic as this are seldom neat and tidy. James Montgomery Boice argues strenuously that Wimber's "power evangelism" is invalid in that it is based on narrative events, rather than "didactic and teaching events": "The bottom line . . . is that 'signs and wonders' are not to be sought for today and that it is a mistake to understand such phenomena, whether truly miraculous or not, as biblical 'signs'" (Boice 1993, 1187).

Often, theological and hermeneutical questions revolve around such topics as the canonicity of the longer ending of Mark's Gospel, uniqueness of the miracles of Jesus and his apostles, the nature of Bible passages linking specific objects or actions with demonstrations of power, and the absence of "territorial spirits" in the New Testament record.

Nor is the debate only theological. Two of the chief voices, Robert Priest and Kraft, are anthropologists. Priest's position is clearly stated in an essay written with Thomas Campbell and Bradford Mullen, "Missiological Syncretism: The New Animistic Paradigm." Their argument is that power encounter/spiritual warfare theory represents a radical "paradigm shift" from a biblical worldview to the worldview of animism, tribalism, folk religion, and magic. According to the animistic worldview, spirit power operates on the principles of contiguity/contagion and similarity/ imitation. Priest maintains that, like animists, power encounter proponents assume a vulnerability to demons through (1) contact with physical objects, (2) curses, (3) genealogical transmission, and (4) geographical location. He argues that both the doctrines and strategies that flow from this worldview reorientation have negative consequences and cannot be justified, either logically or scripturally (Priest, Campbell and Mullen, 1995, 9–87).

Kraft counters that opponents of signs and wonders are incorrect in defining the pro-spiritual warfare view as "animistic" and "magical." He says that "their definitions of these concepts in no way apply to the clear statements I and most of the rest of us who were attacked have made concerning what we believe and practice" (Kraft 1995, 88). Kraft admits that he and his colleagues may have been "sloppy at times" in their choice of illustrations. They may seem to have implied that feelings alone establish the presence and influence of demonic spirits. On occasion, they may have been overenthusiastic about their discoveries. But he develops a number of grounds for his position (Kraft 1995, 88–136).

One of Kraft's arguments is that the Great Commission has *two* parts—"a 'proclaim' part and a 'heal' part (Luke 9:2)." Proponents of spiritual warfare theology believe they are interpreting both the missionary task and the Bible accurately at this two-fold "new and deeper level" (Kraft 1995, 94). Second, although warfare advocates believe that we can learn from animists to open our eyes to areas where Western culture and rationalism have blinded us, they do not believe that the worldview of animism and magic represents the real worldview of the Bible.

A third point made by Kraft is that hermeneutics is a subcategory of worldview. As the worldview of power encounter/spiritual warfare proponents changes to become more reflective of biblical realities, it can be anticipated that there will be differences in the ways in which they will interpret and understand certain Bible passages. Where this is the case, it is incumbent upon fellow believers to try to understand each other and consider the text together.

Kraft is correct that the biblical hermeneutic of some warfare advocates has changed. Whether it should have changed is another question. His suggestion that believers on both sides of the issue study the biblical text together is well taken and, I would think, unchallenged. In fact, were parties on both sides of this and similar controversies to examine the biblical text in the company of fellow believers *before* publishing and promoting their ideas among the general Christian public, much good might result. As it is, very few—including spiritual warfare advocates themselves—have taken the time and exercised the patience required in in-depth Bible study. Failure to do so is at least in part responsible for exchanges that are characterized more by passion than insight.

Truth Encounter in Contemporary Missiology

Even though truth encounter has not occasioned as much controversy as has power encounter in recent conversations among evangelicals, the matter of effectively communicating Christian truth and bringing adherents of false religions or no religion to embrace that truth always remains high on their missiological agenda (Moreau 2000, 23–80).

First, as we noted in chapter 2 (pp. 66–69), the New Testament draws attention to the "truth of the gospel" by repeated use, not only of the

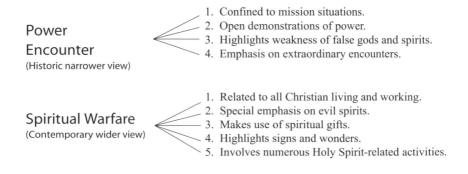

Power Encounter
(Historic narrower view)

1. Confined to mission situations.
2. Open demonstrations of power.
3. Highlights weakness of false gods and spirits.
4. Emphasis on extraordinary encounters.

Spiritual Warfare
(Contemporary wider view)

1. Related to all Christian living and working.
2. Special emphasis on evil spirits.
3. Makes use of spiritual gifts.
4. Highlights signs and wonders.
5. Involves numerous Holy Spirit-related activities.

Figure 6. Power Strategies in Missions

terms *alētheia* ("truth") and *euangelion* ("gospel"), but also of such related terms as *entolē* ("command"), *logos* ("word"), *didachē* ("teaching"), *kerygma* ("proclamation"), and *rhēma* ("word or message").

Second, activities enjoined upon missionaries necessarily entail a truth encounter. These activities include *mathēteuō* ("be a disciple"), *symbibazō* ("prove"), *parakaleō* ("admonish"), *peithō* ("persuade"), and *epistrephō* ("convert").

Third, the Bible insists that Jesus Christ alone is the way, the truth, and the life (John 14:6) so there is no other way of salvation (Acts 4:12). In a climate of relativism, pluralism, and tolerance this missionary claim to the absolute uniqueness of Christ and the gospel in itself constitutes a challenge to all other religions and philosophies. In the engagement that can be expected to ensue, respect, courtesy, cordiality, contrition, kindness are all in order, but absolutes must not be compromised. It follows that truth encounter is inevitable.

John Hermann Bavinck on Truth Encounter

In some respects, modern missions is a replay of what went on in early centuries; in other respects it is not. After the Reformation, Bible translation, production, and distribution came to play an increasingly important role, with the emergence of the Bible Society movement and missions committed to translating and distributing Scripture. Obviously, these activities are intrinsic to any consideration of truth encounter, but so are all endeavors in communicating the gospel cross-culturally.

The prominent Dutch missiologist John Hermann Bavinck devoted the lion's share of his book *An Introduction to the Science of Missions* to communication of the gospel. He does not hesitate to think of communication approaches as "encounters" (Bavinck 1960, 121). In fact, Bavinck does not even deal with what today's missiologists call "power encounter" when he considers missions in the Acts and post-Acts periods. Rather, he emphasizes the person and work of the Holy Spirit in the mission of the church, especially as the Spirit enables apprehension of truth in the Word of God.

Bavinck is persuaded that some apologists, most notably Thomas Aquinas (1225–1274), relied altogether too heavily on philosophy and the operation of human wisdom. While Reformers broke with that approach in principle, some Protestant missiologists, such as Gijsbert Voetius (1588–1676) and Abraham Kuyper (1837–1920), made the same error in stressing philosophy, dialectic, and psychology in the encounter with unbelief. Voetius in particular believed that the proper missionary method is to use reason and "natural light" to refute heathenism and its errors. Bavinck himself believes that reason can be an "opening wedge" where the Bible is not known or recognized. However, the primary missionary appeal must be made to the truth of the revelation of God as found in Scripture (Bavinck 1960, 224–26).

We have introduced Bavinck, but we will return to discuss his elenctic approach (pp. 189–93). At this point, it is sufficient to note that his approach relies heavily on the Holy Spirit, but it emphasizes truth encounter rather than power encounter. And though he does not deny that reason and argument have their place in the truth encounter, Bavinck is of the opinion that the strongest approach "would restrict itself to the direct proclamation of the message of the Bible" (Bavinck 1960, 141).

The Proclamation of the Biblical Message

A mind-boggling variety of approaches to "discipling the nations" has been advocated during the era of modern missions. Some propose that we start with a consideration of the nature and attributes of God; others prefer to begin by introducing Christ and his work. Some propose that we begin by teaching the great themes of Scripture—God, man, sin, Christ, salvation, Christian living, for example—while others settle for some simple formula such as "six things God wants you to know" or the "four spiritual laws." Some begin by introducing people to the "great drama" that unfolds in Scripture from Genesis to Revelation, while others confine themselves to one or another of the Gospels, usually Mark or John. Some make extensive or even exclusive use of the *Jesus Film*; others prefer simple diagrams and charts contrasting the "way of life" with the "way of death." Some tout the virtues of dialogue; others restrict themselves to one-way communication. Some are dedicated to the techniques of mass evangelism, while others expound the virtues of one-on-one personal evangelism. Some target children, since "that is the time when most Christians come to Christ," while others note that, in most cultures, parents must first be won to Christ if childhood conversions are to be meaningful.

With these and other contributions to the discussion, missionary communication becomes anything but the simple enterprise it is often considered to be.

It is certainly easiest to view these various approaches as complementary rather than competing. The problem with that is that some approaches are inherently superior to others. Further, certain approaches cancel out other approaches. I have been most impressed by the way in which, over the last half century, more and more missions and missionaries have come to recognize the importance of "storying the gospel." I also find strength in a chronological Bible study that follows the progress of biblical revelation from creation in Genesis to Christ in the Gospels, and from the church in Acts and the Epistles to the consummation in the Apocalypse. The New Tribes Mission, for example, progressed from a superficial "John 3:16" missionizing approach to a carefully constructed "chronological Bible study" approach to truth encounter within the scope of one generation from the 1940s to the 1970s (McIlwain 1991). My conviction is that gospel communication of the chronological and narrative kinds proposed by such missiologists as McIlwain, Hans-Reudi Weber, Tom Steffen, and John and James Slack is crucial to effective gospel communication (see Hesselgrave 1991, 104–19; 1994, 87–119).

Why so? As suggested above, the chronological-narrative approach most closely follows both the divine message and the method as God the Holy Spirit gave them to us in sacred Scripture. Also, this approach tells the larger story of Jesus clearly while, at the same time, contrasting it with the false fabrications of Satan. Nevertheless, there is a point at which the complexities of cross-cultural communication become overwhelming. At that point, *both* the truth and power of the Holy Spirit must come together in our encounter with the world and its god. Only then will Satan be routed and men and women redeemed.

As occasionally happens among those in ministry, Methodist missionary Marvin Wolford was not truly converted to Christ until he was already serving as a missionary in what was then the Belgian Congo. After his conversion, Wolford became convinced that the establishment of a spiritual church on the mission field is impossible apart from a thoroughgoing knowledge of the Scriptures. Wolford and his wife Jean started the Kafakumba Pastors' School. Then in 1966, along with some Congolese pastors, they began the first translation of the Old Testament and a retranslation of the New Testament into the Uruund language.

During the course of that translation project and in connection with his doctoral studies at Trinity Evangelical Divinity School, Wolford undertook an in-depth examination of sorcery—the number-one problem of many churches in Sub-Saharan Africa. Building on his intimate knowledge of the Uruund language and his acquaintance with scores of African pastors in and outside of Congo, Wolford was enabled by the Holy Spirit to write one of the most thorough analyses of sorcery and its remedies ever prepared. Written with and for African pastors, it is aptly titled *Free Indeed From Sorcery Bondage: A Proven Scriptural Ministry* (Wolford 1999). Wolford's study draws upon both the *truth* and *power* of God to enable ministry to those caught in sorcery belief systems. In doing so, he furnishes a pattern that all should emulate.

Holy Spirit, Believing Disciples, and an Unbelieving World

During the days and hours just before his Passion, the Lord Jesus prepared his disciples for impending events, providing them with essential information and necessary instructions. Matthew focuses on what Christ the coming King will do when he returns to earth to gather his own and inaugurate his kingdom. In his encounter with the forces of evil it will be "no contest." His sword will be unsheathed and he will prevail. In response to the prayers of God's people, Christ's kingdom will indeed be established on earth.

The Setting of John 13–17

On that last evening before His passion, Jesus and his disciples traveled from Bethany to a prepared upper room to eat the paschal meal together. They are nearing Christ's "hour," but only he knows the urgency and importance of what he is about to say and do. The message communicated at that meeting was absolutely critical to the ministry of the apostles in the first century. These words are just as critical to the twenty-first century.

Words That Speak Volumes

The emphasis of Jesus in John 13–17 is upon "another Paraclete" (*paraklētos,* "helper; advocate") whom the Lord Jesus would ask the Father to send after his ascension into heaven (John 14:16). In the encounter with the world, flesh, and Devil, much depended upon Christ's disciples. But in the ultimate sense, nothing depended on them. Everything depended on the one who stood by them, lived in them, and spoke and worked through them. By virtue of the coming of the Holy Spirit, God's purpose would be accomplished.

With the promise of "power" *(dynamis)* in Acts 1:8 and the accompanying signs and wonders of the Acts period in mind, one might think that Jesus would dwell on the power theme here. Such is not the case, however. The word *dynamis* does not appear anywhere in John 13–17. Rather, John quotes Jesus as using the same word he uses in Matthew 28:18, *exousia,* which is best translated "authority," and with reference to his own authority (John 17:2), not the authority of the Spirit. The words *tera* ("wonder; omen") and *semeion* ("miracle; sign; token") do not appear at all in this context.

The noun and verb forms of *agapē* (love) occur some fifteen times in the John 13–17 context, while *phileō* occurs once. One might gather that, from the perspective of "John the beloved disciple" at least, the Holy Spirit was given to enable disciples to "love the world" even as God loved the world when he sent his Son (John 3:16). A more careful reading of the text, however, reveals that another meaning is in view. The reference in these chapters is to Christ's love for believers, believers' love for Christ, believers' love for one another, and the kind of love that prompts someone to lay down his or her life for a friend. It is the kind of love that God uses to convince the world that the Son was sent from the Father (17:21).

Finally, a constellation of words used here revolve around the ideas of "truth" and "revealed truth." Related words appear some twenty-five times in these five chapters. The word *alētheia* ("truth") itself occurs nine times, *logos* eight times, *rhēma* ("word" in the sense of proclamation) four times, and *graphē* ("scriptures, writings") and *martyreō* ("witness") once each. In fact, the Holy Spirit is called the "Spirit of truth" no less than three times (John 14:17; 15:26; 16:13). *In sending the Holy Spirit into the world, the Lord Jesus was preparing the way and equipping the apostles for truth encounter.*

The Holy Spirit in the World

Jesus said that it was to the advantage of the disciples that he go and send the Spirit (John 16:7). At first that might seem unthinkable. But when we consider what the Spirit would do in the world, it all becomes clear.

First, the Spirit would call to the remembrance of the apostles what Christ had taught (John 14:25–26). After his resurrection, Jesus commanded the apostles to disciple the nations by "teaching them to observe all that I have commanded you" (Matt. 28:20). It was the "Spirit of truth" who made it possible for the disciples to remember Christ's commands and teachings and then inspired them to record his teaching in such a way that that all believers would have an authoritative Bible.

Second, the Holy Spirit would witness concerning the Lord Jesus and enable Jesus' disciples to be His witnesses (John 15:26–27). As is generally known, the word for "witness" is *martyreō,* from which we derive the English word *martyr.* At first blush, it would seem simple for both those original disciples and Christians today to testify concerning their faith in Christ and what he has done for them. As important as that was and is, however, more is involved. The significance of the witness of the apostles was that they personally had been with the Lord Jesus. The significance of their witness and ours is that, as apostles, it may entail suffering. In any and all cases, the effectiveness of human witness for Christ is dependent upon the accompanying witness of the Holy Spirit.

Third, the Holy Spirit would convict the world of sin, righteousness, and judgment (John 16:7–11). We often read these words too hurriedly. This convicting and convincing work of the Holy Spirit is so important that it is a distinct area of theology—*elenctics.* Since these verses are so often neglected and because they relate so intimately to elenctics, we return to them shortly.

Fourth, Jesus prays that the Spirit will keep and unify the believers of that day—and all who will believe through their witness through history (John 17:15–23). Much has been made of Jesus' petition "that they may all be one . . . so that the world may believe that you have sent me" and the *kind* of unity for which Jesus prayed (v. 21). Roman Catholics stress *ecclesiastical unity* in the one, authoritative Holy Catholic Church. Conciliar ecumenists emphasize *organizational unity* as in the World Council of Churches. Evangelicals underscore the invisible *organic unity* of all true believers.

All of these interpretations may miss the mark.

According to the full text of John 17, Jesus prayed with at least four aspects of Christian unity in mind. First, Christians are to be sanctified, separated, and distinct from the world, even while being in the world. Second, they are to be sanctified in and through truth, God's Word constituting that truth. Third, their unity is to be a visible expression of the perfect unity that exists between Father and Son. Fourth, their unity inherently bears witness to the fact that God has sent his Son into the world.

It seems to me that the kind of unity for which Christ prayed and which impresses the world is neither the ecclesiastical or organizational types that can be seen nor the organic kind that cannot be seen. Rather, it is a unity based on the truth of God's Word, characterized by separation from a world antagonistic to the true God, and demonstrated when the members of believing churches love and serve one another and reach out in loving service to their neighbors.

Elenctics and the Encounter with the World

The term *elenctics* is not really familiar to most Christians, but the theology (or "science" as Bavinck calls it) of elenctics is pertinent to any consideration of the Christian encounter with the world. Foundational to an understanding of elenctics is a correct reading of the Greek words *elengchō* and *kosmos*.

According to Bavinck, in Homer, *elengchō* meant "bring to shame." In later Attic Greek it meant "bring to guilt." In the New Testament it means "rebuke; convict; convince" with reference to both believers and unbelievers. Its meaning is entirely religious and ethical (Bavinck 1960, 221–22). It occurs only once in John's upper room chapters, but that use in 16:8 is of critical importance if we are to understand the nature of our encounter with the world.

Kosmos ("world") is a very familiar word in the writings of the apostle John. One of the chapters in which it occurs most often is John 16. In that chapter alone it appears some forty times. *Kosmos* is derived from *kosmeō* ("arrange; order; adorn") and predominantly refers to earth as contrasted with heaven. By extension its meaning usually takes in the current *world order* and/or the *world's peoples*. It is used in both of these latter senses in John 14–17, but when John writes that the Holy Spirit will "convict the *kosmos*" (16:8) he obviously means that the Spirit will convict the *world's peoples*. This direct ministry of the Holy Spirit to the peoples of the world is of special interest because Jesus is almost exclusively occupied with the Holy Spirit's ministry to believers in these chapters. Moreover, in his high priestly prayer in John 17, Jesus specifically says that he is *not* praying for the *kosmos* or world, but only for his disciples and those who will later "believe . . . through their word" (v. 20).

Elenctics in Anthropological Perspective: Conscience as Ally

Taking up the elenctic idea from Bavinck, Robert Priest writes, "We as Christians must directly confront and formally recognize that calling people to a new understanding of self as sinner is indeed part of our task" (Priest, Campbell, and Mullen 1995, 292). The article goes on to say that we have an important ally in this difficult task—the human conscience. Building on the truth of Romans 2:14–15 ("Gentiles . . . show that the work of the law is written on their hearts, while their conscience also bears witness") and writing as an anthropologist, Priest shows how this is so. He explains that the dictates of conscience differ, depending on whether the conscience is informed by the missionary's culture, the respondent's culture, or Scripture's teaching.

Nevertheless, there will be areas of overlap. Understandably, unbelievers of other cultures cannot be convicted of sin on the basis that they have not lived up to standards of the missionary's culture, which is foreign to them, or the Bible, which they do not know. But they are guilty, insofar as they have transgressed standards of their own conscience; their conscience has been informed to some extent by the truth of the Creator God.

Elenctics in Philosophical Perspective: Reason as Ally

Ancient apologists and modern theorists such as Voetius and Kuyper notwithstanding, Bavinck is at best ambivalent about the role of reason in confronting "heathendom." He says that "the 'coming to the light' is never yielding to philosophical argumentation, it is rather becoming convinced of the sin hidden behind unbelief, the sin of fleeing from God" (Bavinck 1960, 226).

Nevertheless, Bavinck takes note of the fact that, in their "elenctic attack on idolatry," the prophets of the Old Testament sometimes used reason. Isaiah 44, for instance, sarcastically reviews the process whereby idolaters take one part of a tree to make firewood for burning and another part of the same tree to make a carved image for worship. Idolatry is foolishness, and it is worthwhile to point that out. Though philosophical argumentation has limitations and even dangers, and although it cannot be the bridge to repentance and faith, it can be an ally in bringing people to consider their need for the gospel (Bavinck 1960, 226–30). We already have seen that Carl F. H. Henry agrees with this (p. 108).

Elenctics in Theological Perspective: Revelation as Foundation

The basis of elenctics is nothing more or less than the proclamation of God's revelation in Jesus Christ and a firm trust in the Holy Spirit "who alone is empowered to *elengchein*" (Bavinck 1960, 231). Bavinck goes on to say that, in his view, elenctics comes down to that part of the church's mission that has to do with our approach to the world and, even more specifically, to a specific aspect of that approach: namely, "our direct attack upon non-Christian religiosity in order to call a man to repentance" (Bavinck 1960, 233).

Bavinck devotes some forty pages to a discussion of various aspects of that "direct attack" before he returns to John 16:8–11, and even then much remains to be said. In 16:8–11 Jesus makes it clear that the Holy

Spirit has a vital role in persuading, convincing, and convicting the world of sin, righteousness, and judgment—not just in a general sense but in specifics.

First, the sin Jesus speaks of is the sin of unbelief in Jesus himself. Just about the last thing that the world is prepared to accept is that it is sin not to believe in Jesus. In fact, apart from the work of the Holy Spirit, it is impossible for unbelievers to accept the idea that they *must* believe. We might convince them that they are guilty of other sins, but the Holy Spirit alone can convince them that unbelief in Jesus is sin.

Second, the righteousness he is speaking of is the righteousness of Jesus. Again, to persuade men and women that they need Christ's righteousness is all but impossible. Unbelievers around the world invariably compare themselves to their neighbors and convince themselves that, although imperfect, they are "good enough." In fact, in all of history only one small group of people has had a "perfect Neighbor." No wonder that, compared with him, they did not stack up very well. No wonder they wanted to throw him over a cliff. Who could have convinced them of their need for, and the availability of, the righteousness of Jesus? Who alone can convince people today of that need? Only the Holy Spirit that Jesus sent into the world.

Third, the judgment Jesus is speaking of is the judgment of sin that occurred when he as the Christ of God triumphed over sin and Satan on the cross and in the tomb. The world seems to believe that evil is securely and everlastingly enthroned. Two North American expressions convey this idea: "This is a dog-eat-dog world" and "Good people finish last." In India the expression is "Big fish-eat-little fish world." To be successful, it is understood that one will live by the world's standard. But God says that the *real* world is not that way. Satan is a defeated foe. Christ is Victor. We may not be able to convince the world of that truth, but the Holy Spirit can and does.

That Christ has authority and the Holy Spirit does convict the world of sin are the central points of elenctics. Whether they are aware of it, missiologists are in debt to Bavinck for developing this insight. Bavinck drew our attention to this aspect of ecclesiology and missiology. The principles of elenctics open more pointedly what Scripture says about the place of the Spirit in our encounter with the world. Here we are shown the power of truth in spiritual warfare.

Encounter Addenda

Power and truth encounters are the most significant, but at least four other encounter proposals deserve mention, and to those we now turn.

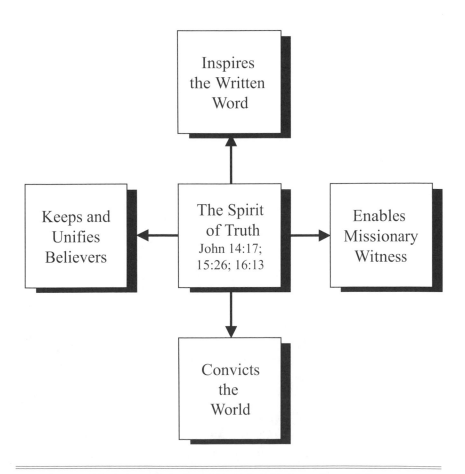

Figure 7. Missionary Ministries of the Holy Spirit According to John 13–17

The Allegiance Encounter

Allegiance encounter involves "the exercise of the will in commitment and obedience to the Lord" (Kraft 1999, 410). Kraft writes, "Jesus fought Satan on a broader front than simply power encounters. If we are to be biblically fair and balanced, we must give two other encounters equal attention—allegiance encounters and truth encounters" (Kraft 1999, 409). In Kraft's view,

- The concern in *power encounter* is for freedom, and the vehicle is spiritual warfare.
- The concern in *truth encounter* is for understanding, and the vehicle is teaching.
- The concern in *allegiance encounter* is for relationship, and the vehicle is witness (Kraft 1999, 409).

The initial allegiance encounter leads to a relationship with God, and successive encounters lead to increased intimacy with God and likeness to the Lord Jesus. Clearly, these are desirable, and even essential, aims of the whole of Christian ministry, whether or not one agrees with Kraft's particular trifurcation.

The Empirical Encounter

Few references to Hiebert's *empirical encounter* can be found in missionary literature. But his excluded middle thesis upon which this theory is based (see p. 178) is both tremendously significant and common grist for missiological mills. It has been published, reviewed, and acclaimed in a great variety of contexts (Hiebert 1999, 414–21).

Hiebert says that the dualistic, two-tiered view of reality characteristic of the Western world grows out of changes dating to the seventeenth and eighteenth centuries. Belief in middle-level supernatural beings and forces has gradually been eclipsed by a philosophy based on Platonic dualism and a science based on materialism and naturalism. Questions having to do with the everyday world of sensory experience have been relegated to science and natural laws. Those having to do with such otherworldly matters as God, miracles, visions, and inner feelings have been relegated to religion.

Among tribalists and animists, however, issues having to do with ancestors, evil spirits, demons, witches, and local gods are neither remote otherworldly concerns nor secular scientific and mechanistic ones. Rather, they are part and parcel of the everyday world and experience. Western-thinking missionaries who are unaware of this middle-tier or unable to interact with people about it are at a great disadvantage in these cultures.

That is where the empirical encounter comes into play. Truth encounter deals with "the ultimate story of the origin, purpose, and destiny of the self, society and the universe." Power encounter has to do with "the uncertainties of the future, the crises of the present, and the unexplainable events of the past." But empirical encounter deals with middle-level concerns having to do with "the nature and order of humans and their relationships, and of the natural world" (Hiebert 1999, 419). At this middle level (not the religious or the science level) tribals seek answers to practical questions: "Which of these seeds will grow?" "How can we make sure this marriage will last?" "Why has my brother suddenly become ill?" Once a tribal learns about Christianity, the daily life questions are the same: "How does the Christian God tell us where to hunt?"

All too often, tribals can get answers to these questions from the local medicine man but not from the foreign missionary. Until the missionary has a worldview theology that can respond to such questions, the result will likely be syncretism or rejection.

The Prayer Encounter

We have seen that prayer is given an important role by those who seek spiritual warfare power encounters (pp. 177–78). Of course, all Christians recognize the importance and power of prayer whether of intercession, adoration, worship, thanksgiving, confession, or repentance. If there is anything new in the current emphasis on *prayer encounter,* it is this linkage to *spiritual warfare* (as that term is understood by those who speak of power encounters). Evangelicals agree that prayer always has a central role in reaching peoples, church renewal, and spiritual awakening, but they divide on some of the practical applications and aims of prayer.

For example, World Vision International's John Robb writes, "Christians have been divided for years over the most effective means of transforming our world. Is it through verbal proclamation of the gospel or with social action? In truth, the two cannot be separated. Without both, there simply is no good news. One thing ties them together—prayer" (Robb 1999, 145). In a few short sentences, Robb makes prayer out to be the agent that inseparably links gospel proclamation and social action.

Both propositions sound good, but both call for careful analysis. We have dealt with the relationship between gospel proclamation and social action in chapter 4. There we said that the relation between them is primarily a matter of Bible interpretation, not of prayer as such.

But what about prayer as the agent that makes the gospel good news and world transformation?

Certainly, *every* aspect of Christian life and witness needs to be conceived in, and carried forward by, prayer. Prayer is an indispensable part of both life and witness. So Robb's admonition certainly has merit, and it does express a widely held conviction. But it also goes beyond traditional evangelical ideas of the nature and mission of prayer. As Stan Guthrie says, "While in earlier mission eras prayer was seen primarily as a way to communicate one's needs to God, as a way to join God in his saving purposes for the world, and as a proving ground for one's faith, today prayer is often viewed as a tool to 'bind' demonic 'strongholds' holding people, cities, and nations in spiritual bondage" (Guthrie 2000, 76).

Some of us read Guthrie's words with nostalgic appreciation for an earlier day when missionary prayers were somewhat more simple, although, we believe, not less availing. No doubt Satan increases his activities as the time becomes shorter. But we do well to listen to Gailyn Van Rheenen that "Prayer should not be viewed as a power tool but as relating to God, the source of all power" (Van Rheenen 2003; cf. Moreau 1997, 161).

The Love Encounter

To speak of a *love encounter* in the "encounter" context may seem a bit strange. As we have seen, Christ's prayer for his followers in John

17 focuses on love for God and one another as believers, not on love for the world (see p. 187). Nevertheless, love for both God and neighbor is essential to all being and doing *as Christians,* so it goes without saying that love is important in missionary operations.

As in the case of prayer, love is often related to special strategies such as incarnational ministry, missionary identification, the servant role, winning a hearing, bridging, and bonding. But love, like prayer, should characterize *all* missionary encounters with the world. It should not be distinct from any of them. Bavinck says as much in relation to his kerygmatic truth encounter:

> Meeting-in-love includes the recognition of myself in the other person, a sympathetic feeling of his guilt and a sincere desire in Christ to do with this man what Christ has done with me. . . . I cannot really look another person in the eye without being reminded of the darkness out of which Christ has called me. In the proper approach there is always an awareness of being on the same level with a person and there is a real consciousness of our common guilt in the eyes of God. It is this which gives the approach a warm undertone. (Bavinck 1960, 127)

Even love, however, must be understood in the light of revealed truth, not in terms of human understanding. For example, the same John who records the words and prayer of Jesus we have considered in this chapter also authors three letters in which he emphasizes love. In addressing the "beloved Gaius" he adds "whom I love in truth" (3 John 1). In fact, in this short letter to Gaius he uses the word *truth* five times and the word *love* only twice. We might say that the letter is about "truth love" or "love in truth."

Note the ways in which that kind of love is expressed. It is expressed in (1) prayer for Gaius's physical and spiritual health, (2) joy over brothers who are walking in truth, (3) support for those spreading the gospel, (4) a severe denunciation of Diotrephes, (5) commendation of Demetrius, and (6) warm greetings to and from Christian friends.

Truth and love, love and truth. In the economy of God it is hard to see how one can exist without the other.

Conclusion

Knowing how little we really know and feeling how weak we really are, we are obliged to accept whatever the God of all truth and power has to say about encounters with the world, as on every other subject. All claims to truth and power emanating from any source must be measured by the truth of God's Word. The truth of God takes first priority in the personal struggle with the world, flesh, and Satan or in any encounter with the world system of which Satan is god.

I am encouraged that even advocates of power and other types of encounter often agree with me at this point. For example, Kraft, with whom I sometimes entertain serious but brotherly disagreements, writes:

> Truth encounters in which the mind is exercised and the will is challenged seem to provide the context within which the other encounters take place and can be interpreted. . . . When we focus on knowledge and truth, we enable people to gain enough understanding to be able to accurately interpret the other two encounters [allegiance and power]. For example, a power demonstration has little, or wrong, significance unless it is related to truth. (Kraft 1999, 410–11).

Timothy Warner, a student of encounter in missions (see Warner 1991), once remarked in conversation with me about the relationship between power encounter and truth encounter, "The longer I live, the more I am persuaded that, as important as power encounter is, truth encounter is even more so." I believe that the apostle Paul would agree. At the same time, he could be expected to add, "To those who are called, both Jews and Greeks, Christ the power of God and the wisdom of God" (1 Cor. 1:24).

Epilogue

Fifty years ago, some of my missionary colleagues in Japan pulled up stakes where they were working and moved to Toyama. There they spent their time concentrating on prayer that God would send a mighty revival to Japan. Other than that desire, I do not know their thinking related to power encounter. I do know that one missionary who possessed outstanding communication skill and unusual facility in the Japanese language left his station and joined the group in Toyama. He decided to pray and wait for divine assurance that when he started to preach once again, large numbers of Japanese would respond to his message. Failing to receive assurance, he soon left the field, as did most of his Toyama colleagues.

What are we to conclude? Probably no more than that God is all-wise, all-powerful, and sovereign. We ourselves are limited, not only in our knowledge and strength, but also in prayer and proclamation. Sometimes there is but a short distance between faith and presumption. While we have not yet witnessed a sweeping revival in Japan, missionaries who faithfully preached the gospel there have been privileged to see many of God's choicest saints come to Christ in that land.

References

Anderson, Neil T. 1990. *Winning Spiritual Warfare: Steps to Freedom in Christ.* Eugene, Ore.: Harvest House.

Bavinck, J. H. 1960. *An Introduction to the Science of Missions.* Translated by David Hugh Freeman. Philadelphia: Presbyterian & Reformed.

Boice, James Montgomery. 1993. *Romans.* Vol. 3, *God and History: Romans 9–11.* Grand Rapids: Baker.

Conn, Harvie. 1984. *Eternal Word and Changing Worlds.* Maryknoll, N.Y.: Orbis.

Guthrie, Stan. 2000. *Missions in the Third Millennium: 21 Key Trends for the Twenty-first Century.* Waynesboro, Ga.: Paternoster.

Hesselgrave, David J. 1991. *Communicating Christ Cross-culturally: An Introduction to Missionary Communication.* Grand Rapids: Academie.

———. 1994. *Scripture and Strategy: The Use of the Bible in Postmodern Church and Mission.* Pasadena, Calif.: William Carey Library.

Hiebert, Paul G. 1999. "The Flaw of the Excluded Middle." In *Perspectives on the World Christian Movement: A Reader,* edited by Ralph D. Winter and Steven C. Hawthorne. 3d ed. Pasadena, Calif.: William Carey Library.

Kennedy, John W. 2003. "Prayer Warriors." *Christianity Today* 47.5 (May): 37.

Kraft, Charles H. 1995. "'Christian Animism' or God-Given Authority?" In *Spiritual Power and Missions: Raising the Issues,* edited by Edward Rommen. Pasadena, Calif.: William Carey Library.

————. 1999. "Three Encounters in Christian Witness." In *Perspectives on the World Christian Movement: A Reader,* edited by Ralph D. Winter and Steven C. Hawthorne. 3d ed. Pasadena, Calif.: William Carey Library.

Latourette, Kenneth Scott. 1953. *A History of Christianity.* New York: Harper.

Lewis, C. S. 1952. *Mere Christianity.* New York: Macmillan.

McConnell, C. Douglas, ed. 1997. *The Holy Spirit and Mission Dynamics.* Pasadena, Calif.: William Carey Library.

McGee, Gary B. 1997. "The Radical Strategy in Modern Mission: The Linkage of Paranormal Phenomena with Evangelism." In *The Holy Spirit and Mission Dynamics,* edited by C. Douglas McConnell. Pasadena, Calif.: William Carey Library.

McIlwain, Trevor. 1991. *Notes on the Chronological Approach to Evangelism and Church Planting.* Sanford, Fla.: New Tribes Mission.

Moreau, A. Scott. 1997. *Essentials of Spiritual Warfare: Equipped to Win the Battle.* Wheaton, Ill.: Harold Shaw.

Moreau, A. Scott, gen. ed. 2000. *Evangelical Dictionary of World Missions.* Grand Rapids: Baker.

Nevius, John L. 1968. *Demon Possession.* Reprint, Grand Rapids: Kregel.

Otis, George, Jr. 1999. *Informed Intercession.* Ventura, Calif.: Gospel Light.

Pierce, Chuck. 2000. "Transferring Wealth from the Queen's Domain." *Global Prayer News,* Winter, 2.

Priest, Robert J., Thomas Campbell, and Bradford A. Mullen, 1995. "Missiological Syncretism: The New Animistic Paradigm." In *Spiritual Power and Missions: Raising the Issues.* Edited by Edward Rommen. Pasadena, Calif.: William Carey Library.

Reddin, Opal, ed. 1989. *Power Encounter: A Pentecostal Perspective.* Springfield, Mo.: Central Bible College.

Robb, John D. 1999. "Strategic Prayer." In *Perspectives on the World Christian Movement: A Reader,* edited by Ralph D. Winter and Steven C. Hawthorne. 3d ed. Pasadena, Calif.: William Carey Library.

Rommen, Edward and Harold Netland, eds. 1995. *Christianity and the Religions: A Biblical Theology of World Religions.* Evangelical Missiological Society publication series, no. 2. Pasadena, Calif.: William Carey Library.

Rommen, Edward, ed. 1995. *Spiritual Power and Missions: Raising the Issues.* Pasadena, Calif.: William Carey Library.

Steyne, Philip. 1995. *Gods of Power: A Study of the Beliefs and Practices of Animists.* Houston, Tex.: Torch.

Tippett, Alan. 1969. *Verdict Theology in Missionary Theory.* Lincoln, Ill.: Lincoln Christian College Press.

———. 1971. *People Movements in Southern Polynesia: A Study in Church Growth.* Chicago: Moody.

Van Rheenen, Gailyn. 1991. *Communicating Christ in Animistic Contexts.* Grand Rapids: Baker.

———. 2003. "A Theology of Power." *Monthly Missiological Reflections,* no. 28. www.missiology.org.

Warner, Timothy. 1991. *Spiritual Warfare: Victory over the Powers of This Dark World.* Wheaton, Ill.: Crossway.

Wimber, John. 1992. *Power Evangelism.* Revised ed. New York: Harper and Row.

Winter, Ralph D. 2000. "Theologizing the Microbiological World: Implications for Missions." Pasadena, Calif.: U.S. Center for World Mission.

Wolford, Marvin S. 1999. *Free Indeed From Sorcery Bondage: A Proven Scriptural Ministry.* Cleveland, Tenn.: Pathway.

Chapter 7

Amateurization and Professionalization

A Call for Missionaries or a Divine Calling?

You ascended on high, leading a host of captives in your train and receiving gifts among men.

—Psalm 68:18

And he gave the apostles, the prophets, the evangelists, the pastors and teachers, to equip the saints for the work of ministry, for building up the body of Christ.

—Ephesians 4:11–12

Prologue

SOME TEN YEARS OR SO AGO, the missions-minded First Evangelical Free Church in St. Louis, Missouri, decided to "jump-start" a church-planting movement in Tatarstan, Russia. Their strategy was both simple and bold. They would send missionary teams on two-week missions trips to assist a national church planter by witnessing and presenting the gospel in a variety of ways. Over time, converts would be organized into small groups for fellowship and Bible study. Out of these groups, one church, or perhaps several, would be organized.

Over a two-year period, the church sent more than one hundred short-termers (mostly laypersons) to Tatarstan with disappointing results.

Providentially, a seminary missions student from another church by the name of Carl Brown was in Tatarstan on a two-month assignment at the time. Aware of the arrangement and its lack of progress, he informed his seminary mentors of the situation. Meanwhile, back in St. Louis, Christians made two decisions. First, they decided to pray that the Lord would raise up a church-planting career missionary with whom they could work. Second, they decided to suspend the short-term program in Russia until the Lord supplied such a missionary.

All of us know the difference between an "amateur" and a "professional." But do we understand the meaning conveyed by "amateurization" and "professionalization"? And what are we talking about regarding "amateurization and professionalization *in missions*"?

The Amateurization and Re-amateurization of Missions

As far as I know, Ralph Winter was the first to use the term *amateurization* (or *re-amateurization*) in connection with Christian missions. In a 1996 editorial in *Missions Frontiers Bulletin* titled "The Gravest Danger: The Re-Amateurization of Mission" (Winter 1996a, 5), he recounted how great numbers of students volunteered for foreign missions toward the end of the nineteenth century.

The Student Volunteer Movement was borne on a wave of enthusiasm and commitment. However, in their enthusiasm, the volunteers tended to ignore the insights of earlier missions workers. They made serious mistakes that resulted in many unnecessary deaths among the missionaries and a demoralization and spiritual decline among national pastors. Their amateurism set missions back instead of propelling the work forward. It took missions educators and institutions forty years to relearn the lessons that had been so quickly forgotten.

Surveying missions today, Winter notes that popular interest in missions is at an ebb, so "we mission professionals are inclined to accept 'interest'—warts and all." The short-term phenomenon has had little careful scrutiny. Missions, he concludes, "has become any Christian volunteering to be sent anywhere in the world at any expense to do anything for any time period." His question is, "Is this re-amateurization?"

In a followup article, Winter elaborated on one primary concern (Winter 1996b, 6). He says that contemporary missions candidates tend to be steered in one of two directions. First they go overprepared, or second, they go with little preparation at all. Either situation places them and their ministries at a decided disadvantage.

The first situation comes because of a tendency in American education to assume that, if a little education is a good thing, more education must be better. Long ago, American colleges normally took students at about thirteen years of age, educated them for four years, and graduated them at seventeen or so. That was the program until the nineteenth century. Today, many candidates ministries have had sixteen to twenty years of education, with a residue of financial indebtedness to pay off before they can leave for the field. The result is that missionaries arrive on the field with minds too old to master either the language or the culture (see Bonk 1990, 138).

In the second situation, to avoid educational expense and time, many missionary candidates forego college and seminary (including the study of missiology). They arrive on the field young enough to learn the language and culture but without the educational tools needed to learn these subjects efficiently or well. Undereducated missionaries lack the broader knowledge and experience needed to work effectively.

Both scenarios tend toward the same result, the *re-amateurization* of the missionary enterprise. Work too often is carried on by missionaries who lack what they need to be effective, either because they have invested too much of their lives in education or too little. Winter's solution, which is echoed by many leading missiologists, is to encourage earlier candidacy (perhaps even before the end of college) and earlier training in language and other needed tools. Deficiencies would have to be met through continuing educational opportunities after candidates are on the field (Ward 1987, 404).

John Piper on the Professionalization of the Ministry

I have coined the word *professionalization* to help explain some important thoughts by a great friend of missions, John Piper (Piper 2002). Piper writes for pastors, but his points apply equally to missionaries.

In the very first paragraph of his book, he says,

> We pastors are being killed by the professionalizing of the pastoral ministry. The mentality of the professional is not the mentality of the prophet. It is not the mentality of the slave of Christ. Professionalism has nothing to do with the essence and heart of the Christian ministry. The more professional we long to be, the more spiritual death we will leave in our wake." (Piper 2002, 1)

At first glance, it would seem that Piper is making a case against professionalization while Winter is making a case for it. Actually, they are on somewhat different wavelengths but make corollary points. Piper's concern is not totally unlike that of Winter. With the increase in education required for ministry, Piper is concerned about the desire among pastors for "parity among the world's professionals." Such a desire "kills a man's belief that he is sent by God to save people from hell and to make them Christ-exalting, spiritual aliens in the world" (Piper 2002, 3).

Piper's ideas are as foundational to missionary service as to pastoral service—perhaps even more so. For example,

> I think God has exhibited us preachers as last of all in the world. We are fools for Christ's sake, but professionals are wise. We are weak, but professionals are strong. Professionals are held in honor; we are in disrepute. We do not try to secure a professional lifestyle, but we are ready to hunger and thirst and be ill clad and homeless. When reviled, we bless; when persecuted, we endure; when slandered, we try to conciliate; we have become the refuse of the world, the offscouring of all things (1 Cor. 4:9–13). Or have we? (Piper 2002, 2)

So in the context of Piper's book, professionalism primarily has to do with attitude. Professionals tend toward pride and self-promotion, instead of humility and self-abnegation.

Amateurization and Professionalization in Context

Certainly we can agree with both Ralph Winter and John Piper. Winter has put his finger on a serious problem in contemporary missions—one that can make both the undereducated novice *and* the well-educated graduate amateurish when it comes to thinking and doing missions. Piper has identified a serious problem in both pastoral *and* missionary ministries—one that can drain both pastor and missionary of those qualities that impact people and bring praise to God.

My perspective here is something of an expansion of Winter's ideas and a change of direction from Piper's. Basically, I am thinking of missionary service as a divine calling. This is more in line with a book called *Give Up Your Small Ambitions* (Griffiths 1970). It was written by Michael Griffiths, a colleague in Japan who later became president of London Bible College. He begins with a discussion of the "missionary call" and then describes the kind of missionary he believed to be most needed. This desired missionary . . .

> is not just one of those bluff, genial, well-meaning Christian men who is unfortunately unable to speak the language and seems rather clueless, but someone who has served an apprenticeship with the national churches and can communicate effectively, using not only the language, but also the thought patterns of the people. (Griffiths 1970, 121).

I do not mean to imply that Griffiths intends this to be anything like a complete description of an "ideal missionary." His basic concern that the missionary be divinely called, a student and servant of national churches, and an effective communicator of the gospel starts us in a good direction, however.

In this chapter the main distinction between *professionalism* and *amateurism* is our assumption that missions work is a divine calling, rather than a human choice. The responsible, professional missionary honors Scripture rather than resorting to opportunism and "sales appeal."

Here is the dichotomy between amateurism and professionalism as I define those opposite terms:

Amateurism	**Professionalism**
A (human) call for workers	A divine calling
Our mission	God's mission
Individualistic	Interdependent
Inadequate preparation	Adequate preparation
Short-term goals	Long-range goals
Based on "supporter-appeal"	Based on biblical priorities
Inclined to proof-texting	Biblically grounded
Self-acclaimed teachers	Learners, then teachers
Monocultural orientation	Bi-(multi-)cultural orientation
Superficial analysis	Competent analysis

Note that, while formal education makes an obvious difference in moving from amateur to professional status, it is not all-important. A deficient formal training does not automatically make the missionary an amateur anymore than an advanced degree in theology, anthropology, or missiology makes someone a professional in the sense in which we are using the term. Common sense, fruitful experience, and spiritual insight may mean far more than a Ph.D. in intercultural studies. A person of modest education sometimes is more qualified than his or her impeccably credentialed counterpart (Taylor 1991, 5). Rather than try to create more elaborate and precise descriptions, we invite the reader to keep in mind the contrasting characteristics for amateurism and professionalism that we have listed. One can see how the presence or absence of these characteristics can be crucial in both theory and practice.

Beginnings of Protestant Missions

Protestant Missions on the Continent

The seeds of both professionalism and amateurism were planted early in the history of Protestant missions. After the Reformation, Protestants were divided as to whether the Great Commission pertained to the church today or was only for the first-century apostles. On the Continent, Hadrian Saravia (1531–1613) and Justinian von Weltz (1621–1668) were among the first to argue that the church was still obliged to carry out the Great Commission. Over a century later in England, when William Carey (1761–1834) put forth his case for foreign missions at a meeting of Baptists in Northamptonshire, he was immediately rebuffed by Dr. John Ryland, who said, "Young man, sit down. When God pleases to convert the heathen, he will do it without your aid or mine."

Roman Catholic religious orders were not just enclaves of monks who copied musty manuscripts and mumbled pedantic prayers. Dominicans, Franciscans, Augustinians, and, especially, Jesuits were active and effective carriers of the Catholic faith to far-flung peoples and places. Protestants had nothing comparable to these Catholic orders. Moreover, given their theological differences, internecine strife, and the struggle for survival, it is easy to understand why Protestant missions agencies were slow to develop.

The earliest attempt to form a Protestant missions group and send them abroad was made by John Calvin. He sent a small group of missionaries to Brazil in 1555, but their work was anything but a success. The group's leader, Villegagnon, abandoned the colony, the Portuguese ravaged it, and Catholic Jesuits killed the few survivors (Kane 1971, 76).

Over a long period, other missions were formed. The Danish-Halle Mission resulted from the efforts of Philipp Jakob Spener (1635–1705) and August Hermann Francke (1663–1727). Moravian missions were formed by followers of Spener and Francke, who were protected from persecution on the estate of Nicolaus Ludwig, Count von Zinzendorf in 1722 and organized into a mission. "The Particular Baptist Society for Propagating the Gospel among the Heathen" was formed in England in October 1792 when William Carey, Reynold Hogg, and Andrew Fuller convinced a small number of supporters meeting in Fuller's Kettering Chapel to help with the enterprise. Chapel members gave ten pounds initially and ten shillings sixpence annually to support the mission.

Protestants were forced to found both the sending agencies and the training schools. In 1622, the Dutch East India Company established a school in Leyden to train chaplains and missionaries, but it lasted only twelve short years. Justinian von Weltz (1621–1668) helped organize a mission and establish a college in which to train missionary recruits. Failing in both endeavors, he went to Surinam as a missionary himself.

The University of Halle and the Danish-Halle Mission resulted from the efforts of Spener and Francke. Their university became the base for spreading Pietism in Germany, Scandinavia, and Switzerland and also for a mission to Tranquebar in southeast India. That mission was inaugurated by the king of Denmark. When he asked for missionaries to India, Francke recommended two of his students— Bartholomaeus Ziegenbalg (1682–1719) and Heinrich Plutschau (1677–1747).

Protestant missions and missionaries were profoundly different in the strategies they employed. Although Plutschau and Ziegenbalg were young, and the work fraught with serious difficulties, their training stood them in good stead. Ziegenbalg in particular combined his Halle education and Tranquebar experiences to develop missionary principles and strategies that are helpful even today. At the other end of the spectrum, without the benefit of formal training, Moravians adopted the strategy of sending small groups of self-sustaining artisans to some of the most neglected and difficult places and peoples on earth. The Moravians became one of the most self-sacrificial and dedicated missionary forces in the history of the Christian church.

In the Catholic tradition, women were severely limited as to the roles they could play in missions. The role of women in early Protestant missions also was restricted at first, but especially in pietistic theological traditions, change came. Women were destined to make an unprecedented contribution to the mission of the church (Beaver 1968).

It would be naïve to disregard the European roots of the Protestant missionary enterprise if one is to understand missions. We are removed from this history in time and space, but in practices, attitudes, and the native churches begun by Europeans, we are still affected by this heritage.

Protestant Missions in North America

One day in 1802 young Samuel J. Mills sensed a divine call to preach the gospel to the nations while plowing on his Connecticut farm. Determined to be "obedient to the heavenly vision," he entered Williams College some four years later to prepare for Christian ministry. There he met with the Society of the Brethren—like-minded students that included Luther Rice, Gordon Hall, James Richards, and others who regularly met for discussion and prayer.

On the way to one of their prayer sessions, these students were caught in a torrential rainstorm and took refuge in a haystack. There they pledged to give themselves to foreign missions, a decision that made that "haystack prayer meeting" the greatest launching point in the history of Christian missions.

At the new Andover Seminary, which was founded to train ministerial candidates in the theological tradition of Puritanism and Jonathan Edwards, these students were joined by Adoniram Judson, Samuel Newell, and Samuel Nott Jr. Together they formed the Society of Inquiry on the Subject of Missions. On June 28, 1810, Judson, Mills, Nott, and Newell announced their candidacy for foreign missionary service and solicited the advice of the "Reverend Fathers" of the General Association of Congregational Ministers of Massachusetts. Unlike the staunch Calvinistic Baptists in England, the Congregational ministers immediately approved their purpose and recommended the formation of a missions society, the Board of Commissioners for Foreign Missions (BCFM).

The new Board of Commissioners found it relatively easy to begin missions to North American Indians. Foreign missions, however, was another matter. Judson was sent to England to take counsel from the established London Missionary Society (L.M.S.) and perhaps establish an association. But the L.M.S. wisely recommended autonomy, and the BCFM selected Burma as its first missions field.

The first problem was financial. Sufficient monies for the mission from North America did not come in until passage of the first missionaries had been announced. Then enthusiasm for the new venture grew. By the time some of the missionaries were ready to sail in January 1812, their passage and salaries for the first year of service were in hand. Before arriving in Calcutta, however, Judson changed his theological position to that of the Anabaptists. He resigned from the BCFM and offered his services to American Baptists. That resulted in the formation of the American Baptist Foreign Missionary Society. Over the next eighteen years, the Methodist Episcopal, Protestant Episcopal, Presbyterian, and Evangelical

Lutherans organized their own missionary societies. The pattern was set for Protestant missions based in North America.

Professionalism and Historical Analysis

Those with an interest in world missions know about the development of missionary societies. We forget the lessons learned along the way at our peril. Anglican bishop and missions historian Stephen Neill analyzed this history and surveyed the challenges the missionaries faced as they related to other missionaries, to other religions, to nation-states, and to the "younger churches." In his book, *Creative Tension* (1959), Neill contended that the tensions that were encountered and somehow overcome in early missions bequeathed to us a foundation for understanding the present and a hope for the future.

The kinds of tensions we have inherited from our forerunners include:

1. *Theological tensions.* Though questions concerning the applicability of the Great Commission are mostly resolved, Christians still disagree over the nature and necessity of Christ's call.
2. *Organizational tensions.* Protestants always have struggled with tension arising out of "two structures of missions." Some missions are operated under the church and denominational agencies and some under parachurch and "faith" missions (Winter 1981, 178–90). History shows that these parallel structures can and should complement each other. But it also shows that problems sometimes occur that are not easily resolved.
3. *Recruitment tensions.* The appeal to undertake missionary service generally has been decidedly different from appeals to many other forms of Christian service. In most cases, recruitment has been directed at students—many of them very young. Students tend to lack a solid basis for realistically understanding what mission actually entails, so they are least able to make that decision.
4. *Training tensions.* From the beginning, missions were well served by training institutions such as the University of Halle, Williams College, and Andover Seminary. Currently, a number of more

advanced schools of mission compete for enrollees. Issues having to do with undereducation and overeducation, as raised in this chapter, have always been around, however. They may be even more of a problem in the future.

5. *Support tensions.* In the earliest missions from Europe and North America, churches rarely had the ready funds required to train and send missionaries. Most of the time, while some volunteers went to the field, others worked hard and long to accumulate the funds needed for their support. As we will see, support-raising has become a major problem for most missionaries.

6. *Strategy tensions.* From very early on, Protestant missionaries of different groups employed decidedly different methods and strategies. The approach of a trading company chaplain in India, for example, was much different from that used by Moravian missionary-artisans in Greenland. The same is true in missions today—some methods are biblically sound and contextually appropriate; these will meet with significant success. Those that are not biblically sound and appropriate will ultimately fail. Earlier, deeper study would steer us away from the latter.

If preaching the gospel so that peoples of the world can understand its meaning isn't enough of a challenge, these and other kinds of tension are the abiding companions of Protestant missions. Given the ecclesiastical and world circumstances in which they were birthed and in which they have continued, these tensions are not surprising. What is surprising is that anyone would undertake such a demanding enterprise without first looking at previous mistakes and so avoid repeating them.

Biblical and Theological Foundations

The Bible—especially the New Testament, but the Old Testament as well—literally bristles with principles and precedents having to do with the mission of the church. To be sure, one must be careful to interpret the text carefully and to avoid confusing that which is normative with that which is simply descriptive. Nevertheless, apart from Scripture, the work of world outreach becomes immediately directionless and ultimately meaningless.

Two Sides of Grace

A golden thread woven all through the tapestry of biblical missions, indeed all through the Bible, is the concept of grace. The Hebrew word is *ḥēn* and the Greek word, to which we devote special attention here, is *charis*. The cultural thinking behind *charis* is the Greek notion that whenever a statue or picture or drama is good or beautiful, it should naturally evoke an appropriate and appreciative response on the part of the beholder. As used in the New Testament, *charis* refers both to the favor, blessing, and goodness that God extends to undeserving creatures *and also* to the appropriate and thankful response of those who receive grace to the One who gave it.

It is especially important to keep both sides of grace in mind when considering missions (Spicq 1994, 503–6). According to the apostle Paul, when God graciously revealed his nature and power to men and women of antiquity, they did not respond by honoring him or giving him thanks. Out of futile minds and foolish hearts, they made idols to take the place of the Creator (Rom. 1:18–27). God's gifts are freely given without regard to merit, but they are to be thankfully received.

This remains true today. When God allows sinners to hear the gospel, their response is commanded. And when Christ gives "gifts" that enable the church to bear that gospel to peoples around the world, the only appropriate response is grateful reception and deployment of the gifts he has given.

Two Kinds of Spiritual Gifts

It is common these days to think in terms of spiritual gifts and to urge Christians to discover and use their gifts. There is a sense in which this is justified. In Romans 12:3–8 and 1 Corinthians 14:1–19, Paul speaks of God's gifts to the church, such as prophecy, exhortation, leadership, tongues, healing, and helps. God gives these gifts so that they might be exercised in accordance with biblical guidelines to strengthen the church.

But another type of gift is given to the church by the ascended Christ— "person gifts," or "gifted persons." Paul identifies these person gifts in Ephesians 4:6–16, explaining why they have been given to the church. Gifted people are called to be apostles (missionaries), evangelists, prophets, pastors, and teachers (or, pastor-teachers). In introducing them, Paul quotes Psalm 68:18: "When he ascended on high he led a host of captives, and he gave gifts to men." The picture is that of a conquering king or general leading captives back to his capital city and giving the spoils of war to citizens. The "gifts" here could be booty, but in terms of the realities of war at the time, Paul likely meant captives to be used as slaves.

Now a larger picture emerges. Jehovah gave priests and Levites to serve Israel. Israel's generals gave captives to certain citizens. Christ himself gives spiritual gifts to individuals and "person gifts" to the church. He conquered the Evil One and took many of his minions captive, people such as the persecutor Saul and the impetuous Peter. He gave them and those who came after them to equip church members for service and build up the church—locally and all around the world.

Two Kinds of Missionaries

The general call for missionary volunteers with which we are familiar in missions is often reinforced by the urgent reminder that "we are all missionaries." This is confusion compounded. In the first place, there is no general call for missionary volunteers in the New Testament. All New Testament missionaries were personally conscripted by Christ, his apostles and their representatives, or by Holy Spirit–directed churches.

In the second place, although all followers of Christ are called to be *witnesses,* it is not true that all are called to be *missionaries*, any more than all are called to be pastors.

This requires some elaboration. The word *missionary* is not ordinarily found in English translations of the New Testament. The English word comes from the Latin word meaning "send" (*mitto*), which, in turn, is a translation of the Greek word for "send," *apostellō*. Actually, two words are used for "send" in the New Testament: *pempō* occurs eighty times and *apostellō* 135 times.

Pempō is the more general verb and refers to the act of sending. *Apostellō* is the more technical term. Originally it may have been used of a ship sent out with a cargo of grain to be delivered to a given port. But by the time the New Testament was written, *apostellō* referred to sending someone with authority to deliver a message or to accomplish some stated mission, much as an ambassador or envoy might be sent to a foreign country.

The New Testament word for "missionary," then, is the noun form of this more technical idea: *apostolos* or "apostle." The critical idea is "sentness." A missionary is not just someone who *goes,* but someone who is *sent.* As sent by the Father, Christ is the "prototype" missionary, the "apostle and high priest of our profession" (Hebrews 3:1). D. A. Carson views the sending out of the Twelve in Matthew 10 as both a preparation and a paradigm for the Great Commission and for missions in general (Carson 1984, 242).

Two kinds of apostles or missionaries are found in the New Testament record. First, some "ear- and eye-witnesses" of Christ were personally commissioned by him. In this regard, note that Luke began "the Acts of the Apostles" by reminding his readers that in his Gospel he had dealt with "all that Jesus began to do and teach" (Acts 1:1). The "apostles" in this special sense were eyewitnesses of Christ's doings and teachings. Included were the eleven, Matthias, who took the place of Judas (vv. 20–26), Paul by virtue of a special revelation of the Lord (Gal. 1:11–17), and perhaps James the brother of our Lord (v. 19). Theirs was a unique and authoritative office, quite distinct from that of deacon, elder, or bishop.

Second, other apostles were sent out by Holy Spirit-directed churches or leaders (Acts 13:4; 2 Cor. 8:23; Phil. 2:25; 1 Thess. 2:6). Apostles or missionaries in this more general sense included Barnabas, Mark, Silas, Timothy, Titus, and Epaphroditus. Paul was an apostle in this general sense, in addition to being a "special apostle." Apostles/missionaries of this type were sent to preach the gospel and establish churches or assist in this work. They are clearly identified as "apostles" in the passages referred to and as "apostles *of the churches"* in 2 Corinthians 8:23.

References in Acts and Thessalonians have evidently been deemed sufficiently ambiguous by translators to allow the word *apostle* to stand in most English translations. In 2 Corinthians 8:23 and Philippians 2:25, however, translators have almost invariably translated *apostolos* as "messenger" or something similar, rather than as "apostle." Very likely they have done so in order avoid confusing these people with the "special apostles." The more literal translation, "apostle," goes into a margin note. Translators have undoubtedly meant well. However, to translate *apostolos* as "messenger" obscures the fact that New Testament writers speak of "apostles of the churches" as well as "special apostles" personally commissioned by Christ (for further discussion, see Peters 1972, 246–58).

Two Crises in New Testament Missions

After Paul and Barnabas returned from their first missionary journey and reported to the Antioch church, Judaizers came from Jerusalem saying that Gentile believers had to be circumcised. This precipitated a theological controversy that could have undermined the entire mission. Then, after that issue was settled, another controversy arose between Barnabas and Paul regarding strategy. They disagreed about where to go and whether to take John Mark.

So who was right? The Judaizers or the "missionizers"? Barnabas or Paul? These are not trivia questions. The future of the early mission depended on getting correct answers. Notice the responses to these critical questions.

1. *The theological crisis.* The Antioch church sent the missionaries and some elders to consult with the apostles and elders in Jerusalem (Acts 15:1–35). Peter offered an opinion based on his experience with Cornelius and his household (perhaps a partial fulfillment of the Lord's promise in Matt. 16:19 to give him the "keys of the kingdom of heaven"). James confirmed that Peter's experience and the report of the missionaries matched what God was doing among the Gentiles. He declared it to be in accordance with the prophetic Word. All agreed that, with some cautions so

Identified:	Sent by:	Characterized as:	To accomplish:
Jesus Christ	God the Father	"The Apostle and High Priest of our profession" (Heb. 3:1)	Salvation and intercession.
The Twelve (incl. Matthias and Paul)	Christ the Son	"The Apostles" (1 Cor. 15:9) "The Twelve" (Matt. 10:5) "Eyewitnesses of his majesty" (2 Pet. 1:16)	Witness for Christ proclaim the gospel, disciple the nations, found the church, write portions of N.T.
Paul, Barnabas, Silas, John Mark, Timothy, Titus, Epaphroditus, et. al.	Holy Spirit-directed churches and leaders	"The Apostles of the churches:" (2 Cor. 8:23 margin)	Witness for Christ, proclaim the gospel, disciple the nations, plant churches, and help those engaged in these tasks

Figure 8. New Testament Apostles

as not to give unnecessary offense, believing Gentiles and Jews were to be accepted as saved apart from circumcision. The decision was made, and a letter was written and sent to the Antioch church. The missionaries and representatives from the Jerusalem church, including Silas, accompanied the letter to give assurance of its authenticity.

2. *The strategy crisis.* Luke reports that Paul and Barnabas differed sharply, although both were of unimpeachable character and possessed unusual giftedness and like faith and vision (Acts 15:36–41). Attracted by his home area and friends, and disposed to forgive his cousin John Mark for not completing his first term of missionary service, Barnabas insisted that they take Mark and go to Cyprus. Drawn by churches previously planted and determined to have a tried and trustworthy team, Paul insisted that Mark be left behind and that they go through Syria and Cilicia.

Who was right? The text shows that Paul had the better case. First, Luke notes that believers in Antioch once again "commended [Paul and Silas] to the grace of the Lord" and sent them on their way (Acts 15:40). No such mention is made concerning Barnabas and Mark. Second, an important part of Great Commission mission is to strengthen planted churches. This is what Paul had in mind (v. 41). Third, aided by a Spirit-directed "in-course correction" that took Paul west rather than east, Paul's strategy resulted in the evangelization of a broad area of the Roman Empire, and, eventually, in the conversion of much of Europe and the Western world. Fourth, Luke's inspired record follows the missionary journeys and ministries of the apostle Paul. Barnabas all but disappears from the New Testament record after this incident. Fifth, Paul's little team faced intense opposition. Paul had good reason for thinking that John Mark might not hold up under the pressure.

All of this bristles with practical lessons for Western missions, infected as we often are by Enlightenment individualism and modern and postmodern cultures. Against the Judaizers, the apostle Paul could have made a strong case for both his message and mission without "taking time out" to be subject to the Jerusalem Council. And the same Antioch church that had sent Paul and Barnabas out at the prompting of the Holy Spirit could have taken action independent of the apostles in Jerusalem. All concerned could have acted on these strategy and doctrinal issues on the basis of long-time friendships, family ties, and the desire to avoid fuss and muss.

But none did. They acted responsibly, spiritually, and "professionally."

Stan Guthrie highlights twenty-one missions trends evident at the outset of the twenty-first century (Guthrie 2000). One issue he raises is "doctrinal drift," but most of the rest relate to strategy. Seen together, the trends noted by Guthrie present a tremendous challenge. God grant future leaders the ability to respond as ably as did the first missionaries.

Pertinent Cultural Factors

Both missionaries and their respondents are "cultural beings." It is no surprise, then, that cultural studies have played an ever-larger role in post–World War II missionary preparation. In 1953 missiologists initiated the publication of *Practical Anthropology,* a bimonthly publication of excellent articles on cross-cultural understanding and communication. Later, some of the best of those articles were collected and published in two separate and important volumes (Smalley 1967; Smalley 1978).

Practical Anthropology was but the beginning. Over the years, missions scholars have produced more and more titles on all aspects of culture and cross-cultural ministry. In spite of critical treatment at the hands of secular anthropologists, missionaries have been well served by the writings of anthropologists and cross-culturalists, both Christians and unbelievers. Among those who have added important understandings are Clyde and Florence Kluckhohn, Francis L. K. Hsu, Anthony Wallace, Edward Stewart, Kenneth Pike, William Smalley, Allan Tippett, Eugene Nida, Charles Kraft, and Paul Hiebert.

Since cultures constantly change, future missionaries will continue to owe much to these anthropologists. One indication of amateurism is an inability to recognize deeper-level cultural differences. One hallmark of professionalism is the ability to recognize and understand culture traits of both home and host cultures. Critical analysis can help diminish problems and promote kingdom purposes.

Two tasks are imperative. First, as members of a source culture, we must understand ourselves and our own culture as it progresses (or regresses). Second, we must endeavor to understand respondent cultures and peoples to whom we take the message of Christ. Something of what is involved in this latter contextualization task will be dealt with in chapter 8. But it is well here that we briefly examine the ever-present danger of ethnocentrism and "cultural overhang." Americans in particular are notorious for unwittingly exporting cultural ideas and values as they try to communicate Christ cross-culturally. Amateurism feeds on ethnocentrism.

"Generations" in North American Culture

All cultures change over time, but North American culture tends to change particularly rapidly and in significant ways. And with our North American penchant for imposing our cultural traits upon the rest of the world, we Americans often act as though changes at home are, or soon will be, mirrored in most other cultures. In some respects that may be true, but it is this kind of myopic approach that plagues many cross-cultural undertakings, whether political or religious.

We begin here by identifying the successive "generations" of North American culture often cited in the literature.

1. Builders born before 1946
2. Boomers born between 1946 and 1964
3. Busters (Gen-Xers) born between 1965 and 1976
4. Millennials born between 1977 and 1994
5. Babies born after 1994

Many recent writings have attempted to show how American culture traits and values have changed with the emergence of these successive "generations." Our take on this will be clear as we proceed, but it seems that American culture is always changing and never changing. Some characteristics of traditional culture are modified or replaced; others persist and may even be strengthened. This process is particularly difficult to analyze when, as is the case now, new "generations" emerge every few years. We now have a "multigenerational generation" and a "multicultural culture," so to speak. For example, some missiologists now insist that missions must change if the gospel is to appeal to Gen-Xers and Millennials, and those who will come next. Though some changes are certainly in order, it is far more important to satisfy the biblical requirements than to satisfy shifting values and tastes of successive "generations."

Traits of North American Traditional Culture

Drawing upon a wide variety of post–World War II studies, including those of the Human Resources Research Organization, Robert Kohls drew up a list of some of the most often cited traits of North American culture at the end of the 1970s:

1. No belief in fate; instead, personal control of the environment.
2. Change seen as inevitable and desirable.
3. Equality/egalitarianism.
4. Individualism.
5. Self-help concept.
6. Competition and free enterprise.
7. Future orientation.
8. Action orientation.
9. Informality.
10. Directness and openness.
11. Practicality.
12. Materialism.
13. Problem-solving orientation.
14. "Cause-and-effect" logic. (Kohls 1981, 14)

As characteristic as these may have been for the Builder generation, however, the emergence of the Boomers was already promoting essential changes when Kohls drew up his list at the end of the 1970s. In fact, before another decade had passed, Herbert Gans concluded that American culture was in a state of significant change (Gans 1988, 1). Frances Moore Lappe (who had grown up in a strong traditional American family in Texas) agreed. She urged Americans to "rediscover their values" (Lappe 1989, 3–17).

To take one example of the kind of change that Gans (and Lappe) observed, consider one of the more obvious traits of traditional American culture: individualism. Back in 1972, Edward Stewart observed that the North American individual was defined in terms of uniqueness, decisions, and accomplishments (Stewart 1972, 10). In contrast, in most Asian, African, and Latin American cultures, the individual was defined more through social links and reciprocal obligations.

At the end of the 1980s, Gans still believed that one of the most stable elements of North American culture was "the continued pursuit of individualism by virtually all segments of the population" (Gans 1988, 1). At the same time, however, Gans felt obliged to explain that individualism had come to be expressed in new ways. First, individuals avoided involuntary conformity, whether required by family, neighbors or government; second, individuals attempted to "sidestep obligatory membership in institutions and organizations, sacred and secular" (Gans 1988, 1–2).

Missions have desperately needed to understand that particular change. However, a still more challenging change was already looming on the horizon.

From Modern to Postmodern Culture

This more significant change occurred with the coming of age of the Busters in the late 1980s and early 1990s—the transition from modernism to postmodernism. It is impossible to read very widely in contemporary Christian literature having to do with evangelism, missions, church growth, preaching, and worship without encountering the notion that our churches and missions must change, and change radically, if they are to minister effectively to postmoderns (see, for example, Johnston 2001; Stetzer 2003, 105–6; Hexham, Rost, and Morehead 2004).

In theologian Millard Erickson's view, postmodernism came about because of the . . .

1. denial of personal objectivity;
2. uncertainty of knowledge;
3. death of any all-inclusive explanation;
4. denial of the inherent goodness of knowledge;

5. rejection of progress;
6. supremacy of community-based knowledge; and
7. disbelief in objective inquiry (Erickson 1998, 19, as quoted in Stetzer 2003, 120).

Erickson's list is certainly correct, but not necessarily complete.

Disenchantment with Western cultural institutions and values was accompanied if not occasioned by a discovery or rediscovery of Eastern religions and philosophy, first on the part of Boomers. Yoga, Transcendental Meditation, Hare Krishna, astrology, New Ageism—these and other Eastern movements found root and flowered in the United States. The West met the East at a new and deeper level than previously. By the time the Busters and Millennialists had come of age, the turn from both revelation and reason was evident. Both epistemological and moral absolutes were largely abandoned. Sequential, step-by-step, cause-effect reasoning was replaced by the desire and even the expectation of grasping the whole of a subject without such exertions. The human quest became a search for *reality* rather than *truth*. The Intellectual Quotient (I.Q.) was replaced by the Emotional Quotient (E.Q.). Reflection centered on the self. "I *think*; therefore I am" was replaced by "I *feel*; therefore I am." Youths were encouraged to *empathize* rather than to *intellectualize* (Pickles 2000, 37–41). Missions strategists and other church leaders were called upon to adjust their message and methods or become irrelevant.

The Self-Orientation of North American Missions

Of course, many cultural values of the Builders remain more or less intact in America. Traditional or contemporary, modern or postmodern, one persistent trait of North American culture that is inimical to biblical missions continues to be the extreme value placed upon the individual self by non-Christians and Christians alike. Rugged (or ragged) individualism has long been a peculiarly ingrained trait of American culture. But if one were to identify the most influential contributor to evangelical "selfism" in the twentieth century, it probably was Abraham Maslow (1908–1970) and his "motivational pyramid" (Maslow 1970).

First put forward in a symposium at the University of Nebraska in

1950, Maslow's humanistic framework for assessing human need became widely accepted. Often overlooking the limitations of his theory, Christians as well as unbelievers went too far in uncritically employing Maslow's ladder from biological needs to needs for security, belongingness, self-esteem, and self-fulfillment. "Self-actualization" became the key to understanding human motivation. To discover whether one was "called to be a missionary" Christians were challenged to "give missions a try" to find out if one "fit." The question to answer was whether missionary work might be "self-fulfilling." Short-terms fit this mind-set and became a primary recruitment tool. But the effects were far more encompassing.

Now think of cultural changes and the challenges involved in confronting postmodern Busters, Millennialists, and, in time, Babies (i.e., future missionaries). A later dimension of Maslow's thinking now comes to the fore. Maslow presaged postmodernism when, after exhausting the potential of "self-actualization," he like many others turned eastward and took to exploring the potential of "peak experiences" (Hesselgrave 1991, 587–612). Accordingly, churches and missions are urged to contextualize both their message and methods in ways that will register with postmoderns who have subscribed to a new kind of "spirituality" that avoids religious dogma and doctrine in favor of "spiritual experience." Bible teachers are encouraged to appeal to postmoderns who insist that to "know God" one must "experience God" and who delight to hear that a simple prayer receiving Christ will "change your eternity." The message we are to press is that, as a child of God, "you bring pleasure to God like nothing else he has ever created" (Warren 2002, 58, 63).

For postmoderns, "full surrender" to the claims and call of God is more readily understood as a "commitment" in which the individual self retains the right to reevaluate and reconsider priorities and options. Preachers and other church leaders are told that to appeal to postmoderns they must tell stories instead of preach sermons. They must give music that worshippers can "feel," fellowship that is satisfying, and service opportunities that are personally rewarding. Missions that want to deploy postmoderns are told that they must be holistic, incarnational, and more congenial to the formation of "communities of service and witness" around the world than they are to planting churches that exhibit the classical "marks of the church" outlined in Acts 2:42–47.

Contextualization there must be. The questions relate to what kind of contextualizing should be done and how much change is acceptable. Popular pastors of postmodern megachurches invite other pastors to attend their seminars, emulate their methods, and duplicate their success. At the same time, statistics from pollsters and analysts show that the impact of American culture on evangelical churches exceeds that of evangelical churches on American culture.

At the very least, therefore, missions leaders should restudy history and the Scriptures. Understanding past errors, they should be careful not to appeal to potential volunteers on the basis of self-interest and cautious lest they export still more North American cultural values through postmodern messages and methods. Those well acquainted with Asian religions in particular should be wary of adopting approaches that appeal to the "inner" or "higher self" and produce little more than subjective religious experiences. Leaders would be well advised to remember that the North American commitment to individualism and selfism does not commend itself to kingdom service.

Biblical Missions: "Like a Mighty Rushing Wind"

In Scripture, the workings of the Holy Spirit are compared to the movings of the wind (e.g., John 3:8). On the Day of Pentecost the Holy Spirit came with "a sound like a mighty rushing wind" (Acts 2:2). In the context of Scripture, a certain mystery about wind, its source and its effects, lends itself to similar comparisons and analogies.

The missions movement has been like a mighty moving of the Holy Spirit—a mighty rushing wind that has blown over the earth through the centuries. Its effects are seen and felt. For all of the foibles and failures attending the missionary enterprise, history has not known any movement to match Christianity in its effect on people and their cultures and societies. It will continue to be so until Jesus returns, for in the final analysis, the Holy Spirit both motivates agents of mission and orchestrates its outcome.

Still, much depends on those to whom this work has been entrusted.

It is incumbent upon inheritors of the past and "creators" of the future to be faithful to the Spirit of God in our being, in our thinking, and in our doing.

"Inheritors of the Wind": The Past Is Still with Us

We have referred to a "legacy." The legacy that our successors will bear is marked with some points of tension, including some we have already considered. These points can be seen either as potential crises or possibilities and opportunities.

First, leaders must address questions regarding the relative authority of churches and missions agencies. The relationship of these two structures of the Protestant missionary enterprise has always been crucial to effective missionizing. It promises to become even more crucial. Nearly seven hundred U.S.-based missions agencies are listed in recent editions of the *Mission Handbook.* The actual number is undoubtedly much higher (Moreau 2000, 33; Moreau 2004, 12). Moreau notes that "agencies describing themselves as denominational are decreasing in their proportion of income for overseas ministries and also long-term missionary personnel contrasted with the 'not-denominational' organizations" (Moreau 2004, 12). Obviously, this shift will have consequences, but that is only part of the story.

Most missiologists would agree that these two structures have roots in the New Testament and not just in the history of missions. They complement each other. That doesn't mean that churches cannot benefit from the extended vision, increased vitality, and heightened creativity often found in parachurch and interdenominational missions organizations. And these more independent agencies profit from the solidity and connectedness found in the denominational boards. But the philosophical difference between these two ways of organizing for mission is profound. Some believe that Paul's "missionary team" was more or less independent. Others emphasize Paul's dependence upon the sending church at Antioch and the "mother church" at Jerusalem.

Whichever view is more accurate, interdenominational parachurch agencies and denominational boards have complementary parts in carrying out the plan of God. For their part, churches should be allowed more of a role than simply funding personnel and operations in parachurch agencies. Paul Beals observes that the missions agency *serves* the church, pointing out important implications of that subservience (Beals 1995, 133–44).

Second, the realities of financing missions create inevitable tension and problems, so we should carefully manage money. In 1998 the total income reported by missions agencies in the United States came within a hair's breadth of the staggering total of $3 billion. By 2003 this had increased to over $3.75 billion (Moreau 2004, 28, 45). Nevertheless, most missions and missionaries continue to report a serious need for support.

What are we to make of this state of affairs?

There can be no doubt but that the Western missionary effort has been both helped and hampered by Western affluence. In the first century, Paul could be self-sufficient when he needed to be and even support his missionary colleagues by tentmaking. Moravian missionaries required only those necessities that enabled them to gain a foothold and care for themselves and their work on the field. Obviously they had no money to give to locals. Since the nineteenth century, missionaries have gone out with funding. For example, various missions hired many Bible women and other Christian workers in China. Communist revolutionaries pointed to these payments and called paid workers "running dogs of the imperialists." They adroitly named their own state-sponsored church the "Three-Self Church" to indicate that it received no foreign money.

Currently, the "influence of Western affluence" is again a subject of serious debate. Critics question the policy of giving financial aid to nationals, the methods used to raise missionary support, and the validity of emotional appeals for funds. Missionary fundraising has become an industry in the United States. Fundraising specialists have their own publications and Web sites. From the U.S. perspective, missions money never meets the need. It always is in short supply. Nationals look at how often missions groups come to their land, and the amount of money spent. Nationals note that the average missionary is far better off than the average local resident. Nationals might be forgiven, then, for thinking that the United States in particular is the source of an inexhaustible supply of funds. Why not try to tap this wealth to meet local needs of all kinds? No wonder astute observers such as Jonathan Bonk view Western affluence as an impediment to ministry (Bonk 1991). We have reached a point at which almost every facet of the American missionary enterprise is significantly impacted by money, money, and money:

- Money is often the most important single factor in determining who does, and who does not, get to the field.
- The potential for obtaining monetary or material gain of some kind marks the way in which many nationals assess the contributions of missionaries and visiting ministers and laypersons.
- High missionary salaries (by local standards) often make national workers envious of missionaries. They want to emulate the missionary lifestyle.
- When financial prosperity is connected with becoming a Christian, the connection between the biblical gospel and a prosperity gospel becomes more confused. This is especially true in economically depressed areas of the world.
- Availability of Western money to nationals often drives a wedge between national workers who receive foreign funds and those who do not.
- Faithful missions supporters are sometimes urged to stop sending missionaries and just support national evangelists in order to "get the job done quickly and efficiently."

Considering much funding to be both unbiblical and ill-advised, Robertson McQuilkin says, "Stop Sending Money" (McQuilkin 1999, 59). The complexity of missions finance calls for a rethinking that is informed, biblical, sensible, and innovative. Of course, some missions such as the International Board of the Southern Baptist Convention, support missionaries from a denominational fund. Some missions, Overseas Missionary Fellowship for example, pool funds and apportion them equally. Most missions, however, require missionaries to raise their own support, and it is they who need to rethink, and perhaps retool. Rather than requiring harried candidates to "sell" themselves and their worthiness for service to potential supporters who do not even know them, perhaps missions-minded Christians who have experience in business, finance, and sales could help alleviate the difficulties of raising personal support. These volunteers could make contacts with potential donors, introduce candidates and their projected ministry, make presentations on their behalf, and otherwise help them in this most time-consuming and difficult aspect of missionary service.

Whatever improvements can be made, the progress of postmodern missions will continue to depend upon the generous but informed stewardship of laity on the one hand, and the honest and wise management of missions monies by missions leaders on the other.

Third, we must recognize the difference between volunteerism *and* voluntarism, *seeing that there are problems and a potential in either.* New Testament missions were *voluntaristic* but not *volunteeristic.* None of the apostles were sent out unwilling; they were *voluntary* evangelists. But neither were any of them recruited by a general call to believers who are "willing to go." Generally speaking, early Protestant missions did not operate through a call for volunteers. More often, dedicated candidates who were willing to pay the price presented themselves to church leaders for consideration and support. From the mid-1800s, however, impassioned appeals for missionary recruits became more common among Protestants.

Michael Griffiths rightly says that "the most that an individual can do is express his *willingness.* Others must determine his *worthiness.* The individual may be *free* to go, but only his church knows if he is really *fitted* to go" (Griffiths 1970). *Availability* is not to be confused with *suitability.*

Currently, the pool of potential volunteers for full-time missionary service of one kind or another is expanding. Between 1992 and 2001, the number of missions-connected volunteers working in the U.S. grew at a rate of 1605.9 percent, from 37,452 to 638,907 (Moreau 2004, 13). Over the three-year period from 1998 to 2001, the number of short-termers going abroad (from two weeks to a year, the most likely pool from which long-term workers will be drawn) grew at a rate of 256 percent from 97,272 to 346,270.

There are several reasons for this astounding increase in the number of missions volunteers. As many as ten thousand volunteers are recruited at each triennial meeting of the Urbana Student Mission Convention. This conference for college students is sponsored by InterVarsity Christian

Fellowship/USA and the world parent organization of InterVarsity, the International Fellowship of Evangelical Students. Other Urbana-like conventions meet in Europe and Asia. Other volunteers are drawn by Perspective courses sponsored by the U.S. Center for World Mission and offered all around North America.

There is a most encouraging aspect to this: Even though the majority of missionary volunteers will never become career missionaries, they nevertheless constitute a vast reservoir of missions interest and support. The minus side to volunteerism is that, once a candidate "feels called," some organizations tend to assume suitability unless there is overwhelming evidence to the contrary. There can be a pressure to send all available and funded candidates to the field, even if there are uncertainties about their suitability.

Availability and suitability are both essential elements of a "missionary call." The monumental challenge is to identify those who are both available and suitable for service. The risen Christ has already separated out these "apostolic gifts" to his church.

Fourth, there is both opportunity and danger in global partnerships, so these efforts must continually be evaluated—especially as Western churches relate to non-Western churches and missions. As a total work of God, Protestant missions has succeeded beyond the wildest dreams of the pioneers of this movement (Johnstone 1998, *passim*). A vast number of churches around the world have been started and helped many to find places of service.

We now understand how crucial this is to the ongoing mission of the church. During the last decade of the twentieth century from 1992 to 2001 the total number of *fully supported* U.S. missionary personnel serving overseas showed a very modest gain from 38,375 to 44,386, or a total of 15.7 percent (Moreau 2004, 13). That increase was largely due to an increase in those short-term workers and others who never take up residence in the receiving country. The number of long-term workers (over four years) increased only 6.5 percent from 32,604 to 34,757.

Meanwhile, more missionaries are being sent out from countries that once were "receivers" of Western missions. There are no accurate statistics, but some authorities believe that more missionaries are being sent from these formerly receiving nations than from all Western nations combined (Guthrie 2000, 137). This sometimes is referred to as the "great new fact" of missions.

Significance, though, extends beyond raw numbers. With increased personnel from non-Western nations, it is obvious that missions and missionaries from all over the world must work together as never before. That fact is readily recognized, but it is not easily realized. "Partnership in mission" is an eloquent slogan but not always an effective strategy.

For one thing, partnership implies equality. Christians confess that all members of the body of Christ are equal in the sight of God. The problem is that the influences of national origin, enculturation, language, and education cause believers from various areas to relate to others in very different ways. For example, Engel and Dyrness are absolutely correct in chiding Americans for their overbearing attitude in relations with Christians from other areas (Engel and Dyrness 2000, 76–78 *passim*). Over the last half of the twentieth century, Americans have tended to initiate the congresses, set the agendas, organize the programs, and supply the representatives with which Christian missions are identified.

Most agree that this American dominance eventually will decline, as it must. But there are other cultural factors that impede the transfer of initiative and authority. Culturally, Easterners and Westerners do not have the same notions of what leadership is and how it is encouraged, recognized, and expressed. All the seminars in the world on "servant leadership" will not help until leaders from the East, and especially from the West, understand why it is that Americans do not hesitate to "take front seats" while Easterners wait to be "urged forward."

Partnership implies mutuality. All true Christians want to give and not just receive. But giving is not to be encouraged when the new "partnership" morphs into the old "paternalism." At this point, Western churches and missions usually supply monies, medicines, material goods, macro-ideas, development programs, and secular and theological education. Non-Western churches and missions supply "manpower." In this exchange, the givers may think they are encouraging the receivers when few "strings" are attached to the resources provided—but that means a lack of accountability.

Partnership is never easy, and global partnership of churches and missions offers particular challenges. As noted above, Paul had important things to say about exchanging material and spiritual "goods." He said that those who shared spiritually should be rewarded materially (1 Cor. 9:12–14). We can assume that the converse is also true. Non-Western church and missions leaders have much of value to share with American Christians if we exercise the patience to listen. They can teach about such things as suffering, true *koinonia,* meaningful worship, Christian lifestyle, and New Testament patience and steadfastness. Moreover, since culture is often best understood from the outside, they can help us understand how secularization affects churches and missions of various cultural backgrounds.

Finally, one of the most important aspects of partnership among churches and missions implies walking, witnessing, worshipping, and working *with one mind.* This implies a togetherness based upon shared doctrine, polity, and ethical practice. Given the shift toward postmodernism and relative truth, it is imperative that partners agree on the way in which they will worship and work (Moreau, Corwin, and McGee 2004, 311).

Fifth, there is great opportunity in the growth of short-term missions, but the resources and management required must be kept in balance with long-term work. It is an open question as to who stands to gain the most from short-term projects—national churches or the short-termers and their home churches. The blunt question must be asked: Are short-term missions worth their cost?

Short-term opportunities were not a feature of Protestant missions until after World War I, and they did not become a significant factor until the 1960s. Since then, availability and reduced cost of international travel, combined with the American penchants to become involved but not to make long-term commitments, have led to an explosion in short-term missions.

The generation of career missionaries that reached the field after World War II has now retired. As noted above (see p. 231), the number of new career workers remains more or less static, while the number of short-term missionaries sent out by U.S. agencies increased by 256 percent during the three-year period from 1998 to 2001. The total is even higher when one counts unreported short-termers sent out by local churches and those who "go on their own." By 2001, the number of full-time staff members that reporting agencies employed to serve short-term efforts reached 582, and another 503 spent at least part time caring for short-term workers.

According to Moreau, "The ongoing growth in personnel devoted to servicing short-term missions work indicates a need for further research into the total cost of such work for missions agencies and the benefits that accrue from short-term mission projects" (Moreau 2004, 36–37). Such research would be especially important to the progress of missions from North America. Are short-termers getting an accurate view of biblical missions during their short-term experiences? When all expenses are taken into account, could short-term building projects (for example) be accomplished more economically by hiring local artisans? If so, do other benefits outweigh the increased cost of sending North Americans?

A large percentage of career missionaries once came from the pool of short-termers. However, that is no longer so. The pool is expanding dramatically, but not the number of career missionaries actually placed on the field. Is it simply that the number of career recruits doesn't keep up with attrition and retirement in the ranks of career missionaries? Or are there other factors?

The time has come to take a careful and candid look at the effectiveness of both short-term and long-term missions. Meanwhile, it might be best that the short-term enterprise be renamed "short-term Christian *education* and mission." That would be a reminder that all of us—including all who go on any project and all who send—must ourselves learn, even as we try to teach others (Hesselgrave 2002, 47–50).

Entrepreneurship and Contemporary Missions

With Nicodemus, Jesus called attention to the fact that one hears the wind but one doesn't know where it comes from or where it goes. Post-World War II missions have been characterized by a number of methodological and theological "winds" that have blown across the landscape. Responsible missiology requires that we examine where these winds are moving us. Here are a few "current wind currents."

The "skeleton key" or "golden key" approach to missionary methods and strategy. People who are really serious about missions tend to be given to the notion that there must be some method somewhere that, if

found and used, will enable us to complete the task of world evangeliza-
tion. The history of post–World War II missions can be told in terms of
the comings and goings of such methods and strategies (Wakely 2004).
But ask the average college-age student of missions today about Church
Growth, Evangelism-in-Depth, Theological Education by Extension,
Key-73, Discipling a Whole Nation, Every Home Crusade, and even
World Class City and Prayer Walk missions movements and methods.
Chances are you will be greeted with puzzlement. At some point, each
of these movements, and others like them, commanded attention. Some
still do.

Many of the strategies were and are viable and helpful. But none has
provided the comprehensive solution to abiding challenges. If these fads
have damaged the Great Commission mission, it is because the hype
diverted attention from less glitzy but more substantive efforts. Such
keys are still being manufactured. Each should be subjected to more
evaluation than was sometimes given in the past. It is doubtful that there
is any "key" to world evangelization that was not known long before we
arrived on the scene.

"Creative access" to closed and partially closed countries. The idea
that our missions need to find creative ways to establish a presence and
maintain a witness in closed or semiclosed countries is valid. Creative
access strategies sometimes work and give results. Some of these
strategies for working in creative access countries (C.A.C.) would work
in other countries as well. Unfortunately, this strategy is widely discussed
and poorly disguised. Oppressive governments are usually quite aware
of what is going on, and they sometimes manipulate these efforts to their
own ends. Missions employing these tactics need to be wise as serpents
and harmless as doves.

Planting church-planting movements. This strategy is easily marketed
with appealing slogans. It draws visionary personnel. David Garrison
gives the "simple, concise definition" that "a Church Planting Movement
(C.P.M.) is *a rapid and exponential increase of indigenous churches
planting churches within a given people group or population segment"*
(Garrison, n.d., 7; see also Mannoia 1994; Garrison 2004). Certain questions must be asked. Exactly what is a church-planting movement? That
definition is clear, and Garrison does a good job of identifying examples

of such movements. But what precisely are the differences between C.P.M. strategy and Pauline church development strategy? What is the difference between planting a "church-planting movement" and planting churches that plant other churches? Given the difficulties of planting indigenous churches, exactly how does an outsider go about planting an *indigenous movement*, as missionaries are encouraged to do (Garrison, n.d., 7)? If it is God who "gives the increase," how can a "planter" or "waterer" determine the time, place, and pace at which a movement will occur? Are any important steps in developing responsible, New Testament churches short-circuited in starting church-planting movements? What are we to say about the marks of the true church as given in Acts 2:42–47?

A generation ago, Tippett, J. Waskom Pickett, and Donald McGavran were among those who demonstrated the effectiveness of people movements in discipleship and evangelism. But church planting movements seem to be different. Before we devote money and personnel to such a strategy, it requires extended study and protracted prayer.

The "oral Bible movement." Literacy and Bible translation have been front and center in missionary theory and practice (Townsend 1998). All or part of the Bible has been translated in nearly three thousand languages, but that is still fewer than half of the known languages of the world. For at least one-third of the world's peoples without a written language, oral communication is the only way to pass information. It is the preferred form of learning and communication for many more. Taking all this into account, it is sometimes claimed that an emphasis on oral communication of Scripture may be the next great advance.

Those who promote the spoken Word in this movement can make a persuasive case for their strategy, but the discussion raises questions about how to invest time, energy and money. This doesn't mean that Wycliffe Bible Translators, New Tribes Mission, Pioneers, and other missions promoting literacy and translating and printing the Bible should fold their tents and go home. Churches must have a translated and printed Bible to become mature in faith.

The emergent (or emerging) church movement. It is quite common to read that American Christian leaders are adopting a "missionary perspective" to reach their own people. North American culture, in particular, is changing so rapidly and thoroughly that we are advised to study and accommodate to new modern and postmodern cultural realities. Otherwise we will be unable to communicate the gospel effectively. Perhaps the best example of this approach is the emergent church and the writings of its chief architect, Brian D. McLaren. McLaren's approach to postmodern culture is explained in various writings and especially in *A Generous Orthodoxy: Why I am a Missional, Evangelical, Post-Protestant, Liberal/Conservative, Mystical/Poetic, Biblical, Charismatic/Contemplative, Fundamentalist/Calvinist, Anabaptist/Anglican, Methodist, Catholic, Green, Incarnational, Depressed-yet-Hopeful, Emergent, Unfinished CHRISTIAN* (McLaren 2005). This title borders on the definitive.

Obviously the emergent church approach does not parallel that of traditional evangelical missionaries abroad, any more than it does that of traditional evangelical churches at home. Leaders do not claim that they have the "old" evangelical message with new methods. They claim that they are "re-discovering the Bible as a human product" and that they are willing to abandon some long-defended battle lines (Crouch 2004, 38).

This is a classic case of over-contextualization. Missiologists have faced this kind of thing before and should be raising flags of caution against such excess (Carson 2005).

Change is necessary. Change will come. But we must be concerned about any open-ended appeal for a completely new paradigm. Satoru Kanemoto concludes his discussion of new paradigms in Japan by saying, "We need to remain confident in the Bible as our guide and continue our mission in hope" (Kanemoto 2003, 11). At a time when evangelicalism is being tested in Japan and worldwide, it is this kind of reasoning that we find most reassuring as we look to the future.

Conclusion

As we have been reminded many times in recent years, this is a "time for risking" (Adeney 1987). By its very nature, evangelism involves risks. In the conflict that lies ahead, the work will demand the risk that accompanies surrender to the living God, dedication to the task, and love for our Lord Christ and world neighbors. Facing the complexities of postmodernity, Christian missionaries will also need to prepare patiently, plan carefully, and model understanding and objectivity.

Only that combination can be expected to merit Christ's "Well done, good and faithful servant."

Epilogue

Carl Brown's mentors sized up the situation in Tatarstan and concluded that the short-term effort from St. Louis had potential, but only if some well-prepared long-term missionary would take up residence in the target area and use carefully selected teams whose ministries could be coordinated with the progress of a well-designed church-planting program. In a relatively short time, the Holy Spirit brought them all together—the church with its old vision and new understanding; Carl and Angela Brown with their field experience, studies in church-planting, and unusual facility in the language and culture; a few national leaders, converts and inquirers; and a ten-step strategy that led from initial contacts to missionary withdrawal. Not just another struggling church, but a solid "church-planting Free Church" became a reality in Kazan, Tatarstan.

References

Adeney, Miriam. 1987. *A Time for Risking: Priorities for Women.* Portland, Ore.: Multnomah.

Beals, Paul A. 1995. *A People for His Name: A Church-Based Missions Strategy.* Revised ed. Pasadena, Calif.: William Carey Library.

Beaver, R. Pierce. 1968. *All Loves Excelling: American Protestant Women in World Mission.* Grand Rapids: Eerdmans.

Bonk, Jonathan. 1990. *Missions and Money: Affluence as a Western Missionary Problem.* Maryknoll, N.Y.: Orbis.

Carson, D. A. 2005. *Becoming Conversant with the Emerging Church: Understanding a Movement and its Implications.* Grand Rapids, Zondervan.

———. 1984. *Matthew.* Expositor's Bible Commentary, vol. 8. Grand Rapids: Zondervan.

Crouch, Andy. 2004. "The Emergent Church: Ministry Fashion Statement of the Church's Future?" *Christianity Today*, November: 37–41.

Engel, James F., and William A. Dyrness. 2000. *Changing the Mind of Missions: Where Have We Gone Wrong?* Downers Grove, Ill.: InterVarsity.

Erickson, Millard J. 1998. *Postmodernizing the Faith: Evangelical Responses to the Challenge of Postmodernism.* Grand Rapids: Baker.

Gans, Herbert J. 1988. *Middle America Individualism: The Future of Liberal Democracy.* New York: Free Press.

Garrison, David. n.d. *Church Planting Movements.* Richmond, Va:. International Mission Board of the Southern Baptist Convention.

————. 2004. *Church Planting Movements: How God Is Redeeming a Lost World.* Midlothian, Va.: WIGTake Resources.

Griffiths, Michael C. 1970. *Give Up Your Small Ambitions.* Chicago: Moody.

Guthrie, Stan. 2000. *Missions in the Third Millennium: 21 Key Trends for the Twenty-first Century.* Carlisle: Paternoster.

Hesselgrave, David J. 2002. "More than a Vacation." *Moody Magazine,* May–June, 47–50.

————. 1991. *Communicating Christ Cross-Culturally: An Introduction to Missionary Communication.* 2d ed. Grand Rapids: Zondervan.

Hexham, Irving; Stephen Rost; and John W. Morehead II, eds. 2004. *Encountering New Religious Movements: A Holistic Evangelical Approach.* Grand Rapids: Kregel.

Johnston, Graham. 2001. *Preaching to a Postmodern World: A Guide to Reaching Twenty-First-Century Listeners.* Grand Rapids: Baker.

Kane, J. Herbert. 1971. *A Global View of Christian Missions from Pentecost to the Present.* Grand Rapids: Baker.

Kanemoto, Satoru. 2003. "The Present State of the Church in Japan." *Japan Update,* Spring, 6–7, 11.

Kohls, L. Robert. 1981. *Developing Intercultural Awareness.* Washington, D.C.: Society for Intercultural Education, Training and Research.

Lappe, Francis Moore. 1989. *Rediscovering American Values: A Provocative Dialogue for Exploring Our Fundamental Beliefs and How They Offer Hope for America's Culture.* New York: Ballantine.

Mannoia, Kevin W. 1994. *Church Planting: The Next Generation: Introducing the Century 21 Church-Planting System.* Indianapolis: Light & Life.

Maslow, Abraham. 1970. *Motivation and Personality.* 2d ed. New York: Harper & Row.

McLaren, Brian D. 2004. *A Generous Orthodoxy.* Grand Rapids: Zondervan.

McQuilkin, J. Robertson. 1999. "Stop Sending Money." *Christianity Today,* March, 59–60.

Moreau, A. Scott. 2000. "Putting the Survey in Perspective." In *Missions Handbook: U.S. and Canadian Christian Ministries Overseas 2001–2003*, edited by John A. Siewert and Dotsey Welliver. 18th ed. Wheaton, Ill.: Evangelism & Missions Information Service.

———. 2004. "Putting the Survey in Perspective." *Missions Handbook: U.S. and Canadian Christian Ministries Overseas 2004–2006*, edited by Dotsey Welliver and Minnette Northcutt. 19th ed. Wheaton, Ill.: Evangelism & Missions Information Service.

Moreau, A. Scott, Gary R. Corwin, and Gary B. McGee. 2004. *Introducing World Missions: A Biblical, Historical, and Practical Survey.* Grand Rapids: Baker.

Neill, Stephen. 1959. *Creative Tension: The Duff Lectures, 1958.* London: Edinburgh House.

Peters, George W. 1972. *A Biblical Theology of Missions.* Chicago: Moody.

Pickles, Helen. 2000. "I Feel Therefore I Am." *Business Life,* July–August: 37–41

Piper, John. 2002. *Brothers, We are Not Professionals: A Plea to Pastors for Radical Ministry.* Nashville: Broadman & Holman.

Smalley, William A., ed. 1967. *Readings in Missionary Anthropology.* Tarrytown, N.Y.: Practical Anthropology.

———. 1978. *Readings in Missionary Anthropology II.* Enlarged ed. Pasadena, Calif.: William Carey Library.

Spicq, Ceslas. 1994. *Theological Lexicon of the New Testament.* 3 vols. Translated and edited by James D. Ernest. Peabody, Mass.: Hendrickson, 3:505–6.

Stetzer, Ed. 2003. *Planting New Churches in a Postmodern Age.* Nashville: Broadman and Holman.

Stewart, Edward C. 1972. *American Cultural Patterns: A Cross-Cultural Perspective.* Chicago: Intercultural.

Townsend, William Cameron. 1998. "Tribes, Tongues and Translators." In *Perspectives on the World Christian Movement: A Reader,* edited by Ralph D. Winter and Steven C. Hawthorne. Pasadena, Calif.: William Carey Library.

Wakely, Mike. 2004. "The Search for the Golden Key." *Evangelical Missions Quarterly,* January, 12–22.

Warren, Rick. 2002. *The Purpose-Driven Life.* Grand Rapids: Zondervan.

Winter, Ralph D. 1981. "The Two Structures of God's Redemptive Mission." In *Perspectives on the World Christian Movement: A Reader,* edited by Ralph D. Winter and Steven C. Hawthorne. Pasadena, Calif.: William Carey Library.

———. 1996a. "The Greatest Danger . . . The Re-Amateurization of Mission." *Missions Frontiers Bulletin,* March–April, 5.

———. 1996b."I Have to Eat Humble Pie." *Missions Frontiers Bulletin,* May–August: 6.

Chapter 8

Form and Meaning

How Does the Inspiration of Scripture "In-form"
Contextualization and Make It "Meaning-full"?

For verily I say unto you, Till heaven and earth pass, one jot or one tittle shall in no wise pass from the law, till all be fulfilled.

—Matthew 5:18 AV

All Scripture is breathed out by God and profitable for teaching, for reproof, for correction, and for training in righteousness, that the man of God may be competent, equipped for every good work.

—2 Timothy 3:16–18

Prologue

HE WAS A STUDENT AT Doshisha University in Kyoto, Japan—a brand-new believer, bubbling with enthusiasm and brimming with questions. His classes at the university occasioned many questions because, although Doshisha had begun as an illustrious Christian institution, the university had long since departed from the faith of its founders.

Particularly troubling to Eizoh Maeda was a class in the Acts of the Apostles. From the Ascension in chapter 1 to Paul's deliverance from the bite of a viper in Acts 28, Maeda's professor explained away every supernatural element with much aplomb and no apology. The teacher insisted that Bible students of the past had been conditioned by their prescientific cultures to interpret these accounts literally, whereas today we understand them as being couched in the "language of appearances." The *form* of the text may be much the same, but it functions differently. Consequently, its *meaning* for premoderns was different than is its *meaning* for moderns.

Language form and language meaning can join in a rather stormy marriage. For a generation or longer, general semanticists have fed a steady diet of relative truth slogans:

- "Meaning is not in words; meaning is only in people."
- "Stamp out 'isness.'"
- "Rather than say 'This is. . . .' say, *'To me* this is. . . .'"

In line with these notions is United States President William Jefferson Clinton's classic line of self justification: "It all depends on what the meaning of *is* is."

Obviously a considerable amount of contemporary thought has focused on linguistic symbols and their meanings. Philosophers used to inquire into the meaning of the universe. Some still do. But more of them now end up inquiring into the "meaning of *meaning."* Over half a century ago, the philosopher Susanne Langer saw this trend and called it "philosophy in a new key" (Langer 1948).

Psychologists are now concerned with the relationship between linguistic and other forms of behavior. They may inquire into ways in which patients respond to certain words and phrases. Or they may concentrate on dialogue and "talking things out." Cognitive behaviorists in particular attempt to change undesirable behavior patterns by changing language patterns. To use a simplistic example, a behaviorist might counsel a pessimist to start referring to the glass as "half full" instead of "half empty."

Likewise, anthropologists make much of how a culture uses linguistic symbols and assigns meaning and function to them. They believe that this tells them much about culture in general and specific cultures in particular. For example, how words function in ritual has something to say about worldview.

This chapter addresses verbal cross-cultural communication and contextualization, particularly as they relate to the Bible and its inspiration, translation, interpretation, and proclamation. We have explained other aspects of communication (see Hesselgrave 1991; Hesselgrave and Rommen 1989). Here we will give special attention to some of the most critical and contentious contextualization problems now facing missions, especially those growing out of the relationship between biblical revelation and gospel communication.

The Bottom Line in Gospel Communication

By Way of Definition

Gospel ministry in general entails Bible interpretation, exposition, and application. Missionary ministry must work harder than other forms of Christian communication to take into account two other elements— contextualization and decontextualization. Yet another aspect of ministry that takes on added significance in missions communication is Bible translation.

As used here, *gospel* refers *both* to the Word of God in the whole of Old and New Testaments *and* to its "heart"—the "good news message" summarized in John 3:16 and 1 Corinthians 15:3–4. Most Christians understand the second of these two meanings. Identification of gospel with the entirety of biblical revelation may be novel to some.

The meaning of *contextualization* is a somewhat different matter. Ralph Winter calls *contextualization* a dangerous word (Winter 1993). Not only does it mean different things to different people, but its users sometimes give the impression that creativity and risk-taking are at the heart of the process. To these contextualizers, the product must command attention and have arresting impact.

That is not what we mean by *contextualization*, however. In its historical meaning, *contextualization* has to do with making a message (such as the biblical gospel) *meaningful* to people who are "foreign" in the ethno-cultural sense or to those who subscribe to a "foreign" worldview. *Decontextualization* has to do with freeing a message (e.g., the gospel) as much as possible from elements of the contextualizer's culture, so that the intended meaning comes through with a minimum of interference.

Contextualization and decontextualization are usually thought of as separate, distinct aspects of the overall process of communicating the gospel cross-culturally. That is certainly a valid way of thinking about them. But in practice they are intimately connected in the translation, interpretation, exposition, and application of Scripture. In order to avoid awkward constructions and tiresome redundancy, our use of the term *contextualization* in this chapter will refer to contextualization and de-contextualization aspects of all four of these operations in communicating God's special revelation.

No Other Gospel

There is no other gospel than that revealed in Holy Scripture. When writing to the Galatians, Paul expressed surprise that some had turned to "another" gospel. Then he quickly added that there is no other gospel— only distortions of the truth that are not "gospel" at all (Gal. 1:6–10). As for the gospel Paul preached, though he sometimes called it "my gospel," it was not *his* gospel in any ultimate sense. Concerning it, he wrote, "I did not receive it from any man, nor was I taught it, but I received it through a revelation of Jesus Christ" (v. 12).

Of course, missionaries today are not in a position to lay claim to direct revelation. But they can and must lay claim to preaching a gospel that emanates from divine revelation rather than human thought or experience. The world is full of gospels of human design. But they are false gospels, or rather, not gospels at all.

As for the true, biblical gospel, one of many passages used by orthodox Christians to reinforce and explain the inspiration of the autographs of Scripture as the only inerrant, authoritative revelation from God is 2 Timothy 3:16–17: "All Scripture is breathed out by God and profitable for teaching, for reproof, for correction, and for training for righteousness, that the man of God may be competent, equipped for every good work." During the past half-century, 2 Timothy 3:16 has probably been quoted as regularly among evangelicals as John 3:16 has been quoted in communicating the gospel to unbelievers. Of course, the case for a fully authoritative Bible is not based on this passage alone, but these verses in context in 2 Timothy are worthy of special attention.

First, the Bible is identified in three ways in this passage: (1) "sacred writings" *(hiera grammata);* (2) "scripture" *(graphē);* and (3) "the Word" *(to logos).* Mahayana Buddhists often speak of a "meaning" or "word beneath the letter" of Buddhist sacred books. Paul's teaching admits of no special word or meaning beneath, above, or beyond the actual words of the Bible. All three of Paul's identifiers refer to one Word of God written.

Second, as observed by the Princeton theologian B. B. Warfield, the Greek word *theopneustos* ("God-breathed") cannot be properly exegeted to mean "breathed into by God," nor does it refer to the product of "in-breathing" into human authors. Paul means that Scripture is the product of the "creative breath of God." Paul isn't referring to the process by which God accomplished this. He is confessing without equivocation that all of Scripture is a divine product. No term could more clearly and emphatically assert divine production. In the Bible "breath of God" always refers to God's mighty power and creative word (Warfield 1967, 133).

Third, with the clear teachings of 2 Timothy 3:16 in mind, we should approach Scripture with the very strong presumption that the autographs contain no errors. It is not necessary to examine all the "facts" before we can examine the doctrine of inerrancy. We believe this doctrine on the basis of the witness of the apostles and prophets. It must be considered as trustworthy as all other doctrines taught by them (Warfield 1967, 215, 406–7). This being the case, Warfield's title for one of his chapters is "'It Says'; 'Scripture Says'; 'God Says.'" His point is that what Scripture says, God says (Warfield 1967, 299).

Fourth, grammatically and contextually, *theopneustos* in this passage can be understood as either part of the subject or part of the predicate, although the natural sense of the Greek makes it part of the predicate. If part of the subject, it would modify *graphē* and be translated something like "All Scripture, being God-breathed, is as well profitable. . . ." The conjunction *kai* argues against *theopneustos* being part of the subject unless it is used in the rare adverbial sense of "likewise" or "as well."

Almost all translations take the normal sense of the words to mean that
"Each/every/all Scripture is God-breathed. . . ."

Warfield argued that whatever one does with *theopneustos,* it still
ends up saying that Scripture is of divine origin and for that reason is
profitable (Warfield 1948, 134). Paul was directly referring to the Old
Testament, the canon of his day. As part of the gospel, even the Scripture
written before the coming of Christ is able to make one "wise for salvation
through faith in Christ Jesus" (2 Tim. 3:15). More than that, Scripture is
"profitable [*ōphelimos,* "beneficial; useful; advantageous"] for teaching,
for reproof, for correction, and for training in righteousness" (v. 16).

Paul says in 2 Tim. 3:16 that the Holy Scripture takes the form of
written, God-breathed words, and that it is efficacious in making the
unregenerate "wise to the salvation" that is in Christ Jesus and also in
making the regenerate "competent, equipped for every good work" (v.
17). Whether times seem to be opportune, Scripture is to be preached
because it is both true and profitable. In fact, the proclamation of the
Word of God is crucial when people are inclined to listen to false teachers
and "turn away from listening to the truth and wander off into myths"
(4:4).

The Verbal-Plenary View of Inspiration

The doctrine of inspiration espoused by Paul in 2 Timothy and affirmed
in the other Scriptures from which we build our doctrine of Scripture is
also confessed in creeds and confessions of the orthodox church down
through history. Revelation and inspiration go together. *Revelation* comes
from the Greek word *apokalypsis,* which literally means "unveiling" or
"making visible." Most often *apokalypsis* is used metaphorically to refer
to making truth known, either "in propositional form, or . . . in the form of
an experience from which propositional truth may be inferred" (Buswell
1962–63, 1:183). The verbal-plenary view of the *inspiration* of biblical
revelation is that, although the words of the autographs are human words
written by human authors, those authors were inspired by the Holy Spirit
of God in such a way that every word they wrote expressed literally and
propositionally the precise thought that God intended to communicate.
As God's revealed communication, all of these writings (as originally

produced) are absolutely true and completely authoritative in expressing what God wants to tell us.

Care must be exercised to differentiate *literal inspiration* and *literal interpretation*. These are two different concepts. The fact that the words and not just the ideas of Scripture were "God-breathed" means that inspiration extended to the words chosen. But these words were still the expressions of the authors, following normal literary conventions for historical writing, poetry, and other forms of literature. That means that some thoughts are expressed metaphorically in Scripture's writings, just as we do in writing today. Some words and phrases are meant to be interpreted metaphorically or firguratively, not literally. For example, when Jeremiah says, "Your words were found, and I ate them" (Jer. 15:16), those words were inspired *literally* but cannot be *interpreted* literally.

The Importance of a "Meaning-full" and Trustworthy Bible

The ability to use linguistic symbols to communicate God's thoughts or ours has always been intrinsic to the human experience. In the biblical account of the creation, God formed the first human from the dust of the ground, after which he "breathed into his nostrils the breath of life, and the man became a living creature" (Gen. 2:7). We read on that God put man in Eden to "work it and keep it" (v. 15). No sooner had God made man than they had conversation. It was rather one-sided at that point, but it was conversation nevertheless (v. 16). Bodily form and its functioning is inextricably linked to the use of linguistic symbols and their meaning. Physically equipped to keep the garden, Adam was linguistically equipped to understand God's words. This was demonstrated when he followed God's instruction to assign names to the animals (vv. 19–20).

Think of the endless and complex theories of the origins of the earth and humankind, and of speech in the human race and in individuals. Think of all our complex and sometimes convoluted questions. God doesn't stop to answer many of them, although he answers those that really matter. His concern is that we understand redemption and sanctification, not that we know all about the origins of the universe or whether ontogenesis and phylogenesis theories of the origins of speech are correct. Having created us, God informs us about the world well enough to superintend it, and his Word well enough to comprehend it. And he holds us responsible for doing both.

With respect to their book *One Faith: The Evangelical Consensus* (Packer and Oden 2004), J. I. Packer and Thomas C. Oden were asked, "An affirmation about the Bible is the first item in some evangelical faith statements. Others put it later. Why does your book place the Bible first?" Oden answered, "The Bible takes the first place in confessional Protestantism. You can go back to the Heidelberg Catechism and similar documents and find the authority of Scripture first or very close to first." Packer added,

> During the last 50 years, the matter has become higher profile and the debate sharper because we're up against liberal episte-mology—which starts from the affirmation that the world has the wisdom and what the church believes has to be relativized to what the world is saying at the moment. Encountering that, all these statements of faith have appreciated that you have to start with an affirmation about the Bible as a fit source to consult for sure knowledge about God. (Neff 2004, 80)

A Brief History of Inspiration and Contextualization

Early Contextualization Efforts

When administrators of the Theological Education Fund of the World Council of Churches launched its Third Mandate Program (1970–78) to encourage the "contextualization of theology," most who responded to that challenge were Third World theologians of a liberal or neo-orthodox persuasion. Their resulting contextualized theologies displayed a pro-found appreciation for indigenous cultures and religions, including black theology, African theology, liberation theology, waterbuffalo theology, third-eye theology, and theology of the pain of God.

However, these contextualized theologies invariably left a great deal to be desired when measured against the biblical text and biblical theology. After carefully examining various sorts of black and African theologies, the evangelical theologian Byang Kato concluded, "African Theology seeks for identity of the African. In order to do this, the advocates exalt African culture, religion and philosophy beyond proportion. Christianity cannot claim a monopoly on revelation or salvation, some claim, though it may be glibly referred to as being unique" (Kato 1975, 51). Little wonder, then, that Kato entitles the chapter that follows this assessment, "'African Theology': Described and Rejected" (Kato 1975, 53).

Evangelicals also tried, with mixed results, to come to terms with the idea of contextualization. A Lausanne Consultation on Gospel and Culture was convened in Willowbank, Bermuda, in 1978 to give direction to evangelical contextualization efforts. Several papers drew sharp criticism and had to be revised. The refined work was published as *Down to Earth: Studies in Christianity and Culture* (Stott and Coote 1980). A new evangelical quarterly publication, *Gospel in Context,* was launched. But such disagreements arose over numerous articles that the publication became too controversial. Funding was withdrawn, and publication ceased.

The most extensive single-author work on contextualization that appeared during those early days was Charles H. Kraft's *Christianity in Culture: A Study in Dynamic Biblical Theologizing in Cross-Cultural Perspective* (Kraft 1979). Well-reasoned but highly provocative, Kraft's book was extremely creative in showing how culture affects Scripture from translation to application. For his colleague Donald McGavran and most other evangelicals, however, Kraft's approach evoked serious questions about how his high view of culture influenced his view of Scripture (McGavran 1974).

Throughout the 1970s and 1980s, some of the most serious questions raised among evangelicals had to do with what the contextualization process means to the authority of Scripture. Evangelical publications and conferences resulted in the publication of critical evaluations by Bruce Nicholls, Morris Inch, Bruce Fleming, Bong Rin Ro, Carl Armerding, Edward Rommen, David Hesselgrave, and others in addition to those of Kato and McGavran. These attempts to define and describe a more evangelical and orthodox understanding of contextualization helped, but they tended to be rather uneven in clarifying the relationship between responsible contextualization and the verbal-plenary understanding of revelation and inspiration.

Evangelical Organizations

The modern "evangelical movement" began with formation of the National Association of Evangelicals in 1942. It grew out of the concern of theologians such as Roger Nicole, Edward J. Carnell, Harold Ockenga, Carl F. H. Henry, and others to distance themselves from some aspects of fundamentalism while maintaining a thoroughgoing commitment to the verbal inspiration and complete trustworthiness of the Bible. That commitment was the touchstone for the Evangelical Theological Society (E.T.S.) when some sixty evangelical scholars founded the organization in 1949 with a single doctrinal statement: "The Bible alone, and the Bible in its entirety (including its explicit and implied propositions) is the Word of God written and is therefore inerrant in the autographs."

A quarter century later, in 1974, Christian leaders from 150 countries meeting in the International Congress on World Evangelization in Lausanne, Switzerland, signed the Lausanne Covenant. It included a statement similar to that of the E.T.S., even though the doctrine of inspiration was not a burning issue at the Congress.

Inspiration and authority of Scripture was, however, a burning issue among theologians who met in Chicago in 1977 to form the International Council on Biblical Inerrancy (ICBI). Believing inerrancy to be "crucial to the life and vitality of the Christian church," the Council produced two strong statements, "The Chicago Statement on Biblical Inerrancy" (International Council on Biblical Inerrancy 1978b) and "The Chicago Statement on Hermeneutics" (International Council on Biblical Inerrancy 1978a; see Radmacher and Preus 1984, viii; appendix, Geisler 1979). Over the decade from 1977 to 1987, the ICBI produced a number of scholarly books and papers on inerrancy, but few referred to contextualization issues. Then the organization was disbanded. Providentially its work was taken up by another group, the Coalition on Revival (C.O.R.). This U.S. group represents Christians from a variety of theological backgrounds who believe that Scripture is without error. An international subsidiary of the coalition, the International Church Council Project (I.C.C.), is working toward producing public meetings all around the world to affirm and build upon the Chicago statements, strengthening the biblical base for national churches and missions.

Those consultations are modeled after the fourth-century Council of Nicea. The first was in Fort Lauderdale, Florida, in 2003. The conviction behind them is that the doctrine of verbal-plenary inspiration is not only "crucial to the life and vitality of the Christian church," but is also basic to contextualization of the gospel and fulfillment of the Great Commission.

The I.C.C. approach to contextualization is built around the essentials of a confession of inerrancy:

1. The autographs of the Old and New Testament were ancient writings, mainly in the Hebrew, Aramaic, and Greek languages. The autographs undoubtedly looked much like other writings of their times—human letters, words, and sentences written in cuneiform and cursive forms.

2. While do not have direct access to the autographs, we are able to reconstruct them very precisely through study of the manuscripts. These copies of copies have been carefully and scrupulously copied and discrepancies between the best manuscripts tend to be few and without major consequence. Weighing internal and external evidence, we can have confidence that we know with considerable precision what the human authors and God intended.

3. The autographs were, and the critical texts we possess are, inspired by God the Holy Spirit in such a way as to make them the very Word of God, completely authoritative, without error, and absolutely unique among all the sacred writings of the world.

We will return to draw some implications about ICBI and the I.C.C. statements.

Types of Revelation and "Holy Books"

A "World-full" of "Holy Books"

One major dimension of contextualization has received scant attention among evangelical theologians and missiologists. We have dealt with it at greater length in other places (See Hesselgrave 1984, 691–738;

Hesselgrave and Rommen 1989, 128–43), but it cannot be completely overlooked here. Just as there are many "gods that are not God" and numerous "gospels that are not gospel," there are also numerous "holy books that are not holy." From the perspective of peoples of other cultures and religions, Christian missionaries bring both a foreign religious message and a foreign religious book. Missionaries continually face the challenge of other books held to be sacred and even revelatory. As Eric J. Sharpe says, "Since virtually all scripture is understood in revelatory terms . . . [the missionary must have] some prior understanding of Hindu, Jewish, Christian, Muslim and other doctrines of God and doctrines of revelation" (Sharpe 1971, 64–65).

As Sharpe correctly observes, missionaries will not go far in their studies or in their travels before they discover that respondent peoples rely on various "holy books" as sources of that knowledge. The missionary must find ways to communicate the truth that, while the true God is not circumscribed in the ways he can communicate, he has chosen to reveal himself most clearly in just one book, the Bible, and in one person, the Christ of the Bible. To do that, missionaries must be able to differentiate between the *kinds* of revelation represented in the holy books of the various religions and be able to explain these differences. This is part of the contextualization process.

Differing Types of Revelation

All sacred books of the major religions of the world can be placed within four categories.

1. *Mythological writings.* Mythological sacred books provide narratives and information (generally fiction and often fantasy) that bind peoples together in common loyalties and destinies. Examples include the Japanese Kojiki, Nihongi, and Engishiki.

2. *Enlightened writings/teachings.* Common to this class of sacred books is the notion that actual knowledge of the divine and reality comes only through personal enlightenment experience. Knowledge of the divine cannot be conveyed through verbal propositions, but personal experiences and understandings can

be reported in writings or reports and teachings that facilitate enlightened knowledge. Examples would be the Hindu Vedas, the Buddhist Tripitaka, and the Chinese Tao-Teh-Ching.

3. *Divine writing.* Divine writing purportedly comes directly from the divine apart from human involvement other than to take down the words in the mechanical process of writing. The most well-known example is the Qur'an, although the Book of Mormon also fits this category.

4. *Divinely inspired writings.* The Old and New Testaments are held by orthodox Christians to differ from all other books in that they are "God-breathed." The Christian conception is unique among religions. Christians teach that the true God has revealed needed propositional truth in the biblical writings, although these revelations are mediated through the personality, background, ideas, and research of the human authors. The agent who "inspires" the human authors and directs what they write is the Holy Spirit of God who dwells and works in them, so that the final product is ultimately the very Word of God.

The importance of these distinctions cannot be overemphasized. Practically as well as logically, the type or kind of revelation contained in sacred books is as important as their teachings. Believers' perception of the type of revelation determines how the words are understood and applied, and how they are translated and contextualized. When the absolute uniqueness of God's revelation in the Old and New Testaments is not recognized, the Bible takes on the characteristics of other holy books. Its God remains hidden, and its message is relative truth.

Contextualization of Mythological Writings

Contextualizing the Kojiki, Nihongi and Engishiki

For centuries, Shintoism has unified the Japanese nation around deities, the emperor, and the collective destiny of Japanese people. The Shinto myth undergirded the Japanese war effort in the 1930s and 1940s. Most Japanese were convinced by Shinto chauvinists that their divinely

Types	Mythological	Reports of the "Enlightened"	"Divine Writing"	Divinely Inspired Writings
Examples	Kojiki, Nihongi Engishiki	Tripitaka, Vedas, Tao-Teh-Ching	Koran (Qur'an), Book of Mormon	Holy Bible (Old and New Testaments)
Characteristics	Combines myth and history	Reflects knowledge gained by Holy Men through mystical experiences.	Records actual words and phrases of the Divine through a human medium.	Inspired or "God-breathed" in such a way as to assure the autographs to be the Word of God.
Functions/ Uses	Facilitates solidarity; provides values and ethics; gives direction	Provides stimuli and methods designed to occasion enlightenment experience.	Makes divine will available and understandable to those who understand the language.	Profitable for teaching, reproof, correction, and training in righteousness.

Figure 9. Written Revelation and the World's Holy Books

ordained destiny was to share the beneficent rule of the *Tenno Heika* ("Heavenly Emperor") with the rest of the world.

The Shinto myth (into which some history is interwoven) is set out in the three sacred volumes of the Kojiki, Nihongi, and Engishiki. How did nationalistic Japanese scholars use those texts to shape wholehearted support and sacrifice of the Japanese people? They did not regard their holy writings as needing objective analysis to study their historicity and trustworthiness. That would be self-defeating. Nor did they publish updated and idiomatic translations. That would achieve nothing. Myths are not potent because they are "true" or historically accurate. Nor are they useful only as they are read and understood. Myths and mythological language provide linguistic symbols out of which scholars can construct a "contemporary" and persuasive faith. As D. C. Holtom makes clear, that is exactly what the Japanese warlords did as they convinced the Japanese people that they were "a race of unique divine attributes" with "a peerless nation structure," and "a sacred commission to save the world" (Holtom 1943, 25).

Contextualizing the Bible (Wrongly) as Myth

Some scholars erroneously view the Bible much as Shintoists view their holy books—a collection of myths. In *Toward a Recovery of Christian Belief,* Carl F. H. Henry writes about "theistic atheism, or deconstructionism," the position of scholars who have attempted to "overturn the whole history of Western thought by turning it loose from God and logic, from verificatory criteria and shared signification" (Henry 1990, 30). Included in the category are such "Bible as myth" theologians as Paul Tillich and Rudolf Bultmann and such "God is dead" theologians as Thomas Altizer. According to these theologians, the language of the Bible is not to be understood literally. It cannot be, for objective knowledge of God is impossible, and moderns no longer have the option of believing in the God of the Bible and traditional theology.

For Tillich, God is not to be understood in the literal sense presented in Scripture but in a symbolic construction of the biblical texts. He is the "Ground of all Being" in Tillich's terminology. John Warwick

Montgomery is reported to have quipped in response that "the only 'ground of all being' I know of is hamburger."

I heard Tillich present a series of lectures at the University of Kyoto in the late 1950s. He went to great lengths to explain that the Bible is not a book of historical and ontological knowledge as taught by misguided Christian "fundamentalists." The real meaning of the Bible is to be found in its "myths," as is the case with most holy books. In one of his lectures, he referred to Rudolph Bultmann, saying,

> My friend, Professor Bultmann, says that one must "demytholo-gize the Bible" in order to understand its meaning. I told him that would be a mistake. The real meaning of the Bible is in its myths such as "In the beginning, God," "creation out of nothing" and "Christ, the Son of God." Demythologize the Bible and it loses its significance. (from personal notes)

I don't know the overall effect of Tillich's lectures, but I do know that he offered little reason for Shintoists to forsake the Kojiki or for Buddhists to abandon the Lotus Sutra. I also know that a member of my weekly Bible class abruptly stopped coming immediately after the lecture series. She was the daughter of the university president.

Ludwig Wittgenstein had a hand in this. He believed that words are not so much labels for things as they are tools for tasks. The members of any and every linguistic group are engaged in a kind of "language game," and the meanings of their words are to be determined by how people use those words. The proponents of "theistic atheism" mentioned above appealed to moderns by playing a kind of Wittgensteinian "language game" that turned meaning on its head and the Scriptures into mythological writings.

We wonder how far some of our contemporary thinkers now go in playing a similar game to appeal to postmoderns. According to Gordon Lewis, the notion of Stanley Grenz and John Franke that there is no one-to-one correlation between language and the world ultimately makes tenuous any objective knowledge of God that can be attained from creation and Scripture. We are left with the faith of various linguistic and religious communities, each of which relies on its own language to describe God and the world. These theologians would seem to reduce the meaning of Scripture to whatever a particular Christian community might choose to make of it. Such an approach is neither biblical nor missionary (Lewis 2003, 279–83; Grenz and Franke 2001, 23).

Contextualization of Writings of the Enlightened

Translating and Contextualizing the Upanishads

Hinduism holds to two types of sacred literature: *Sruti* (Skt.; lit. "that which is heard," that is, *revelation*) and *Smrti* (Skt.; lit. "that which is remembered," that is, *tradition*).

Sruti is highest and includes the Vedic literature and later commentaries on the Vedas, called the Brahmanas and the Upanishads. As valued as the Vedas, Brahmanas, and Upanishads might be, however, logically they must be approached as dictated by basic Hindu epistemology. According to Hinduism, God and ultimate truth can be known only through the experience of personal enlightenment. The most that any guru or sacred writing can do is to help *occasion* that experience.

Swami Prabhavananda and Frederick Manchester provide us with an "enlightening" example of this approach. They attempt a translation of the Upanishads for Westerners. They explain that all Hindus recognize the Upanishads as the highest written authority. The Upanishads are "concerned with the knowledge of God, the highest aspect of religious truth" (Prabhavananda and Manchester 1947, ix).

Nevertheless, the translators "allow themselves the freedom" as "seems desirable" to do anything possible in order to convey the "sense and spirit" of the original into English. They may render the poetry of the original text into English prose, for example. Why? To do so produces a heightened effect. After all, words and forms are not really important in this view. The "real meaning" is to be found in the way the words and forms *function* in and among those who read them (Prabhavananda and Manchester 1947, xi–xii).

Contextualizing the Bible (Wrongly) as Enlightened Writing

Some Christians view the Bible in much the same way as Hindu scholars view the Upanishads. It is not uncommon for some lay Christians to refer to the Bible as important, but consisting of no more than "dead letters" (especially regarding doctrine) until something happens to make it "come alive" and be really meaningful.

A somewhat similar idea is entertained by Christian scholars, who perhaps state it with more nuance and sophistication: The Bible is not actually the Word of God; rather it *contains* the Word of God or *potentially is* the Word of God. Only by virtue of a special work of the Holy Spirit or the creativity of Bible scholars does it effectively *become* the Word of God to readers and hearers. The neo-orthodox doctrine of the inspiration of the Bible lends itself to this view. Extreme understandings of "dynamic equivalence" take this idea into the realm of Bible translation and contextualization theory.

The origins of dynamic equivalence are not to be found in Scripture but in the human sciences. The term *dynamic equivalence translation* was coined by one of the most insightful and influential linguistic scholars of our times, Eugene A. Nida, "to describe a 'meaning-based' approach to translation—one that looks for *functional equivalence* rather than *formal equivalence* in translation" (Neff 2002, 46). In answer to the question, How did you develop your ideas about Bible translation fifty years ago? Nida responds as follows:

> When I was at the University of California, Los Angeles, our professors would never let us translate literally. They said, "We want to know the meaning. We don't want to know just the words." I found that a number of the Greek classics had been translated very meaningfully, much better than the Bible had been translated. . . . I studied linguistics, Greek, Latin, and Hebrew, and I decided that we've got to approach the Scripture as though it is the message and try to give its meaning, not just repeat the words. (Neff 2002, 46)

Nida studied anthropology, in addition to linguistics, communications, and lexicography, because "words only have meanings in terms of the culture of which they are a part" (Neff 2002, 46). In the article from which the above quotation is drawn, Nida doesn't explain his understanding of revelation and the inspiration of Scripture. We can assume that he has a high view of Scripture, but it seems obvious that he doesn't subscribe to the verbal-plenary view espoused by Warfield and founders of the Evangelical Theological Society. That is an important point. Evangelicals often follow scholars such as Nida uncritically, never thinking what rejection of verbal plenary inspiration means in epistemological practice. Definite limits are imposed naturally by a belief in the divine inspiration of the *very words* of Scripture. Those who do not recognize those limitations sometimes lead us astray.

To see the extreme to which dynamic equivalence can be taken, consider the translation and contextualization approach of Charles Kraft as outlined in *Christianity and Culture* (Kraft 1979). To his credit, Kraft provides a clear explanation of his own view of revelation and inspiration as well as his philosophy of language and contextualization. He believes revelation to be subjective and continuing (Kraft 1979, 184). The Bible is "like the ocean and supracultural truth like the icebergs that float in it" (Kraft 1979, 131). It is *potentially* the Word of God, not error-free except in its intended teachings (Kraft 1979, 208).

Taking this view of the Bible, Kraft holds to the kind of "dynamic livingness of Scripture" and "vital Christian experience" supported by recent "behavioral insights" but not allowed for by the "static philosophical presuppositions" of conservative scholars (Kraft 1979, 211). In keeping with his "dynamic" view of revelation, Kraft does not hold to grammatical-historical interpretation but to what he calls "ethnolinguistic interpretation." The Bible is an "inspired casebook" of events that were time- and culture-specific (Kraft 1979, 134, 202). Today's translators and interpreters have the responsibility to analyze the events of those ancient writings in context, so as to correctly read their ahistorical functions and meanings. The question is how the original hearers or readers understood and reacted to the words. Armed with that information, the contemporary "contextualizer" must reproduce in modern hearers and readers the same or similar understanding and response.

According to Kraft, this is what dynamic and functional equivalence is all about. Meaning, after all, is not in words. Meaning is in people. Forms—especially ancient forms—are relatively unimportant. Function is all-important. Revelation occurs whenever the message of the text is made meaning-full and especially *impact-full* to an audience, ancient or modern. *Impact-full* is stressed because in Kraft's view, unless the message is contextualized in an arresting and powerful way, it accomplishes little or nothing.

Kraft is to be applauded for being forthright, and he has many, often brilliant, insights. But in his approach, the God-breathed words of Scripture are scarcely more important than the special insights of their modern interpreters—*perhaps no more important.* If his understanding of biblical revelation and inspiration is not the same as a Hindu understanding of the Vedas, it is close enough to be scary.

A recent controversy in North American evangelicalism plays out this controversy in Bible translation. One of numerous problems facing Bible translators and exegetes in the West is the Bible's perceived "maleness." So debate has long raged over the validity of a "gender correct" translation, such as that of the *Today's New International Version* (with emphasis on the words *Today's New*).

Take the simple greeting of Paul in Galatians 1:1–2 as a case in point. In his greeting (v. 2), Paul wrote, *kai hoi syn emoi pantes adelphoi,* literally, "and all the brethren who are with me." We can assume that the "maleness" of this greeting occasioned no special problem in first-century Galatia, nor would it occasion a problem in most of the non-Western world today. But it *is* a problem in the gender-conscious United States and Europe generally, and among feminists especially.

If Paul's greeting did not communicate "male bias" in first-century Galatia, the sensitive TNIV translators employed a "dynamic equivalent" lens to ensure that Paul does not communicate "male bias" in twenty-first-century California. The phrase becomes "and all the brothers *and sisters* with me" (emphasis mine). Anyone who reads the Greek text knows that this is not what Paul actually wrote, but when Paul referred to his colleagues, he did not intend to offend Galatian women. Therefore, the change is deemed appropriate, so that the ancient *form* conveys equivalent *meaning* in Western culture today to the meaning it conveyed in first-century Galatia.

The contextualizing principle at work is that the translation must not have an impact on contemporary culture that the original text did not make on first-century Galatian culture. For that reason, the form of the text has been changed. In correspondence to the Greek, the TNIV translation is not correct. Is it more historically and theologically correct? I am sure that Kraft would say that the TNIV is more accurate.

I would suggest that this opportunity to rework the text carries with it a strong temptation. Whether consciously or unconsciously, accuracy becomes less important than the acceptability of Paul and the Galatian epistle. Historical accuracy, in fact, depends on whether women actually were among those "with Paul." If Chrysostom, Luther, Alford, Lightfoot and other leading scholars through church history are right in their exegesis of Paul's words, the apostle here is referring only to his traveling companions. We know who was traveling with Paul (Acts 20:4). If Paul is referring only to those people, the TNIV text is historically inaccurate.

The point is important because, though not determinative, both the grammar and history of Paul's greeting relate to the theological question of male leadership. And that is the debate that the gender neutral version was supposed to help resolve in the first place! The TNIV translation has not helped resolve anything. By playing with the wording, the version only makes some parties to the controversy feel that they are on better exegetical ground than they really are.

Whether the words "and sisters" occurs in Galatians 1:2 may seem like a splitting of hairs, especially to laypeople. However, the approach and its result reflects a careless attitude about biblical revelation that Bible believers can't afford. Thoughtful missionaries can't either. To be sure, contextualizers must pay attention to "meaning in culture." But if the very words of Scripture are *God-breathed*, then textual accuracy is more important than supposed cultural relevance. In fact, when it comes to the biblical text, accurate translation and interpretation will, by definition, be culturally relevant. Accurate text will be free to speak, confirming or correcting cultural values and practices.

Some missionaries may be tempted to think that the discussion about Galatians 1:2 does not concern them because gender is not an issue in their respondent cultures. But look at verse 1 again. The Greek speaks of *"Theou patros"* ("Father God"). Many feminists would complain that this phrase also represents a male bias. Moreover, some radical function-alists in Latin America assert that a better understanding of God in Latin America would result from translating "Father God" as "Mother God." The word *father* carries negative connotations in Latin America, while mothers are loved and revered. Going even further, a leader of "goddess religion," Carol P. Christ, says that Christ reconciled traditional polari-ties. On that basis, she proposes the adapted translation "Goddess/God" (Christ, 2004, 38; cf. Mollenkott 2003).

Vern Poythress speaks precisely to our basic concern at this point. He writes: "Political correctness can, I believe, influence Bible translation *in spite of* contrary intentions on the part of translators. The influence mainly affects details of meaning, so it may not seem too serious at first glance. But in the end it threatens the vital doctrine of the *plenary* inspi-ration of Scripture" (*Christianity Today* 2002, 37).

In the final analysis, that is what is at stake, isn't it? It is not just, or primarily, What is your philosophy of translation and/or contextualiza-tion? It is rather, What is your doctrine of the inspiration of Scripture?

Contextualizing Scriptures Wrongly as "Divine Writing"

Translating and Contextualizing the Qurʾan

Though not often dealt with in popular literature, there are actually two types of inspiration in Islam: "lower-level" inspiration, or *ilham,* and "higher-level" inspiration, or *wahy. Ilham* is a gift of Allah to various holy men and prophets, but it is subjective and therefore trustworthy only to a point. *Wahy,* on the other hand, is a gift of Allah to certain prophets only and is objective and fully trustworthy. From a Muslim perspective, a problem accrues to the fact that the *wahy* writings of prophets prior to Muhammad (e.g., Moses and Jesus) have been corrupted and therefore we are left with the Qurʾan as the only final and fully authoritative divine revelation.

According to W. Montgomery Watt, the essential features of Muhammad's *wahy*-type inspiration were "the words in his conscious mind, the absence of his own thinking; and the belief that the words were from God" (Watt 1969, 69–70). The upshot of all of this is that, in the Muslim view, the Qurʾan is "the language of Allah" and "made in heaven." It is, in fact, a replica of the "Mother of the Book," which is in heaven. As such the Arabic Qurʾan can be read, memorized, preached, and taught, but it cannot be translated. Inquirers into the faith themselves must ultimately become "contextualized" in the sense that they must learn Arabic and read the Qurʾan for themselves. Versions of the Qurʾan in other languages are not translations at all. They are only "interpretations" and, therefore, not completely trustworthy.

Though not a Muslim himself, as a faithful "translator" of the Qurʾan, A. J. Arberry recognizes all of this and does his best to reproduce or to "imitate, however imperfectly, those rhetorical and rhythmical patterns which are the glory and sublimity of the Koran" (Arberry 1955, 28). In other words, Arberry admits that the precise *form* in which Muhammad is said to have received the Qurʾan is absolutely vital to the way in which the Qurʾan *functions*. In the end, Arberry settles for calling his work *The Koran Interpreted*.

Bible Translation and the King James Version

Though conservative evangelicals are sometimes accused of believing in dictation theory and are sometimes called "word worshipers" (Neff 2002, 46), I personally am not acquainted with any such person, and I believe this is a "straw man" argument. Those who might appear to be guilty are simply very conservative when it comes to their doctrine of inspiration—scholars of the likes of Edward Hills (1956) and Wilber Pickering (1977). Their case for the superiority of the King James Version does sound somewhat akin to Arberry's assessment of the Qurʾan. They say that the King James or Authorized Version is both the most trustworthy and enduring translation of the Bible available. They call special attention to its beautiful prose, its majestic rhythms, and its influence upon English language and literature over the centuries. And they project that, somewhat updated and slightly revised, it will be the standard translation for many years to come.

But their argument goes deeper than that. They are rightly concerned with manuscript evidence and providential preservation of the biblical text in the face of higher criticism. They believe that in his providence,

God chose the Greek church to become guardian of the New Testament. They are persuaded that the King James Version, based as it is upon the Byzantine text and the *Textus Receptus,* is the purest and most accurate version. They agree that periodic updating on the basis of new manuscript evidence and language change is warranted, but that changes should be minimal and introduced only with great care.

All of this devotion to, and all of these arguments for the superiority of the King James Version do not merit the charge that these scholars believe in dictation theory, nor that they are "word worshippers." Inspiration by divine dictation is not an issue in this particular debate. The issue ultimately has to do with the inerrancy of the autographs and the trustworthiness of Bible manuscripts and translations. Most conservative Bible scholars will not agree with arguments of King James Version supporters, but we can appreciate their concerns.

Contextualization of "Inspired Writings" of the Bible

As for the Old and New Testament "inspired writings," they are unlike any of the "holy books" mentioned above. They are absolutely unique—the only works in this class of holy books in the history of the world.

How then are they to be treated? How are they to be translated, interpreted, explained, and applied? How are they to be contextualized? Certainly they should receive a different treatment than are other so-called holy books. To approach the Bible as one might approach the Kojiki or the Upanishads or even the Qurʾan is to do it a gross injustice. The Bible is the very Word of God and must be approached differently.

We must approach it with something of the reverence with which ancient copyists approached the early manuscripts—something considerably beyond the seriousness with which even the most respected translator might approach any other religious book. Following Warfield, we should assume that the claims the Bible makes for itself are true and treat the text in that light. Any and all reasonings and opinions stemming purely from human origins, however scholarly and well intentioned, cannot claim more than secondary or tertiary importance.

Here we will point out some things that should and should not be done in contextualizing, using the teachings of Scripture and statements on inerrancy and hermeneutics. We will especially look at I.C.C. topic 13 on "Culture, Contextualization and the Gospel" (available with related documents at churchcouncil.org).

The Person of Christ and Contextualization

One aspect of the uniqueness of Scripture is that it is personal communication from the Son of God through Holy Spirit-inspired human writers. Drawing closely on Hebrews 1:1–2, the ICBI begins its affirmations section in The Chicago Statement on Biblical Inerrancy with this relationship of Scripture to its source in God the Father and God the Son:

> We affirm that God has inspired Holy Scripture to reveal Himself through Jesus Christ as Creator and Lord, Redeemer and Judge. (Topic 1, Short Statement 1)

Paul speaks in the Athenian address in Acts 17 as an apostle personally chosen and sent forth by Christ to proclaim his gospel. He, among others, would be chosen and inspired to make an enduring written record of that gospel, explaining who Christ is and what he said and did as Messiah and Lord. As Paul spoke that day, the apostolic record remained to be completed, but Paul was operating under direct, personal authority from the risen Lord. The Son of God himself had called Paul to be the "apostle to the Gentiles." Therefore, the Son himself was a vivid revelational basis for Paul's message. He and the other apostles would bring to their writings this same inspired source of mission and message.

Through his writings, Paul's apostolic authority was extended to the church. Following in Paul's train, others would be directly equipped by the word of God in Christ that had been in Paul's own commission. Future leaders could preach the gospel of Christ and build his church upon the same personal apostolic authority, not because they had an apostolic commission but because they were handling the thoughts of authors with such a commission.

Paul writes that the church is "built on the foundation of the apostles and prophets, Christ Jesus being the cornerstone" (Eph. 2:20). Christ Jesus is the cornerstone and Scripture is the foundation of the Christian church, and also of gospel contextualization.

Propositional Revelation and Biblical Truth

All Scripture is true, including all of its propositions. Jesus asked the Father to "sanctify them in the truth; your word is truth" (John 17:17). The Chicago Statement on Inerrancy offers this testimony:

> We affirm that the Bible expresses God's truth in propositional statements, and we declare that Biblical truth is both objective and absolute. (Topic 2, Article 6)

Of course, the Bible contains much more than propositional statements. Some of the Bible is poetry, some is narrative, some is command, and some is exhortation. But the propositions of Scripture have occasioned most of our problems in modern and postmodern times. Propositional statements are judged to be true or false in a way that poetic and hortatory statements, for example, are not, and that constitutes a special problem for many.

Theological modernism represented an attempt to make Christianity acceptable to moderns. Therefore, it was inclined to judge and reject historical propositions of the Bible, and some of its doctrinal propositions as well. Postmoderns are less interested in sequential thought, objective truth, and propositional statements than were moderns. In order to reach them, even some evangelicals (as in the emergent church movement) deemphasize propositional truth, especially creedal or doctrinal propositions. Rather postmoderns emphasize narrative, symbols, images, and mystery (see Carson 2005, 40 and elsewhere in his discussion).

The judgments of theological modernists and evangelical emergents are erroneous, but perhaps the latter constitutes the greater threat to evangelical orthodoxy today. So we cannot leave a discussion of contextualization without some thoughts on postmodern epistemology.

Opposing mistaken views of inspiration and of the nature of biblical doctrine, Gordon Lewis argues that propositional revelation is essential to evangelical spiritual formation (Lewis 2003, 269–98). Lewis shows that propositionless spirituality has no foundation in meaning. Historically, evangelicals have a solid source for making spiritual insights in the tri-unity of God: The Creator is the Author of universally valid propositions. The Son became the incarnational basis for revelational propositionalism by becoming man, dying, and rising from the dead. The Holy Spirit leads directly through biblical propositions.

For those who truly believe the presuppositions from which Lewis argues, the logic is incontrovertible. Those presuppositions are (1) that the Bible is without error and (2) that it is completely trustworthy. For Lewis, propositions sharpen the goals of spirituality, reveal love to be normative, direct us to sources of strength, show us how to live by faith, encourage us to practice the presence of God, and encourage us to love the church. Postmoderns who cannot philosophically accept Lewis's presuppositions cannot be brought to authentic spiritual truth by contextualization. They inevitably come to a false view of God and reality. True spirituality is precisely what the Holy Spirit works through the Bible and Bible doctrine. Jesus prayed that his people would be sanctified in the truth and immediately added, "Your word is truth" (John 17:17). The apostle Paul declared, "All Scripture is breathed out by God and profitable for teaching, for reproof, for correction and for training in righteousness that the man of God may be competent, equipped for every good work" (2 Tim. 3:16–17).

If missionaries are to be *Christian* contextualizers, and especially if they are to be true *evangelical Christian* contextualizers, they are obligated to respond to postmodernist spirituality of the West and mystical religiosity of the East by reverently studying and fervently teaching Bible doctrine in propositional form.

The Work of the Spirit and Bible Interpretation

"The Spirit is the one who testifies, because the Spirit is the truth" (1 John 5:6). The Chicago Statement on Hermeneutics declares,

> We affirm the necessity of interpreting the Bible according to its literal, or normal, sense. The literal sense is the grammatical-

historical sense, that is, the meaning which the writer expressed. Interpretation according to the literal sense will take account of all figures of speech and literary forms found in the text. (art. 15)

Too often the hard work of studying the biblical text is divorced from the necessity of trusting the Holy Spirit for guidance and illumination. In the various documents of the ICBI and I.C.C., the work of the Holy Spirit in inspiring and illuminating Scripture is set alongside the human work of interpreting and applying Scripture in accordance with normal rules of historical inquiry and literary interpretation. Breaking this connection works havoc with biblical meaning and significance.

For example, about half a century ago, the writings of rhetorician and literary critic, Kenneth Burke, became prominent in Western academies. Burke's thought ranged over a vast expanse of literary works, including theological writings. In one context Burke notes four kinds of "medieval interpretation" defined by Thomas Aquinas in his *Summa Theologica:* literal, allegorical, moral, and anagogical. For Burke, Aquinas's definitions illustrate how ordinary descriptive language can be "socioanagogical." In socioanagogical interpretation, a "mystical interpretation" can be used to justify sweeping social change (Burke 1962, 774).

In Burke's view this mystical interpretation need have no connection to the intention of the original author. After all, the author's "scene"—the total situation or set of circumstances in which he or she wrote—was very different from that in which a reader now discovers meaning in the writing. So the intention of the author is not crucial to the interpretation of what was written. It is more important to know the "scene" in which the author wrote. But neither the author's intention or the original scene is as important as the reader/interpreter's scene and intention.

Burke greatly influenced both secular and Christian literary criticism. Before the middle of the twentieth century, W. K. Wimsatt and Monroe Beardsley were speaking about the "intentional fallacy" in Bible interpretation. Applying Burke's ideas to Bible interpretation, they concluded that what the Bible writer meant or intended to say has become irrelevant with the passage of time. It is the meaning and application of the text as determined by the reader in his or her world that is important. Their point, then, is that the ancient authors of the Bible are not as important as are contemporary interpreters in determining and applying meaning. Sometimes called "formalist criticism," this approach to Bible interpretation invaded many theological schools in the late 1960s and 1970s, just as Baby-Boomers were getting their education. Its ideas still are widely influential. As a result, schools, churches, and Bible study groups stress meaning for you, meaning for me, meaning for our times, meaning for this generation.

But that is not the extent of mischief. Burke's "rhetoric of motives" underscores the intentions of author-speakers and also reader-listeners. He recalls Blaise Pascal's criticism of certain Jesuits who proposed to "direct the intention" of wayward believers of their day (the mid-seventeenth century). Since church members would not change their ways, these Jesuits proposed to teach wayward believers how to apply Christian motives to their un-Christian behaviors. By doing so, worldly believers could stay in the church while living un-Christian lives (Burke 1962, 680–81). Unlike Pascal, who denounced ethical word games, Burke believes there is merit in bringing current behavioral norms to the work of interpreting Scripture, not to condemn but to give a contextual patina of acceptability.

A contemporary illustration of the implications of Burke's idea comes to mind. One of my students was preparing to be a missionary and maintained that he was serious about being a good witness for Christ as commanded in Acts 1:8. But this man had what those of us who mentored him regarded as a grave moral weakness: He habitually attended X-rated movies. He argued that what he was doing was justified by the Bible as part of his Great Commission calling. His intention, he said, was to witness for Christ. He always tried to attend these movies in the company of unbelievers and use the movie to demonstrate that the Bible is true when it says that all people are sinners.

It is little short of amazing. Almost any ethical standards can be justified by Scripture when the text and its meaning are divorced from the intent of its authors and clear grammatical-historical denotation of the words. Meaning intended by the authors is prior to meaning interpreted by the readers. *Meaning then* has precedence over *meaning now* if literary communication, let alone biblical authority, means anything at all.

Little wonder, then, that the framers of both the ICBI and I.C.C. statements use the language, "We affirm the *necessity* of interpreting the Bible according to its literal, or normal, sense. The literal sense is the grammatical-historical sense, that is, the meaning which the writers expressed . . ." (Chicago Statement on Biblical Hermeneutics, art. 15; see also I.C.C. art. 18).

The Christian Church and Orthodoxy/Orthopraxy

. When Christian missionaries go into the world, they are duty-bound to deliver God's Word of redemption. But that is not all. They also must encourage formation of a corporate body that has identification with the visible church of Jesus Christ. On what foundation is the church to be built? Paul tells us in Ephesians 2:19–20 that Christians are "members of the household of God, built on the foundation of the apostles and prophets, Christ Jesus himself being the cornerstone." Implications of Paul's understanding of unity are addressed by the I.C.C. in its paper "Concerning Unity of the Body of Christ" (topic 11):

> We affirm that true Christian unity must be based on a doctrinal foundation that includes historic Christian doctrine as revealed in the inerrant Scriptures and expressed in the Apostles' Creed. (art. 6)

The framers of this affirmation attest to the fact that the inerrant Word of God is integral, not just to the *saving faith of individuals,* but also to the *time-tested faith of the church.* Of many reasons why such a statement is biblical and appropriate, let me focus on two, (1) linkage with the historic church and (2) critical contextualization.

First, each biblical mission links the emerging church around the world with the historical church, the church of the twenty-first century with the church of the first century. From the lips of Jesus we hear, "Thy Word is truth." From the pen of Paul we read, "All Scripture is breathed out by God" (2 Tim. 3:16a). From the early church we learn the essentials of faith from Scripture contained in early versions of what eventually was called the Apostles' Creed. From the works of Papias, second-century bishop of

Hierapolis, we read, "Mark made no mistake when he thus wrote down some things as he remembered them; for he made it his especial care to omit nothing of what he heard and to make no false statement therein" (Bettenson 1947, 38).

Local churches are not spiritual islands. The universal church of Christ through history, and sending and receiving churches today, are best served by a conscious and careful linkage with each other. This linkage fundamentally includes common confession of the authority of Scripture, the deity and lordship of Jesus Christ, and other cardinal doctrines that have stood through history.

Second, missionaries and leaders of the emerging church should jointly decide how to apply Scripture to specific elements of culture. This means meeting for regular discussions on the meaning of the biblical text as it relates to cultural practices and expectations. Paul Hiebert's term for this process is "critical contextualization" (Hiebert 1987, 287–96).

Once converts are being incorporated into forming churches, these discussions become critical. Rituals and revels, ceremonies and celebrations, and monuments and meetings of indigenous cultures have cultural meanings and functions. Those from outside the culture may not understand the importance of these events. The underlying meaning may not be just the superficial idea that is reported. Missionaries, pastors, and laity all need to share knowledge on all levels of meaning, as well as how Scripture teachings relate to them. Together they should decide how the church will respond to these practices, either as obstacles to Christian living and testimony or as opportunities for communicating the gospel of Christ.

This discussion of ICBI and I.C.C. affirmations of biblical inspiration and authority and their significance for Christian contextualization could be greatly extended. For example, we might go on to show how they reinforce the practical importance of the kind of biblical theology that "describes God by recounting what God has done. . . . the acts of God in history, together with what must be inferred from those acts" (Wright 1991, 101). Discussion is needed on discerning nonnegotiable universals and the culurally-nuanced formulations in Western theologies (Davis 1978). With Tite Tiénou, we must recognize that Western ideas in theology are not universally normative and theologians in other cultures must explain the universals in meaningful non-Western terms (Tiénou 1992, 261).

Conclusion

Missionary contextualization that is authentically and effectively Christian and evangelical does not begin with knowledge of linguistics, communications theory, and cultural anthropology. It begins with a commitment to an inerrant and authoritative Word of God in the autographs of Old Testament and New Testament Scripture. From the starting point of a commitment to the authority of that Word and its truth and dissemination, tools afforded by relevant sciences are necessary additions to enable us to understand Scripture and communicate it meaningfully and effectively across cultures (Hesselgrave 1984, 3–13). But apart from that commitment, using the tools will not enhance understanding. In fact, it may take away from knowledge of truth.

Epilogue

Missionary colleagues—especially from Japan—know that many believing students have been subjected to the kind of testing that Eizoh Maeda experienced at Doshisha University. Most come through it unscathed. It is for their encouragement that I began, and now close, this chapter with this young man's story.

After graduation, Maeda determined to study theology and become a pastor. As a result of his decision, he was alienated from his parents for a long time. Nevertheless, he completed his seminary training in Japan and then matriculated at Trinity Evangelical Divinity School in Deerfield, Illinois. His master's thesis at Trinity focused on gospel preaching in Japan, studying evangelistic preaching principles that fit the Japanese context (Maeda 1971). He discovered some twenty-three such principles, but concluded that almost all of them must be modified significantly in Japanese culture (Maeda 1971).

However, two principles require the *least* modification and seem to be applicable in every culture: (1) To be effective, the evangelistic sermon must have clear objectives; and (2) to be effective the evangelistic sermon must have sound theological presuppositions (Maeda 1971, 154–58). Assuming the objectives and presuppositions are anchored in the Word, these two principles must work together in Christian contextualization.

References

Arberry, Arthur J. 1955. *The Koran Interpreted.* New York: Macmillan.

Bavinck, J. H. 1960. *An Introduction to the Science of Missions.* Translated by David Hugh Freeman. Philadelphia: Presbyterian & Reformed.

Bettenson, Henry, ed. 1947. *Documents of the Christian Church.* London: Oxford University Press.

Burke, Kenneth. 1962. *A Grammar of Motives and a Rhetoric of Motives.* New York: World.

Buswell, J. Oliver. 1962–63. *A Systematic Theology of the Christian Religion.* Grand Rapids: Zondervan.

Carson, D. A. 2005. *Becoming Conversant with the Emergent Church: Understanding a Movement and Its Implications.* Grand Rapids: Zondervan.

Christ, Carol P. 2004. Review of *She Who Changes: Re-Imagining the Divine in the World. Christian Century,* 1 June: 38.

Christianity Today. 2002. "The TNIV Debate," October 7, 35–45.

Davis, John Jefferson, ed. 1978. *The Necessity of Systematic Theology.* 2d ed. Grand Rapids: Baker.

Geisler, Norman L., ed. 1979. *Inerrancy.* Grand Rapids: Zondervan.

Grenz, Stanley J., and John R. Franke. 2001. *Beyond Foundationalism: Shaping Theology in a Postmodern Context.* Louisville: Westminster John Knox.

Henry, Carl F. H. 1990. *Toward a Recovery of Christian Belief: The Rutherford Lectures.* Wheaton, Ill.: Crossway.

Hesselgrave, David J. 1984. "Contextualization and Revelational Epistemology." In *Hermeneutics, Inerrancy, and the Bible: Papers from ICBI Summit II,* edited by Earl D. Radmacher and David D. Preus. Grand Rapids: Zondervan.

———. 1991. *Communicating Christ Cross-Culturally: An Introduction to Missionary Communication.* 2d ed. Grand Rapids: Zondervan.

———. 1994. *Scripture and Strategy: The Use of the Bible in Postmodern Church and Mission.* Pasadena, Calif.: William Carey Library.

Hesselgrave, David J., and Edward Rommen. 1989. *Contextualization: Meanings, Methods, and Models.* Grand Rapids: Baker.

Hiebert, Paul G. 1987. "Critical Contextualization." *Missiology* 12.2: 287–96.

Hills, Edward F. 1956. *The King James Version Defended.* Des Moines, Iowa: Christian Research Press.

Holtom, D. C. 1943. *Modern Japan and Shinto Nationalism.* Chicago: University of Chicago Press.

International Church Council Project. 2001. *Timeless Truth for the Twenty-first Century: The Documents of the International Church Council Project.* Hathaway Pines, Calif.: International Church Council Project.

International Council on Biblical Inerrancy. 1978a. "The Chicago Statement on Biblical Hermeneutics." Dallas, Texas: Dallas Theological Seminary Archives. At churchcouncil.org/ccdocuments.

———. 1978b. "The Chicago Statement on Biblical Inerrancy." Dallas, Texas: Dallas Theological Seminary Archives. At churchcouncil.org/ccdocuments.

Kato, Byang H. 1975. *Theological Pitfalls in Africa.* Kisumu, Kenya: Evangel.

Kraft, Charles H. 1979. *Christianity in Culture: A Study in Dynamic Biblical Christianity in Cross-Cultural Theologizing.* Maryknoll, N.Y.: Orbis.

Langer, Susanne K. 1948. *Philosophy in a New Key.* New York: New American Library of World Literature.

Lewis, Gordon R. 2003. "Is Propositional Revelation Essential to Evangelical Spiritual Formation?" *Journal of the Evangelical Theological Society* 46.2: 269–98.

Maeda, Eizoh. 1971. *A Study of Evangelistic Preaching of Selected American Evangelists in an Attempt to Discover Evangelistic Preaching Principles Which Would Be Effective in Japanese Evangelism.* Master of Arts thesis, Trinity Evangelical Divinity School.

McGavran, Donald A. 1974. *The Clash Between Christianity and Culture.* Washington, D.C.: Canon.

Mollenkott, Virginia Ramey. 2003. *She Who Changes: Re-Imagining the Divine in the World.* New York: Macmillan.

Neff, David. 2002." Meaning-full Translations." *Christianity Today,* October 7: 46–49.

———. 2004. "Discovering Unity: Two Theologians Are Bullish on Evangelical Futures." *Christianity Today* 19 January: 75–76.

Packer, J. I., and Thomas C. Oden. 2004. *One Faith: The Evangelical Consensus.* Downers Grove, Ill.: InterVarsity.

Pickering, Wilbur N. 1977. *The Identity of the New Testament Text.* Nashville: Thomas Nelson.

Prabhavananda, Swami, and Frederick Manchester. 1947. *The Upanishads: Breath of the Eternal.* Hollywood, Calif.: Vedanta.

Sharpe, Eric J. 1971. *Fifty Key Words: Comparative Religion.* Richmond: John Knox.

Stott, John R. W., and Robert T. Coote, eds. 1980. *Down to Earth: Studies in Christianity and Culture.* Grand Rapids: Eerdmans.

Tiénou, Tite. 1992. "Which Way for African Christianity: Westernization or Indigenous Authenticity?" *Evangelical Missions Quarterly* 28.3: 256–63.

Warfield, Benjamin Breckenridge. 1967. *The Inspiration and Authority of the Bible.* Philadelphia: Presbyterian & Reformed.

Watt, W. Montgomery. 1969. *Islamic Revelation in the Modern World.* Edinburgh: University of Edinburgh Press.

Winter, Ralph D. 1993. "The Theology of the Law of God." In *Foundations of Global Civilization: Semester One.* Mentors Handbook 27.1. Pasadena, Calif.: Institute of International Studies, U.S. Center for World Mission.

Wright, G. Ernest. 1991. "Biblical Theology (OT)." In *New Twentieth Century Encyclopedia of Religious Knowledge,* edited by J. D. Douglas. Grand Rapids: Baker.

Chapter 9

Countdowns and Prophetic Alerts

If We Go in Force, Will He Come in Haste?

And this gospel of the kingdom will be proclaimed throughout the whole world as a testimony to all nations, and then the end will come.
—Matthew 24:14

And the gospel must first be proclaimed to all nations.
—Mark 13:10

Prologue

IT WAS EARLY AUGUST 1968—the year following the Six Day War. For the first time in the modern era, the Jews were observing the ninth day of the Jewish month of Ab with access to the Western Wall of the Temple Mount, called the Wailing Wall. It is not a wall of the temple, but it was built in the second temple period near where the temple rose. The Western Wall is as close as Jews can come to the actual temple grounds, where mosques now stand.

According to an especially accommodating Jewish rabbi standing nearby, the pilgrims at the wall that day were reading the book of Lamentations and praying that God would destroy the mosque on the

Temple Mount. Finding my companion, Professor Edward Goodrick of Multnomah, and me to be interested listeners, the rabbi explained that his people would rebuild their temple but that they themselves would never destroy the holy place of any religion. God himself would somehow destroy that magnificent mosque, called the Dome of the Rock, so that the temple could be rebuilt.

Suddenly the solemnity of the occasion was broken by a group of young girls singing "Jerusalem the Golden," one of the songs sung frequently around the time of the war. An elderly Jewish lady began to loudly berate the singers for their disregard of the true nature of what was going on. The singing stopped as quickly as it had begun.

Our rabbi friend sought to explain: "It's the generation gap in Jerusalem. These young girls sing in celebration of victory in the recent war, but they have little sense of history and the times in which we live. Those who are older know that much bloodshed still lies ahead."

Time can be viewed from various perspectives. Anthropologists identify great cultural differences. The Indian cyclical view of time, with its seemingly endless rounds of births and rebirths, is very different from the tribal view, with its orientation to the past and abbreviated future. Both differ from the American linear view, according to which, "time is money," a commodity to be spent.

The psychologist, on the other hand, doesn't see time so much as a cultural construct. Time existentially has an impact on a person's feelings, psyche, or sense of wellbeing. After all, an hour in the dentist chair is manifestly not the same as an hour spent in a theme park. People react to severe time restraints and accelerated schedules differently from one another. Some people want carefully laid out work schedules. Others chafe under such regimentation.

The philosopher/theologian has yet other interests related to time. To the seminal Christian minds of Augustine, Aquinas, Calvin, and Hodge, time has serious theological implications. Augustine held that, because God is equally knowledgeable about past, present, and future, temporal distinctions are not real so far as God is concerned. Hodge, on the other hand, held that, though all things are known and ever present in God's view, he nevertheless sees them within a framework of proceeding moments (Buswell 1962, 1:45) To the average layperson this may seem like a distinction without a difference, but it bears mightily on questions having to do with the omniscience and immutability of God. We touched on some of these issues in chapter 1.

Our concerns in this chapter are theological and missiological. Regarding time, God has a redemptive purpose and "program" in time that was conceived in, and has ramifications for, eternity. He not only invites but commands us to share in his purpose and participate in his program—a "missiological view of time." Christian missions began before this generation came upon the scene. The mission of the church will come to an end when Jesus returns, probably after this generation has passed on.

A missiological view of time mediates the tension between *working* in missions and *waiting* in hope for Jesus' second coming. This larger time perspective helps resolve the tension between wanting to see many coming to the Lord in a hurry and patiently building a self-sustaining, disciple-making church. Missions confronts the theological time question about whether we can somehow "hasten" the day of his coming or whether we must simply serve while "patiently awaiting his appearing." Every generation of missions-minded Christians has experienced similar tensions, and modern technology and theology have given missions theorists some especially thorny time discussions over the last generation.

When Yahweh covenanted with and commissioned Abram, he said, "In you all the families of the earth shall be blessed" (Gen. 12:3). After reaching out to the Samaritan woman, Jesus said to his disciples, "Do you not say, 'There are yet four months, then comes the harvest'? Look, I tell you, lift up your eyes, and see that the fields are white for harvest" (John 4:35). Before his Passion, he said, "And this gospel of the kingdom will be proclaimed throughout the whole world as a testimony to all nations, and then the end will come" (Matt. 24:14). And before his ascension, he commanded "Go therefore and make disciples of all nations. . . . And behold, I am with you always, to the end of the age" (28:19–20).

So what about programs designed to expedite or even complete the divinely mandated task of world evangelization within a specified time frame? Countdowns certainly appeal culturally to a Western, and particularly an American, view of time. Time objectives are psychologically engaging and challenging for many of us. Setting a goal of reaching all the world seems to be in conformity with relevant biblical and eschatological expectations of the Second Coming.

The Great Century and Beyond

Kenneth Scott Latourette described the years from 1792 to 1910 as "the great century in missions." (Latourette 1941). Ralph Winter has referred to the burgeoning missions movement after World War II as "the unbelievable years" from 1945 to 1969 (Winter 1970). After that period, parachurch organizations in particular seriously contemplated the completion of the Great Commission task to all the world by the close of the twentieth century. Obviously the present and several preceding generations of Christians have lived through some of the most remarkable times in the history of missions. It is well that we reflect on them.

Progress in Modern Missions

Modern missions as we know them began with William Carey at the end of the eighteenth century. We have seen that hyper-Calvinists in England argued that the conversion of the heathen would be God's work in his time, and that nothing we could do would accomplish it (see p. 29). Carey's answer was contained in his treatise *An Enquiry into the Obligation of Christians to Use Means for the Conversion of the Heathen* (1792).

Toward the end of the nineteenth century, the United States assumed an increasingly prominent role in world missions (Latourette 1941, 94–100). In significant measure, this was due to the inception of the Student Volunteer Movement (S.V.M.) and the influence of men like Dwight L. Moody, Robert P. Wilder, and John R. Mott (Johnson 1988). The watchword of the S.V.M. was "the evangelization of the world in this generation," and its challenge was "all should go and go to all."

By the time of World War II, the S.V.M. was pretty much a spent force, and its slogan had become an empty phrase. But after the war, conservative evangelicals first and then Pentecostals revived the slogan, pressed forward with renewed vigor, and accomplished great things for God and his church (Winter 1970, 51–57). InterVarsity Christian Fellowship and Campus Crusade for Christ became powerful international college and university student organizations. The Church Growth Movement and Evangelism-in-Depth were among missions strategy movements. Fuller Theological Seminary and Trinity Evangelical Divinity School led the way to establish theological education programs that had a world outreach philosophy.

These and many other missionary entities propelled Christian missions forward. Indigenous evangelical movements around the world added tremendously to a missions surge through the rest of the twentieth century and into the twenty-first century.

Apocalypticism, Millennialism, and Missions

The nineteenth century witnessed not only a great move forward in world missions, but also a proliferation of apocalyptic cults such as the Shakers, Latter-Day Saints, and Jehovah's Witnesses—each of which had its own views concerning the Second Advent. Especially well known for setting dates on which prophecies were not fulfulled were the Jehovah's Witnesses and the Millerites. Several organizations were spun off from the Millerite movement, including the Seventh-Day Adventists.

Three very different eschatological perspectives and schools developed as mutually antithetical theological perspectives during the nineteenth century—premillennialism, amillennialism, and postmillennialism. A full explanation of these complex theological frameworks is impossible here, but a few highlights can help us understand the development of missions.

Premillennialists believe that the thousand-year reign of Christ prophesied in Revelation 20 refers to an earthly kingdom (usually thought to last for one thousand years) inaugurated by Christ at his second coming and extending until a final conflagration and the Final Judgment. Not all premillennialists are dispensational in eschatology, but dispensationalists dominated premillennialism and had the most impact on missions.

Shortly after the beginnings of modern missions from England and then America, John Nelson Darby of England gave rise to the Plymouth Brethren movement and the dispensational premillennialism that became most widely accepted among North American Protestants by the 1870s. Darby taught that Christ's church will be raptured or taken out of the world and a period of Great Tribulation will precede the setting up of the millennial kingdom. Unlike some apocalyptic cultic groups of the nineteenth century, dispensationalists were more concerned with "signs of the times" than with setting precise dates for the Lord's return. *One of those signs was the completion of world evangelization.*

Most important in the progress of dispensationalist theology in America was C. I. Scofield (1843–1921). He wrote and edited dispensational notes for the best-selling *Scofield Reference Bible* (first published in 1909); participated in various Bible conferences; and influenced numerous leaders among conservative Protestants, such as Dwight L. Moody, Frederick Franson, and Lewis Sperry Chafer. Scofield's particular take on dispensationalism profoundly influenced institutions of his time, including the Chicago Evangelization Society (1887; now Moody Bible Institute) and other institutions of the Bible school movement. He had an impact on some of the important missions organizations, notably Central American Mission (1891; now usually referred to as CAM International). When Dallas Theological Seminary began in 1924, its theological foundations owed much to Scofield.

It is impossible to fully appreciate the twin emphases on world evangelization and the Second Coming in closure strategies of the nineteenth and twentieth centuries apart from dispensational premillennialism.

The eschatological perspective that more strongly influenced Anglican, Lutheran, and Reformed communions was that of *amillennialism*. From an amillennialist perspective, Revelation 20 is to be interpreted symbolically as having to do with the present time during which Christ rules in heaven but also on earth through his church. The world will never be fully Christianized until the Second Coming, and until that time the earth will be the scene of a contest between good and evil. As compared with ages past, however, this world is becoming more Christian. As the gospel progresses, the church grows in numbers and influence, Satan is, in a sense, being "bound" (Matt. 12:29). Christ's rulership is becoming more evident as his second coming draws nearer.

Postmillennialism had many proponents among the Puritans and such notables as theologian Jonathan Edwards and revivalist Charles Finney. With amillennialists, postmillennialists also held that the thousand-year reign in Revelation 20 is to be understood figuratively. However, their view was that the kingdom of God is being extended through the preaching of the gospel and the saving work of the Holy Spirit. Gradually the world will be Christianized, a long period of peace and righteousness will ensue, and at the close of that period of peace the world will witness Christ's return, a general resurrection, and the Final Judgment.

Postmillennialism seemed a viable option at the turn of the twentieth century. The Civil War was over. America stood poised on the threshold of greatly expanded influence and power in the world. An optimistic reading of the times engendered hope for an age of peace and prosperity on earth. The time seemed ripe for a new thrust in the mission of the church as the curtain began to fall on the "great century of missions." However, with widespread social upheaval and, especially, with the onset of World War I, postmillennialism lost its appeal. Today, few postmillennialists remain other than those to be found in a few conservative theonomist movements, mostly presbyterian in polity, such as *Christian reconstructionism.*

A Nineteenth-Century "Countdown Strategy"

In parallel with hopes for a "golden age," whatever that might look like, some leaders were preoccupied with the relationship between the return of Christ and the progress of world evangelization. One of the most influential of these leaders was an eclectic Presbyterian-turned-Anabaptist minister-theologian by the name of Arthur T. Pierson (1837–1911).

Profoundly disappointed with the spiritual state of some prominent congregations, Pierson was one of a group of American leaders influenced to embrace premillennialism by British Plymouth Brethren in the 1870s and 1880s. His "conversion" did not dampen but rather heightened his concern for, and involvement in, endeavors designed to remedy social ills. It also provided him with a different perspective on extremely optimistic views of America's role in the future, some of which were supported by a utopian postmillennialism. And it reinforced themes that characterized his preaching: the Bible as a book of prophecy; the need for believers to separate from the world; the "signs of the times"; and the imminent return of Christ.

This is not to imply that the impulse for world evangelization and the great student movement came from only one theological and eschatological stream. Various student Christian organizations appealing to young people were involved, including the Young Men's Christian Association and Young Women's Christian Association and especially the Student Missionary Inquiry and Young People's Societies of Christian Endeavour. All of these and others made important contributions. But most important to our discussion is the fact that Pierson became an indefatigable promoter of world missions while ministering to a rapidly growing, evangelistic, and socially active Philadelphia church started by businessman John Wanamaker (1838–1922). Pierson soon became a prominent speaker at Bible and missionary conferences. He challenged young men such as Robert Speer, Samuel Zwemer, and T. C. Horton to go into missions. He became closely associated with evangelical leaders such as J. H. Brookes, A. J. Gordon, Robert Wilder, Henry W. Frost, Moody, and John R. Mott. He wrote *The Crisis in Missions* (1886), one of the most significant missions books of his day. And he was editor of the influential journal *The Missionary Review of the World* from 1887 until his death in 1911.

At the second American Prophetic Conference in 1886, Pierson gave an address, "Our Lord's Second Coming a Motive to World-Wide Evangelization," which was later published by Wanamaker. This teaching "laid the groundwork for the vital connection between premillennial biblical exegesis and the cause of foreign missions" (Roberts 2003, 135). That same year, Moody invited college students to his summer conference for lay workers. Uncertain that he could hold the interest of students, Moody asked Pierson to give lectures on "the Bible and prophecy."

Pierson's impassioned and yet rational approach to the world's need for Christ appealed to students. Before a week was out, one hundred students had decided to become missionaries. The "Mount Hermon 100" changed the course of missions and, indeed, the course of world Christianity (Roberts 2003, 149). In 1888 the Student Volunteer Movement for

Foreign Missions was organized—a movement that launched thousands upon a career in foreign missions.

Pierson coupled his theology of the Second Coming with the phrase "the evangelization of the world in this generation." In fact, Pierson himself coined the slogan, although Mott and the S.V.M. popularized it. In 1877 Pierson devised a plan to evangelize the world by 1900. The plan grew out of his calculation that, if all Protestant Christians would give just one dollar a year and if one in every one hundred Christians would become a missionary, world evangelization by 1900 would be an attainable goal. More than that, world evangelization could be expected to hasten Christ's coming and "bring back the King." Over the ensuing years, Pierson reluctantly came to the conclusion that churches lacked the spiritual vitality required to carry out his plan to achieve world evangelization by 1900. Pierson's program was more or less abandoned in the mid-1890s, but the idea of closure lived on.

The impact of Pierson on world missions was considerable. He had a passion for evangelization and for developing the kind of biblical theology, missions strategy, and Christian unity to sustain it. In public he was a most enthusiastic promoter of the great Ecumenical Missionary Conference held in New York in 1900. However, as a participant he privately expressed misgivings in his notes: "Thus far no *spiritual* impression on conference. Word of God not read. The whole air post millennial [*sic*], undue stress on culture. Fatherhood of God. Brotherhood of Man. Education, etc. Too much like Congress of Religions" (Roberts 2003, 293). Nevertheless, his influence was to be felt in Edinburgh 1910, in the formation of the International Missionary Council, in the S.V.M., and through various efforts. Pierson's shadow extended to the Lausanne Movement of the mid-1970s and especially the A.D. 2000 and Beyond Movement.

Pierson did not attend the conference in Edinburgh in 1910. *The Missionary Review* was represented by his son Delavan. But that year Pierson celebrated the fiftieth year of his ordination to the ministry. As part of that celebration, the general assembly of the Presbyterian Church in the United States of America—the denomination that had expelled him fifteen years before after his baptism by immersion, sent "affectionate greetings" with gratitude for his work on behalf of world missions.

The celebration of Pierson almost amounted to exoneration, for very different theological worries besides baptism were troubling the Northern Presbyterians. As Roberts puts it:

> Not only was Pierson's protégé, Robert Speer, head of the mission board, but the convergence of conservative forces against modernism meant that Pierson's controversial views on baptism, spirituality, and prophecy had become less important to the denomination than his spirited and consistent defense of an infallible Bible, and his promotion of foreign missions. Passage of the "five points of fundamentalism" occurred at the same General Assembly that held out an olive branch to the elderly Bible teacher. (Roberts 2003, 295)

Closure and Countdown Strategies in the Twentieth Century

Todd M. Johnson, director of the World Evangelization Research Center, writes that the closure idea has been kept "before the Christian public almost continually through the twentieth century in the form of confident slogans, plans and documents" (Johnson 1988, 26). He shows a progression of plans and slogans through the twentieth century.

1900—"The evangelization of the world in this generation."
1910—"The whole church taking the whole gospel to the whole world."
1912—"Reaching every home."
1914—"Inauguration of the kingdom of God on earth."
1929—"Each one teach one."
1930—"Bringing Christ to the nations."
1934—"Evangelize to a finish to 'bring back the King.'"
1943—"Into all the world."
1946—"Complete Christ's Commission."
1956—"The gospel to every creature."
1957—"Global conquest."
1959—"Two thousand tongues to go."
1967—"Crusade for world revival."
1974—"Let the earth hear his voice."

1976—"Bold Missions Thrust."
1980—"A Church for Every People by the Year 2000."
1984—"Strategy to Every People."
1986—"One million native missionaries."
1990—"Decade of Evangelization."
1995—"A Church for Every People and the Gospel for Every Person by A.D. 2000."

Winter, of the U.S. Center for World Mission, also reviews this history and concentrates on conferences, events, and strategies that focused in one way or another on the evangelization of the world and, more specifically, on the completion of that task. He takes a very positive view of the 1910 World Missionary Conference in Edinburgh. Unlike subsequent conferences that brought together church leaders but not missions leaders, this meeting was exclusively for delegates of agencies. Edinburgh 1910 directed attention solely on topics related to world evangelization and what it would take to "finish the job." Winter said that an understandable deficiency of the 1910 conference was that leaders and delegates thought in terms of "unoccupied fields" rather than in terms of "unreached peoples." Since they thought in "field terms" rather than in "people terms" they overlooked the Indians of the Americas and minority peoples in other countries (Winter 1995, 14). Although he focuses on precursors of the A.D. 2000 and Beyond Movement, Winter recounts a number of evangelization-closing events and strategies that developed following Edinburgh 1910 (Winter 1995, 29–34):

1972—Proposal for a 1910-type conference to be held in 1980.
1973—Founding of the Asia Missions Association.
1979—EFMA Executives Retreat on Unreached Peoples.
1980—Three Edinburgh 1910-type conferences.
1982—Formation of the IFMA Frontier Peoples Committee; Lausanne committee-sponsored retreat designed to standardize key terms referring to unreached peoples.
1984—Founding of *International Journal of Frontier Missions*.
1986—Founding of the International Society for Frontier Missiology; celebration of the founding of the Student Volunteer Movement

by four U.S. bodies; world meeting of the Asian Missions Association produces the Third-World Mission Association.

1987—First continental Americas missions conference, COMIBAM *(Congreso Missionero Americano)* in São Paulo, led by Latin Americans.

1989—Singapore Global Consultation on World Evangelization (GCOWE); founding of the A.D. 2000 and Beyond Movement; the Lausanne 2 meeting at Manila.

1989–1995—"An incredible whirl of activities by the A.D. 2000 and Beyond Movement, leading to a May 1995 meeting in Korea—the Global Consultation on World Evangelization (GCOWE 2).

These are only some of the more visible events. According to Luis Bush of Partners International, this "late-twentieth-century catalytic movement" for world evangelization by 2000 involved as many as two thousand "individual plans" and took shape in the 1980s and early 1990s (Bush 2003, 17). Representatives of some of these plans were the ones meeting in Singapore in January 1989. They committed themselves to "The Great Commission Manifesto" to "seize the moment toward fulfillment of a saturation church planting movement among every people and the proclamation of the Gospel to every person" (18). The A.D. 2000 and Beyond Movement (sometimes shortened to A.D. 2000) was born.

That is the gist of the story, but more is required to understand the movement and what happened to and through it (see, e.g., Starling 1981; Gary and Gary 1989; Wang 1989; Stearns and Stearns 1991; Winter 1995).

Counting Down and Up: The A.D. 2000 and Beyond Movement

It is no easy task to summarize an evaluation of the "incredible whirl of activities" relating to the A.D. 2000 Movement. But critical to the larger story was the 1972 proposal for a 1980 meeting to be patterned after the 1910 "missions only" conference in Edinburgh. Meetings in 1980 of the World Council of Churches (Melbourne) and the Lausanne Committee for World Evangelization (Pattaya) overshadowed and almost derailed plans for a meeting of exclusively missions agency delegates focused on "hidden" or "unreached" peoples. Still, strengthened by the vision of Winter and other respected missions leaders, and managed by Larry Allmon, Leiton Chin, Roy Spraggett, and others, the World Consultation on Frontier Missions was held in Edinburgh in 1980.

This "conference that almost wasn't" proved most significant in taking the next steps toward the future developments. Unlike Edinburgh 1910, when non-Western agencies were overlooked, all of the major non-Western missions agencies were represented at Edinburgh 1980. Fully one-third of the delegates came from Third World missions agencies—the largest number of Third World delegates ever to meet in a world-level conference of this kind. Three of the four plenary speakers were non-Westerners and one of them, Thomas Wang, was destined to play a crucial role in subsequent developments of the A.D. 2000 and Beyond Movement. A complete record of the proceedings and presentations of Edinburgh 1980 is compiled in Alan Starling's edited volume *Seeds of Promise* (1981).

Wang, the international director of the Lausanne Committee for World Evangelization, was the link between Edinburgh 1980 and the Global Conference on World Evangelization in Singapore (1989). Edinburgh 1980 had awakened within him an unshakable commitment to evangelizing unreached people groups by the year 2000. However, achieving the required unity and synergy was not to come easily. Jay Gary reports that, in an interview with David Barrett in 1989, Barrett said, "The century from 1871 to 1971 saw at least 60 major clarion calls to evangelize the world by a certain date. The history of world evangelization is littered with hundreds of well-intentioned plans and pronouncements that aroused enormous interest but came to nothing" (Gary and Gary 1989, 19).

After hearing that pessimistic appraisal by the well-known statistician on world missions, Gary realized "something more" would be needed if the contemplated countdown to world evangelization by the year 2000 plan were to succeed. Wang, Bush, R. Keith Parks, Bill Bright, and Ralph Winter were among other leaders who entertained similar plans to accomplish world evangelization by the year 2000. In 1988 some of these leaders got together to lay plans for a 1989 Singapore meeting, the Global Consultation on World Evangelization.

In anticipation of the Singapore meeting, Todd Johnson analyzed the efforts then underway to evangelize the world at the end of the nineteenth century. He found that a chief cause of failure was that leaders of that effort had conferred with each other but failed to take united action. Now united action seemed unlikely once again. But a turning point was reached when some of the leaders pledged themselves to take a number of action steps (especially the adoption of specific segments of the world's unevangelized people groups) both together and separately. These action steps constituted the "something more" that Gary deemed to be necessary if the plan was to succeed (Gary and Gary 1989, 19, 66–71).

The January 1989 consultation in Singapore promoted a decisive vision that was advanced further at the Lausanne II Conference in Manila the following summer. The vision of Edinburgh 1980 had been realized: The A.D. 2000 and Beyond Movement had been born. The Edinburgh 1980 purpose statement, "A Church for Every People by the year 2000," had been enlarged to "A Church for Every People and the Gospel for Every Person by the Year 2000." New leadership had been secured.

Under the leadership of Wang and Bush, the movement attracted interest from many church leaders and laity. Hundreds of missions agencies and local churches "adopted" unreached people groups. As Bush later reported, "Christian leaders responded worldwide from large, medium, and small organizations, ministries, churches, denominations, and movements. Laymen and women became involved. Formal and informal relationships were established" (Bush 2003, 20). Ultimately, the movement was an umbrella for a number of closure-oriented organizations and efforts. These organizations launched such operations as Adopt-a-People, People Clusters and Affinity Groups, the Joshua Project, the 10/40 Window, Praying Through the Window, and Prayer Profiles.

For all its success in planting functioning churches among previously unreached people groups, a more significant long-range result of the A.D. 2000 effort may yet prove to be its unifying effect. As never before, Two-Thirds World leaders and missions-minded Christians talked and worked in concert through national, regional, and global consultations. At the international level, the Global Consultation on World Evangelization met in Korea in 1995 and the Global Consultation on World Evangelization II was convened in Pretoria, South Africa, in 1997. These consultations demonstrated the ongoing feeling of urgency that momentum toward achieving an evangelized world must be advanced, not lost. Both conferences attracted as many as four thousand delegates from well over one hundred nations.

The Korea gathering undertook an "in-process assessment of the unfinished task." It was carried on in a mood of fervor that spilled over into Korea's churches. Before it ended some seventy thousand Korean young people had committed their lives to world missions. The 1997 meeting in Pretoria was a more subdued and "chastened" gathering and a time of self-analysis and critique. Winter urged that a more contextualized and less Western gospel be presented, especially as Christians approached unreached segments of the Muslim, Hindu, and Buddhist world. Emphasis shifted to the "and beyond" of the A.D. 2000 and Beyond designation. Leaders wanted to be certain that the year 2000 was not viewed as a deadline, but rather as a springboard into twenty-first-century evangelism.

If there was an element of "chastening" at Pretoria, however, the meeting also might be regarded as something of a harbinger of what might yet come to pass. It was the largest and most globally representative gathering of Christians in history.

In accord with the intent of its organizers, the A.D. 2000 and Beyond Movement disbanded with the close of the "Decade on World Evangelization." Much happened that would not have been accomplished had goals not been set, had closure not been in view, and had a countdown not been initiated. More analysis than that, however, will be necessary to determine whether it might be called truly successful, so we will revisit these strategies and events after looking at what Scripture might have to say about all of this.

A Premillennial View of Evangelization

Most of those who were so motivated to work toward fulfillment of the Great Commission have been operating from a premillennial perspective. Within this perspective, central importance is given to Jesus' teaching on the Mount of Olives during the final week before his crucifixion and resurrection (Matt. 24–25; Mark 13; Luke 21:5–36).

It has become apparent that the Lord's purpose in what is traditionally called the Olivet Discourse, was to give important preparation for the

Great Commission. Of course, Jesus also was preparing his disciples for the events of his passion a few days later. But Jesus spelled out quite clearly what would happen during the interval between his first and second comings. The explanations and instructions on the Mount of Olives provided the disciples with all the background information they needed to act, once they received their specific marching orders and the empowerment of the Holy Spirit. The marching orders came in the form of the Great Commission. Empowerment came at Pentecost.

"What Will Be the Sign?"

Jesus' disciples were confused and very curious. After experiencing the grandeur of the temple, their effusive appraisals were interrupted by Jesus. He abruptly announced that the temple would be completely laid waste. Startled by this prophecy, they responded in wonder, "Tell us, . . . what will be the sign of your coming and of the end of the age?" (Matt. 24:3 NIV).

Jesus answered that there would be false Christs, wars, famines, earthquakes, persecution, false prophets, apostasy, spiritual declension—and a worldwide preaching of the gospel. The entire litany of events is negative and ominous, except for one element, *world evangelization.*

There is little to indicate that his disciples really understood his answer to their *when?* question and even less that Jesus was answering precisely the question they had asked. Not many weeks later, on that same "mount called Olivet," the disciples' curiosity once again got the best of them. They inquired, "Lord, will you at this time restore the kingdom to Israel?"

This time Jesus responded, "It is not for you to know times and seasons that the Father has fixed by his own authority" (Acts 1:7). Then he repeated the Commission and told them to wait for the promised Holy Spirit.

After the passing of twenty centuries, our contemporaries still are often confused when it comes to the same questions. As might be expected, scholars interpret our Lord's words in the light of their preferred eschatological frameworks. For some, these prophecies were fulfilled when Titus and his Roman soldiers invaded Jerusalem and destroyed the temple in

A.D. 70. For others, the destruction of Jerusalem in 70 presaged another, more salient fulfillment in the future. For some, those caught away in a future rapture of the church will meet the Lord in the air and the rest will remain on earth to endure the sufferings of the Great Tribulation. For others, those caught away will be taken into judgment, and those left behind will enter the millennial kingdom.

There are varying interpretations of the "end of the age," the "abomination of desolation," the "lesson of the fig tree," the "generation that will not pass," and so forth. Laypersons, meanwhile, often give up on prophecy or resign themselves to following the lead of some favorite Bible teacher or fiction writer.

We can take heart that those early disciples and other first-century Christians did not show that they had come to a complete understanding of all that Jesus was saying either. But there is every indication that they came to a better understanding of its meaning to their own lives.

So can we. *And so should we, because much is at stake.*

The End Times and the Second Coming

Without even attempting to resolve knotty detail issues that attend Christ's answer to the *when?* question, we can understand the essentials that Jesus wanted to communicate and appreciate their importance for our time.

The first essential is that we should understand the difference between the "end of the age" and the "end of the ages." The disciples' question focused on the end of the age (singular). Both Jesus and his disciples used the singular *time* and *age* when speaking of the culmination of the present age and the events attending Christ's parousia or second coming. Accordingly, when Jesus gave the Great Commission, he promised to be with his sent ones until "the end of the age" (Matt. 28:20). The entire period between his two comings, on the other hand, is in view in such expressions as "the last days" (Acts 2:16–17; 2 Peter 3:3), "the end of the ages" (1 Cor. 10:11; Heb. 9:26), and "the last hour" (1 John 2:18). Our age in its entirety constitutes the eschatological age that looks back to the First Advent and ahead to the Second Advent.

It is clear, then, that the disciples were inquiring as to the end of the age and "end-time" events. What has not been so clear is the fact that Jesus' answer also took into account the "the last days" or "the end of the ages,"—that is, the entire period between Christ's two advents. Why? Because, though the disciples were not aware of it, they and we need to understand the characteristics, contours, and course of this entire period called "the end of the ages."

The second essential is that we should distinguish between the "signs of the times" and the "sign of Christ's coming." Recent events around the world, and especially in the Middle East, have occasioned many questions concerning so-called "signs of the times," such as wars, famines, earthquakes, pestilence, persecution, false christs, and so on. But it should be noticed that Jesus did not call any one of these events singly, or all of them together, a "sign" as such. Though the disciples asked, "What will be the sign [*sēmeion*] of your coming and of the close of the age?" in verse 3 (of Matt. 24), Jesus himself did not use that term until verse 30 when, in connection with catastrophic events in the heavens, he said, "Then will appear in heaven the sign [*sēmeion*] of the Son of Man, and then all the tribes of the earth will mourn, and they will see the Son of Man coming on the clouds of heaven with power and great glory."

Differences of interpretation will persist at this point until unfolding events make clear which interpretation is correct. But personally I am persuaded that the events catalogued in verses 4–14 are not really signs in any special sense at all. Rather, Jesus was pointing to the kind of events that would characterize the whole of history from his first to his second comings. Only later in chapter 24 did he deal with really unique eschatological events, such as the "abomination of desolation" and the "budding of the fig tree." Even in that context, only the actual appearance of the Son of Man in the clouds of heaven is identified as a "sign."

The third essential is that we should understand the difference between "times" and "seasons." It is easy to give but scant attention to Jesus' words to his disciples in Acts 1:7, "It is not for you to know times and seasons." But most students of New Testament Greek learn the difference between times and seasons very early on. "Times" in this case is the English translation for the Greek word *chronoi*, from which we derive English words such as *chronology*, and *chronometer*. It has reference to ongoing time, periods of time, and the course of time. "Seasons" is the translation for the Greek word *kairoi,* which refers to special, appointed, favorable, opportune, or critical times.

The importance of this distinction becomes clear when we realize that, in his version of the Olivet Discourse, Luke quotes Jesus' words concerning the coming destruction of Jerusalem, that the Jews "will fall by the edge of the sword and be led captive among all nations, and Jerusalem will be trampled underfoot by the Gentiles until the times of the Gentiles [*kairoi ethnōn*] are fulfilled" (Luke 21:24). Jesus was pointing forward to "times" that were more than just ongoing and unfolding; they were to be the appointed times for Christians to preach the gospel around the world and opportune times for the world's people to hear and believe it.

Those earliest disciples didn't get it. They were too preoccupied with the *when?* question. They got it later on, as did other first-century Christians (1 Thess. 5:1; 2 Peter 3:1–13). But, whether in the first century or the twenty-first century, believers who are primarily motivated by curiosity will find that in focusing on signs they lose sight of Christ and what he really wants us to know, be, and do.

The fourth essential is that we must distinguish between "countdowns" and "prophetic alerts." We do not know the number of earthquakes or the intensity of the pestilence or the extensiveness of the testimony that our Lord had in view, even if we are persuaded that the events enumerated in Matthew 24:4–14 are "signs" of the end and of Christ's coming. If, on the other hand, those events are characteristic of the whole of this eschatological age, then every time we see or experience them we will be reminded that the Lord Jesus who predicted them actually knew the shape of history beforehand. And we will be reminded that he is coming again and warned to be ready for his coming. Instead of counting the number and frequency of so-called signs, we will be encouraged to count them as "signals" that Jesus is indeed coming, and we must be ready.

With that in mind, Stephen Travis calls these events "prophetic alerts" (Travis 1974, 44). In his understanding, we could say that these events are something like the "alert system" that was set up in the United States after the terrorist attacks of September 11, 2001. Different "levels of danger," which in the U.S. are indicated by colors indicating how likely the threat of attack is at the moment, impress upon us the urgency of being ready, and the frequency with which they occur is an additional

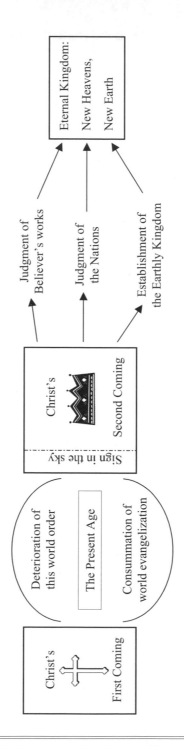

Figure 10. History: Heading From and Heading To

prod to heighten the sense of urgency. That Jesus himself was thinking in "prophetic alert" terms seems evident from the fact that three times he admonished the disciples to "stay awake" ("be on the alert," Matt. 24:42–43 NASB), "be ready," and "watch" for his coming (vv. 42–44; 25:13). Nevertheless, as the angel chided them in Acts 1:11, Jesus did not mean that they were to simply look into the sky. The greatest long-term task in human history was about to commence. The gospel of the kingdom was to be preached in all the world as a testimony to all nations. Then and only then would occur the "great consummation"—the "sign in the sky," the "coming of the Son of Man," and the "end."

The Right Question: What Kind of Persons?

Like many of us, the early disciples were slow learners. Only with time did Peter, for example, understand that the wrong question had been asked on the Mount of Olives. Instead of "When will these things be, and what will be the sign?" their question should have been "What kind of people ought we to be?"

Why can we be quite confident that that is the case? Because, when Peter becomes an experienced apostle he writes through the inspiration of the Holy Spirit to believing Jews dispersed throughout the Mediterranean world about the eschatological age (the "last days"). He prophesies that many will call the promise of Christ's return into question and insist that history is only a meaningless repetition of events. Nothing really changes; history is going nowhere (2 Peter 3:3–4). But Peter counters that view of history by recounting that, just as the world was once destroyed by water, it will one day be destroyed by fire. More than that, the proper measurement of *chronos* time until the end is the salvific purpose of God. God wants all to repent and be saved. That being true, with him a day is as a thousand years and a thousand years as a day (vv. 8–10).

In light of all of this, the apostle Peter asks "What sort of people ought you [we] to be in lives of holiness and godliness, waiting for and hastening the coming of the day of God?" (vv. 11–12). Notice how Peter's question and even his language fit hand in glove with our interpretation of the first part of the Olivet Discourse. Notice that Peter's question turns

out to be the question that Jesus as the Master Teacher actually answered
in the last part of his discourse on Olivet.

Christ's Perspective on His Second Coming (Matt. 24:43–25:13)

There were three parts to the answer that Jesus gave. *First, his followers should be watchful (Matt. 24:43–44).* "Know this," Jesus said,
"that if the master of the house had known in what part of the night the
thief was coming, he would have stayed awake and would not have let
his house be broken into." But the householder did not know when the
break-in would occur, so he was not "on the alert" (v. 42 NASB), and his
goods were stolen.

For Christians to be caught unawares at Christ's second coming would
be both lamentable and unnecessary. In Christian missions, as in every
other endeavor, we carry out world witness, knowing *that he will come*
even though we do not know *when he will come.*

*Second, no one who knows that the Master is coming should presume
that he will not come now (Matt. 24:45–51).* A servant is put in charge
of the affairs of a large estate while the owner goes on an extended trip.
If the servant is faithful, he will conduct affairs in such a way that all
will be in good order whenever the owner returns. Or, as the owner says
in the parallel passage of Luke 19:13, "occupy till I come" (KJV). Who
knows? The servant's temporary appointment may become a permanent
one. But if the servant says to himself, "The owner won't be returning
for a considerable time; so this is my chance to 'live it up' and do what
I want," and then proceeds to hang out with the wrong crowd and beats
up on his underlings, what then? The obvious answer is that he will be
punished.

People make a great mistake if they delude themselves into thinking
that Christ's coming and the end of the age are far enough in the future so
that they will have a future opportunity to get their priorities straightened
out and to do his bidding. For many there *will not be time.* All of us are
to serve Christ today. We do not know about tomorrow.

*Third, no one should make decisions on a presumption that Christ
must come right away (Matt. 25:1–13).* Ten young ladies (bridesmaids?)
were invited to be part of a wedding party, but only five of them made

it. Why? Because five of them neglected to take extra oil for their lamps. Without lighted lamps they could not be a part of the procession. So when the bridegroom was detained for some reason, they found it necessary to go off to the store to buy more oil. But in that culture, weddings did not begin at the tick of a clock but when the notables showed up. While the young ladies were shopping, the bridegroom appeared and the wedding started. Imagine their disappointment when they found themselves outside the banquet hall looking in. Their mistake was the opposite of the servant's when he thought the master would never return, but it had a similar result.

Those young bridesmaids were really no more foolish than are many Christians of the past and present. Some Christians are so sure that Christ is coming at a certain time—or within a certain time period—that they neglect to prepare for their own assignment. It might be something of a "stretch," but think of the "amateurism" discussed in chapter 7. Think of all the dedicated young people who hurriedly get their support and equipment together and head for the missions field but do not take the time required to get the mental and spiritual equipment required for missionary service. They are so sure the time is short that they go half-prepared. And they are so busy on the field that they do not take time to nurture mind or spirit. The months pass; perhaps even years. Sooner or later, they have "run out of oil." Some return to school to "buy more oil." But for others it is simply too late. The opportunity to prepare and remain prepared to meet the challenges of missionary service has passed.

It is right to look for Christ's coming. *But it is wrong to make important decisions on the basis of calculations as to the exact time of his coming.* Someone has said, we should act as though he is coming today, but we should *plan* as though he is not coming for a thousand years. There is a tension there, but, rightly understood, that must be close to what Jesus meant.

Investing Wisely in the Work of Christ (Matt. 25:14–30)

Our part in fulfilling the Great Commission can be thought of as investing in the future kingdom. To think of it that way gives more of a feeling of expectancy or even urgency. We should not waste time. Timely investments will reap eternal rewards.

In the Olivet Discourse, Jesus makes a direct point of this, as recorded in Matthew 25:14–30. Before leaving on an extended tour, a wealthy man entrusted his finances to three servants in accordance with the ability and faithfulness they had demonstrated in the past. He gave five talents to one, two to another, and one to the third. These amounts represented an enormous investment—the equivalent of twenty years of income for a laborer even in the case of the servant who received one talent. He instructed them to put the money to work and then he departed.

Immediately the first two put their talents to work, but the third buried his talent in the ground for "safekeeping."

After a long time the rich man returned and asked for an accounting. The two employees who had doubled their holdings by wise planning and hard work were rewarded in accord with what they had done. Jesus was saying that, when he returns, his people will face what the Bible calls the "judgment seat of Christ," where each one will "receive what is due for what he has done in the body, whether good or evil" (2 Cor. 5:10). This is all too easily forgotten.

Our Lord "invested" his very life in this business of reclaiming his planet and redeeming his people, and he anticipates that we will use the opportunities, gifts, strength, and substance that he has placed at our disposal in this same divine business. Great rewards will attend good stewardship.

Misuse of God-given talents will result in eternal loss. The third employee excused himself on the grounds that he knew his master to be a successful and exacting man. Rather than risking his talent, he was content to bury it and return it to his employer—unmarked, untouched, and unused. But his carefully contrived confession was unavailing. He claimed to know his employer but he did not really know him at all. Had he really known him, at the very least he would have put the talent in a bank and gained some interest. The master's response to his ignorance and indolence was anger. The servant was reprimanded, divested of his lone talent, and severely judged.

All Christian service entails sacrifice. Some service, especially when it comes to world evangelization, also entails risk. But, lest we forget, the Lord took the greatest risk when he delegated so many resources and so much responsibility to his often erring people. And yet he did.

Correct Expectations About Christ's Coming (Matt. 25:31–46)

If believers generally, and missionaries in particular, have a proper understanding of their task, they should be careful to have the right expectations.

This brings us to Matthew 25:31–46, one of the most misinterpreted, misunderstood, and misapplied passages in the entire New Testament. For example, T. Paul Verghese reflects a widespread but erroneous interpretation of these verses when he writes, "The ultimate judgement . . . is not in terms of conscious acceptance of the Lordship of Christ and membership in the believing community. It is rather in terms of one's active compassion for the poor and needy (see the parable of the judgement of the nations in Matt. 25:31–46)" (Verghese 1968, 416).

Verghese is correct in recognizing this as the "ultimate judgment of the nations," but he is incorrect in making works the primary basis for that judgment. Many commentators make not one but two mistakes here. First, they fail to recognize that the ultimate or Final Judgment is in view. Second, they proceed to interpret the passage as though it had to do with the judgment of the believers' works. No wonder confusion abounds with reference to this passage.

We need to keep in mind our interpretive perspective, that the Olivet Discourse was used by Jesus to prepare the disciples to receive the Great Commission, according to which they were to be sent to disciple the *ethnē*. We need to remember also that the present age presents an unprecedented *kairos,* the "mother of all opportunities," for the church to proclaim the gospel and for the world to receive it. And we need to recognize that Christ will "gather the *ethnē*" at the Great White Throne and render his Final Judgment upon them (Matt. 25:32; Rev. 20:11–15). What will happen is likened to the action of a rancher who separates his sheep from his goats in order to deal with both types of animals in an appropriate fashion.

Jesus identified three classes of people who will be at the Final Judgment: (1) Christ's sent ones; (2) those who will come to him because they accept the message of the sent ones; and (3) those who will reject the message of salvation.

Christ's "sent ones" or missionaries, are described here as the "least of these my brothers" (Matt. 25:40) or simply the "least of these" (v. 45). Matthew 25:31–46 closely parallels an earlier Matthean passage where Jesus sends out his disciples to minister to the "lost sheep of the house of Israel" (10:6). At that time Jesus sent his disciples to the people of Israel (not to Gentiles or Samaritans) to minister by preaching the kingdom message, exorcising evil spirits, and healing the sick. Difficulties and discouragements there would be. Some people would receive them; others would not. But, Jesus says, "Whoever receives you receives me, and whoever receives me receives him who sent me. . . . And whoever gives one of these little ones [or, as in the margin of some Bibles, "humble folk,"] even a cup of cold water *because he is a disciple,* truly, I say to you, he will by no means lose his reward" (vv. 40–42, emphasis mine).

This standout incident in the mission of Christ to Israel at his first coming should not be overlooked when interpreting Matthew 25:31–46. The ambiguous rendering "little ones" in some translations should not be allowed to confuse us. The Greek word used in these verses is *elachistos,* the superlative form of the word for "small." A better translation would be "least" in the sense of "quite unimportant or insignificant." Paul uses the word in 1 Corinthians 15:9 when he says that he is the "least of the apostles." And that is the connotation when Jesus speaks of his representatives as those who are willing to be thought of as the "least of his brothers" (Matt. 25:40). Christ's "sent ones" or missionaries are in view in this passage, just as they are in Matthew 10.

Some scholars take the idea a step further to propose that the missionaries in view here are 144,000 Jewish missionaries who will preach the gospel during the Great Tribulation. That interpretation does mesh with the parallel passage, with Matthew's special concern for the place of the Jews in the divine plan, and with the fact that Matthew mentions that it is the "gospel of the kingdom" that is to be preached (though Mark simply says "gospel" in Mark 13:10). Evaluation of that argument is beyond the scope of this volume. Whether all missionaries or a particular group of missionaries is in view, what is clear is that Jesus is referring to *missionaries* and their treatment at the hands of the *ethnē.* Jesus is not referring here to poor and weak people or little children, but to his "sent ones" or missionaries and those people of the world who either receive or reject them and their message.

It is quite a stretch for Western Christians and missionaries to accept this interpretation. By virtue of our cultural and economic background, we Westerners will not readily accept an interpretation that pictures missionaries as experiencing hunger, thirst, nakedness, and imprisonment. But consider those early believers and missionaries to whom Jesus was speaking. What happened to them? Recall also the stories of missionaries like Adoniram Judson and the fate of thousands of other missionaries in the nineteenth century. Tens of thousands of Christian martyrs from many lands have fallen to persecution in recent times. Actually, this closing portion of the Olivet Discourse introduces us to a sobering reality about the Christian mission that is easily lost when we are inclined to think of missions in ways that invariably makes others out to be the sufferers and Christian witnesses to be their benefactors.

The second group of people to whom Jesus refers have accepted Christ's representatives and their message. From whence will they come? How will they be assembled? There is much that we do not know. But all the peoples of the world will be gathered at the Great White Throne. According to the text, they will be divided into two groups—the "sheep," who are positioned on the King's right hand, and the "goats," on his left. The King will first commend the "sheep" for accepting him and ministering to his needs. Their puzzlement at these words is soon dispelled. They did so when they invited his missionary representatives into their hearts and homes. And when they ministered to his missionary representatives according to their needs. The sheep *ethnē* will inherit the kingdom prepared for them from the foundation of the world.

The third group collects those who rejected Christ's representatives and their message. They are on the King's left hand and identified as "goats." The metaphor has no cultural connotations familiar to our culture. The sad truth is that these people are lost and will be consigned to eternal punishment. By turning away the King's representatives, they rejected the King himself. Consequently, there will be no place for them in his kingdom. This kingdom business is serious indeed, far more serious than any of us can imagine. We can take Christ's word for it.

Countdowns, Alerts, and the Commission

Countdowns to World Evangelization: An Accounting

Countdowns to world evangelization are more biblical than countdowns to the Second Coming. A history of the latter sort reveals that when Christ does not return on the date predicted, the results are disillusionment, cynicism, and a rush to regain some measure of credibility. This should not be the case when it comes to setting goals for evangelizing the world. In both the A.D. 1900 and A.D. 2000 movements, leaders understood well before the target date that the goal would be only partially realized. That recognition allowed for tempered assessments and certain adjustments. In the A.D. 1900 case, Mott himself was instrumental in adopting the catchphrase "the evangelization of the world in this generation." In the A.D. 2000 case, the phrase *and beyond* was added so as to make the goal independent of the arbitrary year that was selected. The movment was about "the evangelization of the world by A.D. 2000 and beyond."

Admittedly, the addition of the words *and beyond* made for a degree of ambiguity, but the words recognize the fact that the task of evangelization is ongoing until Christ's coming. As far as Winter is concerned, the A.D. 2000 Movement had neither the return of Christ nor the completion of the Great Commission in view: "The Bible clearly teaches that His Return will be unexpected for everyone." And, although the completion of the Great Commission is what we are all working for, since it is "not an idea that is specific enough to make into a measurable goal the A.D. 2000 Movement has wisely chosen a purpose statement which is eminently measurable" (Winter 1995, 5–6)

Setting dates for the Second Coming is quite a different matter. It would be absurd to say, "Christ will come by the year 2000 *and beyond.*" Equally absurd is the idea of setting a date at all when our Lord himself said that he did not know the date of his return. Nevertheless, the completion of the Great Commission for which we are all working and the return of our Lord for which we are all waiting are clearly conjoined in Scripture.

What should we conclude about these things? What about conferences, congresses, and consultations focusing on the completion of world evangelization and the Great Commission, or even on measurable goals that anticipate those events? Are they worthwhile? Who should be involved? What outcomes can be anticipated?

It seems to me that either of two perspectives is legitimate. One view is that such conferences can be worthwhile, especially if participants can focus on carrying out the Great Commission (as at Edinburgh 1910), and provided that Two-Thirds World agencies have significant representation (as at Edinburgh 1980). Such meetings only accomplish something if the agenda is set by church leaders and theologians who are concerned and actively involved in the "Great Commission mission." But the agenda must be set by those who best understand the issues that all missionaries face everywhere. Then the discussion can result in some positive action steps.

The other perspective is somewhat less positive for at least two reasons. First, critics take a rather dim view of their accomplishments. Second, critics observe that the absence of academic theologians at such meetings is often attended by a disregard for, or even abrogation of, "Great Commission theology."

Undergirding biblical missions with biblical theology is so central that the theological basis of such conferences should be clear and the relationship between biblical teachings and strategy/action proposals should be discussed. It is not quite enough that participants have a personal reputation for holding to the cardinal doctrines of the church. Their basic doctrinal positions should be made explicit as these relate to the issues being discussed. Even though the conveners of Edinburgh 1910 may have been united in their commitment to Christ and Christian missions, the conference had neither a doctrinal basis for participation nor a place on the agenda for discussion of what the Scriptures say as to the exact nature of the Christian mission. Indeed, in the aftermath of 1910, it became apparent that doctrinal deviation would eviscerate not only the church but also its mission.

Insofar as Edinburgh 1980 mirrored the earlier conference, it shared this weakness. In place of identifying participants through their doctrinal commitments, organizers preferred to identify them as "Great Commission Christians, leaders, and organizations" or leaders of groups with a "focus on the world" and a stake in "world evangelization" (Gary and

Gary 1989, 29, 51, 185 *passim*). It was pointed out at the time that, on this basis, Jehovah's Witnesses and Mormons would qualify. And, even if completion of the Great Commission were not in view, the churches would benefit from a relevant discussion of the extent of biblical Christian unity. Perhaps in the twenty-first century, missiology and theology will come closer together.

What about the practical results of an emphasis on closure, the setting of goals, and the adoption of a countdown missionary strategy? Is this approach warranted? Will it pay off in the long run?

The A.D. 2000 slogan already has been relegated to the missiological dustbin, but it produced results that are still positive and hopeful. If we accept David Barrett's definition of "evangelized" as becoming "aware of Christianity, Christ and the gospel," 49.2 percent of the population of the world fit the definition of "evangelized" in 1914. By 2000, the percentage had increased to 73.1 percent (Barrett and Johnson 2001, 149, 193). If we think in terms of the stated GCOWE 2 goal for A.D. 2000 of "a church for every people and the gospel for every person" there was definite movement. By the end of the A.D. 2000 effort, approximately 90 percent of 1,739 "people groups" previously targeted for church planting either had such a program or had been "adopted" by some church or mission for a planting effort (Guthrie 2000, 394). If we agree with Luis Bush's optimistic assessment, as of December 31, 2000, "80 percent of the world had heard the Gospel" and "nearly 99 percent of the world's population lived in a people group that had an actual or planned on-site church planting team" (Bush 2003, 35–36).

In addition to statistical gains, the countdown to A.D. 2000 effort had numerous effects that will need to be evaluated over time. First, scheduled near the turn of the third millennium, A.D. 2000 obviously had the kind of psychological advantage that accrues to efforts undertaken at really significant hours of world history (Stearns and Stearns 1991, 147). Second, A.D. 2000 represented a major advance in the sense that world evangelization was seen in terms of reaching people groups. The Pierson strategy in the 1880s and 1890s had revolved around evangelizing individual persons. Third, the participation of non-Western missions and church leaders, so often overlooked or eclipsed by Western colleagues in the past, represented an important step. Fourth, A.D. 2000 certainly bore out traditional management wisdom about setting goals: Set a measurable goal for a specific time period. At the end of that period the goal may not be reached, but there will be more progress than if no goals had been set.

What about the relationship between "countdowns" and "prophetic alerts," and between world evangelization and the Second Coming of Christ? Jesus juxtaposes them in the Olivet Discourse and elsewhere, but what is their proper relationship and how should we deal with these often-divisive issues?

Church and missions leaders will have to continue to wrestle with such questions. The A.D. 1900 and A.D. 2000 movements emanated from vastly different theological perspectives in respect to them. The 1900 campaign was designed by leaders who had strong premillennial commitments. They looked to the "signs of the times," and the conjoining of world evangelization and the Second Coming played an important role in both justifying and motivating a countdown strategy. As for A.D. 2000, world evangelization was largely seen as a goal to be achieved in and of itself. Instead of conjoining the fulfillment of the Great Commission with the imminent coming of Christ, these two great eschatological events were seen as separate parts of God's plan. Some devoted more energy to the return of Christ and some to a special concern for the Great Commission. This was true even among premillennialists. The prophecy emphasis of earlier twentieth-century Bible teachers, such as William E. Blackstone (1841–1935), was still reflected in the ministries of teachers and authors such as Hal Lindsay, Tim LaHaye, and Jerry Jenkins. Countdowns to the Rapture, Great Tribulation, Parousia, and Armageddon were their preoccupation. Countdowns to world evangelization and the fulfillment of the Great Commission, on the other hand, came to be associated with the missions leaders to whom we have referred.

In the future, this and other types of "disconnect" between theology and missiology, and between eschatological and missiological concerns, could foster a parochial attitude of professionalism that will be deleterious to the fulfillment of the Great Commission. Time will tell.

Conclusion

On the basis of relevant Scripture, at least three conclusions would seem to be warranted.

First, we know that we are constantly to be on the alert, anticipating the return of Christ. Our Lord Jesus said so. No one except God the Father knows the day nor the hour (Matt. 24:36, 50; 25:13; Mark 13:32; Luke 12:46). The Lord Jesus said that he is coming "as a thief in the night" (Matt. 25:43). Peter said the same thing. Jesus said that we should be on the alert, awake and watchful. Peter wrote that we should be "waiting for" (ESV) or "looking for" (NASB) the "coming of the day of God" (2 Peter 3:12).

By their very nature, countdowns have to do with calendars and clocks, with days and hours. In spite of limitations, we do well to give more attention to "times and seasons." Whatever else they might indicate, world events are reminders of the fact that he is coming and will come on the Father's "schedule." Preachers, teachers, missionaries, laymen and laywomen all should point to that coming and encourage one another to good works and godly living. An awakened and committed church is tremendously important, if not absolutely imperative, to world evangelization.

Second, we know that the Great Commission will be completed and the world will be evangelized before Christ returns. Exactly what that means and when it will occur is not known by the most astute missiologists and studied Bible scholars. Within the parameters of our limited knowledge of such matters, countdowns to the completion of world evangelization can be very helpful. Religious movements never experience straight-line growth. Human nature being what it is and human cultures being what they are, world evangelization campaigns such as those of A.D. 1900 and A.D. 2000 can be used of the Lord to propel the church forward in missions.

But we must remember that countdown efforts are not enjoined by Scripture. We also must remember that such movements succeed only to the degree that they do not become ends in themselves and that sound doctrine and commonsense thinking are not sacrificed to inflated projections and overriding pragmatism. They succeed to the degree that the church is prophetically aware, spiritually alive, and missionally committed.

Third, obedience to Great Commission mission will hasten the day when Christ will return and inaugurate his kingdom. Whether extraordinary or ordinary, all consultations and conferences, all campaigns and crusades designed to encourage and expedite world evangelization should be undertaken in anticipation of Christ's glorious return and coming kingdom. *Christ's commission to go is meaningful only in the light of his promise to come.* The apostle Peter wrote, "But do not overlook this one fact, beloved, that with the Lord one day is as a thousand years and a thousand years as one day. . . . Since all these things are thus to be dissolved, what sort of people ought you to be in lives of holiness and godliness, waiting for and hastening the coming of the day of God?" (2 Peter 3:8, 11–12a). Henry Alford argues that in some sense believers can hasten the day:

> They hasten it by perfecting in repentance and holiness, the work of the Gospel, and thus diminishing the need of the *makrothumia* ver.9 ["patient wait, forbearance"] to which the delay of that day is owing. . . . It is true that the delay or hastening of that day is not man's matter, but God's; but it is not uncommon in Scripture to attribute to us those divine acts, or abstinences from acting, which are really and in their depth, God's own. (Alford 1968, 4:417)

Readers may find it interesting that some older translations add the Greek word *eis* to the text and translate Peter's admonition as "hastening *unto* the coming of the day of God" (e.g., KJV). Newer translations, however, usually omit the unwarranted *eis* and also render *speudō* more arrestingly as "speeding the day" (e.g., NIV, TNIV).

Jesus said that we should *pray* for the coming of God's kingdom. Peter said that we could and should actually *speed* its coming. So James McGranahan (1840–1907) was right on when he wrote the hymn "Go Ye Into All the World."

God speed the day when those of
every nation
    "Glory to God," trium-
    phantly shall sing;
Ransomed, redeemed, rejoicing
in salvation,
    Shout "Hallelujah, for the
    Lord is King."

All pow'r is given unto Me,
    All pow'r is given unto Me,
Go ye into all the world and
preach the gospel,
    And lo, I am with you
    alway.
    (Peterson and Johnson, no. 504)

Epilogue

The rabbi's explanation provided an opportunity to inquire cautiously as to whether the modern unrest in Israel and the world might be different had his people accepted the Lord Jesus as their Messiah some two thousand years ago. It was a risky question at best, and the rabbi's demeanor changed at the suggestion. Reaching for all the height his five foot two- or three-inch frame would allow, he curtly replied: "We Jewish people will never consider him a possibility." And with that he quickly moved away.

It is entirely possible that when our Lord said, "Truly, I say to you, this generation will not pass away until all these things take place" (Matt. 24:34) he was speaking of the Jewish people. Certainly *genea* ("generation") can have a wide range of meanings, including "race." It need not be understood as referring to all those people living at one period of history. Not all eschatological systems would allow for it, but as Edward Goodrick and I walked back to our room on the side of Mount Zion, our conversation focused on the unique experience we had just shared. After all these centuries, here they were again—God's chosen people . . . at their temple site but without their temple. Back on Zion, but without their King.

Modern Israel is an arresting reminder of the *course* of history, of its present *kairos,* and its impending *climax.*

References

Alford, Henry. 1968. *The Greek New Testament.* Revised by Everett F. Harrison. 4 vols. Chicago: Moody.

Barrett, David B., and Todd M. Johnson. 2001. *World Christian Trends, A.D. 30–A.D. 2200.* Pasadena, Calif.: William Carey Library.

Bush, Luis. 2003. "The A.D. 2000 Movement as a Great Commission Catalyst." In *Between Past and Future: Evangelical Mission Entering the Twenty-first Century,* edited by Jonathan J. Bonk. Pasadena, Calif.: William Carey Library.

Buswell, J. Oliver. 1962. *A Systematic Theology of the Christian Religion.* Vol. 1. Grand Rapids: Zondervan.

Gary, Jay, and Olgy Gary, eds. 1989. *The Countdown Has Begun: Global Consultation on A.D. 2000.* Rockville, Va.: A.D. 2000 Global Service Office.

Guthrie, Stanley M. 2000. "Global Consultation on World Evangelization '97 (GCOWE II)." In *Evangelical Dictionary of World Missions.* A. Scott Moreau general editor. Grand Rapids: Baker.

Johnson, Todd M. 1988. *Countdown to 1900: A History of World Evangelism.* Birmingham, Al.: New Hope.

Latourette, Kenneth Scott. 1941. *A History of the Expansion of Christianity.* Vol. 4, *The Great Century (A.D. 1800–1914): Europe and the United States of America.* New York: Harper & Brothers.

Peterson, John W., and Norman Johnson, comp. 1979. *Praise! Our Songs and Hymns.* Grand Rapids: Zondervan.

Roberts, Dana L. 2003. *Occupy Until I Come: A. T. Pierson and World Evangelization.* Grand Rapids: Eerdmans.

Starling, Alan, ed. 1981. *Seeds of Promise: World Consultation on Frontier Evangelism, Edinburgh '80.* Pasadena, Calif.: William Carey Library.

Stearns, Bill, and Amy Stearns. 1991. *Catch the Vision 2000.* Minneapolis: Bethany House.

Travis, Stephen. 1974. *The Jesus Hope.* Downers Grove, Ill.: InterVarsity.

Verghese, T. Paul. 1968. "Salvation: The Meanings of a Biblical Word." *International Review of Mission* 57 (October): 228.

Wang, Thomas. 1989. *Countdown to A.D. 2000: The Official Compendium of the Global Consultation on World Evangelization by A.D. 2000 and Beyond.* Pasadena, Calif.: William Carey Library.

Winter, Ralph D. 1970. *The Twenty-Five Unbelievable Years, 1945 to 1969.* Pasadena, Calif.: William Carey Library.

———. 1995. *Thy Kingdom Come: A Church for Every People and the Gospel for Every Person by the Year 2000.* Pasadena, Calif.: U.S. Center for World Missions.

Chapter 10

The Kingdom of God and the Church of Christ

What on Earth Is God Building—Here and Now?

Your kingdom come, your will be done, on earth as it is in heaven.

—Matthew 6:10

I will build my church and the gates of hell shall not prevail against it.

—Matthew 16:18

All authority in heaven and on earth has been given to me. Go therefore and make disciples of all nations, baptizing them in the name of the Father and of the Son and of the Holy Spirit, teaching them to observe all that I have commanded you. And behold, I am with you always, to the end of the age.

—Matthew 28:18–20

Prologue

> I want to lay before you, David, a very important item. . . . I think
> that the evangelical professors of missions need to establish a
> nationwide organization called openly and courageously "The
> American Society of Christian Missiology.". . . What is needed in
> North America and indeed around the world is a society of mis-
> siology that says quite frankly that the purpose of missiology is to
> carry out the Great Commission. Anything other than that may be
> a good thing to do, but it is not missiology. (McGavran 1988a)

The ministry of the late Donald Anderson McGavran (1897–1990)
spanned almost three-quarters of the twentieth century. After service as
a Disciples of Christ missionary to India, he became founder of the Institute of Church Growth, and, finally, director and professor of the School
of World Mission at Fuller Theological Seminary. Known as "father of
the Church Growth Movement" and as one of the foremost missiologists
of his time, McGavran was mentor to hundreds of missions scholars and
practitioners.

McGavran already was a member of at least two missiological societ-
ies whose membership included conciliar, evangelical, and Pentecostal
Protestant as well as Catholic scholars. So the obvious question is why
McGavran would call for the organization of still another such society.
Why would he suggest that it be called a society of *"Christian* missiol-
ogy"? Why would he say, "The purpose of missiology is to carry out the
Great Commission"?

To answer such questions, we are obliged to take a last look at
twentieth-century missions/missiology through the eyes of some who
lived it. Then, perhaps, we will be in a position to understand the threat
to what McGavran called "Great Commission mission" as he perceived
that threat.

~

In this chapter we will trace the course of missions connected with
mainline conciliar denominations such as the older Methodist, Presbyterian, Episcopal, Baptist, Congregational, and Disciples of Christ com-

munions and the ecumenical movement of the twentieth century. This does not include missions of groups who are biblically conservative and connected to these denominational categories by polity tradition only. We will include a brief analysis of missiological issues encountered by those missions and the reason their efforts declined to almost nothing.

Then we will turn to missiological developments in those churches and missions now usually lumped together by the word *evangelical* and including "fundamentalist-evangelical-Pentecostal-Baptist-conservative Protestant denominations" (Marty 2004, 38). We will particularly refer to four books, two of which mirror a more traditional evangelical approach to missiology and two of which reflect a more recent neo-evangelical approach.

It is only fair to warn readers that the issues involved are both exceedingly simple and amazingly complex, as is usually the case when scholars are involved. My aim here is to write to be understood, not to please everyone.

Twentieth-Century Conciliar and Ecumenical Missiology

What a change a century can make. As we have seen in the previous chapter, at the very beginning of the twentieth century in the year 1900 a large Ecumenical Missionary Conference was convened in New York. One hundred sixty-two missions agencies were represented, and the total attendance over the ten days reached nearly two hundred thousand. The mainline denominations represented supplied 80 percent of the American missionary force. President William McKinley spoke of the hope for civilizing and Christianizing the peoples of Asia, Africa, and Latin America.

By the close of the twentieth century, mainline denominations supplied no more than 6 percent of the missionary force from North America while agencies categorizing themselves as evangelical, Baptist, or Pentecostal alone accounted for almost 29,000 or approximately 70 percent of the total of U.S. missionaries (Pierson 2003, 67; Moreau 2000, 34, 4).

How is one to account for such cataclysmic change? It is almost as though one great segment of the church forgot its mission completely while another suddenly awakened to the fact that it has a mission. Of course, it is not nearly that simple. Nothing is. But this "forgetting" and "awakening" is part of the answer. And for this part of the answer, history reveals tremendously important lessons for both conciliar ecumenists and for conservative evangelicals.

Ecumenical History: Progress and Regress

Despite the inroads of liberalism, the social gospel, and higher criticism into mainline churches by 1900, the missions arms of the churches were still committed to winning people to Christ and gathering them into churches as the primary goal of their mission. That was certainly true of most boards represented at the World Missionary Conference in Edinburgh in 1910.

The chairman of that conference was John R. Mott (1865–1955), secretary of the Young Men's Christian Association (YMCA), cofounder and chairman of the Student Volunteer Movement (S.V.M.), leader in establishing the World Student Christian Federation, and author of the book *The Evangelization of the World in This Generation* (1910). Mott later became chairman of one of Edinburgh's outgrowths and the fulfillment of his dream with Arthur T. Pierson— the International Missionary Council (I.M.C., 1921). The I.M.C. was the first ongoing ecumenical organization dedicated to world missions and evangelism. Still later he chaired the I.M.C.'s Jerusalem Missionary Conference (1928) and was named honorary president of the newly formed World Council of Churches (W.C.C.) (1948). His active career stretched over six decades.

Conservatives who know the stories of these organizations can readily see that Mott's dedicated service to the cause of world evangelization met with great success, and equally significant failures. Edinburgh 1910 was a huge success in numbers of delegates representing missions agencies, the concentration on strategies for reaching into unoccupied fields, the emphasis on completing the Great Commission task, and the impetus toward formation of the I.M.C. It was not a success in the sense that it more or less assumed an unbiblical "Great Commission theology," misdefined the areas and peoples that needed to be reached, and helped inaugurate ecumenical programs that were anything but friendly to world evangelization.

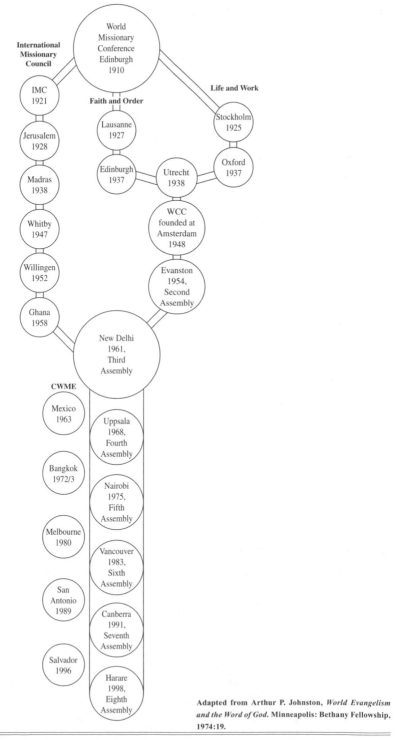

World
Missionary
Conference
Edinburgh
1910

**International
Missionary
Council**

IMC
1921

Jerusalem
1928

Madras
1938

Whitby
1947

Willingen
1952

Ghana
1958

Faith and Order

Lausanne
1927

Edinburgh
1937

Life and Work

Stockholm
1925

Utrecht
1938

Oxford
1937

WCC
founded at
Amsterdam
1948

Evanston
1954,
Second
Assembly

New Delhi
1961,
Third
Assembly

CWME

Mexico
1963

Bangkok
1972/3

Melbourne
1980

San
Antonio
1989

Salvador
1996

Uppsala
1968,
Fourth
Assembly

Nairobi
1975,
Fifth
Assembly

Vancouver
1983,
Sixth
Assembly

Canberra
1991,
Seventh
Assembly

Harare
1998,
Eighth
Assembly

Adapted from Arthur P. Johnston, *World Evangelism
and the Word of God.* Minneapolis: Bethany Fellowship,
1974:19.

Figure 11. The Organizational Development of the Ecumenical Movement

Formation of the I.M.C. in 1921 was soon followed by the controversial Commission on Faith and Order and Commission on Life and Work. Begun with good intentions, each of these three groups was infiltrated by modernist theologies that filled the vacuum left by their ambiguous stands on the authority of Scripture and the truth of historic doctrines of the Christian faith.

Many in missions looked to the often brilliant insights of exponents of the "new orthodoxy" of theologian Karl Barth and missiologist Hendrik Kraemer, but these theologies did not rescue institutionalized ecumenism and conciliar missions from their downward spiral. That downward trajectory became more pronounced after World War II because innovations introduced by neo-orthodoxy and the "new hermeneutic" were added to the infection of classic liberalism.

In postwar years, ecumenical issues were compounded by the fact that "younger churches" had sprung up. These groups now were becoming organizationally established and maturing ecclesiastically. Old aspirations for a global partnership between the sending churches of the West and indigenous churches seemed to be within grasp. The new aspiration was that these indigenous churches would become centers of missionary authority and activity. Accordingly, the younger churches themselves assumed an ever-increasing role in directing the activities of Western missionaries. They also figured prominently in deliberations of the I.M.C. and its successor, the Commission on World Mission and Evangelism (CWME) of the World Council of Churches.

Looking back, James Scherer says that soon after World War II an ecumenical stamp of approval was placed on a *church-centered* view of missions. This replaced the *personal conversion* view that had been so prominent in Protestant missions (Scherer 1993, 83). But that is not the end of the story.

The decade of the 1960s was as revolutionary for ecumenical missions thinking as it was for the surrounding Western society. In the wake of World War II, vast needs required a Christian response. Interchurch aid and world relief efforts became more important. By the mid-1960s R. Pierce Beaver exclaimed, "Service or relief programs, so closely associated with interchurch aid, *are* mission" (Beaver 1964, 110; emphasis his). Postwar conciliar studies on the nature of the church were powerfully influenced by Johannes Hoekendijk (1912–1975). Hoekendijk criticized the prevailing church-centric theology, insisting that the church exists for others, not itself (World Council of Churches 1967). The church itself is mission. The kingdom of God and *shalom* in the world are integral to evangelization, but not so much the church itself.

Missio Dei or "mission of God" theology has been variously attributed to Martin Luther and/or Karl Barth. At any rate, it was popularized in the mid-1960s by George Vicedom and others. Most simply stated, *missio Dei* missiology viewed missions as being first and foremost God's mission and only secondarily the mission of the church. Note how these and similar notions were reflected in ecumenical assemblies and discussions during the post–World War II era.

1. Whitby, Ontario, Canada (I.M.C. 1947). The theme "Partners in Obedience" embraced a "global church-centered mission" and enjoined a "partnership" between older and younger churches to fulfill the unfinished task of world evangelization. At the same time, it promised to cooperate with all movements designed to achieve social justice and overcome all forms of oppression.
2. Amsterdam, the Netherlands (W.C.C. 1948). This formative meeting of the World Council of Churches met with the theme "Man's Disorder and God's Design." Evangelism was proclaimed as an imperative, but social concerns were coming to center stage.
3. Willingen, Germany (I.M.C. 1952). The focus moved from a church-centered mission to a global one. A church-centered framework was "no longer adequate for dealing with the problems facing churches engaged in missions *in, from,* and *to* all six continents in the post-colonial era" (Scherer 1993, 85; emphasis his). The place of the kingdom in the plan of God began to supersede that of the church.
4. Evanston, Illinois, U.S.A. (W.C.C. 1954). The theme "Christ the Hope of the World" encouraged some leaders of the I.M.C. but caused problems for others. Ultimately, dialogue with other faiths was encouraged and conversionist views of missions were largely thought to be outdated.
5. Ghana (I.M.C. 1958). The emphasis was on making churches so

missions-minded that the church itself would "become mission." Missions themselves were deemed to be more or less dispensable. The decision was made by the I.M.C. to become part of the W.C.C. organizationally. In effect, this decision marked the end for Mott's and Pierson's dream of an ongoing organization of leaders and delegates of missions organizations who, by virtue of their position, interest, and involvement, would be able to concentrate on strategies for world evangelization.

6. New Delhi, India (W.C.C. 1961). The International Missionary Council was integrated into the W.C.C. as its Division of World Mission and Evangelism, later the Commission on World Mission and Evangelism (Visser 't Hooft 1962, esp. 26–31). Some missions leaders, such as Max Warren and Stephen Neill, entertained great misgivings, believing that, rather than infusing the W.C.C. with a missions vision, the W.C.C. would cease to see the need for missions agencies separate from the churches at all. Their fears would prove to be well founded.

7. Mexico (CWME, 1963). The slogan was "Mission on Six Continents." Since the church was already found all around the world, the need for reaching new people in new places was not of great concern (W.C.C. n.d., a).

8. Uppsala, Sweden (W.C.C. 1968). The message for this important gathering was "Behold, I Will Make All Things New." The Christian mission was placed on its head. The world was to be allowed to set the agenda. Instead of the divine order of God-church-world, the new order was to be God-world-church. Instead of taking its marching orders from God directly, the church was to take its marching orders from God as mediated through the world. Just as Jesus was the "Man for others," the church should be, to borrow Bonhoeffer's phrase and to reflect Hoekendijk's missiology, the "church for others" (W.C.C. 1968, esp. 27–51).

9. Bangkok, Thailand (CWME, 1973). This meeting carried the theme of Uppsala to its logical conclusion. At Bangkok, "Salvation Today" was interpreted as "humanization"—a divine invitation to all people to develop their "full humanity" (W.C.C. n.d., b).

10. Nairobi, Kenya (W.C.C. 1975). The "Confessing Christ Today"

theme of the conference represented a continuation of ecumenical ambiguity and ambivalence (Johnson 1975). On the one hand, the conference featured a call for evangelism by Mortimer Arias. On the other, a play was presented that "linked Christian missions with the evils of colonialism and gave the impression that many African problems were the result of the coming of Christianity" (Pierson 2003, 79).

11. Melbourne, Australia (CWME 1980). The conference demonstrated the close relationship between kingdom and sociopolitical gospel that had come to characterize ecumenism. The conference title was "Your Kingdom Come." Special emphasis was given to "Good News to the Poor."

12. Vancouver, British Columbia, Canada (W.C.C. 1983). The theme "Jesus Christ—the Life of the World" ignited hope among some conservatives that world evangelization would once again be a major concern. However, no major speaker even referred to it. Instead, the focus was on "world affairs in ecumenical perspective" (Glasser, 2000, 1026).

Subsequent CWME meetings in San Antonio, Texas, U.S.A. (1989), and Salvador de Bahia, Brazil (1996), and W.C.C. assemblies at Canberra, Australia (1991), and Harare, Zimbabwe (1998), continued to feature themes that raised "Great Commission expectations" on the part of more conservative and evangelical participants. But the reality of each meeting betrayed those expectations by promoting a social and political agenda.

Meanwhile, the successor of the I.M.C.—the CWME—disappeared as a separate entity before the end of the century, having been absorbed into W.C.C. Programme Unit No. 2 (Churches in Mission, Health, Education and Witness). Only the future will tell, but to many observers it seems that ecumenical missions have largely run their course as a force for world evangelization. The missionary endeavor was marginalized in part because the ecumenical vision of mission was gradually broadened by the W.C.C. to include everything the church does in the world—and even what God does outside the church. The effort to carry out *missio Dei* came to be divorced from obedience to God's Great Commission.

Warning Signals Along the Way

The near demise of ecumenical missions came despite numerous warnings about the road being taken. As a matter of fact, the various meetings to which we have referred often featured small group Bible studies, even when major addresses made little reference to the biblical text. In that respect, ecumenical gatherings were sometimes superior to those of their evangelical counterparts. All along the way, more conservative communions and individuals made significant appeals to the conciliar conscience. Five examples are representative.

First, before New Delhi in 1961, the Greek Orthodox Church warned the W.C.C. to look to the weakness of its confessional basis and its missionary vision. In response, the W.C.C. amended its own organizational description definition. To the sentence "The World Council of Churches is a fellowship of churches which confess the Lord Jesus Christ as Lord and Savior" was added "according to the Scriptures and therefore seek to fulfill together their common calling to the glory of the one God—Father, Son and Holy Spirit." The W.C.C. having responded in what seemed a positive way, the Greek Orthodox Church applied for membership. Scherer viewed these as positive developments as he looked back on them in the early 1990s.

> The Orthodox vision of God's mission sees the salvation of the world as the "program" of the holy trinity for creation. The kingdom of God is the eschatological goal. Attention always focuses on the central act of confessing the incarnate, crucified and risen Christ as the one who restores our broken communion with God. . . . The contention of this essay is that the special Orthodox contribution to ecumenical mission theology, at a decisive moment in the history of the ecumenical missionary movement, has helped to save ecumenical mission theology from serious aberration by bringing it back to solid moorings in scripture and apostolic tradition. (Scherer 1993, 87–88)

But such an assessment seems far too optimistic, given the ways in which the revised confessional statement was interpreted and reinterpreted by W.C.C. leaders. The Orthodox proposal was indeed accepted *pro forma,* but little attention was paid to its meaning and implications.

Second, during the months leading up to the meeting in Uppsala, Donald McGavran attempted to get planners to take a more scriptural position on the need for world evangelization. McGavran openly challenged W.C.C. leaders to include a concern for the 2 billion unevangelized in their deliberations. McGavran's pleadings fell mostly on deaf ears. Ecumenist leaders already had turned a corner and had little patience for the outspoken advocates of Great Commission missiology, either at Uppsala 1968 or at Bangkok 1973.

Third, another rebuffed missiologist was Peter Beyerhaus, despite his prestige as a German Lutheran professor at the University of Tübingen. His experience is revealing. On March 4, 1970, Beyerhaus and certain other European church leaders adopted the "Frankfurt Declaration on the Fundamental Crisis in Christian Mission." The "crisis" referred to was the new direction for missions that had been charted at Uppsala. They could already see where this movement was going in advance of the "Salvation Today" conference at Bangkok. Bangkok study materials highlighted humanization as essential to salvation and an aim, or even *the* aim, of missions. (Beyerhaus 1972, 63ff.; Sovik 1973, 50–53, 64–68).

As the attitude toward dissent had been dismissive at Uppsala, however, so it was at Bangkok: Beyerhaus and the formulations of the "Frankfurt Declaration" were largely ignored.

Fourth, we have already mentioned Mortimer Arias's challenge to reconsider the place of evangelism in the mission of the church at Nairobi 1975 (see p. 323). This call was reinforced by John R. W. Stott. In a response to Arias's paper, Stott listed five missions emphases that the W.C.C. needed to recover: (1) the doctrine of man's lostness; (2) confidence in the biblical gospel; (3) the uniqueness of Christ; (4) the urgency of evangelism; and (5) the need to personally experience Jesus Christ (Pierson 2003, 81).

Fifth, my former colleague, Arthur P. Johnston, was not affiliated with the W.C.C. when he wrote books calling the conciliar ecumenists back to evangelism. But Johnston had cultivated close relationships with those in the ecumenical movement while he served as a missionary in France and studied at the universities of Paris and Strasbourg. Johnston aptly titled one of his books *World Evangelism and the Word of God* (1974) and the other *The Battle for World Evangelism* (1978). In books and articles evaluating current events in missions, he maintained that conciliar ecumenists had failed to base deliberations and activities on a fully authoritative and inerrant Bible. He warned that, until that failure was recognized and the problem rectified, their movement would never really find its way.

Crises in Conciliar Ecumenical Missiology

The literature of conciliar ecumenical missiology is replete with such words as *crosscurrents*, *crossroads*, and *crisis*. One might add another word to this lexicon— *confusion*. There was terminological confusion, theological confusion, missiological confusion. Time and again, the W.C.C. and the I.M.C. and its successors came to forks in the road. Most of the time, they chose the right words but the wrong way.

Reasons for the downward spiral in the message and influence of conciliar missions could be analyzed in various ways. At least one option is to look at its conceptualizations (or reconceptualizations) of *church*, *kingdom*, *Scripture*, and, ultimately, *mission*.

Church. The church did not fare well in ecumenical theology and missiology. Sometimes the church was deemed to be all that was really important to the plan of God, as at Amsterdam. Sometimes the church was all but expendable, as at Uppsala. Sometimes "mission is church," as at Whitby. Sometimes "church is mission," as at Ghana.

Charles Van Engen notes that three factors were important in the loss of mission as historically defined and the adoption of a new idea that everything the church does is mission (Van Engen 1996, 157ff.; Pierson 2003, 84). First was integration of the I.M.C. into the W.C.C. at New Dehli 1961. That muted the voice of missionaries and missiologists. Second was incorporation of the *missio Dei* idea, which rapidly came to be reinterpreted in accordance with Hoekendijk's twin ideas. These ideas were that it is illegitimate for missions to have the church at the center of its work and that kingdom, *shalom,* and service are at the heart of mission. Third, various studies on the nature of the church concluded that mission is the very nature of the church and, therefore, Christian world evangelization does not need any distinctive attention or consideration.

Kingdom. According to Archibald Robertson, Christians have operated under three main understandings of the kingdom of God: The kingdom is (1) the perfect reign of God in heaven, to be realized after the Last Judgment; (2) the visible reign of Christ on earth between the time of the second coming of Christ and the Last Judgment; and (3) the church. Premillennialists generally adopt the second understanding. Augustine's idea that the *visible church* is the kingdom fits under the third. Sixteenth-century reformers edited Augustine's idea to say that the *invisible and universal church* is the kingdom (Robertson 1901, 119; cited in McClain 1968, 7).

But if these are the major understandings through church history, they are by no means the *only* understandings of the kingdom. Alva J. McClain deals with *eight* views of the kingdom, including two or three (in addition to the above) that are especially important to our discussion.

The "Liberal Social-Kingdom" idea, as McClain calls it, was associated with the social gospel movement in the United States. According to this conception, the kingdom of God represents a progressive improvement of humankind in which society takes precedence over individuals. The task of the church is to work to establish a new and Christian social order. This idea of the kingdom is an important point of reference, although it has proved to be as impractical as it is unbiblical. As the eminent John Bright once stated, the early church never imagined that it could, through its labors, bring in the kingdom of God. "That is a modern delusion of grandeur which the early church simply would not have understood" (Bright 1984, 233).

Since the liberal social kingdom proved unfeasible, it has been largely displaced by other, similar understandings. There are several varieties of one that McClain calls the "Modern Eschatological-Kingdom" idea. For example, Albert Schweitzer held that Jesus tried and failed to establish a kingdom. In dying, he put an end to the hope for a kingdom of God in human history. Another version is the "realized eschatology" of Rudolf Bultmann and C. H. Dodd. According to this, eschatology as such is symbolic and mythological. Still another variety, based on Kierkegaardian existentialism, was put forward by Barth and Emil Brunner. They held that nothing eternal can ever enter historical time. The kingdom of God is being realized now, but outside of time and space. To the extent that the kingdom is realized in the church itself, it is so only as an indirect and invisible expression of this "supra-historical" kingdom. The kingdom will be fully realized in the future but never in time and not on earth. McClain expresses misgivings when using the term *eschatological* to refer to most of these notions but bows to popular usage (McClain 1959, 7ff.; Ladd 1974, *passim*).

The twentieth-century ecumenical movement was caught in a web of confusion as to the meaning and nature of the kingdom of God. *Kingdom* basically means "God's rule," and there is not any single expression of it in time and space or beyond time and space. It is difficult enough to sort out the various expressions of God's kingdom as they are revealed in the Bible. When extrabiblical ideas not only intrude into the discussion, but are given equal weight with the Bible, ambiguity is inevitable. This is what happened in conciliar ecumenical discussions.

Scripture. Disagreements about the authority of the Bible (inspiration) and the interpretation of the Bible (hermeneutics) occasioned much of the conciliar confusion. Even when the older liberal views of the Bible no longer prevailed in certain mainline circles, churchmen did not return to the historical, orthodox view of Scripture's authority. Most took up the *new* orthodoxy of Barth. Barth's view of Scripture was higher than that of classic liberalism, but it remained far from a Bible that would give confidence to God's people. Barth did not consider the Bible itself to be the Word of God so much as a "witness to the Word of God." He built his theology on "the Word of God as *event* (Christ), as *witness* (Scripture) and as *proclamation* (apostolic preaching)" (Johnson 1989, 20).

Consequently, even the "orthodox" within the ecumenical camp approached Scripture with a "historical-critical bias." They assumed that the Bible contains errors that only scholarly higher criticism is qualified to correct (Johnston 1974, 255). The door was open to all kinds of aberrant interpretations, even after the W.C.C. added the phrase "according to the Scriptures" to its self-definition in 1961.

The response to Beyerhaus's objections to the "humanization" understanding of salvation at Bangkok is a case in point. In effect, Beyerhaus and the framers of the "Frankfurt Declaration" charged that ecumenists had abandoned the Reformation *sola scriptura* principle in favor of human knowledge. He said that theological method "went bad" by virtue of three fatal moves. First, it placed humans at the center of the search for knowledge. Second, it sought to understand what a given Bible text means by discovering how the theology of one biblical author can be pitted against that of another. Mutual contradictions among authors and their competing traditions are assumed, making room for numerous theologies but no "biblical theology." Third, "historio-critical" interpretation attempted to discover the "intention" of the text by imposing some foreign "principle" onto the text, rather than by asking questions for the text to answer and using its own interpretive principles (Beyerhaus 1972, 7–11).

Mission. Talk about a trumpet sounding an uncertain note! If the trumpet is twentieth-century ecumenism, and the note is mission, think of its uncertain sounds:

- "The mission is church."
- "The church is mission."
- "Everything the church does is mission."
- "Everything the church is sent to do is mission."
- "The mission is to build the kingdom and establish *shalom.*"
- "Let the world set the [mission] agenda."
- "The mission is humanization."
- "The mission is *missio Dei,* the mission of God."
- "The church's mission is to fulfill the purposes of God."

Similar to what happened with the Laymen's Inquiry in 1928 (see p. 83), the good word *mission* was "reconceptualized" by conciliar ecumenists to mean something other than "Great Commission mission." The result was predictable. *Mission* came to mean anything its users decided it should mean, until it was devoid of significance. Stephen Neill's well-known and oft-quoted aphorism was true: "When everything is mission, nothing is mission" (Neill 1959, 81).

That is why, after long involvement in ecumenical missions studies and organizations, in 1988 McGavran wrote the personal letter to me from which an excerpt was taken to begin this chapter (McGavran

1988a). Approximately a month later, in April 1988, McGavran wrote again, this time including his manuscript "Missions Face a Lion," subsequently published in *Missiology: An International Review* (McGavran 1988b). McGavran describes a Third World village with its false gods, poverty, sickness, illiteracy, social inequities, and antiquated agriculture. He affirms that Christians should work to alleviate all of these sorry conditions. . . .

> However, [the village's] crucial need is none of these. Its crucial need is to cease worshiping the stone idols, to cease believing that all sickness is caused by the acts of these gods. The crucial need is to believe on God the Father Almighty, who is made known to us in Jesus Christ, His Son. The great need is to move off the animal and human platform and mount the platform of the divine life. Then and then only will these other advances be made quickly and permanently. (McGavran 1988b, 7)

McGavran's "lion" to be faced is the kind of mission/missiology that "devours" evangelism and church growth efforts by insisting that everything else that is good and desirable is equally or more important.

Church and Kingdom in Evangelical Missiology

We have mentioned Scherer's idea of the evolution of ecumenical missiology from an *individual conversion orientation* in the nineteenth century to a *church orientation* in the first part of the twentieth century to a *kingdom-oriented* mission in the last part of the twentieth century (see p. 320). Now we turn to evangelical missiology. It may be that some new evangelicals have already begun to tread a path similar to that followed by conciliar ecumenists in the past and that some traditional evangelicals are in danger of doing so. All alike would do well to pause and ask, "Is this the direction in which we should be moving?"

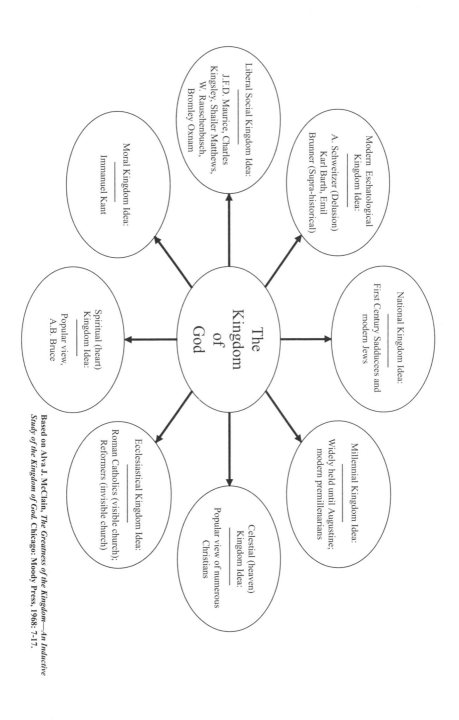

The Kingdom of God

- Modern Eschatological Kingdom Idea:
  A. Schweitzer (Delusion) Karl Barth, Emil Brunner (Supra-historical)

- Liberal Social Kingdom Idea:
  J.F.D. Maurice, Charles Kingsley, Shailer Matthews, W. Rauschenbusch, Bromley Oxnam

- Moral Kingdom Idea:
  Immanuel Kant

- Spiritual (heart) Kingdom Idea:
  Popular view, A.B. Bruce

- Ecclesiastical Kingdom Idea:
  Roman Catholics (visible church); Reformers (invisible church)

- National Kingdom Idea:
  First Century Sadducees and modern Jews

- Millennial Kingdom Idea:
  Widely held until Augustine; modern premillenarians

- Celestial (heaven) Kingdom Idea:
  Popular view of numerous Christians

Based on Alva J. McClain, *The Greatness of the Kingdom—An Inductive Study of the Kingdom of God*. Chicago: Moody Press, 1968: 7-17.

Figure 12. Eight Views of the Kingdom of God

Motivation and Method

My own thinking has been challenged by life experience. My parents were brought up in Universalist and liberal Methodist circles but came to a saving knowledge of Jesus Christ in the context of what I call "biblical revivalism." My undergraduate major in philosophy brought me into almost weekly contact with several internationally acclaimed professors. Their philosophical positions ranged from Kierkegaardian existentialism to a logical positivism of the Vienna school. Most of my missionary career was lived in the Japanese religious context after higher criticism had wreaked havoc on the Protestant church there. Already at the end of the nineteenth century, higher criticism, direct from German universities, had joined a universalism direct from American pulpits and seminaries to divide the Japanese Christian community. All but a remnant of Japanese Christians had compromised with Shinto chauvinism before and during World War II. Most established Japanese schools of theology had settled for one or another form of liberalism or neo-orthodoxy after the war.

I returned to the North American theological context when I joined the faculty of Trinity Evangelical Divinity School in Deerfield, Illinois, in 1965. The evangelical movement was then at the height of its internal controversy over the authority of Holy Scripture. These developments were more important to me because I had seen what theological drift had done in Japan and how heresy had poisoned the relationship between theology and missiology.

In regard to this relationship, a number of books have challenged my thinking. Four sources in particular have seemed quite helpful. I have chosen these books because they represent ways in which contemporary evangelical missiology is commonly being encouraged to move.

1. Alva J. McClain, *The Greatness of the Kingdom: An Inductive Study of the Kingdom of God* (1968). McClain was president and professor of theology at Grace Theological Seminary in Winona Lake, Indiana. His premillennial theology of kingdom and church reflects the theology and eschatology of a large segment of conservative evangelicals during much of the twentieth century. The position still is held by many today.

2. Robert D. Culver, *A Greater Commission: A Theology for World Missions* (1984). Culver was professor of theology at Grace Theological Seminary. He has also taught at Northwestern College, Trinity Evangelical Divinity School, and Winnipeg Theological Seminary. He is a systematics theologian of the same theological bent as McClain. *A Greater Commission* deals with New Testament passages in Matthew and the Pauline literature that Culver deems to have been neglected by missiologists.

3. George Eldon Ladd, *Jesus and the Kingdom* (1964); revised as *The Presence of the Future* (1974; the revised edition used here). Ladd was professor of New Testament exegesis and theology at Fuller Theological Seminary in Pasadena, California. Ladd is identified by Daniel Reid as a premillennialist (see Reid 1990), but his book draws on amillennial and some postmillennial themes. The ideas more or less represent "modern eschatological-kingdom" orientation toward "supra-history" and "realized eschatology" (see figure 12). Ladd himself prefers to speak of "biblical realism" and "consistent eschatology." This book has been singularly influential, even causing some conservative evangelicals to rethink their positions on kingdom, church, Scripture, and mission.

4. James F. Engel and William A. Dyrness, *Changing the Mind of Missions: Where Have We Gone Wrong?* (2000). A marketing expert and missions consultant, Engel taught at Ohio State University and Eastern College. He is founder and president of Development Associates International. Dryness served as a missionary to the Philippines before going to Fuller as dean of the school of theology and professor of theology and culture. Although *Changing the Mind of Missions* is not a missiological clone of Ladd's kingdom theology, it does agree with most of Ladd's main ideas and kingdom-building missiology.

While the authors chosen can be identified as premillenialists, and I take that position myself, it is not that part of their theology that I want to consider here. I am not writing to make a case for premillennialism's understanding of the Second Coming, Rapture, Great Tribulation, or duration of the earthly kingdom. I have great appreciation for the insights of many missiologists who do not share my eschatological perspective. And sometimes I find myself in disagreement with missiologists whose basic eschatological perspective I share.

Let me be clear as to my reasons for choosing these authors and books and for dealing with them as I do. Primarily it has to do with their differing understandings of the nature of revelation, hermeneutics, and sometimes contextualization. McClain and Culver take a more traditional, conservative, evangelical view of the authority of Scripture. They would be in general agreement with the position defended in chapter 8 of this volume. In their consistent hermeneutic, I believe that they provide helpful and sometimes brilliant insights regarding Christian mission. They provide the kind of guidance sorely needed, given the twists and turns of the missiological road we travel.

The views of Scripture's authority of Ladd, Engel, and Dyrness, on the other hand, do not qualify as representing a verbal plenary view of the Spirit's role in the inspiration of Scripture. As a result, they show altogether too much confidence in the role that human scholars play in determining the Bible's fundamental accuracy and meaning. We can benefit from their insights. However, if evangelicals uncritically follow the markers they have laid out, we may well take a wrong turn and end up in a swamp alongside some of our hapless ecumenical forebears.

McClain and Culver

The Greatness of the Kingdom

McClain and Ladd begin their respective books with overviews of perspectives on the kingdom of God that form the backdrop for current discussion. McClain chooses to identify and categorize a wide variety of viewpoints and cite representative theologians.

Church. McClain indicates that the Lord announced to his disciples the building of a "new thing," the *ekklēsia*, after receiving their gloomy report of their ministry to Israel (Matt. 16:13–14). In doing so he presaged the church age to come. The church that Christ prophesied in Matthew 16:18–19 is built upon Peter as a representative of the "apostles and prophets" (Eph. 2:20). Authority is given to the whole church, and this authority will extend even into the millennial/messianic kingdom to be established on earth.

But all of this has to do with the universal church. As far as the local church is concerned, in his earthly ministry Christ first mentioned it and gave instructions concerning it in Matthew 18:15–20. Extended instruction would come later, in the writing of the Epistles (McClain 1968, 326–30).

Kingdom. McClain's understanding of Scripture is that the kingdom basically has to do with the rule of God but that it has various expressions throughout history. The kingdom of God has always existed (e.g., Ps. 10:16) and is universal in its scope (e.g., 103:19). Kingdom is sometimes expressed as the direct rule of God, and sometimes as his indirect rule through a mediator (e.g., 2:4–6; 59:13). It is both present and future (e.g., 29:10; Zech. 14:9). At times it represents God's unconditional rule; at other times it is based on a conditional covenant between God and his people (e.g., Ps. 89:27–29; Dan. 4:34–35).

McClain rejects both the realized eschatology of Karl Barth, Emil Brunner, and others and the amillennialist position of Benjamin Warfield and Louis Berkhof. In spite of his appreciation for Berkhof's repudiation of Barth and Brunner's position, he believes that all of these views of the kingdom are "tarred with the same brush," because their only hope is for a divine kingdom *after the close of history*. In *The Greatness of the Kingdom* history itself is going somewhere both *within time and on earth* (Ps. 72:1, 7, 17). After this church age, the promise to Israel will be fulfilled. Christ will come and reign with his church on earth. Following the Final Judgment, the purpose of Christ's mediatorial kingdom will have been fulfilled and the eternal kingdom ushered in (McClain 1968, 491–515).

Scripture. McClain subscribes to verbal plenary inspiration and grammatical-historical interpretation and demonstrates his fidelity to Scripture in what he writes. McClain's use of the prophecies of Daniel is an example. Beyond the larger issue of inerrancy, the critical debates over the historicity of Daniel are central to developing his eschatological understanding. Without Daniel, biblical eschatology becomes almost impossible to discern. McClain rests his entire case rest on the authenticity of Daniel's visions and the validity of Daniel's interpretation of them.

Mission. McClain teaches that the church's mission is made clear in the Great Commission. He sees these elements: *witnessing* to the messianic King, his death and resurrection; *proclaiming* the gospel; *discipling* the nations; *going* in stages throughout the world; *baptizing* in his name; "feeding the flock" by *teaching* all that Christ commanded; *warning* of divine judgment; *being empowered* by the Holy Spirit; and *experiencing* the presence of Christ. If one accepts the longer ending of Mark as part of the authentic book, the task also includes experiencing miraculous and confirming signs (McClain 1968, 392).

McClain concludes by quoting the Jewish Christian scholar Adolf Sapir, who writes concerning Christ: "We believe that He will come, and with Him the Kingdom, and with the Kingdom the fulfillment of the prayer 'Thy will be done on earth as it is done in heaven'" (McClain 1968, 531).

A Greater Commission

Culver proposes a missiology that is consonant with McClain's theology and eschatology.

Church. During this age of the church, God's rulership takes visible form. The church is the instrument of God's saving power in the world. In this age, all members of the church as the universal body of Christ are members of the kingdom, and all citizens of the kingdom are members of the church. The church and its mission are to be understood through Christ's teaching in Matthew 10 and 13, his prophecy in Matthew 16:18, the marks of the early church in Acts 2:42–47, and the Great Commission ministries of the apostles, especially Paul.

Kingdom. "The Kingdom is God's kingship working salvation" (Culver 1984, 14). Before Christ's first coming, the special sphere of that saving action was the nation of Israel. Because of Israel's unbelief, the kingdom was taken from the nation of Israel and given to the Gentiles (Matt. 21:41). Culver quotes Erich Sauer that God's government "is a living and powerful divine action, revealing itself in ever new forms of self-manifestation, in the course of many dispensations and periods" (Culver 1984, 14). In the future, God's rulership will take visible form in a millennial kingdom—an earthly kingdom that follows the Second Coming and precedes the Final Judgment.

Scripture. What has been stated about McClain's view and use of Scripture applies to Culver and his book as well. Culver has, in fact, written a book upholding premillennialism, defending the authenticity of the book of Daniel, and expounding the significance of Daniel's visions (e.g., the "great image," "four beasts," and "seventy weeks") and prophecies concerning the Jews and the time of the end (Culver 1954). Actually, Culver's missiology can only be fully understood in the context provided by his book on Daniel.

Mission. Concerning the mission of the church, the Great Commission texts were not only applicable to the apostles but still apply to believers throughout this age. The texts tell believers how to carry out God's mission for his people and what to expect when they do. Culver devotes two chapters to a careful interpretation and application of the Great Commission, especially as it appears in Matthew 28, and the "Greater Commission" as Paul advocates it in Romans 10 and 15.

With careful historical and grammatical analyses of the text, Culver concludes that there is no question but that the primary task of Great Commission mission is evangelism—a sowing, even a lavish sowing, of the "good seed" of the Word of God (Culver 1984, 152–54). The "Greater Commission" in Romans 10 and 15 is not greater because it is more important but because it is more encompassing. It has to do with Paul's concept of the church's *sending* of missionaries (i.e., "If you cannot go yourself, then send someone else.") to declare the Word of God to those who still need to hear it. He sees the same implications in these instructions for the early church and for the church today (Culver 1984, viii).

Missions personnel would do well to take to heart the exegetical principles of McClain and Culver, whatever they think of the details of their missiology or eschatology.

Ladd, Engel, and Dyrness

The Presence of the Future

As we have said, in his discussion of the kingdom, Ladd prefers to follow historical developments and avoids the categorization of kingdom views found in McClain.

Church. Ladd says that the church is not the kingdom; rather, it is a "society of men." In the Matthew 16:18–19 prophecy Jesus was not speaking "of the creation of an organization or institution, nor is it [i.e., the prophecy] to be interpreted in terms of the distinctively Christian *ekklēsia* as the body and the bride of Christ, but in terms of the Old Testament concept of the people of God" (Ladd 1974, 259). The conception of Jesus was that his own disciples would take the place of Israel as the "true people of God" (Ladd 1974, 260). That being the case, his disciples were the incipient church, if not the church itself.

Ladd expresses his view of the church through five characteristics (Ladd 1974, 260ff.). First, the church is not the kingdom, although it is composed of the people of the kingdom. Second, the kingdom creates the church, not vice versa. The dynamic rule of God present in Jesus' mission and message brings those who respond into this new fellowship. Third, the church's mission is to witness to the kingdom, not build it. Fourth, the church is the instrument of the kingdom. After the Resurrection and Pentecost, Jesus' blessings and power are demonstrated through the church. Fifth, the church is the custodian of the kingdom. The authority given to Peter in Matthew 16 is grounded in revelation. It has to do with the authority to lead others into the knowledge of Jesus' messiahship and the realm of kingdom blessings. It is on this knowledge that Christ builds his *ekklēsia*.

Kingdom. With reference to the kingdom, Ladd begins with an overview of various interpreters of the kingdom as does McClain. But Ladd confines his discussion to three basic eschatological views that form the backdrop against which he sets forth his understanding: (1) The *apocalyptic and eschatological view* sees the kingdom as future (e.g., Martin Dibelius, Rudolf Bultmann, and R. H. Fuller). (2) A *realized eschatology* views the kingdom in terms of a present experience of God. Accordingly, eschatology becomes more or less superfluous (e.g., T. W. Manson, C. H. Dodd, Rudolf Bultmann when understood existentially, and F. C. Grant). (3) A *synthesis* or in-between view holds that both the futuristic *and* present aspects of the kingdom are essential to a correct or "consistent" eschatology (e.g., Rudolf Otto, Joachim Jeremias, Manson, and W. G. Kummel).

Ladd's sympathies lie with the "in-between" view, but both the eschatological or futuristic aspects and the present or existential aspects of the kingdom turn out to be different from what one might expect. After examining Old Testament and intertestamental Jewish expectations, Ladd attempts a "reconstruction" (cf. Ladd 1974, 42) of Jesus' mission and message, using the kingdom of God as a focal point.

Like McClain and Culver, Ladd notes that the kingdom of God first has to do with "kingly rule" or "reign" and not "territory." For Ladd, however, this rule has ethical, life-changing import as it "unites" the ethical to the salvific. The righteousness of the Sermon on the Mount is not merited but offered as a free gift to those who humbly desire it. Jesus' teaching concerning the tax collector (Luke 18:14) "is the same as the Pauline doctrine of free justification, with the exception that there is no mention of the cross" (Ladd 1974, 216). All is of one piece. The ethic of Jesus is the ethic of the kingdom. It has to do with the inner life and also with "active righteousness." This ethic does not produce utopia, but it makes an impact on society as Christians live as salt and light (Matt. 5:13–16).

With regard to timing, the kingdom is present as well as future, apocalyptic as well as spiritual. The kingdom will be fully realized in the future, but it is concerned with both spiritual and physical wellbeing in the present. A "social gospel" is implicit in kingdom responsibility because the "reign of God" is concerned with the total man and the conquest of evil in whatever form evil may manifest itself (Ladd 1974, 304). Christ "is never interested in the future for its own sake, but speaks of the future because of its impact on the present" (Ladd 1974, 327).

In essence, then, the kingdom is the "breaking in" of God's rulership that attended the coming and ministry of Jesus. Ladd says that his "central thesis" is "that before the eschatological appearing of God's Kingdom at the end of the age, God's Kingdom has become dynamically active among men in Jesus' person and mission" (Ladd 1974, 139). That kingdom is the outworking of God's reign in the present world, but it will be perfected in his universal reign *beyond this world of space and time*. He says, "This is the meaning of the presence of the Kingdom as a new era of salvation. To receive the Kingdom of God, to submit oneself to God's reign means to receive the gift of the Kingdom and to enter the enjoyment of its blessings. The age of fulfillment is present but the time of consummation still awaits the age to come" (Ladd 1974, 217).

That consummation is what is known as the Second Coming of Christ. With respect to "signs of Christ's coming" Ladd's interpretation of the Olivet Discourse resembles our own (see ch. 9), but with respect to the objective of Jesus' discourse, Ladd's interpretation is entirely different. According to Ladd, Jesus' objective was not to prepare his disciples for the Great Commission and his ascension. His objective was entirely ethical. For example, consider Christ's exhortation to be watchful and ready for the imminent coming of the "master of the house." This readiness was not to be achieved by a preoccupation with "signs," which can only misdirect and mislead. It was to be achieved by an awareness of the nearness of the kingdom and the need to be ready for the Last Judgment. "Participation in discipleship to Jesus is not a guarantee of salvation. The foolish maidens were invited to the wedding; the idle servant was called a servant. Salvation cannot be taken for granted; it will be given only to those who are awake and spiritually prepared" (Ladd 1974, 328).

Scripture. It is perhaps easier to understand *The Presence of the Kingdom* if one understands that, as Donald Reid says, Ladd's book "was intended to bring him the cherished recognition of the broader community of biblical scholars" (Reid 1990, 627). Reflecting this desire for the "recognition of a broader community," Ladd says, for example, that the dating of the book of Daniel is of little moment, and the book of Daniel itself is a collection of traditions that relate to "allegedly" historical events (Ladd 1974, 85, 95). Such statements present a suborthodox view of the inspiration and authority of Scripture. They also help account for seeming amillennial (if not postmillennial) aspects of his eschatology even though Reid identifies Ladd as a premillennialist. Perhaps all of this must be factored in when Ladd insists that his is a "consistent eschatology" based on *"biblical realism."*

Mission. With reference to mission, Ladd concludes that the church's mission is to witness to the kingdom, not actually to build it, yet he actually says little about witness as it relates to evangelism or the Great Commission. The missionary message, like the message of Jesus, is the gospel of the kingdom, the good news of God's redemptive acts in history, and the fact that the reign of God has broken into the affairs of men (Ladd 1974, 267). Its power is the same power that was demonstrated in Jesus' authority over sickness and evil spirits. Its promise is the promise of the kingdom—all the blessings of divine rule. Like Jesus, who revealed himself in his saving actions, the "church is an eschatological community not only because it witnesses to God's future victory but because its mission is to display the life of the eschatological kingdom in the present evil age" (Ladd 1974, 337).

In Ladd's view, the problem is that "the church is in the world and has become a worldly phenomenon" (Ladd 1974, 339). As a "fellowship of men" the church gets caught up in its own affairs and in self-aggrandizement. It finds itself engaged in the struggle between good and evil, but it often fails to display the character of the kingdom either in its actions in the world or in its fellowship within the church. Only a true sense of the nature and imminence of the kingdom will preserve the church. "The Kingdom creates the church, works through the church, and is proclaimed in the world by the church" (Ladd 1974, 277).

Changing the Mind of Missions

Changing the Mind of Missions: Where Have We Gone Wrong? introduces the context of modern and postmodern missions into the discussion. The book presents a fictional case study to guide its discussion. The new director of Global Harvest Mission, Bud Anderson, who is himself beset with the task of facing the realities of change, counsels the missions committee of First Church of Rollingwood.

First Church has many things to commend it, but it is captive to the past, beholden to "old paradigms," and experiencing declining missionary interest. About the only thing that encourages the missions-minded people of First Church is that a growing number of younger believers in their twenties "express real concerns about the victims of unrighteousness around the world" (Engel and Dyrness 2000, 13). Only to the extent that missions are able to tap this reservoir of Christian concern do they have a real future. Bud Anderson is willing and able to lead First Church in the adoption of a radically new missions paradigm that both appeals to these concerned younger believers and promises to meet the needs of the new millennium.

Church. Engel and Dyrness have a distinct place for the church, and especially for local churches, in their theory and practice of missions.

They envision churches as being (or becoming) "communities of common people doing uncommon deeds." Such churches do not follow the institutional model inherited from the Reformation, which is characterized by such things as sacraments, preaching, organization, authority, discipline, programs, a preoccupation with numbers, and resistance to change. Rather, they are patterned after pietism and revivalism. They are sensitive to the Spirit; share a vision for Christ's reign; comply with the Beatitudes; identify with the poor and marginalized; and share in witness and social transformation with like communities around the world (Engel and Dyrness 2000, 79–80, 89, 123).

Kingdom. Like others we have met, Engel and Dyrness understand kingdom in terms of divine rule. Unlike Ladd but with McClain and Culver, they do allow for a future kingdom *on earth* in connection with the Second Coming. But they are not greatly concerned with the particulars of the establishment of that kingdom (Engel and Dyrness 2000, 40, *passim*). With Ladd, they concentrate on the "nowness" and ethical nature of God's kingdom. They refuse to recognize a dichotomy between social action and evangelism, insisting that this position is in accord with the model kingdom ministry and mission of Jesus.

Scripture. Changing the Mind of Missions gives pause for concern, even alarm, about the way in which it reflects the presuppositions and hermeneutic of Ladd's *Presence of the Future* and especially David Bosch's influential *Transforming Mission* (1991, 23–24).

One critic of Bosch, Charles Van Engen, says that Bosch's "critical hermeneutic" goes beyond the explicit early Christian definitions of the New Testament in order to encourage dialogue between those definitions and all subsequent definitions, including our own. Bosch himself says that the challenge to missions today is to practice this critical hermeneutic by relating "the always-relevant Jesus event of twenty centuries ago to the future of God's promised reign by means of meaningful initiatives in the here and now" (quoted in Van Engen 1993, 32).

The thing that is both fascinating and frustrating is that, as Van Engen observes, Bosch tantalizes us by suggesting that a variety of paradigms could be constructed by means of his critical hermeneutic. But he never constructs even one such paradigm himself (Van Engen 1993, 32). One wonders whether Bosch would have come up with an entirely new paradigm had he lived longer, and one wonders what his paradigm would have looked like.

I believe that *Changing the Mind of Missions* is an example of how a critical hermeneutic (as over against a traditional grammatical-historical hermeneutic) can be employed to yield a new missions paradigm.

First, Engel and Dyrness select relevant themes, such as the kingdom of God and themes related to it, like incarnation, Great Commission, church, and mission. Second, they look at related Scripture passages. On the bases of their own understandings of Jesus and his ministry, as well as the challenges to mission in the first century, they look for the meaning and significance that those themes, terms, and ideas might have had for Bible authors in the source context. This yields a "first-century" or "apostolic" missions paradigm for the New Testament.

Third, by comparison or "dialogue" between ancient and contemporary contexts and with an awareness of challenges to missions today, they construct an "entirely new missions paradigm" tailored for today.

To see how the critical hermeneutic actually works, consider the interpretation of the Great Commission that Engel and Dyrness use to inform their dialogue between the old and the new. They give very little space to grammatical-historical exegesis of the relevant texts. In fact, they do not hesitate to insert words and even whole new points of significance into the biblical text. According to their interpretation of the Great Commission in Matthew 28:18–20, we are commissioned to "do Jesus' work" (Engel and Dyrness 2000, 31). That phrase does not actually appear in the original text, and even if it had appeared there, sound exegesis could not be expected to yield the meaning assigned to the phrase by Engel and Dyrness. After all, Christ's primary "work" was to fulfill the law and prophets and give his life a ransom for many (Mark 10:45).

To take another example, according to *Changing the Mind of Missions,* in two passages (John 20:21–22; 21:15–21) the apostle John first calls us to "incarnate the reality of God, even as Jesus himself did." Then, in the "feeding of Jesus' sheep" reference, they say that John adds what "may contain the most important element of the Christian's commission." Out of love for the Lord and the world, the Christian is invited into the "very trinitarian life of God"—the life that "incarnates itself and seeks to see realized there works that glorify the Father" (Engel and Dyrness 2000,

35–36). The ideological stretch here is almost as great as the historical stretch from the first century to the twenty-first.

Mission. The authors' "radically new missions paradigm," proposed in *Changing the Mind of Missions*, is indeed *radical.* Engel and Dyrness say that they are "disturbed by the flood of church planting teams into various people groups in the world" (Engel and Dyrness 2000, 151). One reason for their distress is that church planting teams are not taking into account existing national churches and communions. They have a point in that complaint. But they are also disturbed because, in their estimation, the "right kind" of church is not being planted.

In the view of Engel and Dyrness, missions is nothing less than "the establishment and extension of God's kingdom reign on earth" as announced in "Jesus' own mission statement" in Luke 4:18–19 (Engel and Dyrness 2000, 89–90). This is to be accomplished by developing and encouraging the kind of "ecclesial communities" that are not preoccupied with creeds and discipline, but rather characterized by shared witness and social transformation. Planting the "right kind of church" demands that missionary agencies undergo radical, top-down, bottom-up organizational transformation. Engel and Dyrness want agencies to rethink goals, outcomes, and donor relations. They must respond to the concerns of churches and value persons more highly than programs.

In fact, their warning is that missions have a future only insofar as they undergo this kind of reorganization and undertake this kind of mission. The authors add that this understanding is rooted in the *missio Dei*, and has two corollaries:

> First, missions grows out of all that God has done in creation and new creation. And since it has to do ultimately with God and God's purposes, the second corollary is that a complete understanding of missions (and therefore an appropriate missions strategy) must be sensitive to the breadth of God's activities from creation to consummation. (Engel and Dyrness 2000, 37)

Engel and Dyrness perform a service in depicting the postmodern context of contemporary missions. They also point out numerous egregious mistakes made in evangelical missions over the second half of the twentieth century. For example, they lament the dominance of Western churches, missions, personnel, and money, complemented by the dominance of Western approaches and strategies to win souls, add to church rolls, and increase the number of "reached" people groups. They say that even the strategies of the Church Growth, Adopt-a-People, and A.D. 2000 and Beyond movements missed the need to recognize new "centers of power" for missions in the Two-Thirds World. Nor did evangelicals see the need to hear the cries of the world's poor for redress and, especially, the need to model missions after the pattern established by Christ in his kingdom ministry.

But *Changing the Mind of Missions* goes too far—much too far. The world has changed, and missions must change, to be sure. But to make the wholesale changes promoted in this book would be to go backward, not forward. The social action and radical contextualizations to which those changes point is a road already traveled, as we have seen. It has numerous detours and intersections where mishaps occur. Moreover, as noted above (p. 327), John Bright is correct that the early church simply would not have understood the kind of mission envisioned by these changes. It is questionable that the twenty-first-century church will understand it either.

Preserving Biblical Missiology and Performing Biblical Missions

A year or two ago I asked a knowledgeable observer what he thought about the recent emphases on the kingdom of God and *missio Dei* in evangelical missiology. He was noncommittal but replied, "I rather think that I like the kingdom emphasis at least." Well, I "rather think" as he does. In a way, I like both emphases. But therein lies the difficulty. It is much more difficult to choose between alternative "goods" than to choose between good and evil—especially in missions. And that is precisely what we are being called upon to do.

Results of Differing Views and Applications of Scripture

According to Paul Pierson, the first lesson to be learned from the ecumenical history we have reviewed in this chapter is "that mission can go forward only if based on an adequate biblical and theological foundation" (Pierson 2003, 83). He is right, of course. But the key word here is *adequate*. At the urging of Greek Orthodox leaders, the WCC added the phrase *according to the Holy Scripture* to their faith statement in 1961. But what difference did it make?

There is no question that both McClain and Ladd build their respective eschatologies on the Bible, *but the two differ markedly in their respective views as to the nature of biblical authority*. Again, both *The Greater Commission* and *Changing the Mind of Missions* are based on a "biblical and theological foundation," *but as understood according to differing views of the authority of Scripture and radically differing rules of interpretation.*

All of this is of critical importance. My trepidation at this point is exactly that expressed by Edward Rommen. He writes, "I agree fully with the suggestion that a flawed hermeneutic and sub-orthodox view of Scripture allow for a definitional free-for-all in which terms can be redefined without regard for the clear intention of the biblical authors—in which case the world, not the kingdom, sets the agenda" (Rommen 2003). That is precisely what has happened in ecumenical circles. It could happen again.

Lessons Learned from Revisiting the Biblical Text

Of course, even those who adopt orthodox views of Scripture and its interpretation still come up with differing views. *All* of us see through a glass darkly. But take note of the fact that, historically, conservative evangelicals whose positions on the millennium question have been very different have nevertheless been able to agree on the nature of the Christian mission. Liberal conciliars, on the other hand, often have found it difficult, if not impossible, to agree on a definition of exactly what the mission of the church really is.

With respect to *missio Dei,* for example, many liberal scholars have taken this helpful idea and bent it into a shape that conforms only distantly to the teaching of the biblical text. Adhering to the biblical text, evangelical scholars Köstenberger and O'Brien insist that there is "the one mission of God who has sent his Son Jesus as the missionary par excellence and in whose mission the twelve apostles and Paul participate as 'witnesses'" (Köstenberger and O'Brien 2001, 147). But to them, that does not mean that the Twelve and Paul witnessed to the kingdom. The church emerged as a by-product of their successful witness and its converts.

On the contrary, according to Köstenberger and O'Brien,

> Paul knew that he was entrusted with God's "mystery," the eschatological revelation that *now* Jews and Gentiles alike were gathered together into one body, the church. . . . The first task included within the scope of his missionary commission was primary evangelism. Paul's ambition was to go where the gospel had not yet been preached (Rom. 15:20–21). His strategy focused on preaching and evangelizing Jews as well as Gentiles and God-fearers in local synagogues. The apostle proclaimed the gospel, and, under God, converted men and women. *But he also founded churches as a necessary element in his missionary task.* Paul's aim was to establish Christian congregations in strategic (mostly urban) centres from where the gospel could spread further to the surrounding regions. Conversion to Christ meant incorporation into him, and thus membership within a Christian community. Furthermore . . . it is clear that Paul sought to bring men and women to full maturity in Christ. . . . In the Pastoral Epistles, Paul emphasizes that God is the Saviour of all . . . and provides the post-apostolic church with a pattern of organization and qualifications for its leadership. (Köstenberger and O'Brien 2001, 258–59; emphasis mine)

Jesus spoke of the *basileia* or kingdom over one hundred times in connection with his own person and mission. He spoke of the *ekklēsia* or church only three times. The apostle Paul, on the other hand, spoke of the *ekklēsia* some forty-five times (plus two times in Hebrews if he was the author) but of the *basileia* only fourteen times.

This difference in emphasis is significant (Hesselgrave 2000; Howell 1998; Little 2005). Though God is always building his kingdom, he is in this age building his church as an expression of that kingdom. Nowhere in Scripture are we specifically called upon to obey "kingdom mission" in the way we are called upon to obey the Great Commission. "Kingdom mission" was and remains uniquely the mission of Christ, though we are to witness to it in very practical ways. "Great Commission mission" is uniquely ours and requires us to make disciples by preaching, baptizing, and teaching the peoples of the earth. Christ will *bring* his kingdom and so he teaches believers to pray that God's kingdom will come *on earth as it is now in heaven.* Christ is *building* his church so he commands believers to witness and work for its completion, now and in this age. God's kingdom will come because his "is the kingdom and the power and the glory, forever" (Matt. 6:13). His church will be built because God will be glorified "in the church and in Christ Jesus throughout all generations, forever and ever" (Eph. 3:21).

Lessons to Be Learned from Luther, Edwards, and Carey

Martin Luther. Scherer agrees with the nineteenth-century Lutheran missions historian Gustav Plitt (1838–1880) that there are good reasons for considering Martin Luther to be the "Father of Evangelical Missions" (Scherer 1987, 54ff.). Plitt conceded that, unlike Carey, Luther did not support missions society endeavors as such, but he insisted that Luther did support the fundamental task of world evangelization, the central task of the church. During his life, the pure Word of God had not been preached in Germany and only a church grounded in Scripture and the gospel could actually carry out Christian missions. Therefore, "Luther's obedience to mission meant reestablishing the church on its one true foundation in Jesus Christ and the gospel" (Scherer 1987, 55).

Furthermore, Plitt said that Luther anchored *missions* in the "mission of God" *(missio Dei),* which will prevail over Satan's kingdom and every evil power. God will accomplish this goal quite apart from our feeble efforts and even our prayers. "For Luther the final victory of the kingdom is not based on any calculation of the odds, or any frantic call for human cooperation with God to overcome the powers of evil, but solely on confident hope in the ultimate victory wrought by Christ" (Scherer 1987, 57).

We can certainly agree with both of Luther's propositions as interpreted by Plitt and Scherer. We take issue with the notion of conferring "fatherhood status" on Luther, however. Carey remains the best candidate for the honor of being called "Father of Evangelical Missions." Although he did many things to demonstrate and even further God's kingdom purpose, Carey was the one who was committed specifically to fulfilling Great Commission mission by actively sending out missionaries to accomplish it.

Jonathan Edwards. Considered one of the keenest theological minds in American history, Edwards was also one of America's greatest revivalists and most insistent advocates of Great Commission mission. From 1751–1757, Edwards was an enthusiastic missionary to, and founder of a congregation among, Indians living in villages near Stockbridge, Massachusetts. He set aside this work somewhat reluctantly to take the presidency of what is now Princeton University and then died of smallpox after being a willing participant in testing an early form of vaccination. He thus gave his life for another kind of missional work, the promotion of human wellbeing through medical research.

The latter role is of special interest currently because Ralph Winter has called to the attention of the missions community Edwards's willingness to be inoculated for smallpox despite the dangers. Winter makes an impassioned appeal to give serious attention to scientific work on the eradication of killer microbes. He classifies this support of medical research as being part of "kingdom mission" (Winter 2000, 529). Winter's proposal certainly is worth reflection, and his passion is commendable. Nevertheless, the implications of his use of terms has occasioned some appropriate debate.

Inevitably some will seize upon Winter's use of the term *kingdom mission* as meaning that service to humanity is an acceptable alternative to traditional evangelical missionary work. It is indisputable that Edwards's own understanding was in accordance with the Great Commission. He spent himself seeking the salvation of the lost, and he fought battles against what he saw as threats to the purity of the church. His famous sermon "Sinners in the Hands of an Angry God" does not represent the totality of his ministry philosophy, but it encapsulates one high priority. As for Winter, it is to be remembered that he has been a foremost advocate of "reaching the unreached" and growing a church among every people group on the face of the earth.

William Carey. Carey's title "father of modern missions" rests on the fact that his book *An Enquiry into the Obligation of Christians to Use Means for the Conversion of the Heathen* and his own dedication to that task as a missionary to India from 1793 to 1834, resulted in the formation of numerous missionary societies and actually initiated a new era in the history of missions. Given his pioneering missiology, it is important that we grasp Carey's understanding of the task. Every word in the title of Carey's study is significant to that understanding, and none is more significant than the two words *means* and *conversion.* Carey did not have missionary strategies or methods in mind when he referred to "means." His "means" were groups of concerned people—missionary societies—that would send, support, and engage themselves in the missionary task, much as is enjoined on us today in Culver's *Greater Commission.* Most succinctly stated, for Carey the missionary task was to "convert the heathen."

Carey studied Indian culture and languages, preached the gospel, did Bible translation, started schools, initiated medical and relief efforts, planted churches, and trained pastors. He also contributed significantly to the outlawing of the cultural practices of widow burning and infanticide. Because of the diversity and significance of his accomplishments, his name is being invoked as justification for every conceivable sort of missionary endeavor. And, indeed, one would be hard pressed to find a better example of kingdom-building and culture-transforming mission than the work of William Carey.

Except for one thing, that is. Carey himself did not think of his mission that way.

Through all his testings and activities, Carey sustained his initial understanding that his task was primarily to be an instrument in the conversion of Indians and the establishment of Indian churches. At the age of thirty-seven, he wrote to a friend that, although he found it necessary to register as an indigo planter, if ever he found himself in the company of the governor general, he would not hesitate to declare himself a "missionary of Christ."

That opportunity came when, at the age of forty-three and as the founder of a great college, he addressed the governor general and his full court (in Sanskrit). Though the governor general was not in full sympathy with Carey's mission and some on the court greatly resented his presence in India, Carey spoke not only as the scholar he was but as the missionary he had come to India to be. In a manner reminiscent of Luke's report concerning Paul's abbreviated ministry in Athens, Carey courageously gave clear indication of his missionary status and ministry in dialogue with the intellectual elite of India. "I have been in the habit of preaching to multitudes daily, of discoursing with the Brahmins upon every subject, and superintending schools for the instruction of Hindu youth." That instruction was to secure their salvation first and then to train pastors for Indian churches (Walker 1951, 195–96).

Conclusion

Martin Marty looks back to the 1970s and reports that Harvard sociologist Talcott Parsons, speaking to ecumenists in 1978, said, "You won! What are you grousing about? You won!" Parsons continued:

Major elements of the Protestant social gospel, the Catholic Bishops' Program, the black Christian civil rights leadership had "won" as governments enacted what they stood for. Culturally, the same churches had "won" by having contributed to the liberal or open society, which mixed secular thinking and religious prophecy; support for tolerance and respect among religions; celebration of individual freedom; and select affirmations of popular culture. (Marty 2004, 38)

Currently, Marty surveys a North American Western religious landscape composed of "Catholics, Protestants, Jews, African American Protestants, Mormons, secular moralists and citizens who possess eyes and consciences in all camps." He concludes that it is the evangelicals who have "won" in that they have "chosen to adapt more to the main lines of American cultural life than most other groups" (Marty 2004, 39). But the byline of Marty's article is "evangelicals have become major players in American culture, and that may be their biggest problem." Indeed, it may be. It raises all sorts of questions, not the least of which is the question that we have posed in the subtitle of this chapter, "What on Earth Is God Building—*Here* and *Now?"*

With that question in mind, J. Robertson McQuilkin's encouragement to join in dialogue that focuses on areas of agreement but does not compromise the uniqueness of Christ and the necessity of evangelism is well taken (McQuilkin 1993, 165–70). Dialogue that does not compromise the essentials of faith but rather allows for their full expression should always be an option.

Actually, however, the kind of evangelical dialogue that is firmly based on the integrity of Holy Scripture and historic doctrines of the Christian faith is no longer just an option. It is necessarily the kind of dialogue advocated by Kevin Vanhoozer when he says that, at its best, *evangelical theology* is a matter of deliberating well (i.e., canonically) about the gospel in a noncanonical way (e.g., concerning contemporary situations—Vanhoozer 2000, 84). The same can be said for *evangelical missiology.* Unless conservatives dialogue canonically, both theological and missiological dialogues are as apt to compound confusion as they are to dispel it

Epilogue

Donald McGavran was a prominent figure in both ecumenical and evangelical circles through much of the conciliar and ecumenical history summarized in the overview at the beginning of this chapter. It was an experienced—and after witnessing the decline in conciliar missions, a chastened—McGavran who ultimately had a vision of the "lion" that stalks contemporary missions (McGavran 1988b). It was he who, on the basis of his experience and vision, proposed the formation of an "American Society of Christian Missiology" as a forum for missiological discussions based on the verities of the Christian faith.

Speaking personally, I have sometimes wondered why my colleague and friend McGavran approached and challenged me with his proposal. I had not been especially identified with any one of the grand missions strategies that, each in its turn, captured the attention and engaged the effort of the larger evangelical missions community over the years. Moreover, privately and occasionally in public I had criticized McGavran's

Church Growth strategy as overly dependent upon the social sciences and not dependent enough on the biblical text.

Upon reflection, I now think I understand something of his reasoning. Most of my extracurricular efforts had gone into bringing conservative evangelical missions teachers together in the Association of Evangelical Professors of Mission. Perhaps after over sixty years of experience in all kinds of missions situations and a wide variety of missiological discussions, McGavran's passion for what he called *"Great Commission* mission" and *"Christian* missiology" outweighed other considerations. At any rate, the kind of forum he desired came into being in 1990 at the formation of the Evangelical Missiological Society. And that means that McGavran should not be remembered for his leadership in Church Growth endeavors alone. He should also be remembered for his challenge to build the missiology of the future on God's Word and the historic doctrines of the church. For that challenge, all missions leaders and missiologists will forever be in his debt.

References

Beaver, R. Pierce. 1964. *From Missions to Mission: Protestant World Mission Today and Tomorrow.* New York: Association.

Beyerhaus, Peter. 1972. *Shaken Foundations: Theological Foundations for Mission.* Grand Rapids: Zondervan.

Bosch, David J. 1991. *Transforming Mission: Paradigm Shifts in Theology of Mission.* Maryknoll, N.Y.: Orbis.

Bright, John. 1984. *The Kingdom of God.* Nashville: Abingdon.

Culver, Robert D. 1954. *Daniel and the Latter Days.* Westwood, N.J.: Revell. Revised edition 1977, Chicago: Moody.

———. 1984. *A Greater Commission: A Theology for World Missions.* Chicago: Moody.

Engel, James F., and William A. Dyrness. 2000. *Changing the Mind of Missions: Where Have We Gone Wrong?* Downers Grove, Ill.: InterVarsity.

Glasser, Arthur F. 2000. "World Council of Churches Assemblies." In *Evangelical Dictionary of World Missions.* A. Scott Moreau, general editor. Grand Rapids: Baker.

Hesselgrave, David J. 2000. *Planting Churches Cross-culturally: North America and Beyond.* 2d ed. Grand Rapids: Baker.

Howell, Don N. Jr. 1998. "Mission in Paul's Epistles: Genesis, Pattern, and Dynamics," and "Mission in Paul's Epistles: Theological Bearings." In *Mission in the New Testament: An Evangelical Approach.* Edited by William J. Larkin Jr. and Joel F. Williams. Maryknoll, N.Y.: Orbis.

Johnson, David Enderton, ed. 1975. *Uppsala to Nairobi 1968–1975: Report of the Central Committee to the Fifth Assembly of the World Council of Churches.* New York: Friendship Press; London: SPCK.

Johnson, Elliot E. 1989. *Expository Hermeneutics: An Introduction.* Grand Rapids: Zondervan.

Johnston, Arthur P. 1974. *World Evangelism and the Word of God.* Minneapolis: Bethany Fellowship.

————. 1978. *The Battle for World Evangelism.* Wheaton, Ill.: Tyndale.

Köstenberger, Andreas J., and Peter T. O'Brien. 2001. *Salvation to the Ends of the Earth: A Biblical Theology of Mission.* Leicester, England: Apollos.

Ladd, George Eldon. 1974. *The Presence of the Future: The Eschatology of Biblical Realism.* Grand Rapids: Eerdmans.

Little, Christopher. 2005. *Mission in the Way of Paul: Biblical Mission for the Church in the Twenty-first Century.* New York: Peter Lang.

Marty, Martin E. 2004. "At the Crossroads: Evangelicals Have Become Major Players in American Culture, and That May Be Their Biggest Problem." *Christianity Today* 48.2 (February): 38–40.

McClain, Alva J. 1968. *The Greatness of the Kingdom: An Inductive Study of the Kingdom of God.* Chicago: Moody.

McGavran, Donald A. 1988a. Personal letter to David J. Hesselgrave, 7 April.

————. 1988b. "Missions Face a Lion." Manuscript in the possession of David J. Hesselgrave. A version of this manuscript was published as "Missiology Faces the Lion" in *Missiology: An International Review* 17.3 (1 July 1989): 335–56.

McQuilkin, J. Robertson. 1993. "An Evangelical Assessment of Mission Theology of the Kingdom of God." In *The Good News of the Kingdom: Mission Theology for the Third Millennium,* edited by Charles Van Engen, Dean S. Gilliland, and Paul Pierson, 172–78. Maryknoll, N.Y.: Orbis.

Moreau, Scott. 2000. "Putting the Survey in Perspective" in *Mission Handbook:*

U.S. and Canadian Christian Ministries Overseas, 18th ed., 2001–2002. John A. Siewert and Dotsy Welliver, eds. Wheaton, Ill. EMIS, 33–80.

Neill, Stephen. 1959. *Creative Tension: The Duff Lectures, 1958.* London: Edinburgh House.

Pierson, Paul E. 2003. "Lessons from the Twentieth Century: Conciliar Missions." In *Between Past and Future: Evangelical Mission Entering the Twenty-first Century,* edited by Jonathan J. Bonk, 67–84. Pasadena, Calif.: William Carey Library.

Reid, Daniel G. 1990. "George Eldon Ladd." In *Dictionary of Christianity in America,* edited by Daniel G. Reid et al. Downers Grove, Ill.: InterVarsity.

Robertson, Archibald. 1901. *Regnum Dei: Bampton Lectures.* New York: Macmillan.

Rommen, Edward. 2003. Personal letter to David J. Hesselgrave, 16 December.

Scherer, James A. 1987. *Gospel, Church, and Kingdom: Comparative Studies in World Mission Theology.* Minneapolis: Augsburg.

————. 1993. "Church, Kingdom, and *Missio Dei.*" In *The Good News of the Kingdom: Mission Theology for the Third Millennium,* edited by Charles Van Engen, Dean S. Gilliland, and Paul Pierson, 82–88. Maryknoll, N.Y.: Orbis.

Sovik, Arne. 1973. *Salvation Today.* Minneapolis: Augsburg.

Van Engen, Charles. 1993. "The Relation of Bible and Mission in Mission Theology." In *The Good News of the Kingdom: Mission Theology for the Third Millennium,* edited by Charles Van Engen, Dean S. Gilliland, and Paul Pierson, 27–36. Maryknoll, N.Y.: Orbis.

————. 1996. *Mission on the Way: Issues in Mission Theology.* Grand Rapids: Baker.

Vanhoozer, Kevin J. 2000. "The Voice of the Actor: A Dramatic Proposal About the Ministry and Minstrelsy of Theology." In *Evangelical Futures: A Conversation on Theological Method,* edited by John G. Stackhouse Jr. Grand Rapids: Eerdmans.

Visser 't Hooft, W. A., ed. 1962. *New Delhi Speaks: About Christian Witness, Service, and Unity.* New York: Association.

Walker, F. Deaville. 1951. *William Carey: Missionary Pioneer and Statesman.* Chicago: Moody.

Winter, Ralph D. 1999. "The Mission of the Kingdom." In *Perspectives on the*

World Christian Mission: A Reader, edited by Ralph D. Winter and Steven C. Hawthorne. 3d ed. Pasadena, Calif.: William Carey Library.

————. 2000. "Theologizing the Microbiological World: Implications for Mission." Unpublished manuscript. Pasadena, Calif.: U.S. Center for World Mission.

World Council of Churches. 1967. *The Church for Others: Two Reports on the Missionary Structure of the Congregation.* Geneva: World Council of Churches.

————. 1968. *Drafts for Sections: Prepared for the Fourth Assembly of the World Council of Churches.* Geneva: World Council of Churches.

————. n.d. a. *From Mexico City to Bangkok: Report of the Commission on World Mission and Evangelism 1963–1972.* Geneva: World Council of Churches.

————. n.d. b. *Bangkok Assembly 1973: Minutes and Report of the Assembly of the Commission on World Mission and Evangelism of the World Council of Churches, December 31, 1972 and January 9–12, 1973.* Geneva: World Council of Churches.

Subject Index

357

Scripture Index